The Modelling and Analysis of Security Protocols

Vinay. M. Igure

The Modelling and Analysis of Security Protocols: the CSP Approach

03/22/2001

P.Y.A. Ryan and S.A. Schneider
with
M.H. Goldsmith, G. Lowe and A.W. Roscoe

▲▼▼ **Addison-Wesley**

An imprint of **Pearson Education**

Harlow, England · London · New York · Reading, Massachusetts · San Francisco · Toronto · Don Mills, Ontario · Sydney
Tokyo · Singapore · Hong Kong · Seoul · Taipei · Cape Town · Madrid · Mexico City · Amsterdam · Munich · Paris · Milan

PEARSON EDUCATION LIMITED

Head office:	London Office:
Edinburgh Gate	128 Long Acre
Harlow CM20 2JE	London WC2E 9AN
Tel: +44 (0)1279 623623	Tel: +44 (0)20 7447 2000
Fax: +44 (0)1279 431059	Fax: +44 (0)20 7240 5771

Website: *www.aw.com/cseng*

First published in Great Britain in 2001

© Pearson Education Limited 2001

The rights of P. Y. A. Ryan and S. A. Schneider to be identified as Authors of this
Work have been asserted by them in accordance with the Copyright, Designs and Patents
Act 1988.

ISBN 0 201 67471 8

British Library Cataloguing in Publication Data
A CIP catalogue record for this book can be obtained from the British Library

Library of Congress Cataloging in Publication Data
Applied for.

10 9 8 7 6 5 4 3 2 1

Typeset by HK Typesetting Ltd.
Printed and bound in Great Britain by Biddles Ltd.

The Publishers' policy is to use paper manufactured from sustainable forests.

Contributing authors

Preface   Peter Ryan and Steve Schneider

Introduction   Peter Ryan

Chapter 1   Bill Roscoe

Chapter 2   Bill Roscoe

Chapter 3   Steve Schneider

Chapter 4   Michael Goldsmith

Chapter 5   Gavin Lowe

Chapter 6   Michael Goldsmith

Chapter 7   Steve Schneider

Chapter 8   Gavin Lowe

Chapter 9   Peter Ryan

Chapter 10   Peter Ryan

Appendix A   Peter Ryan

Appendix B   Tool generated

Appendix C   Steve Schneider

Contents

x

Preface

The value of information and the power that it can convey has long been recognized. Now, more than ever, information is a driver of society and its integrity, confidentiality and authenticity must be ensured.

Security protocols are a critical element of the infrastructures needed for the secure communication and processing of information. They are, of course, not the only components needed to ensure such security properties: for example, good cryptographic algorithms and systems security measures to protect key material are also needed. Protocols can however be thought of as the keystones of a secure architecture: they allow agents to authenticate each other, to establish fresh session keys to communicate confidentially, to ensure the authenticity of data and services, and so on.

Aims of the book

This book is about the role of security protocols, how they work, the security properties they are designed to ensure and how to design and analyze them.

It was recognized very early on, almost as soon as they were conceived, that the design and analysis of security protocols was going to be a very delicate and error-prone process. Security protocols are deceptively simple-looking objects that harbour surprising subtleties and flaws. Attempts to develop frameworks and tools to reason about their properties goes back over 20 years, but the topic remains a highly active and fruitful one in the security research community. An overview of the historical background can be found in Chapter 9.

In this book we present the particular approach to security protocol verification that has been developed by the authors. It was the first to apply process algebra and model-checking to the problem. The process algebra in question is CSP (Communicating Sequential Processes).

There is a widespread misconception that pouring liberal libations of cryptographic algorithms over an architecture will render it secure. Certainly, good cryptographic algorithms are important but, as we will see, it is quite possible to have an architecture employing high grade algorithms that is still wide open to exploitation due to poor protocol design.

We hope that our readers will come away with a good understanding of the role of security protocols, how they work and the kinds of vulnerabilities to which they are prey. In particular we hope that they will better appreciate the subtleties in making precise the security goals that such protocols are intended to ensure and the importance of making these goals – as well as the assumptions about the underlying mechanisms and environment – precise.

Ideally we hope that the reader will gain sufficient understanding (and enthusiasm!) to apply the tools and techniques presented here to their own protocols, real or imaginary. Perhaps also some readers will be sufficiently intrigued to go on to pursue research into some of the open problems that remain in this challenging and fascinating area.

Structure of the book

This book is concerned with the particular approach to analysis and verification of security protocols based around the process algebra CSP. There are a number of facets to this approach, and the book uses a running example, the Yahalom protocol, to link the material.

The Introduction introduces the general topic of security protocols. It covers the issues that arise in their design, the cryptographic mechanisms that are used in their construction, the properties that they are expected to have, and the kinds of attacks that can be mounted to subvert them. It also discusses the CSP approach and the tool support. The chapter introduces the Yahalom protocol and several other protocol examples.

Chapter 1 provides a general introduction to the main aspects of CSP relevant to the approach. CSP consists of a language and underlying theory for modelling systems consisting of interacting components, and for supporting a formal analysis of such models. This chapter introduces the building blocks of the language which enable individual components to be described, and discusses how components are combined into systems. Specification and verification through refinement, and with respect to property-oriented specifications, is also covered. The chapter finishes with a brief discussion of how discrete time can be modelled.

Chapter 2 shows how to use CSP to construct models of security protocols, which consist of a number of communicating components and are thus well suited to analysis in CSP. The variety of possible attacks on protocols must also be built into the model, and the chapter shows how to incorporate the Dolev-Yao approach to modelling a hostile environment and produce a system description which is suitable for analysis.

Chapter 3 covers the kinds of properties that security protocols are expected to provide, and how they can be expressed formally within the CSP framework. Secrecy and authentication are the main concern of the approaches in this book, and various forms are covered. The properties of non-repudiation and anonymity are also discussed.

Chapter 4 introduces the model-checking tool support available for CSP, the Failures-Divergences Refinement checker (FDR). It discusses how this tool works, and the nature of refinement checking.

Chapter 5 is concerned with the Casper tool. This is a compiler for security protocols, which transforms a high-level description of a security protocol, and the properties required of it, into a CSP model of the protocol as described in Chapter 2, and a number of assertions to be checked. This model can then be analyzed using the model-checker FDR discussed in Chapter 4.

Chapter 6 discusses in more detail some of the CSP modelling that is carried out by Casper, particularly how the hostile environment is modelled to allow efficient analysis by the model-checker.

Chapter 7 is concerned with direct verification of CSP models of protocols. It introduces the 'rank function' approach to proving protocols correct. This allows proofs to be constructed that verify protocol descriptions of arbitrary size against their requirements. The theorem-proving and bespoke tool support available for this approach is also discussed.

Chapter 8 addresses the problem of scale. Real-world protocols are very large and their analysis is difficult because of the volume of detail contained in their description. This chapter is concerned with 'simplifying transformations', which allow extraneous detail to be abstracted away when checking a protocol against a particular property in such a way that verification of the abstract protocol implies correctness of the full protocol. The approach is illustrated with the CyberCash main sequence protocol.

Chapter 9 discusses the literature on security protocol verification and its historical context. There are a number of different approaches to the problems addressed in this book, and this chapter covers many of those that have been most influential in the field.

Chapter 10 discusses the broader issues, open problems and areas of ongoing research, and gives indications of areas for possible further developments and research. One area of current research discussed in this chapter, of particular importance to the model-checking approach of this book, is the development of techniques based on 'data independence', which allow the results of model-checking to be lifted to protocol models of arbitrary size.

There are three appendices. The first covers some background mathematics and cryptography, introducing the RSA and the ElGamal schemes; the second is an example of Casper applied to the Yahalom protocol, containing the input file and the CSP model produced by Casper; and the third contains a verification using rank functions of the simplified CyberCash protocol descriptions produced in Chapter 8.

The book has an associated website:
`www.cs.rhbnc.ac.uk/books/secprot/` This website provides access to all of the tools discussed in this book, and to the protocol examples that are used throughout (as well as others). Readers are recommended to download the tools and experiment with protocol analysis while reading the book. The website also provides exercises (and answers!), as well as a variety of other related material.

Acknowledgements

The authors would like to thank DERA (the Defence and Evaluation Research Agency, UK) and the MoD for funding the Strategic Research Project (SRP) 'Modelling and Analysis of Security Protocols' under which the foundations of the approach were laid down, and the EPRSC (UK Engineering and Physical Sciences Research Council) and ONR (US Office of Naval Research) for funding subsequent developments of the approach. Thanks are also due to Inmos, ONR, DERA and ESPRIT, for funding developments to FDR over the years.

Peter Ryan would also like to thank the Department of Computer Science, Royal Holloway, and Microsoft Research, Cambridge, for hospitality during the writing of this book.

This work has benefited from collaboration with Philippa Broadfoot, Neil Evans, James Heather, Mei Lin Hui, Ranko Lazić and the staff at Formal Systems. It has also been influenced by discussions with and comments from Giampaolo Bella, Steve Brackin, Dieter Gollmann, Andy Gordon, Roberto Gorrieri, Joshua Guttman, Richard Kemmerer, John McLean, Cathy Meadows, Larry Paulson, Matthias Schunter, Paul Syverson and Paulo Verissimo.

Finally, special thanks are due to Coby, Helen and Liz, Kate and Eleanor for moral support.

0 Introduction

0.1 Security protocols

As with any protocol, a security protocol comprises a prescribed sequence of interactions between entities designed to achieve a certain end. A *diplomatic* protocol typically involves some exchange of memoranda of understanding and so on, intended to establish agreement between parties with potentially conflicting interests. A *communications* protocol is designed to establish communication between agents, i.e. set up a link, agree syntax, and so on. Even such mundane, everyday activities as withdrawing money from an ATM or negotiating a roundabout involve protocols.

The goals of *security* protocols, also known as *cryptographic* protocols, are to provide various security services across a distributed system. These goals include: the authentication of agents or nodes, establishing session keys between nodes, ensuring secrecy, integrity, anonymity, non-repudiation and so on. They involve the exchange of messages between nodes, often requiring the participation of a trusted third party or session server. Typically they make liberal use of various cryptographic mechanisms, such as symmetric and asymmetric encryption, hash functions, and digital signatures. In some cases further devices like timestamps are also used. We will explain these terms more fully shortly.

The difficulty of designing and analyzing security protocols has long been recognized. This difficulty stems from a number of considerations:

- The properties they are supposed to ensure are extremely subtle. Even the apparently rather simple notion of authentication turns out to harbour a number of subtleties and comes in various flavours. The precise meaning, or rather meanings, of this concept remain hotly debated.

- These protocols inhabit a complex, hostile environment. To evaluate them properly we need to be able accurately to describe and model this environment and this will have to include the capabilities of agents deliberately trying to undermine the protocol. In this book we will refer to such a hostile agent as an *intruder*; in the literature other terms such as 'spy', 'enemy', 'attacker', 'eavesdropper' and 'penetrator' are also used.

- Capturing the capabilities of 'intruders' is inevitably extremely difficult. Arguably it is impossible, but at least we may hope to make good approximations that can be progressively enhanced as new styles of attack come to light. Besides manipulating messages passing across the network,

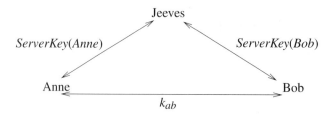

Figure 0.1 Setting up a secure channel

> they could include cryptanalytic techniques, monitoring tempest emanations, timing, power fluctuations, probabilistic observations and other nefarious activities as 'rubber hose-pipe cryptanalysis' (non-mathematical techniques for extracting cryptographic variables).

> ■ By their very nature security protocols involve a high degree of concurrency, which invariably makes analysis more challenging.

Security protocols are, in fact, excellent candidates for rigorous analysis techniques: they are critical components of any distributed security architecture, they are very easy to express, and they are very difficult to evaluate by hand. They are deceptively simple looking: the literature is full of protocols that appear to be secure but have subsequently been found to fall prey to some subtle attack, sometimes years later. In Roger Needham's remark 'they are three line programs that people still manage to get wrong'.

Security protocols have taken on a role for the formal-methods community analogous to that of fruit flies to the genetic research community. They are compact and easy to manipulate whilst embodying many of the issues and challenges to the tools and techniques for the analysis and evaluation of security critical systems.

To make things rather more concrete let us consider an example: the Needham-Schroeder Secret-Key (NSSK) protocol. This is one of the earliest such protocols and has, aside from a rather subtle vulnerability that we will discuss later, stood the test of time. It forms the basis of the well-known Kerberos authentication and authorization system [65]. It uses purely symmetric encryption algorithms and is designed to enable two agents, Anne and Bob say, to set up a secure channel of communication with the help of a trusted server, Jeeves. This situation is illustrated in Figure 0.1.

To start with, all the registered agents, including Anne and Bob, share private, long-term keys with Jeeves. These are pair-wise distinct so although each can communicate securely with Jeeves they are not able to communicate directly with each other. Now suppose that Anne wants to start talking privately with Bob. One obvious possibility is for them to communicate via Jeeves: she sends an encrypted message to Jeeves using the key she shares with him; he decrypts this and then encrypts the plaintext using the key he shares with Bob. This works but rapidly gets very cumbersome: it involves a lot of computation and means that Jeeves becomes a bottleneck and single point of failure.

The trick then is just to use Jeeves as and when necessary to establish a new key between Anne and Bob so that they can then communicate directly without further recourse to Jeeves. An obvious question is: why not just supply each pair of agents with a key at the outset? Again this works up to a point but requires roughly N^2 distinct keys to be distributed from the start, where N is the number of agents. If N is large this rapidly becomes impractical, especially as it is likely that most of these keys will never be used. It is even worse as we may not know at the outset what the set of users is going to be. Typically, registered users will come and go. Another important point is that it is desirable to change keys frequently to make the task of cryptanalysts harder and contain the effect of any compromises. Having a mechanism like the Needham-Schroeder Secret-Key protocol to set up new keys as required makes this easier. The long-term keys, *ServerKey*(*a*), *ServerKey*(*b*) etc., can be stronger and should less susceptible to cryptanalysis as they tend to carry only a small volume of traffic.

Returning then to the protocol we see that if we start with N users only N keys need be set up initially and it will be fairly straightforward to supply each new user with a new private key as and when they register.

Suppose that Anne shares the key *ServerKey*(*Anne*) with Jeeves, whilst Bob shares *ServerKey*(*Bob*) with him.

The protocol proceeds as follows:

$$\text{Message 1} \quad a \rightarrow J \; : \; a.b.n_a$$
$$\text{Message 2} \quad J \rightarrow a \; : \; \{n_a.b.k_{ab}.\{k_{ab}.a\}_{ServerKey(b)}\}_{ServerKey(a)}$$
$$\text{Message 3} \quad a \rightarrow b \; : \; \{k_{ab}.a\}_{ServerKey(b)}$$
$$\text{Message 4} \quad b \rightarrow a \; : \; \{n_b\}_{k_{ab}}$$
$$\text{Message 5} \quad a \rightarrow b \; : \; \{n_b - 1\}_{k_{ab}}$$

This requires some explanation. First let us explain the notation. Each step of the protocol is represented by a line in the description. Thus

$$\text{Message } n \quad a \rightarrow b \; : \; data$$

indicates that in the nth step of the protocol agent a dispatches a message *data* to b. The message in general consists of a number of parts concatenated together. In practice it is of course possible that this message will not reach b or might reach someone else. For the moment however we are only concerned with presenting the intended progress of the protocol.

Terms of the form n_a denote so-called nonces: freshly generated, unique and (usually) unpredictable numbers. The subscript indicates who generated it, but notice that this is just a notational convenience; in the real protocol there will typically be nothing in the actual value to indicate that it was created by a. We will discuss the role of nonces more fully shortly.

Compound terms can take the forms:

■ {*data*}$_k$, which denotes the value *data* encrypted under the key k;

■ *m.n*, which denotes the text *m* followed by (concatenated with) the text *n*.

Now we are in a position to walk through this protocol step by step. In the first step Anne tells Jeeves that she would like to talk to Bob and she supplies the nonce n_a. Jeeves now creates a new key k_{ab} and returns the message with nested encryption indicated in step 2 to Anne. The outer encryption is performed using *ServerKey*(a) which Anne can strip off. Inside Anne finds the following:

$$n_a.b.k_{ab}.\{k_{ab}.a\}_{ServerKey(b)}$$

The first term is just the value of the nonce she sent to Jeeves in message 1. She is expected to check that this value agrees with the value she originally sent out. We will return to the significance of this a little later. The second term should be Bob's name. Again she should check that this agrees with the name in her request of message 1. The third term is the new key k_{ab}. The last term is encrypted using the key that Bob shares with Jeeves. Anne can't read this last term but in accordance with the protocol, and assuming that all the other checks have succeeded, she simply forwards it to Bob in the third step. When Bob receives this he is able to strip off the encryption to reveal: $k_{ab}.a$.

So he now knows the value of the new key k_{ab} and knows that it is intended for communication with Anne. He now dreams up a new nonce of his own n_b and sends it back to Anne encrypted under k_{ab} in message 4. Anne decrypts this to extract n_b. She modifies this in some standard way – the convention is to subtract 1 – and sends this modified value back to Bob, again encrypted under k_{ab}. Finally Bob decrypts this and checks that the resulting value agrees with what he expects for $n_b - 1$.

So, what has all this frantic activity achieved? In informal terms, and assuming that all has gone smoothly, Anne and Bob end up with shared knowledge of k_{ab}. In fact they share this knowledge after message 3 has been received by Bob. So why a further two messages and yet another of these nonces? Messages 4 and 5 are really just acknowledgement messages to assure each other that the other also knows k_{ab}. We see that by the time Bob receives message 3 he knows that Anne knows k_{ab}. Once Anne gets message 4 she knows that Bob knows k_{ab} and, further, she knows that he knows that she knows k_{ab}. And so on. We can see that we could go on constructing an infinite chain of acknowledgement messages leading to a tower of states of knowledge about knowledge.

We should stress though that the conclusions reached by Anne and Bob above are based on very informal reasoning. On receiving message 3 Bob is reasoning something along the following lines:

Apart from me only Jeeves knows *ServerKey*(b) so only he could have generated these terms. Assuming that Jeeves is being honest he would only have generated them in response to a request from Anne and so they must have been included in a message to Anne encrypted with her long-term key. Hence it could only have reached me if it was forwarded to me by Anne. So

Anne received the appropriate message from Jeeves with k_{ab} ...

Such chains of reasoning are extremely error prone as we will see in, for example, the analysis of the Needham-Schroeder Public-Key (NSPK) protocol. We will see in this book how one can reason about protocols in a fully formal and indeed largely automated way.

The goal of this protocol is authenticated key distribution. In particular it should fulfil Anne's request to provide the means for her to have a private, authenticated conversation with Bob. What she wants at the end of the protocol run is to be sure that Jeeves has supplied her and Bob, and only her and Bob, with a freshly generated session key K that they can now use in further exchanges. As long as this key is only known to her and Bob she can be confident that messages she sends out encrypted with K can only be read by Bob, and furthermore that messages she gets back encrypted with K must have come from Bob and will also be safe from prying eyes.

This protocol illustrates a number of interesting issues that will crop up repeatedly throughout this book. Ensuring that Anne and Bob are really justified in having confidence in the services provided by this protocol is no easy task. First, we need to be sure that intruders can't undermine this goal by manipulating the messages in various (non-cryptographic) ways. This depends on the correctness of the protocol design, and is the principal concern of this book. It is also possible that poorly designed or unsuitable cryptographic primitives might lead to vulnerabilities that can be exploited. By and large we will not deal with such problems except to discuss to some extent how features of the crypto algorithms might interact with the protocol itself to give rise to vulnerabilities. We should also note that, from Anne's point of view say, she needs to place confidence in certain, remote parts of the system. She has to trust Jeeves to act according to the protocol description and to employ a 'good' key generation scheme. She also needs to trust Bob. If Bob is going to compromise his key, either deliberately or simply through carelessness (insecure storage of the key material), then all hope of secrecy or authentication is lost. On the other hand she should not need to place any great faith in the communications medium. Quite the contrary: she should typically assume that the medium is entirely open to malicious agents trying everything in their power to undermine the security goals.

Notice that the first message from the initiator, Anne, goes out in the clear. There is thus nothing to ensure the secrecy or integrity of this message. We are assuming that the intruder learning that Anne wants to talk to Bob is not a problem. We will also see later that there is no use to the intruder of learning the value of n_a. Thus lack of secrecy of these values is not a problem unless we are worried about traffic analysis. As to the integrity, it is certainly the case that there is nothing to prevent the intruder altering these values. However the only effect will be for Anne to back out when she finds that the values in the reply from Jeeves do not agree with her records. A denial of service attack can be launched in this way, but secrecy and authentication are not breached.

Another point is that we are assuming that the protocol is using a form of block cipher (which operates on fixed length blocks of plaintext and ciphertext) rather than say a stream cipher (which converts plaintext to and from ciphertext one character at a time). We will discuss the distinctions in more detail in Section 0.3 but this is important for Bob's nonce challenge to work. If a stream cipher were used the intruder would most likely be able to fake $\{n_b - 1\}_{k_{ab}}$, without even knowing either n_b or k_{ab}, by simply flipping an appropriate bit of the ciphertext of message 5.

We are further assuming that encrypting a number of terms together has the effect of binding them together, that is, it is not possible to cut and paste a chunk of the ciphertext in order to replace one of the terms without garbling the whole encipherment. Where the length of the terms exceeds the length of the block cipher, a suitable encryption mode will be needed to achieve this and we will discuss this in more detail a little later. Without such a mechanism the intruder, Yves, might be able to cut and paste a chunk of ciphertext that he knows will decrypt to his identity rather than Anne's, so as to fool Bob into thinking that he has a secure channel with Yves rather than with Anne.

This example served to give the flavour of the role of security protocols and how they are typically implemented. This particular protocol enables principals to authenticate each other and, if required, communicate in secrecy. Other security goals are of course possible and we will see several more in the next section. A number of cryptographic primitives have made an appearance here serving a number of roles: encryption to achieve secrecy, bind terms and ensure authenticity; nonces to foil replays; and so on. Such primitives will recur throughout the book and we will give an overview of the cryptographic background required to understand how these primitives are implemented in Section 0.3.

0.2 Security properties

Here we give an intuitive description of a number of important properties or services that security protocols may be required to provide. Typically, of course, a protocol will only be expected to provide a subset of these, depending on the application.

The meanings of these terms are frequently taken as obvious and widely understood. One typically finds that when pressed people find it remarkable difficult to make precise their understanding. Furthermore it often turns out that these supposedly widely understood terms are given different interpretations, sometimes within a single document or design. It is for these reasons that it is so essential to give precise, formal meanings. It is not sufficient, for example, to assert that a particular protocol is 'secure', or worse 'correct'. A protocol can only be claimed to be correct with respect to a given, precisely defined property and even then only against certain classes of threat and subject to various assumptions.

In the following sections we outline possible formalizations of these properties. These should be regarded as indicative rather than definitive. More detailed descriptions, along with formalizations in CSP, can be found in Chapters 2 and 3.

Secrecy

Secrecy, or confidentiality, has a number of different possible meanings and which is appropriate will depend on the application. We might have a very strict interpretation in which the intruder should not be able to deduce anything about the legitimate users' activity. In effect he should not even be able to perform any traffic analysis, let alone be able to derive the content of any messages. For this a non-interference style characterization is required that asserts that a high-level user's activity should not result in any observable effect on low-level users or outside observers of the system. See for example [82] for a detailed discussion. This is a very strict interpretation and requires correspondingly elaborate implementations. In the case of a communications network it would require, for example, hot-line style dummy traffic, or anonymized routeing.

This tends to be an overly strong characterization for most applications, and typically simpler, safety-style formalizations are sufficient. Such properties are both simpler to understand and to check and also seem more appropriate to most applications, so we will confine ourselves to these in the bulk of this book.

In most cases it is sufficient to prevent the intruder from being able to derive the plaintext of messages passing between the honest nodes. That is, Yves may be able to tell that Anne has sent a message to Bob and maybe even have a good idea of how long it was, but he is unable to read its contents. A property of this kind can be formulated as a safety or trace property. Such properties can be stated as predicates over the behaviours of the system. They state which behaviours are acceptable and which are not. Such properties are generally easier to understand and analyze than say liveness and non-interference, both of which must be formulated as properties over the ensemble of system behaviours and cannot be reduced to a predicate on individual traces.

We can capture a simple notion of secrecy as follows. Suppose that there is some set M of data items that we regard as sensitive and that the users will be encouraged to transmit to each other encrypted under-session keys established using a key-establishment protocol. We want to ensure that no message from this set can be obtained by the intruder in unencrypted form. We will see later how this is formalized in CSP. For the moment we can think of it as follows: if there is any behaviour of the system that reaches a state in which an item from the set M shows up in plaintext form in the intruder's set of knowledge this is deemed to represent a breach of the secrecy property. We of course suppose that the intruder does not have any elements of M in his original knowledge set so if he does learn a value it must be through observation of messages between the legitimate nodes. We are not concerned that the intruder may be able to get hold of encrypted version of sensitive data items, indeed we fully expect this to happen, as long as he doesn't also get hold of the corresponding decryption key.

Authentication of origin

Intuitively authentication of origin is taken to mean that we can be sure that a message that purports to be from a certain party was indeed originated by that party. Furthermore we will typically also require that we can be sure that the message has not been tampered with between times.

We can turn this around and phrase it as follows: a protocol maintains authentication of origin if it is always the case that if Bob's node accepts a message as being from Anne then it must indeed be the case that earlier Anne sent exactly this message. A stronger property is to further require that Anne actually intended the message for Bob. These can be formulated as predicates on system behaviours.

Notice that here we have made no mention of time so there is no measure of the time that might have elapsed between Anne sending her message and Bob receiving it. We tend to assume, for example, that if an agent is still prepared to accept a response to a nonce challenge then the challenge itself was sent out only 'recently'. To take more detailed account of the freshness of the message when it reaches Bob, and to express timed requirements, we typically need a timed model (*see* Chapters 1 and 5).

Another point to note is that there is nothing in this formulation to prevent Bob receiving the message several times even if Anne only sent it once. For many applications this may not be a concern so this formulation is adequate. Sometimes it may be an issue. For example, if the messages represent money transfers then clearly we don't want to allow one deposit to lead to multiple increments to Anne's account. For such applications the predicate can be strengthened in a straightforward fashion, as discussed in Chapter 3.

Entity authentication

The term 'entity authentication' crops up frequently in the literature and its meaning is often unclear. In particular the distinction between entity authentication and authentication of origin is not obvious. Intuitively the notion is that you can be confident that the claimed identity of an agent with whom you are interacting is correct. To a large extent this is already captured in the notion of authentication of origin: you are able to verify the origin of each message you receive from an agent during the course of an interaction.

Entity authentication carries with it a notion of timeliness that is absent in the simple formulation of authentication of origin given above. There also seems to be an implication that it is a one-off process: you establish the identity of your interlocutor and proceed with your interaction. For some forms of communications media this might make sense, if for example once a link is established it is difficult for a third party to tap into it and start masquerading. Terms like 'trusted channel' are sometimes employed to indicate such a link. Such links can be implemented, but great care needs to be taken if you are incorporating the assumption of such links in your analysis. Even if you do have such a link set up, there remains the possibility, for example, that your interlocutor gets overpowered by an intruder and again authentication is undermined.

It is actually rather difficult to capture the notion of entity authentication in a precise mathematical way and for most purposes it seems enough to regard it as a repeated form of origin authentication at each step of the interaction between agents. This is the approach that we will adopt in this book. Gollmann has studied the notion of authentication in great detail in, for example [36]. Much of the confusion surrounding the notion of entity authentication seems to arise from differing models of communication: some people think in connection-oriented terms, others in connectionless terms. The way that we model communications in this book corresponds to the connectionless approach: each message is separately consigned to the medium and the fate of every message is independent.

Integrity

Integrity is usually taken to mean that data cannot be corrupted, or at least that any such corruption will always be detected. In this sense integrity is seen as a corollary of our authentication property above. This follows from the fact that in this formulation we required that the contents of the output message match that of the input message. Notice that we are thinking of the occurrence of an event such as *receive.Anne.Bob.m* as indicating that the node has not detected any corruption of the message and has output it to Bob. If it were possible for a corrupted message to be accepted then this would show up as a violation of the property above and we would have to deem the protocol to be flawed. We could relax the condition in our definition of origin authentication that the data values match. This would give us something akin to entity authentication: it would establish that the other party is alive and responding, but would not guarantee the authenticity of any contents we might receive. This may be useful in some circumstances, for example if you want to check that an alarm is active.

This captures the notion of integrity of communicated messages. Integrity can also be taken to encompass the immunity from corruption of stored data. We will not explore this further as it is really a systems security issue rather than a security protocols problem.

Authenticated key-exchange

One of the major roles of security protocols is to enable authenticated, confidential communication across networks by setting up key material between the various players. To some extent this can be viewed as a special case of secrecy as described earlier, where the sensitive data items are the keys. However, it is a bit more subtle as we have to be precise about who should get knowledge of the keys and who must not. It is also often the case that further properties besides secrecy of the keys are called for. Slightly different terminology is used to reflect the differing requirements.

Secrecy alone is not enough, or at least we have to be far more precise about what secrecy means. Pure Diffie-Hellman key establishment (*see* page 20) does provide a form of secrecy in that only the two interlocutors know the session key at the end of the protocol. The problem is that it is all very well knowing that you share a secret with another person but not much use if you do not know for sure who this other person is.

Thus the essential properties to be upheld by a key-establishment protocol are the secrecy and authenticity of the resulting session keys. More precisely: suppose that Anne starts up a protocol to agree a key to talk to Bob. We need to be confident that whenever Anne reaches a commit state in which she thinks that she shared a key K with Bob, then K should indeed be known at most to Anne and Bob. Similarly for Bob. Thus key establishment and authentication must be inextricably bound up in the protocol to avoid any danger of one of the players being fooled into associating the key with the wrong agent. We will refer to such requirements as authenticated key establishment.

Many authenticated key-establishment protocols are based on a cryptographic primitive like Diffie-Hellman to provide the secrecy of the session key with additional features to ensure the authentication. A prime example of this is the Station-To-Station (STS) protocol due to Diffie, Van Oorschot and Wiener [24]. The reference is in fact an excellent summary of authentication and authenticated key-exchange protocols and recommended reading for anyone interested in the subject.

One of STS's key features is the intertwining of the authentication with key exchange, which would seem vital in order to assure that authentication is maintained.

Assume first (as in Diffie-Hellman, page 20) that a cyclic group along with a primitive element a are publicly known. Assume further that public keys of users are available (for example via certificates issued by a certifying authority). With this in place we proceed as follows:

Anne chooses a random number x and sends a^x to Bob. All calculations are of course performed modulo p. Bob now chooses a random number y and calculates $k = a^{xy}$. He then sends Anne a message of the form:

$$a^y.\{Sign_{Bob}(a^y.a^x)\}_k$$

where $Sign_{Bob}(X)$ denotes the application of Bob's signature to X.

Anne can now compute $k = a^{yx}$ and thence decrypt the token and then finally check Bob's signature from her knowledge of his public key. Anne now sends Bob:

$$\{Sign_{Anne}(a^x.a^y)\}_k$$

Finally Bob can decrypt and check Anne's signature. Figure 0.2 summarizes the exchanges involved. The outcome of all this is that Anne and Bob should be confident of each other's identities and that they share a key k that can now be used for subsequent communication using a symmetric encryption scheme.

The security of the scheme can be enhanced by allowing each user to use a distinct field. The most powerful attacks against these Diffie-Hellman style schemes involve the pre-calculation of a large look-up table to speed up the calculation of logarithms. If a single field is used over a network then clearly such attacks become

Anne   Bob

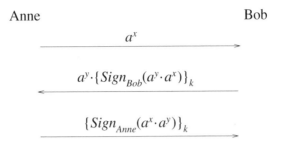

Figure 0.2 Station-To-Station protocol

more attractive. If this proposal is adopted then of course a minor modification to the protocol is needed to ensure that both parties use the same field and primitive element. Thus the first message must include a statement of p and a. So Anne starts the protocol by sending: $a^x.p.a$. Other variants of the protocol are also suggested, such as an authentication-only version. A version in which certificates are shipped across with the messages is also proposed for a situation in which the public keys are not already distributed.

The term 'key-agreement' often also carries an additional connotation: that both players contribute to the final value of the session key, ideally in a symmetrical fashion. In particular, in the absence of some form of collusion, neither can determine the final value. Protocols based on the Diffie-Hellman scheme are a prime example. When Anne supplies her a^x term she cannot predict what y value Bob will use. Arguably if Bob could compute discrete logs he could choose a y to give a particular value for K but we are in any case supposing that this is intractable.

Sometimes Anne, say, may want to know not only that the key is at most known only to her and to Bob but further to be sure that Bob does indeed know it and associates it with communication with her. This kind of requirement is often referred to as key-confirmation. What typically happens is that the agents' knowledge grows as the protocol unfolds. Consider the following toy protocol:

$$\text{Message 1}\quad Anne \rightarrow Bob \quad : \quad Sign_{Anne}(Bob.a^x)$$
$$\text{Message 2}\quad Bob \;\;\rightarrow Anne \quad : \quad Sign_{Bob}(Anne.a^x.a^y)$$
$$\text{Message 3}\quad Anne \rightarrow Bob \quad : \quad \{data\}_K$$

where $K = a^{xy}$.

After receiving the first message Bob knows that Anne wants to talk to him and that she has supplied the Diffie-Hellman term a^x. He responds with the second message and can already infer that if Anne gets this message uncorrupted she should be able to calculate the session key K. Arguably, he could already try sending some data to her along with this message encrypted with K. In fact this would be rather dangerous as, at this stage, he has no assurance of the freshness of the first message from Anne. However, when she receives this second message from Bob she knows that he has acquired her a^x term and has provided his a^y and so he presumably knows

K and associates it with her. Furthermore, she has assurances of freshness of message 2 because her Diffie-Hellman term in effect doubles as a nonce. She could now transmit some data to Bob encrypted with K. On receiving this Bob can now infer that Anne did indeed receive his message and so has constructed K and associates it with him. It may be preferable, of course, just to have some innocent data value here.

Note how the Diffie-Hellman terms double as nonces, so providing assurances of freshness. Note further that we can perform an authentication analysis on this protocol to check that if Bob accepts a^x as originating from Anne then it really was created by Anne and vice versa. We can then invoke the Diffie-Hellman problem to infer the secrecy of the term K between Anne and Bob.

The terms 'key distribution' and 'key transport' are sometimes used to denote schemes in which the keys are generated in one place and shipped out as requested. Here we are thinking more of some central server creating keys as required. There is no notion of the various participants all contributing to the resulting keys, as with the Diffie-Hellman scheme, for example. The Needham-Schroeder Secret-Key or Yahalom (see p. 33) protocols provide examples of key distribution protocols in which the key is generated solely by the server with no input from the principals.

Non-repudiation

For most security goals we are making assumptions that the legitimate participants are honest, i.e. behave according to the protocol rules. Usually it will be in their interests to do so. If, for example, Anne and Bob want to have a private conversation then it is in their interests not to disclose their keys or stray from the protocol rules.

Non-repudiation is rather different however. Here we are concerned with protecting one participant against possible cheating by another. Consequently we cannot assume that the 'legitimate' participants will not cheat. In essence the idea is to provide the parties with evidence that certain steps of the protocol have occurred. For example, non-repudiation of transmission should provide the recipient with proof that the message was indeed sent by the claimed sender, even if the sender subsequently tries to deny it. Furthermore, this proof must be convincing to a third party, not just to the recipient himself. It is essential therefore that the evidence should not be forgeable by the recipient.

As such we see that non-repudiation appears to be very similar to authentication. This suggests that we may be able to capture this property as a variant of authentication, but ensure that our model endows the principals with intruder-like capabilities. That is, the participants are given capabilities to fake messages up to the usual cryptographic constraints. If we can then show that Bob could only have come into possession of a message of a certain form if Anne had actually sent an appropriately related message to him then we will have shown that the non-repudiation property holds. This will usually call for some signature-type mechanism to ensure that Bob can only come into possession of such a message if Anne really had previously signed and sent it to him. Alternatively, a trusted notary can be used, but this adds communication overheads and so on.

Fairness

Occasionally protocols are required to enforce certain fairness properties.   In electronic contract signing, for example, we will want to avoid one of the participants being able to gain some advantage over another by halting the protocol part-way through. Bob could, for example, refuse to continue after Anne has signed up, but before he has signed. Various protocols have been proposed to address this, some involving Trusted Third Parties (notaries). Others avoid this but use instead some form of incremental commitment mechanism. See for example [102]. There tends to be a trade-off here between, on the one hand, the need to involve a third party and, on the other, the need for rather a lot of communication. The former calls for an extra entity to be trusted and to be available. The latter tends to require a large number of messages to pass back and forth. More recent protocols seek to provide fairness efficiently by only resorting to a third party in the event of dispute as discussed in [6].

Anonymity

Anonymity is a property that seems to have been explored comparatively little from a formal point of view.   Intuitively a system that is anonymous over some set of events E should have the property that when an event from E occurs then an observer, though he may be able to deduce that an event from E has occurred, will be unable to identify which. Of course this will in general depend on the status of the observer so we must be clear about the observer viewpoint in formalizing such a property. Typically the set E will be an indexing set of users, so we are asserting that although an observer may be able to tell that a certain class of action has occurred, he is not able to identify which of the agents was associated with it.

An elegant formalization of this property can be given in CSP. The key idea is to use the renaming operator of CSP to shuffle the events of the set E. We then assert that if the observer's view of the system is unchanged after an arbitrary shuffling of the set E then the system provides anonymity with respect to the set E and that observer.

A number of examples of systems displaying various degrees of anonymity, such as Chaum's 'dining cryptographers', have been analysed using FDR (*see* Chapter 3).

The CSP approach is essentially 'possibilistic' in style, that is to say it abstracts away from issues of probability and considers only whether or not certain events are possible. Other approaches have taken a probabilistic style, for example Pfitzmann and Waidner [72].   Here the idea is to show that the *a posteriori* probability distribution over some event set that some observer can assign after an observation is equal to the *a priori* distribution before the observations.

Up to now we have assumed that anonymity should apply to each occurrence of the events in question, in effect that the events from the anonymity set could be freshly shuffled on each occurrence. In some situations we might not expect the occurrence of events from the set to be wholly independent. Voting provides a good example: we do not want a particular vote to be associated with an individual, but on the other hand we want to prevent double voting. The events are thus not independent but are subject to the constraint that for a given run each event should occur at most once.

This and other similar conditional forms of anonymity are most elegantly formalized as constrained forms of the strong anonymity outlined above. Here we construct a process that embodies the constraint and compose it in parallel with the system and again impose the anonymity condition on this. Any behaviours that violate the constraint will fall outside the condition. This allows for the possibility that if an agent violates the constraint then his anonymity will be broken and his identity revealed.

Alternatively we may want to design the system so that such behaviours are not possible. In this case we simply do a refinement check of the system against the constraint.

Availability

Thus far we have discussed the rather negative properties of protocols: establishing that they do not allow certain undesirable behaviours. It is clearly also important to be able to establish that, under appropriate assumptions, the protocol will achieve some desired goal. Thus, for example, for a key-exchange protocol, we would like to be confident that a session will indeed be established. We need to use the more sophisticated semantic models of CSP that deal with such liveness issues. Thus we might have a specification along the lines of: if Anne requests the server to set up a session key between her and Bob then the system must subsequently reach a state in which Anne and Bob both have knowledge of the fresh session key.

Of course, for a system to be able to guarantee such a property we will need to curtail the intruder capabilities to some extent, in particular we cannot allow him unlimited ability to kill messages. It is fairly straightforward to construct models of intruders with curtailed capabilities, e.g. able to kill only a finite number of messages or only over some finite period.

0.3 Cryptography

For the purposes of this book we will treat cryptographic algorithms in a very abstract way. We will be concerned with what properties such algorithms provide and not with the details of how they are implemented. In particular, details of their cryptographic strength will not really concern us; we will typically assume that the algorithms are secure (though in some of the more elaborate analyses we can take account of possible compromises).

In recent decades the science of cryptography has moved from being the exclusive preserve of governments and security agencies into the open world. This has been prompted partly by the increase in the importance of secure communications, but also in large part by the discovery of public-key cryptography (PKC) [23]. It is now widely studied and taught in academia and industry and as a result there is now a substantial open literature on cryptography.

For the most part the two topics of protocol analysis and cryptanalysis have developed quite separately, that is the two styles of analysis are typically conducted quite independently. This is partly to keep the analysis tractable: a model that encompasses aspects relevant to both is likely to be virtually intractable. It can also be attributed in part to the fact that the two communities – the formal analysts and the cryptologists – are largely disjoint and attend separate conferences etc. This is starting to change gradually, with some collaboration and interchange of ideas and techniques taking place between these communities.

For most of this book we will be making this separation, in common with virtually all work in this field. It should be noted though that potentially there can be subtle interactions between protocols and cryptographic algorithms, leading to flaws that would not show up in either style of analysis conducted separately. We will return to this issue in Chapter 10.

Here we will outline the features of cryptographic primitives that we will need later. Our outline is necessarily rather shallow and will not cover all aspects of the subject. We are seeking only to give the reader sufficient feel for the nature and role of these primitives in security protocols. Anyone wanting to delve deeper into the fascinating subject is referred to [89], [100] or [97], for example. An excellent reference book that gives a very rigorous treatment of the whole subject is the *Handbook of Applied Cryptography* [63]. Less mathematical and technical expositions, but excellent introductions with plenty of historical background, can be found in [45] and [94], for example.

Symmetric cryptography

Until the advent of public-key cryptography all cryptography was what we now class as symmetric or secret-key. In effect this means that for two parties to communicate securely they need to share some secret: the cryptographic key. The process of encryption is essentially the same as that of decryption; in particular if you can do one you can necessarily do the other. To take a simple example: in the Caesar cipher you encrypt by shifting each plaintext letter three forward in the alphabet. Clearly, to decrypt you shift back three in the alphabet.

This is rather like the situation with ordinary locks and keys: locking and unlocking can be done with a single key, you just twist in opposite directions. It is not usual to have locks that require one key to lock and a different one to unlock, though in principle such a lock could be constructed. It is of course common to have locks that do not require a key to lock but do to unlock, and indeed this does have some analogy with the notion of public cryptography. We will return to this in the next section.

A distinction is often drawn between the notion of a code, in which the syntactic objects that are manipulated may be letters, syllables, words or phrases, and a cipher, in which (blocks of) letters, alphanumerics, bits etc. are manipulated. Codes in this sense will not be relevant to us.

Ciphers can be classified into substitution and transposition. In the former the letters of the plaintext are replaced by ciphertext equivalents according to some algorithm. In the latter the letters are unchanged but their position is shuffled. Transposition ciphers will not concern us, but it should be noted that modern block ciphers typically involve substitution and transposition to achieve appropriate levels of confusion and diffusion.

Substitution ciphers are further divided up into stream and block ciphers. The distinction is only important to us in as much as it affects integrity issues: the extent to which attempts to manipulate the ciphertext and hence the decrypted plaintext can be detected.

In a stream cipher each symbol is encrypted individually in turn. The Caesar cipher is a simple example in which the same transformation is applied to each symbol of the plaintext. Such ciphers are usually referred to as monographic. A more sophisticated stream cipher would involve applying a varying transformation as you move through the plaintext, for example the Vigenère cipher in which the substitution is determined by a cyclic key. Another example, with a vastly longer, mechanically generated key cycle, is the German Second World War Enigma machine. This is referred to as polyalphabetic. A one-time-pad in which the numerical representation of the plaintext letters are added modulo 26 to a random, letter key stream is another. Such ciphers can provide very high-grade secrecy, indeed a genuine one-time pad system is known to provide perfect security when properly used [92]. However, the key stream has to be truly random, at least as long as the plaintext, and never reused.

What precisely we mean by 'random' here is itself a deep topic that we will not delve into. Crudely speaking, it can be taken to mean that the stream cannot be compressed without loss of information. Thus a pseudo-random stream is not truly random, in that an arbitrarily long sequence can be generated once you know the appropriate algorithm and key. Nor is a cyclic key for which it suffices to know the cycle pattern.

Although stream ciphers can provide a very high level of secrecy they tend to be very weak in providing integrity. As a stream cipher encrypts each element of the plaintext separately it may be possible for the ciphertext to be altered in a way that is not detectable by, for example, changing letters of the ciphertext or cutting out, inserting or reordering chunks. This may not be easy, as most such manipulation will lead to obvious garbling of the resulting plaintext, but there are scenarios in which this is a real danger. Subverting Bob's nonce challenge in the Needham-Schroeder Secret-Key protocol is an excellent example. Another concerns financial transactions involving messages of fixed format in which certain fields represent amounts of money. These fields could easily be altered in a way that would not be readily detectable. Clearly, redundancy in the message space helps, but the point is that the encipherment does not of itself provide any integrity assurances.

In a block cipher, encryption is performed on blocks of plaintext rather than on each letter or bit individually. A well-known, classical example is the Playfair cipher in which the encryption is performed on pairs of letters. The alphabet (minus J) is written into a five by five table. The order of the letters in this table constitutes the key. Suppose that we choose the table (scrambled using the keyword 'dyslexia'):

```
D  Y  S  L  E
X  I  A  B  C
F  G  H  K  M
N  O  P  Q  R
T  U  V  W  Z
```

To encipher a pair of letters, PL say, we first situate them in the table. Typically a pair of letters will occupy different rows and columns, as is the case here, and so form opposite corners of a rectangle. The ciphertext letters are taken to be the other corners of the rectangle ordered according to some suitable convention. Thus PL enciphers to QS in this case. Different rules apply when the letters fall on the same row or column. Double letters in pairs can be eliminated by inserting nulls.

The Playfair cipher is thus a simple substitution cipher acting on pairs of letters, digraphs, rather than single letters. It is simple in the sense that the mapping $A \times A \to A \times A$ remains constant. It of course considerably more complex than a simple monographic cipher, which is a constant mapping $A \to A$. The complexity and security can be made greater by working with larger blocks.

Computers allow us to construct ciphers that work with far bigger blocks than would be practical with pen and paper. Ciphers that work with 64 or 128-bit blocks are typical. The Data Encryption Standard (DES) system is a well-known example. Here the ciphertext is first translated into binary streams using, for example, the ASCII standard. Encryption is now performed on strings of 64 bits at a time and involves an iterated sequence of complex transformations designed to ensure a high degree of confusion and diffusion. In particular, altering a single bit in the plaintext string influences the value of all the ciphertext bits of the block. It is thus extremely difficult to manipulate the ciphertext to produce a given change in the corresponding plaintext.

With the rapid growth in computing power DES is now widely thought to be vulnerable to current cryptanalytic techniques and tools and to have reached the end of its useful life. Another symmetric, block algorithm that is widely thought to be very strong is the IDEA algorithm [50] that works with 128-bit blocks. At the time of writing a competition is being staged by the US National Institute for Standards and Technology to establish a new encryption standard AES (Advanced Encryption Standard) [67].

Asymmetric or public-key cryptography

Prior to 1976 it was taken as an unwritten axiom that all cryptography had to be symmetric: to communicate securely the participants would have to share a common secret. So ingrained was this assumption that it was not even recognized as such.

In 1976 a paper was published by Diffie and Hellman [23] that was to take cryptography into entirely new realms. Here, for the first time in the open literature, the possibility of forms of secret communication without a prior shared secret was aired.

The idea of public-key cryptographic systems had in fact been invented slightly earlier at GCHQ, but was not made public. Indeed this fact was not publicly announced until 1998. Details can be found in [94].

Public-key systems open up possibilities that would previously have been regarded as absurd. For example, it is possible for two complete strangers who do not have any prior shared secrets to establish a shared secret using only open lines of communication. Superficially, this sounds manifestly impossible: any information available to them will equally be available to anyone who can monitor the traffic. Any knowledge they can derive can also be derived by the intruder. However, this ignores the issue of the complexity of deriving information from given information.

First we describe how the concept can be used. Later we will outline some of the mathematical concepts that are used to actually realize the idea. Finding workable, secure implementations of the concept was non-trivial and indeed refinements and new approaches are still being developed.

In public-key cryptography keys come in pairs, one that we will refer to as the private key SK_i and the other the public key, PK_i. The subscript i is drawn from some indexing set that will typically correspond to the set of names of users. Decryption using the private key undoes the effect of encryption with the public key:

$$\{\{X\}_{PK_i}\}_{SK_i} = X$$

However, knowledge of PK_i, say, does not entail knowledge of SK_i and vice versa. This gives us a possibility that was not available with shared-key cryptography: we can make PK_i publicly known whilst keeping SK_i private. Anyone who knows Anne's public key PK_a can send her a secret message by simply encrypting it under PK_a. Assuming that Anne has kept SK_a private and only she knows it then only she can undo the encryption and so read the contents. Some asymmetric schemes such as the RSA scheme, devised by Rivest, Shamir and Adleman [74], have the additional property that:

$$\{\{X\}_{SK_i}\}_{PK_i} = X$$

but this is not true of all public-key schemes.

In fact, using public-key techniques to exchange secret information in this way tends to be very inefficient due to the effort required to perform the necessary computations. Public-key techniques are far more effective when used for authentication and for establishing session keys that can then be used with a symmetric algorithm to do the actual exchanges of secret information. Many of the protocols we will be seeing through this book are designed to achieve various flavours of this.

Coming up with the notion of public-key cryptography is one thing, coming up with a mathematical scheme to actually realize it is yet another. James Ellis of GCHQ, one of the co-inventors of public-key ciphers, gives an account that is interesting here. Having conceived of the possibility, he was stumped as to how to realize it in an effective way. He did come up with an existence theorem, however, by noting that one possibility is simply to have a pair of vast code books, one the inverse of the other. The decryption book can be thought of as the private key, the encryption book as the public key. The former will be organized in lexical order according to the ciphertext, the latter according to plaintext. We assume that these books embody random permutations, one being the inverse of the other. Now we note that with the encryption book it is easy to encrypt a message. However to decrypt a message will be extremely difficult because you do not have the appropriate lexical ordering. In effect you have to search the entire book to decrypt each element. With the decryption book decryption is easy of course – you have the right lexical ordering.

This is fine in theory, but to provide a good degree of security these books will have to be astronomically large to ensure that searching is infeasible. The required size means that it is not practical actually to construct them so this remains a proof of existence rather than a practical possibility. What is really needed is a mathematical procedure to generate the elements of the books as and when they are required. Given that this procedure must also be infeasible to run in reverse it is still not clear that this can ever be realized in a practical way.

The mathematical trickery that enables us to realize the PKC idea in a workable way is the notion of one-way functions and in particular trap-door functions. A one-way function is one that is easy to compute in one direction but intractable in the other. A trap-door function has the added feature that it can be reversed quite easily if you possess a suitable secret, the trap-door, but of course this trap-door has to be extremely difficult to discover. Of course, whoever constructs the function can incorporate the trap-door quite easily. Devising mathematical functions that are one-way and for which a trap-door can be incorporated and effectively concealed is really the key breakthrough here. First let us describe two mathematical operations that were identified early on as having the one-way property:

- calculating the product of a pair of numbers is easy whilst the inverse process of factorizing a number into prime factors is, in general, thought to be intractable;
- taking an exponent in a finite field is easy whilst computing the log of an element of such a field is thought to be intractable.

See Appendix A for further details of these operations, in particular what exactly is meant by intractable.

Just having a one-way function does not advance you very far in the quest for a way of realizing public-key encryption: the legitimate recipient of the message is not going to be any better off than the intruder when it comes to decrypting. An extra ingredient is needed: the notion of a trap-door, a secret that enables the reverse of the one-way function to be calculated easily. Of course, the trap-door has to be hard to discover just from knowledge of the encryption algorithm. We describe two ways to achieve this.

The best known is the RSA algorithm. Here we sketch how it works (the details of the number theory that lies behind it can be found in Appendix A):

1 Two 'large' distinct primes p and q are chosen and their product $n = pq$

computed.

2 An integer e is chosen that is relatively prime to $(p-1)(q-1)$.

3 An integer d is found such that $ed = 1 \, \mathbf{mod} \, (p-1)(q-1)$. Using Fermat's Little Theorem it can be shown that, for all m:

$$m^{ed} = m(\mathbf{mod} \; n) \tag{1}$$

4 n and e are publicized whilst p, q and d are kept secret.

Encryption of a message m (modulo n) can now be performed by anyone knowing the public values n and e by computing:

$$c = m^e(\mathbf{mod} \; n)$$

If the message does not encode to a number less than n then it must be chopped into a suitable number of blocks such that each can be so encoded and each block is enciphered separately.

Decryption is effected by taking the dth power modulo n of the ciphertext (number) which, thanks to equation 3 above equals the original message:

$$c^d = m^{ed} = m(\mathbf{mod} \; n)$$

If you know the factorization of n it is comparatively easy to find a d that is 'inverse to' e, in effect to construct the decryption algorithm corresponding to the encryption with e. The details are in Appendix A. Without the knowledge of the factorization it is thought to be intractable to find a suitable d. In turn, the factorization of the product of a pair of large, suitably chosen primes is thought to be intractable. In effect the factorization of n constitutes the trap-door for this algorithm and its concealment depends on the difficulty of factorization. The description of another trap-door one-way algorithm for encryption, the ElGamal algorithm based on the difficulty of taking discrete logarithms in a finite field, is also given in Appendix A.

It must of course be stressed that the belief that problems like factorization and taking discrete logs are intractable remain unproven conjectures, albeit supported by strong circumstantial evidence. As yet nobody has come up with an effective algorithm for their solution, but equally no proof exists that no efficient algorithm could exist. Indeed any such proof would presumably have to be relative to some model of computation. Thus even if such a proof were found and if effective alternative models of computation were found – quantum computation, to take a random example – then all bets would be off.

An alternative way of using one-way functions is for key establishment. This is rather more straightforward as it is not actually necessary to devise a trap-door: it suffices to have a family of one-way, commutative functions. The Diffie-Hellman key establishment scheme is based on the difficulty of taking discrete logs: finding the exponent l (for a given a, b, and n) such that $a^l = b \, \mathbf{mod} \, n$.

1 A prime p and a primitive root a modulo p are chosen and made public (a being primitive simply means that all numbers between 1 and $p-1$ can be generated by taking exponents of a modulo p).

2 Anne chooses at random an integer x and sends Bob the message: $m_1 = a^x(\mathbf{mod}\ p)$.

3 Bob chooses an integer y and sends Anne the message: $m_2 = a^y(\mathbf{mod}\ p)$.

4 Now Anne, who knows x and has been sent m_2 by Bob can calculate: $K = m_2^x$.

5 Similarly Bob, who knows y and m_1, can calculate: m_1^y.

6 But now we have that $m_2^x = m_1^y$, because $a^{xy}(\mathbf{mod}\ p) = a^{yx}(\mathbf{mod}\ p)$.

7 So we let $K = m_2^x = m_1^y$ and K can now be used as the shared key.

Notice that both Anne and Bob played an essentially symmetric role in the generation of K. More precisely, neither of them can dictate or predict what the final value of K will be, barring collusion or solving discrete logs.

It is thought that for an eavesdropper, who only sees the values m_1 and m_2, calculating the K would require taking a discrete logarithm of either m_1 or m_2. Taking logarithms in a discrete field is thought to be intractable, in the general case. This means the process of taking exponents in a discrete field generates a pseudo-random permutation of the field and so gives us one of our code books. It does not, however, give us the inverse book, but for this scheme we don't need the inverse function. All that we need is that operation of taking exponents commutes to ensure that Anne and Bob arrive at the same value.

This suggests that one could try other large, commutative groups as a source of structures on which to base such a key establishment scheme, and indeed elliptic and hyper-elliptic curves have been proposed, for example [90]. Elliptic curves appear to provide a rather attractive framework, as the equivalent of the discrete logs problem here appears if anything to be harder than for finite fields. The most powerful techniques for tackling the problem of taking logs in a discrete field is based on the so-called index calculus. There is no known equivalent of the index calculus in the context of elliptic curves.

As it stands, the scheme described is flawed in that it is open to man-in-the-middle attacks, which we will describe shortly, due to the lack of authentication. Elaborations of this scheme that avoid such attacks are described in the section on authenticated key exchange.

A number of other 'hard' problems have been proposed as the basis for public key encryption or key establishment. These include variants of the knapsack packing problem, coding theory problems, and so on. These have tended to fall foul of various vulnerabilities and so have not really taken off or been implemented. We will not discuss them further here. The interested reader can find further details in [89, 97, 100], for example.

0.4   Public-key certificates and infrastructures

In our discussion above we have glossed over a difficulty of how the agents acquire the public keys of other users and be sure that they are valid, i.e. associated with the correct user. This is quite tricky, but a standard solution is to set up a trusted authority, known as the Certification Authority (CA), that issues certificates that authenticate public keys and binds them to the names of the users. A public-key certificate is basically a digital document that contains the name of the user along with their authorized public key and perhaps information about the lifetime of the key etc., all signed by the CA using its public key. We discuss digital signatures later. As long as the CA does not cheat and is trusted by the users, the problem reduces to being sure that you have a valid public key for the CA which you can use to check certificates. When you need to acquire someone's public key you simply request a copy of the relevant certificate from some publicly accessible library, say, and verify the signature. Alternatively people just keep a copy of their own certificate and supply it as required. This idea can be applied recursively to establish hierarchies of Certification Authorities, but of course ultimately the recursion has to be cut off. The public key of the root authority has to be distributed in some off-line manner, for example by being published in hard copy [4].

A rather different approach is adopted by Zimmermann [103] in his PGP (Pretty Good Privacy) system. Rather than depending on a central, trusted authority, PGP works by recommendations: if someone you trust passes you the public key for another user in some authenticated fashion then you will tend to trust that key. Thus users gradually build up networks of trust. If you get someone's key from several sources then of course you tend to have a correspondingly higher level of confidence in the validity of the key.

Revocation of certificates remains a tricky problem: how to call in compromised or invalidated certificates. There is no entirely accepted solution to this problem. An obvious step is to give certificates a lifetime. This helps, but getting the lifetime right is not easy: too long and an invalid certificate might survive in the wild for quite a while, too short and you spend a lot of effort refreshing certificates.

For the purposes of this book we will usually assume that each user has a unique private key and associated public key. We further assume that some suitable infrastructure exists to associate reliably the correct public key with the correct user. It should be borne in mind that this may not always be an appropriate or safe assumption. Sometimes there will be good reasons for users to have more than one private/public key pair, for example, and we may then have to take care that this cannot be exploited. It may also be that the mechanisms for associating public keys with users are flawed.

It is possible to design a protocol in such a way as to insulate it from vulnerabilities of the infrastructure for providing public keys. One can, for example, pass certificates with the messages of a key establishment protocol in a way that ensures that they are cryptographically bound to the rest of the message. This ensures that the recipient uses the certificate intended by the sender.

0.5 Encryption modes

Block ciphers can be used in a number of ways or modes. The simplest is the electronic code book mode in which each block is enciphered separately and in turn. This has the merit of being straightforward but does suffer from the drawback of not providing any linkage between successive blocks. As a result, it is comparatively easy to delete, modify or re-order blocks, insert fake blocks, and so on.

Of course for short messages that fit in a single block this is really not an issue. Such messages do occur, particularly if the data is, say, a key or nonce: this might well comprise 128 bits, so if the cipher acts on 128-bit blocks then it is fine. However, many messages will span blocks and so these dangers appear. To foil such vulnerabilities requires more sophisticated modes of encryption that introduce some form of binding between blocks. One such mode is Cipher Block Chaining (CBC) and it works as follows.

Suppose that the cipher acts on blocks of length l. Denote the blocks of the plaintext by $P1$, $P2$, $P3$ etc. up to Pn. Some padding may be necessary to fill out the final block. Typically this mode will also involve the use of an Initialization Vector IV which should be a freshly, randomly chosen value for each message. The first block of the ciphertext comprises IV in plain. The second cipher block is the encryption of the first plaintext block xor'ed with the first cipher block:

$$\{IV \oplus P1\}_K$$

Subsequent cipher blocks are constructed by iterating this process: enciphering the xor of the appropriate plaintext block with the ciphertext output of the previous block:

$$Ci := \{Pi \oplus Ci - 1\}_K$$

Thus the value of the ith cipher block depends on that of the $i - 1$th, and hence on all the previous blocks. As a result any messing with a block of the ciphertext will result in a garbling of the decrypt from that point on. In effect we have built in forward-error propagation.

Other modes exist and have various properties that make them more or less suitable in certain applications. The significant point from our point of view is that cryptographic techniques exist to bind together blocks of text when used in such a way as to ensure that any tampering with any block will be detectable.

0.6 Cryptographic hash functions

Hash functions map inputs of data of arbitrary length into outputs of some fixed length. They serve a variety of purposes in computer science, for example as a way of detecting corruption of data. Suppose that the data is stored alongside its hashed value. If the data is corrupted, a re-computation of the hash will almost certainly not agree with the stored value. We are assuming, of course, that the range of the hash function is some reasonably large space so the chance of accidental agreement is small. We are also assuming that small changes in the data input produce some large change in the hash value. As a result it is unlikely that an arbitrary change in the input data will result in the same hash value, even if the hash value itself has also been corrupted.

To detect accidental corruption of the data, the hash function does not have to be particularly sophisticated: a glorified parity check such as a Cyclic Redundancy Check (CRC) will do. Where we are trying to guard against malicious alteration of the data we have to be more careful in our choice of hash. For a simple hash function it will be fairly easy for someone to choose an alteration of the data that yields the same hash value, which will thus go undetected. To avoid this we must choose a function for which, given some input, it is extremely difficult to find another input that gives the same hash output. Such hash functions are referred to as cryptographic hashes. Designing such functions and establishing that they do have such characteristics is quite an art in itself. Even defining these characteristics in a precise mathematical way is rather delicate. We will not discuss this in any detail but will merely assume that they exist and are readily available. Again references like [89] and [63] give full details.

Various cryptographic hash functions have been proposed and extensively analyzed, for example MD5, SHA1, RIPEMD-160 and so on. Their role is usually to map texts of arbitrary length to a length suitable for a block cipher. Another role is to serve as a way of committing to a certain text or value without necessarily revealing it. A long established role is in the storage of password material. Rather than store the raw password, which would be vulnerable to snooping, the hash value is stored. Checking can be done by computing the hash of the putative password and checking this against the stored value.

0.7   Digital signatures

These are the analogues in the digital world of conventional signatures and seals of the pen and paper world and supposed to prove the origin and authenticity of the data to which they are bound. Digital signatures are usually implemented using public-key cryptography, though a form of signing that does not provide non-repudiation is possible using private-key encryption. We will stick to the PKC version here. A signature algorithm takes a document and a private key *SK* and produces a signed document. A signature verification algorithm takes a signed document and a public-key *PK* and delivers valid or invalid as output. If the output is valid then we should be entitled to conclude that the document was indeed signed with the matching private key *SK* and furthermore this document has not been corrupted or tampered with.

A well-known implementation of a digital signature is to use a combination of cryptographic hash function and the RSA algorithm. The role of the hash function serves to compress the given message to the size of the block handled by the encryption. Suppose that Anne wants to sign a message M. She first applies a publicly known cryptographic hash H to give:

$$H(\![|M|]\!)$$

which is arranged to match the block size of the encryption algorithm. She then encrypts this with her private key to give:

$$\{H(\![|M|]\!)\}_{SK_{Anne}}$$

and finally she appends her name and the original message to give:

$$Sign_{Anne}(M) := A, M, \{H(\![|M|]\!)\}_{SK_{Anne}}$$

Someone receiving this and knowing Anne's public key is now able to confirm that it is authentic, i.e. that it was indeed signed with Anne's private key and that the value of M has not been tampered with in transit. The checking proceeds as follows:

1 Apply the hash function H to the second term to give $H(\![|M|]\!)$. The function H is publicly known so this is straightforward.

2 Now encrypt the third term using Anne's public key, to give $\{\{H(\![|M|]\!)\}_{SK_{Anne}}\}_{PK_{Anne}}$

Given that for RSA $\{\{X\}_{SK_y}\}_{PK_y} = X$, i.e. encrypting with the public key undoes the effect of the private key encryption as long as the pair of keys match, we see that the outcome of these two calculations should be equal. If the value of any of the terms $Sign_{Anne}(M)$ have been tampered with or if the encryption was not in fact performed using Anne's private key then the equality will fail.

To be sure that this check does actually give a good guarantee that the message is authentic we need to be sure that it would be very hard to forge and very hard to alter M in some way that would not be detected by the check. Informally we can argue that this will be true as long as the encryption and hash functions have the properties we claimed earlier:

▓ Given some W it is very difficult for anyone but Anne to compute $\{W\}_{SK_{Anne}}$ (assuming that SK_{Anne} has not been compromised, i.e. is known only to Anne).

▓ Given a W it is extremely difficult to find W' such that $H(\![|W|]\!) = H(\![|W'|]\!)$.

The scheme would clearly fail if someone other than Anne could apply the encryption. Another way it might fail is if Yves could find an M', different from M, for which $H(\![|M|]\!) = H(\![|M'|]\!)$ and such that M' was somehow more advantageous to him than M.

Note that this verification serves to show that the document was signed with the private key that we have associated with Anne. There remains the problem of whether we have been correct in associating the key with Anne. Even if this issue is solved there remains the further question of whether we can be sure that it really was Anne who did the signing. If Anne has compromised her key then it may be that the document was indeed signed with her key but by someone else. Here we are straying into rather legal, non-technical waters but is is important to be aware of such issues. For example, it may be that it does not matter for some applications that we cannot be sure if it really was Anne who performed the signing. As long as we have performed the verification we might still be guaranteed payment. This is the sort of business model that applied to credit-card payments.

Nonces

The *Oxford English Dictionary* defines the phrase 'for the nonce' as meaning for the time being or for the present occasion and a 'nonce-word' is one coined for one occasion. In the context of security protocols a nonce can informally be taken to be a fresh, random value. It is created as required in a way that is supposed to guarantee that it is unpredictable and unique. Giving precise formal meaning to terms like 'unpredictable', 'fresh' and 'unique' is itself rather subtle and we will see later how this can be done in a number of frameworks, including our own. For the moment the intuitive understanding will suffice. The exact properties we require of nonces can vary somewhat, depending on how exactly they are used. In some cases it may not be necessary to make them unpredictable and so a simple counter might suffice.

Roughly speaking, nonces are usually used to establish causal relationships between messages. Take the example of the nonce in the first and second messages of the NSSK protocol. When Anne checks the nonce value embedded in the message she receives back from the server against her record she can feel confident that this message was indeed generated by the server in response to her latest request. The point of this is to guard against replay attacks: if the nonce was not included in the protocol then Anne is open to an attack as follows.

Suppose that earlier she had invoked the protocol and been provided with a session key k_{ab} to talk to Bob. She and Bob will presumably have long since discarded this key. The trouble is that Yves can cryptanalyze their exchanges at his leisure and eventually break the key. Assuming that the strength of the keys has been chosen to be sufficiently strong to guard the information for as long as it is likely to be useful, this isn't really a problem. By the time Yves finally breaks the key, the information is well past its use-by date. The problem arises when Anne subsequently sends out a new request to Jeeves. Now Yves intercepts Anne's latest request (or alternatively Jeeves's reply) and replays the old message with the old session key back to Anne:

$$\text{Message} \quad J \rightarrow a \;:\; \{b.k_{ab}.\{k_{ab}.a\}_{ServerKey(b)}\}_{ServerKey(a)}$$

Now, unless she has been diligently squirrelling away all her old session keys and checking them all for repeats, Anne has no way of telling that this isn't a fresh message from Jeeves with a fresh key. Consequently she goes ahead and exchanges secret information with Bob that Yves can now read immediately, as easily as Bob in fact.

We now clearly see the role of the nonces and why they have to have unique and unpredictable properties. If they failed to be unique, then Yves could launch a similar replay attack. If they are unique but are predictable, then Yves could fake a request from Anne ahead of time and then simply wait for Anne actually to issue the request at some later time. With luck this will again give him enough time to break the key.

Typically nonces are implemented as freshly created random values drawn from some large space of possible values. Strictly speaking this will not guarantee uniqueness, but if the space is sufficiently large – bit strings of length 128, say – then the chance of a nonce failing to be unique is sufficiently small to be ignored.

Timestamps

Nonces are in some sense local markers in time that an agent lays down as the protocol unfolds. They are local in that they are really only meaningful to whoever created them. In the NSSK protocol, N_a means nothing to either Jeeves or Bob. In fact the value isn't even communicated to Bob. To Anne, though, it is highly significant: she knows that it first saw the light of day when she transmitted her request containing it. As a result, any message that she later gets back that depends on it can only have been created after this point in time.

For some applications such a local reckoning of time is fine, but for many a more global notion is required. For example, suppose that we are using a protocol designed for electronic contract negotiation. Here we may want to assert that an offer will remain valid for a certain time after it is issued. For this we need a global notion of time and a mechanism for marking messages with the time that they are submitted, for example.

A timestamp is simply a way of attaching the current time value to a message. Sometimes it is used as an alternative to nonces: the freshness of a message can be calculated by subtracting its time-stamp from actual time.

For time-stamps to work we need a reliable way of maintaining consistency between clocks across the network. We often also need a reliable way of ensuring that timestamps are valid – guaranteed to give the true time of creation of the message. Two requirements arise from this: that there is some automatic mechanism to attach accurate stamps and that once attached they are difficult to modify or forge.

If we are using time-stamps to help maintain the security of the protocols we need to bear in mind ways that an intruder might try to subvert the mechanisms. He might, for example, try to meddle with the agent's notion of time. He might try to modify or fake timestamps or subvert the time-stamping mechanism. Countering such vulnerabilities can be quite difficult and the designer of protocols must bear this in mind. There has been something of a debate in the community as to whether nonces or timestamps are better. The debate is somewhat vacuous in that they serve rather different purposes. Where they are both candidates for mechanisms to establish freshness it is worth remarking that it tends to be easier to establish a high level of assurance with nonces than with timestamps. For nonces it is sufficient, roughly speaking, to ensure that the random number generation is done carefully. With timestamps we need to worry about maintaining global time, ensuring validity of the stamps, and so on. Even in a benign environment it can be difficult to maintain accurate time across a distributed system. In a hostile environment it is even harder.

0.8 Security protocol vulnerabilities

To illustrate the kind of attacks to which security protocols can fall prey we outline a number of well-known strategies that an intruder might employ. Note however that the style of analysis that we are presenting in this book does not depend on knowing these strategies. In particular we do not need to worry about whether the list is exhaustive. In fact we can be pretty sure that it is not exhaustive. It will, however, serve to illustrate the various styles of attack. We should also note that we are only dealing here with vulnerabilities due to flaws in the protocol design. There are, of course, other styles of attack, such as cryptanalytic, monitoring timing, EM radiation or fluctuations in power consumption. These are typically outside the scope of our formal models.

Man-in-the-middle

As implied by the name, this style of attack involves the intruder imposing himself between the communications between Anne and Bob. If the protocol is poorly designed he may be able to subvert it in various ways; in particular he may be able to masquerade as Bob to Anne, for example.

To illustrate this, consider a naïve protocol in which Anne wants to send a secret message X to Bob using public-key techniques but where Anne and Bob do not even need to know each other's public keys. Using an algorithm like RSA, for which encryption and decryption are inverse and commute, the following protocol suggests itself:

1. Anne sends Bob a message $\{X\}_{PK_{Anne}}$, where $\{X\}_{PK_{Anne}}$ represents the message X encrypted with Anne's public key.

2. When Bob receives this he cannot decrypt it to read the message, only Anne can do this. What he can do is to further encrypt it with his public key:

$$\{\{X\}_{PK_{Anne}}\}_{PK_{Bob}}$$

this he duly does and sends this back to Anne.

3. Now, using the commutative property of RSA we have:

$$\{\{X\}_{PK_{Anne}}\}_{PK_{Bob}} = \{\{X\}_{PK_{Bob}}\}_{PK_{Anne}}$$

and so now Anne can strip off her encryption to give:

$$\{X\}_{PK_{Bob}}$$

4. Anne can send this back to Bob and he, and only he can decrypt it.

At first glance this protocol looks like it might work as a means to enable Anne to communicate securely with Bob given the properties that we have stated. It turns out that Yves can easy subvert it by intercepting the messages between Anne and Bob and inserting some of his own. The attack works as follows:

1 Yves intercepts the first message from Anne to Bob and applies his own public key encryption:

$$\{\{X\}_{PK_{Anne}}\}_{PK_{Yves}}$$

2 This he returns to Anne and she has no way of knowing that this is not the reply she expects from Bob. One random stream looks pretty much like another. So she duly strips off her encryption according to the protocol and sends back to Bob:

$$\{X\}_{PK_{Yves}}$$

3 Now Yves again intercepts this before it reaches Bob and strips off his own encryption to reveal X.

This attack arises due to the lack of any form of authentication in this protocol: Anne has no way of checking that the message she gets back is really from Bob as she expects. The Diffie-Hellman key-establishment protocol that we presented earlier is similarly vulnerable. We leave it as an exercise for the reader to fill in the details.

Reflection

The trick here, as the name suggests, is to bounce messages back at an agent. Sometimes this can fool the originator into revealing the correct response to his message. A simple analogy might be responding to a sentry's 'what is the password?' with 'what is the password?' to which, if he is conditioned to respond automatically to that request, he might respond with the password. You can then supply the password to him. This is a bit simple-minded but just such an attack has been used against some real friend-or-foe type protocols.

The attack depends very much on the symmetry of the situation. In our simple example we are supposing that the sentry is prepared to authenticate himself and does so with the same password as people approaching. Breaking the symmetry by, for example, ensuring that sentries authenticate themselves with a different password to everyone else, would foil at least this attack.

Oracle

Here the intruder tricks an honest agent into inadvertently revealing some information. The honest agent is induced to perform some step of a protocol in a way that helps the intruder to obtain some data he could not otherwise obtain. We will illustrate this shortly with an attack that uses a combination of oracle and interleaving of protocol interactions.

Notice that such an attack may involve the intruder exploiting steps from a different run of the protocol, or indeed may involve steps from an entirely different protocol. The latter tends to be rather more unusual as it is clearly necessary for there to be some commonality between the protocols for this to work, but this is by no means unheard of. This is a distinct danger where key material is shared across protocols.

Countering such vulnerabilities typically involves making the roles of every atomic term of a protocol explicit so that it is clear to which run of which protocol it belongs. The paper by Abadi and Needham [2] discusses explicitness as one example of good practice in protocol design, among others. We discuss how to characterize more precisely the conditions that ensure that there will not be such unfortunate interactions of security protocols in the 'strand spaces' section of Chapter 9.

Replay

Here the intruder monitors a (possibly partial) run of the protocol and at some later time replays one or more of the messages. If the protocol does not have any mechanism to distinguish between separate runs or to detect the staleness of a message, it is quite possible to fool the honest agents into rerunning all or parts of the protocol. We have already seen an example of this with the attack on the weakened NSSK protocol with Anne's nonce removed.

Devices like nonces, identifiers for runs and timestamps are used to try to foil such attacks.

Interleave

This is perhaps the most ingenious style of attack in which the intruder contrives for two or more runs of the protocol to overlap.

Let us illustrate with a famous attack that combines interleaving with oracle techniques.

The protocol in question is the Needham-Schroeder Public-Key protocol. It should not be confused with the Needham-Schroeder Secret-Key protocol that we described earlier. In particular, as the name suggests, it uses public-key algorithms rather than shared secret-key. It proceeds as follows:

$$\text{Message 1} \quad a \rightarrow b \ : \ \{a.n_a\}_{PK_b}$$
$$\text{Message 2} \quad b \rightarrow a \ : \ \{n_a.n_b\}_{PK_a}$$
$$\text{Message 3} \quad a \rightarrow b \ : \ \{n_b\}_{PK_b}$$

In the first step Anne creates the nonce, n_a, and encrypts it (along with her name) under Bob's public key. When Bob receives this he, and only he, can decrypt it and so ascertain the value of n_a. He in turn creates a nonce of his own n_b and encrypts the pair n_a, n_b under Anne's public key which he then sends back to Anne. On receiving this message Anne can decrypt it and check that the value in the first field agrees with the value she has recorded. The other term, Bob's nonce, she encrypts under Bob's public key and sends back to him. When he receives this he can decrypt the message and check that the value is correct. At the end of all this they might be inclined to feel confident that:

■ they know with whom they have been interacting;

■ they agree on the values of n_a and n_b;

■ no one else knows the values n_a and n_b.

These beliefs seem plausible given that only Bob can strip off an encryption using his public key and similarly for Anne's public key. Anne and Bob could presumably now go on to use these values, either for later re-authentication purposes or even maybe to use some hash of them as a shared session key for later secret communications.

For many years this protocol was widely thought to provide exactly these properties. In fact the protocol has be shown to be subject to a rather neat vulnerability discovered by one of the authors [54]. It runs as follows:

$$
\begin{array}{llll}
\text{Message } \alpha.1 & A \rightarrow Y & : & \{A.N_A\}_{PK_Y} \\
\text{Message } \beta.1 & Y(A) \rightarrow B & : & \{A.N_A\}_{PK_B} \\
\text{Message } \beta.2 & B \rightarrow Y(A) & : & \{N_A.N_B\}_{PK_A} \\
\text{Message } \alpha.2 & Y \rightarrow A & : & \{N_A.N_B\}_{PK_A} \\
\text{Message } \alpha.3 & A \rightarrow Y & : & \{N_B\}_{PK_Y} \\
\text{Message } \beta.3 & Y(A) \rightarrow B & : & \{N_B\}_{PK_B}
\end{array}
$$

Note that in this attack Yves is actually a recognized user, that is, he is known to the other users and has a certified public key. We suppose that Anne innocently starts off a protocol run with Yves, thinking of him as a trusted user. Yves however is not interested in playing by the game and instead of responding to Anne in the expected way he uses Anne's nonce to initiate another run with Bob but inserting Anne's name instead of his own. The notation $Y(A)$ denotes Y generating the message, making it appear to have come from A. Bob duly responds with his nonce N_B, but he will of course encrypt it with Anne's public key as he thinks that this run was initiated by her. This is now exactly what Anne is expecting from Yves and so she dutifully proceeds to the next step: she decrypts it and shoots a message back to Yves that contains N_B encrypted with Yves' public key. Yves can of course decrypt this and so he can extract the value of N_B. He can now construct the final message of the run he initiated with Bob: encrypting N_B under Bob's public key.

So, at the end of this we have two interleaved runs of the protocol with Yves sitting at the centre of the web. Anne thinks that she and Yves exclusively share knowledge of N_A and N_B. Bob thinks that he exclusively shares knowledge of N_A and N_B with Anne. This is not the case, even though the agent B believes he ran the protocol with Anne, who is honest. Thus, at the very least, the attack has created a mismatch in Anne and Bob's perception.

This vulnerability has stirred up considerable interest and some controversy in the community. The protocol first saw the light of day in the seminal paper [68] by Needham and Schroeder in 1978. The protocol was subjected to an analysis using the BAN logic of authentication and given a clean bill of health. As a result the protocol was widely regarded as providing a sound mechanism for authentication.

We will discuss in more detail in Chapter 9 how this attack slipped through the BAN analysis. In essence the attack falls outside the assumptions made by the BAN logic. However, the attack provides a nice illustration.

Let us examine more closely how the attack works. It is a combination of interleaving and oracle. Clearly two runs have occurred and completed successfully (the runs are labelled α and β). In steps 2 and 3 Yves is using Anne as an oracle to decrypt the message from Bob that he cannot himself decrypt. She is thus innocently fooled in one run into providing Yves with information that he can use to complete successfully another run with Bob.

Failures of forward secrecy

The attacks described above all work without any cryptanalysis on the part of Yves. He has managed to subvert the protocol purely by manipulating the traffic. Inevitably key material will be compromised, either due to successful cryptanalysis or by other means, for example the three Bs: burglary, blackmail and bribery. An analytic framework needs to be able to model key compromises and allow us to establish the consequences. We can then design mechanisms to contain such compromises as far as possible and to recover as effectively as possible.

Some consequences will be rather obvious: any messages encrypted under a compromised key must be regarded as compromised. Where key transport or distribution has been used with keys being transmitted in encrypted form then we must chain through the effect of a compromise: any key encrypted with a compromised key must itself be regarded as compromised. In effect we need to form a transitive closure of a graph representing the dependencies between keys.

Besides these rather obvious consequences there may well be far more subtle ones. The weakness in NSSK that was identified by Denning and Sacco [22] is a prime example. This is a violation of the goal of forward secrecy: that compromises should not propagate into the future. The attack is somewhat similar to the attack we outlined earlier on a weakened form of NSSK with the initiator's nonce removed. Here we exploited the fact that, with her nonce removed, Anne could not detect the staleness of a replayed message and enclosed session key. If we examine the protocol more carefully we note that the responder, Bob in our example, does not have any way of establishing the freshness of the first message that he sees, number 3 of the protocol. This suggests that we might be able to fool Bob with a stale message, and this is indeed the case. Suppose that Yves has broken an earlier session key K, long since discarded. He can simply replay message 3 to Bob and then masquerade as Anne.

This is an example of quite a general vulnerability: even if we think that we have restored a system's security after a compromise by replacing all compromised keys, or even all session keys, there may still be a way for Yves to leverage an earlier breach and so violate forward secrecy. The counter to this particular attack that was adopted by the Kerberos protocol was to use timestamps in place of nonces. An alternative to counter such an attack is to use nonces in a different way, as with the

Yahalom protocol:

Message 1 $a \rightarrow b$: $a.n_a$
Message 2 $b \rightarrow J$: $b.\{a.n_a.n_b\}_{ServerKey(b)}$
Message 3 $J \rightarrow a$: $\{b.k_{ab}.n_a.n_b\}_{ServerKey(a)} \cdot \{a.k_{ab}\}_{ServerKey(b)}$
Message 4 $a \rightarrow b$: $\{a.k_{ab}\}_{ServerKey(b)} \cdot \{n_b\}_{k_{ab}}$

Here we see that both Anne and Bob get to inject nonces before the request reaches Jeeves. They both get a handle on the freshness of the key that Jeeves generates in response to the message from Bob. That freshness is really guaranteed needs to be carefully verified of course. *We will use the Yahalom protocol as a running example throughout the book.*

Algebraic attacks

Cryptographic functions often satisfy various algebraic identities. Sometimes these are essential for the correct functionality of a protocol. The fact is that exponentiation in a finite field is commutative and this is essential for Diffie-Hellman key establishment to work. However, it may be possible for intruders to exploit such identities to undermine the security of the protocol. A number of examples of this are known, e.g. [34].

In order to be able to identify such attacks it is necessary to represent such identities within the modelling framework. In effect this means extending the intruder's capabilities to include knowledge of such identities and endowing him with a certain facility with algebra. This will be discussed in detail in Chapter 2. There is still the difficulty of being sure that all relevant identities have been identified and correctly modelled. There does not seem to be any easy way to deal with this. A naïve possibility would be to include the functions and algorithms in the model in their full glory. This would certainly be entirely intractable.

The above sections should serve to give the reader an idea of the variety and subtlety of the attacks to which protocols may be vulnerable. There are many other known styles of attack and presumably many more that have yet to be discovered. Many involve combinations of these themes. As we saw, Lowe's attack on the original Needham- Schroeder Public-Key protocol involves a combination of interleaving and oracle attacks, for example. We will see further illustrations of many of these later. Often these are remarkably subtle and in some cases they have gone unnoticed by even the best experts for many years. In many ways spotting an attack on a cryptographic protocol is rather like solving a deep chess combination. The combination is often very subtle, but obvious when you've seen it. As with chess puzzles, a number of standard themes tend to crop up. And it of course helps a lot to have the analogue of a good chess analysis program like Fritz.

0.9 The CSP approach

The approach that we present in this book is centred on the use of the process algebra Communicating Sequential Processes (CSP) and the model-checker FDR. CSP is a mathematical framework for the description and analysis of systems consisting of components (processes) interacting via the exchange of messages [41, 76, 87]. An introduction to CSP is provided in Chapter 1.

In this section we introduce the reader in informal terms to how a system is modelled in CSP. More detailed descriptions in CSP will be given later in Chapter 2.

Nodes and servers, at least honest ones, are fairly straightforward to model as CSP processes, as they merely enact a simple sequence of actions. A little care is needed in treating exceptions, especially where, as is often the case, the design fails to be specific about these. We have to be explicit about what checks are performed by the nodes and what is their intended behaviour if checks fail.

The default behaviour of the medium is to deliver messages correctly to their destination, by which we mean that when it receives a message $i.j.m$ from the node i it will duly output $i.j.m$ to the node j. Note that we generally assume an open addressing scheme. That is to say messages carry address fields that specify the source and destination in the clear. These are not bound to the messages but can be manipulated freely by the intruder. In particular, he can alter the source field to make a message appear to come from a different source. To guard against agents being fooled by such tricks we will need to incorporate suitable cryptographic mechanisms in the protocol.

A number of other behaviours are possible that can be thought of as being controlled by the intruder. The protocol may:

- kill a message, i.e. prevent it from being delivered;
- sniff a message, i.e. obtain his own copy;
- intercept a message, i.e. sniff and kill a message;
- re-route a message;
- delay delivery of a message;
- reorder messages;
- replay a message;
- fake a message.

These are not all independent but we list them all to make clear the full capability. It may be appropriate in some applications to modify the intruder's capabilities. For example, it may not be possible for the intruder to kill messages if we are dealing with a protocol for communications broadcast over the airwaves.

It is sometimes convenient, though it may seem a little bizarre, to identify the intruder and the medium. This follows the approach of Dolev and Yao [25]. When it suits him he will pass messages on correctly.

The intruder is the most fascinating character in this game. His aim is to subvert the protocol. Exactly what powers we imbue him with can be varied according to circumstance, but typically we will perform a worst-case analysis: we allow him to manipulate messages passing through the medium as outlined above, limited only by cryptographic considerations. That is to say, his ability to extract terms from messages he sees or construct new terms will be limited by cryptographic constraints. He can only extract the contents of an encrypted term if he possesses the relevant key. Conversely, he can only construct an encrypted term if he has the appropriate key. He can compute a hash but not its pre-image, and so on. In some models we may even allow him to acquire keys in certain circumstances to mimic the possibility of keys being broken or compromised.

Note that in some analyses we may want to allow the intruder, in addition to the capabilities described above, the status and capabilities of a legitimate user. In particular we may give him a recognized identity and corresponding keys, certificates, and so on. The server and other nodes thus regard him as a legitimate player and will communicate with him accordingly. We see this in Lowe's attack on the Needham-Schroeder Public-Key protocol for example.

From an abstract point of view we can include as many intruders as we want. In some cases it can be shown that we can restrict the model to a single intruder process without loss of generality: it can be shown that a single intruder is equivalent to n intruders. Occasionally it may be necessary to include more than one if we need to consider the possibility of collusion attacks. This might occur if, for example, we are considering a protocol designed to enforce an n-man rule (e.g. the agreement of at least n different agents). Even here it is often sufficient to give a single intruder access to multiple identities.

The intruder will be provided with certain initial knowledge and will subsequently be able to deduce further knowledge from traffic that he observes through the medium. The intruder is equipped with an inference system that governs what he can deduce from given information as indicated earlier. This system will be spelt out formally in Chapter 2.

Besides passively overhearing traffic, the intruder can construct fake messages from the information he can deduce and try to use these to trick the other principals. He can thus mount interleaving, replay, oracle, man-in-the-middle attacks, and so on. Note that such strategies are not coded explicitly but are emergent. In this respect the intruder is more like Deep Blue than Kasparov: he tries everything until something works.

Where appropriate we may include algebraic identities in the intruder's inference system. Some crypto-algorithms are commutative, for example, and this fact may be exploitable by the intruder. Vernam encryption (bit-wise exclusive-or of the message and the key) is self-inverse, and so on. For some protocols such facts may actually be vital to allow the protocol to function: Diffie-Hellman key exchange depends on the commutativity of exponentiation in a finite field, for example.

Our intruder will be rather obliging in that whenever he discovers some sensitive data item he reports it to us. This is of course not typical intruder behaviour but is a modelling device to allow us to detect when a breach has occurred.

Another attractive feature of this style of analysis is that an explicit and flexible model of the hostile capabilities is incorporated. This allows us to tailor a realistic threat model appropriate to the application. For example, if we are dealing with a system using broadcast messages, then it might be deemed unreasonable to give the intruder the ability to kill messages. This is in contrast with many other approaches in which the intruder has fixed and often only implicit capabilities. In the BAN logic, for example, there is no explicit statement of the intruder's capabilities – they are implicit in the choice of logical axioms.

Having defined the components of the systems as CSP processes we can now construct the entire system as the parallel composition of these components: the nodes, the intruder and the medium (if it hasn't already been incorporated in the intruder).

Having formulated a model of the system and the properties of interest in the framework of CSP the next problem is to find effective ways of reasoning about and analyzing such descriptions. Two, complementary approaches have been developed and will be described in this book: one is highly automated based on model-checking (essentially exhaustive search over behaviours), the other is rather more interactive, involving theorem-proving techniques to establish properties of the designs.

Model-checking

The automated tool support for the approach is provided by the model-checker FDR[1]). Given two CSP specifications, *Imp* and *Spec* say, FDR checks whether *Imp* is a refinement of *Spec*, that is whether the behaviours of *Imp* are contained in those of the *Spec*. In Chapter 1 we will make precise what is meant by refinement. Put very simplistically, the check is performed by enumerating all the behaviours of *Imp* and checking that they are allowed by *Spec*. If the check fails it returns a behaviour that violates the property encoded in *Spec*.

To perform a CSP/FDR analysis of a security protocol against a given security property, a CSP model of the system in question, including hostile intruders along with a CSP process that encodes the security properties required, are input into FDR. If the check fails FDR returns a counterexample: a trace that violates the refinement. In the context of security protocols such a counterexample represents the interactions of the intruder in an attack.

The great advantage of such an approach is that it is highly automated. Once the system model and specification have been constructed the checking is essentially push-button. This means that it is highly effective for debugging designs: we can start with a putative design and run a check. This will almost certainly come back with an attack that will suggest a modification to counter it. This can then be run through the checker prompting further, incremental improvements to the design until a version is found that passes the checks.

---

[1] Marketed by Formal Systems (Europe) Ltd.

An alternative technique is to start with a (possibly over-designed) protocol and check various weakenings. This will indicate either that certain details of the design are overkill, if no attack is found, or will make clear why they are necessary, if an attack is found.

The drawback of model-checking is that the models have to be finite and indeed rather small. This means that in practice considerable ingenuity may be required to keep the models compact enough whilst not sacrificing any significant behaviour. Indeed in many ways this is the major challenge facing this approach. We will discuss how such reductions can be performed in more detail in Chapter 4 and future directions in tackling this in Chapter 10.

Proving protocols

The FDR approach has been used principally as an efficient and reliable way to uncover vulnerabilities – to debug protocol designs in effect. This is very valuable in itself, but ultimately we would really like to be able to prove that, modulo the assumptions of the models, a given protocol does ensure a given security requirement.

Techniques like data-independence, induction, simplifying transformations, and so on, all help broaden the class of systems that can be analyzed using model-checking, but complete proofs using model-checking are still difficult to establish.

The alternative is to take a theorem-proving approach rather than a model-checking approach. In Chapter 7 we will discuss an approach that uses rank functions. These are functions from the space of messages to the integers. They are used to formulate certain invariants whose validity implies the property of interest. Rank-function techniques have been encoded in the PVS theorem prover enabling mechanical support for the approach. In addition, for a particular class of protocols a decidable procedure can either generate the appropriate rank function automatically (where it exists), or can establish that no valid rank function can exist. This approach is also supported by a tool, the RankAnalyser. This is discussed in detail in Chapter 7.

0.10   Casper: the user-friendly interface of FDR

The construction of the FDR code corresponding to a given protocol requires specialist skills. However, the production of such a code from the description of the protocol is largely systematic. Based on this observation, one of the authors (Lowe) [56] developed a compiler that takes a description of the protocol and the security property and automatically generates the corresponding FDR code.

In practice this is not entirely straightforward:

- The standard notation for describing protocols is notoriously ambiguous.
- Security protocols differ widely in their security goals and the mechanisms they employ. This means that it is difficult to have a general-purpose compiler able to handle them all.

Lowe introduces an enriched notation to describe the protocols that resolves the ambiguities and makes explicit certain aspects of the protocols. This has much in common with the CAPSL notation [64] proposed originally by Millen as the basis for a standard notation for describing security protocols.

Casper has considerable theoretical as well as practical significance as it addresses the issue of ensuring a clear correspondence between the formal framework and a notation accessible to the protocol designers and implementers. The process of analysis is thus much more efficient and less error prone. Chapter 6 gives a detailed description of Casper, along with worked examples.

0.11 Limits of formal analysis

It is quite possible to implement a perfectly secure protocol using high-grade crypto-algorithms in such a way that the result is hopelessly flawed. A real example of this is an implementation proposed by a company called APM of a protocol that had been verified by Paulson [69]. This was found to have a glaring vulnerability. Paulson's analysis was perfectly valid, but the way APM proposed to implement the encryption gave rise to some additional algebraic identities not included in the model. It was these identities that the intruder could exploit. This is documented in [81].

More generally, security properties tend not to be preserved by conventional refinement techniques. This is a widely recognized problem for which no general solution is yet available and an area of ongoing research. In Chapter 10 we will discuss this in more detail.

Our models are, like all mathematical models, only ever approximations to reality. We are usually assuming that the intruder's only source of information is through monitoring traffic. In reality he may have other sources such as EM radiation, power fluctuations or timing information, or indeed extracting information using 'rubber hose' tactics. In principle such possibilities could be incorporated in the models, but that would inevitably tend to vastly complicate them. It seems best to deal with such vulnerabilities separately, i.e. to establish that EM radiation cannot leak out, and so on. There is always the danger, of course, that there may be aspects of reality that may be relevant that we have overlooked but that some smart hacker might light on. Thus we must bear in mind that the validity of our analysis will always be relative to the threat model and to the faithfulness of our system model, so proofs of security will never be absolute. Of course, as and when new modes of attack are uncovered, they can be incorporated into the analysis.

0.12 Summary

CSP has been shown to be a very effective framework in which to formulate the behaviour and properties of security goals. The CSP framework readily encompasses a whole host of different architectures, mechanisms and security properties. Furthermore, the model-checking technique based on FDR has been shown to be very effective in identifying vulnerabilities.

When faced with a new security protocol for evaluation a good methodology is as follows:

- Establish exactly how the protocol works and what security properties it is intended to provide and against which threats.

- Examine it for obvious flaws. It can be surprising how much can be picked up just by eyeballing a protocol.

- Once any obvious flaws are eliminated then try to analyze the protocol using Casper. This may require some intervention in the Casper output in some cases (for more exotic protocols and properties).

- Once any further flaws identified by the Casper/FDR analysis have been ironed out, go on to construct a proof using the rank-function techniques.

Later in this book you will be taken through a number of worked examples of this process.

The effectiveness of this approach has been demonstrated by the uncovering of several new attacks on well-established protocols (see e.g. [55]). Its utility as a design tool is also apparent, as exemplified by its use to strengthen progressively the TMN protocol [61]. Here a weak version of the protocol was progressively strengthened in the light of vulnerabilities revealed by the analysis until a version was arrived at that stood up to analysis. Alternatively, an over-engineered design can be progressively 'weakened' to probe for redundancies and help better understand the role of the cryptographic primitives.

1 An introduction to CSP

CSP (Communicating Sequential Processes) is a notation for describing systems of parallel agents that communicate by passing messages between them. In this book we will be seeing it mainly as a descriptive language: a natural way of writing down the type of systems we study. However, it is also an excellent vehicle for studying the theoretical problems that arise from *concurrency* (the study of parallel and interacting systems), which means that it provides just about all the machinery required for the formal study of systems described in it. We will get glimpses of this mathematical side of CSP every now and again when we formalize security properties.

This chapter gives a basic introduction to CSP, and should give sufficient detail for readers of this book. Much fuller descriptions can be found in three different textbooks. Hoare's [41] is the original presentation, and gives an insight into the subject from the point of view of its inventor. It was, however, written before many of the most interesting developments in CSP, for example the modelling of time and the use of tools. Two up-to-date treatments, which cover these and much more besides, are by Roscoe [76] and Schneider [87]. Schneider's book gives many more details about time (and especially modelling continuous as opposed to discrete time), whereas Roscoe's covers a wider range of theory and applications for untimed modelling. Both of these last two books have websites with links to and from that of this book.

CSP is traditionally written in a fairly mathematical notation, with special symbols representing its operators, and is typeset more like mathematics than a typical programming language. We will be following this style for most of this book. All implementation (for example in the scripts obtainable from this book's website) is done in CSP_M, an ASCII version of the notation (*see* [76]) which mimics this mathematical style and the appearance of the operators, but also provides the features necessary to make it into a language for programming large-scale practical system models. Readers are advised to familiarize themselves with CSP_M as well as the mathematical style of notation that we will be seeing in this chapter.

CSP is, fundamentally, a notation for describing *interaction*, and can be used to describe a huge range of systems whose only feature in common is that there are different components that influence each other. Thus it can be used to write programs for components of distributed computing systems, such as the protocols that are the main focus of this book, can describe interactions between humans and machines (as in the vending-machine examples of Hoare's book), or provide models of safety-critical control systems like railway networks (where things such as points, signals, segments of track, and trains interact with each other) or of combinatorial puzzles like peg solitaire (*see* Roscoe's book). We will also find that it is useful to use the language of CSP to form *specification* processes that set out another system's intended behaviour. You can deduce from all of this that the processes we describe in CSP sometimes behave like you might expect a 'real' parallel process to behave, but at least as often they do not. We will find that the notation contains enough constructs for both classes of process, including some that would look a little eccentric if all we wanted to build was the first sort.

1.1 Basic building blocks

The only way in which one CSP process interacts with others, or with us as observers, is by communicating. Communications take the form of visible *events* or *actions*; processes can often also perform invisible actions that represent some sort of internal progress, but these have no direct effect on the outside world. The set of all visible events is called Σ (the Greek capital letter *sigma*). There is usually no reason to have any more than one internal action, and it is conventionally written τ (the Greek letter *tau*).

The language of CSP provides us with a way of describing the states in which processes might be. What the language describing the state has to do is to allow us to work out what actions are immediately possible for the process and what the result state or states of any action is or are. The process then 'runs' by the selection of any of its initial actions, waiting to see what state it ends up in, selecting one of the actions of that state, and so on.

If two different programs produce patterns of visible actions that cannot be distinguished by an observer then they are to be thought of as *equivalent*. In other words, formally speaking, it is only the communications of a program that really matter.

Communication and recursion

The simplest process of all is *Stop*, which does nothing: no internal actions and no visible actions. By itself it is pretty useless, of course! We will see, however, that it plays some unexpectedly useful roles in constructing programs and in forming specifications. Thanks to the principle set out in the last paragraph it also serves the important purpose of being a simple process equivalent to any other that simply sits there and refuses all external communications. The best known example of this is the phenomenon of *deadlock*, in which a network of parallel processes cannot agree on any action to perform next. Thus you can think of *Stop* as the pure expression of deadlocked behaviour – we will see some more interesting examples later.

Obviously we need a way of introducing communications into our programs. This is done by *prefixing*: given a process P and a communication a, $a \rightarrow P$ is the program that performs a and then behaves like P. Thus if *in* and *out* are two actions in Σ, the process

$$in \rightarrow out \rightarrow Stop$$

performs the actions in turn and then does nothing else. In fact it is a little bit more complicated than this, since the process's environment might choose not to accept one or other of these actions, so it might get stuck earlier.

In the usage seen so far, all we can do is to create processes that offer a finite succession of 'take it or leave it' choices to its environment, before finally stopping. It is easy to build processes to go on for ever: all we have to do is to provide some way of them looping back to a state they have been in before. In CSP the most usual way of doing this is to give names to one or more of the states our program can reach, and allow these named processes to be used in the program itself. We can thus create several processes, all of which (except *Malt2*) describe simple and equivalent machines that performs *to*s and *fro*s alternately for as long as its environment wants:

$$Alt = to \rightarrow fro \rightarrow Alt$$
$$Dalt = to \rightarrow fro \rightarrow to \rightarrow fro \rightarrow Dalt$$
$$Malt1 = to \rightarrow Malt2$$
$$Malt2 = fro \rightarrow Malt1$$
$$Nalt = to \rightarrow fro \rightarrow Dalt$$

The *Alt* recursion is the most obvious presentation of this simple process, while *Dalt* is a more complex recursion with the same result. The pair of processes *Malt1* and *Malt2* together form a *mutual* recursion: they are defined in terms of each other. The final process is not recursive on its own name, instead relying on the already-defined process *Dalt*.

A further presentation of the same recursive process as *Alt* is

$$\mu P.to \rightarrow fro \rightarrow P$$

This is exactly the same recursive definition as that of *Alt*, but represents the process only, in a form that can be used as part of a larger process definition directly, rather than having to give the process a name and then separately use the name in any larger definition.

The communications in the prefix construction can take more interesting forms than simply offering a single action. We can, instead, offer a choice: if $A \subseteq \Sigma$ is any set of visible actions the process $?x : A \rightarrow P(x)$ offers the environment all of the actions in A and, when any $a \in A$ is chosen, goes on to behave like $P(a)$. Here, of course, $P(x)$ must be a recipe for building the next state, whichever $a \in A$ is chosen.

A particularly simple example of this is the process

$$RUN_A = ?x : A \rightarrow RUN_A$$

which is always prepared to offer any event from $A \subseteq \Sigma$. This is, of course, a rather uninteresting process by itself, but we will find it is a useful building block.

In $?x : A \rightarrow RUN_A$, the state that results from each choice of action is the same, but in general this is not true, of course. You should think of x as being a *parameter* of $P(x)$. It can be used to decide what to do based on cases: the parameter can be used in events in the program, or it can be manipulated by applying a function to it and any other parameters. We can also give programs other parameters that are not introduced directly by input. For example, suppose we have a coding machine with some internal state s that has keys $L \cup \{off\}$ where L is the alphabet of individual characters it supports. Then we can define the machine

$$CM1(s) = ?x : L \cup \{off\} \rightarrow CM1'(s, x)$$

$$CM1'(s, off) = Stop$$
$$CM1'(s, x) = crypt(s, x) \rightarrow CM1(newstate(s, x)) \quad (x \in L)$$

where $crypt(s, x)$ is the output communication the machine produces from x in state s, and $newstate(s, x)$ is its new state.

Presumably, here, $crypt(s, x)$ is not in L, since otherwise we would be confusing the input actions and output actions of our machine. However, they probably both have similar form as data, and in general it is essential that we have a simple way of incorporating ordinary data – such as characters, numbers and truth values – into both our programs and actions in a simple way. Programs are easy: just add necessary data values as parameters to named process states, as we did with the state s in the example above. In order to allow the same freedom with actions, CSP allows compound events in which the components are put together using a dot. In general, an action is a channel name c followed by zero or more (but always finitely many) data components drawn from the list of types corresponding to c. Thus a simple communication (such as *to* or *fro* as used above) has no data components, and it would be more natural to write our coding machine with input and output channels *in* and *out* of type L.

Forgetting for the time being about the event *off* and its consequences, we can now build a machine with the same functionality as follows:

$$CM2(s) = in?x \rightarrow out!crypt(s, x) \rightarrow CM2(newstate(s, x))$$

This introduces two new ways of building communications: $in?x$ allows the environment any communication of the form $in.x$, where x ranges over the type of in (or, where a channel has more than one data component, it ranges over the type of the component to which x refers). This construct binds the identifier x to whatever data value is chosen by the environment so that it can be used in the process following the prefix (and, indeed, in most treatments, in any components of the same action that follow it, as in $c?x!x + 1$). Thus ? models a process inputting data. In the corresponding output form, $c!x$, the effect is to offer the compound action $c.x$. While it is good practice to use ! to denote the output of data, it is usually immaterial whether it or a simple dot is used[1] and many processes and scripts use the two forms fairly interchangeably.

The use of parameters allows us to build mutual recursions that define infinitely

---

[1] The only difference comes in multiple data component communications where there is an input (via ?) of an earlier component since then $c?x!y$ and $c?x.y$ have different meanings. The latter assumes that a compound object $x.y$ is being input rather than x being input and y output. For further explanation see [76]. In practice all you need to remember is always to make the input or output nature of each data component following a ? explicit with either ? or !.

many different processes. This is already true of $CM(s)$ and its relations, if the set over which s ranges is infinite, and is certainly true of the following example of a counter, parameterized over the natural numbers $\mathbb{N} = \{0, 1, 2, 3, \ldots\}$ which uses the choice operator of the next section:

$$Count_0 = up \rightarrow Count_1$$
$$Count_{n+1} = up \rightarrow Count_{n+2}$$
$$\square \; down \rightarrow Count_n$$

This is a useful example because it is just about the simplest possible process that is evidently infinite-state: all of the states $Count_n$ are, in a clear sense, behaviourally distinct.

Choice operators

By naming one process P_i for each state, and using the $?x : A \rightarrow P(x)$ construct to set out the possible actions of each state and the new state that results, it is possible to describe any deterministic finite state machine over a finite Σ using only the notation we have already seen. All you have to do is set $P_i =?x : A_i \rightarrow P'_i(x)$ where A_i is the actions possible in state i, and give a case-by-case definition of which P_j each resulting value $P'_i(x)$ is. The word 'deterministic' here means that there only is one possible result of each action: no ambiguity about what a given action leads to. As we have already seen with our coding machine, this sort of program for a state machine can be clumsy, and mixes badly with the input of data.

We can do a lot better by introducing an operator $\square$ whose job it is to give us the choice between the actions of two processes, and then behaves like the one chosen. If $A = B \cup C$ then

$$?x : A \rightarrow P(x) = (?x : B \rightarrow P(x)) \;\square\; (?x : C \rightarrow P(x)) \qquad (1)$$

the equality between programs meaning that they always behave equivalently. We can add back the *off* switch into $CM2(s)$, getting a much clearer definition than $CM1(3)$.

$$CM3(s) = in?x \rightarrow out!crypt(s, x) \rightarrow CM3(newstate(s, x))$$
$$\square \; off \rightarrow Stop$$

The style in which $CM3(s)$ is written is how we will see most of the sequential components of CSP programs written throughout this book. Choices of actions in each state are presented by an appropriate mixture of input, output and $\square$, and the process frequently loops back to just being in one of the named states again. This is *tail recursion*.[2]

If $B = \varnothing$ then obviously $?x : B \rightarrow P(x)$ is equivalent to *Stop*, since no options are given to the environment. Since $A = A \cup \varnothing$ we can deduce from equation (1) that

$$(?x : A \rightarrow P(x)) = (?x : A \rightarrow P(x)) \;\square\; Stop$$

---

[2] Tail recursive definitions can also use the other choice and prefixing constructs that we will meet in this chapter, but not the other styles of operator that we will see.

In fact, $P \mathbin{\square} Stop$ is equivalent to P in general, since offering the environment the choice between P's actions and no others is the same as just offering P's.

It is natural to imagine that B and C are disjoint in (1), since then they combine to give all the choices of A without any ambiguity. However, even if they do overlap it would not matter, as the result $P(x)$ of selecting action x is the same either way. Since $\square$ is an operator between pairs of processes, we do have to understand what $P \mathbin{\square} Q$ means whatever P and Q are, so it is necessary to worry not only about the case where $B \cap C \neq \varnothing$ in (1), but about the similar case in which the results of choosing an action $x \in B \cap C$ are different on the two sides:

$$(?x : B \rightarrow P(x)) \mathbin{\square} (?x : C \rightarrow Q(x))$$

This type of situation obviously presents an implementor with a problem, since he has to choose between two options but has no basis on which to make the choice if the environment picks x. The answer CSP gives to this is to allow the implementor to make the choice between the two sides: in the above case the process may behave like $P(x)$ or $Q(x)$ after the action x, and the environment has no control over which.

In practice this sort of case is rare, since it is usually easy to avoid creating this type of ambiguity in programs and it is only in rather eccentric situations that there is any reason to introduce it deliberately. However, it does serve to introduce us to one of the most important concepts that appears in CSP and all other similar notations, that of *nondeterminism*. A program acts nondeterministically when it is unpredictable because it is allowed to make internal decisions that affect how it behaves as viewed from the outside. For example,

$$(a \rightarrow a \rightarrow Stop) \mathbin{\square} (a \rightarrow b \rightarrow Stop)$$

is nondeterministic because after the action a the implementation is allowed to choose whether the next action is to be a or b. We will find later that the way parallel processes run and interact with each other introduces nondeterminism whose effect is rather similar to this.

Since nondeterminism is around in the CSP world whether we like it or not, the language contains an operator for expressing it directly. Like $P \mathbin{\square} Q$, the nondeterministic choice $P \mathbin{\sqcap} Q$ behaves like P or like Q. The difference is that the user has no control over which. The choice in this nondeterminism can be implemented using internal actions: we can imagine the initial state of $P \mathbin{\sqcap} Q$ as having no visible actions and two internal τ actions, one each to the initial states of P and Q. There is, however, no obligation on the implementor to do this and he can implement it as P, or as Q, or even as $P \mathbin{\square} Q$. There is nothing that any of these processes can do that $P \mathbin{\sqcap} Q$ cannot.

Nondeterministic choice is not something a programmer is very likely to use in a practical program, since if his program would work with $P \mathbin{\sqcap} Q$ in it then it would also work with the shorter and simpler process P (or Q) instead. It is, however, useful in modelling components of systems that have a degree of unpredictability and which are outside our control, such as a communication medium that may transmit data correctly or lose it:

$$NDM = in?x \rightarrow (NDM \sqcap out!x \rightarrow NDM)$$

It also plays major roles in the formulation of specifications, in the mathematical theory of CSP, and in cases where we deliberately build models of systems in which some of the deterministic decision-making capability is abstracted away. It can be useful to do this last thing, either to produce a system with fewer states and therefore easier to verify, or in order to prove that its correctness does not depend on which decision is made – for an example see [76].

The processes $P \sqcap Q$ and $P \square Q$ have identical sets of *traces*, namely the sequences of visible communications that can be performed from the start to some point. Therefore the distinction between these two processes is not vital when all one is doing is judging a process by its traces – as we will actually be doing most of the time. It is, however, an issue of which you should try to get an understanding, since conceptually there is a great difference between

$$(a \rightarrow P) \sqcap Stop \quad \text{and} \quad (a \rightarrow P) \square Stop$$

(one can deadlock immediately, the other behaves exactly like $a \rightarrow P$) and because there are many important properties (like deadlock) that do depend on the difference.

One of the most important roles of CSP is to make sense of nondeterminism and allow us to reason about it cleanly. It argues that in most circumstances there is no way how we can tell *when* a nondeterministic choice was made by observing a process, either immediately before its effects become visible or a long time before. So, for example, the processes

$$a \rightarrow (b \rightarrow Stop \sqcap c \rightarrow Stop) \qquad (a \rightarrow b \rightarrow Stop) \sqcap (a \rightarrow c \rightarrow Stop)$$

are equivalent. Just about all CSP operators satisfy the so-called *distributivity* principle, which says that it does not matter whether a nondeterministic choice is made before or after applying them. In other words $F(P \sqcap Q) = F(P) \sqcap F(Q)$ for any such operator $F(\cdot)$. The equality above is an example of the distributivity of prefixing, and the distributivity of $\square$ is set out in the following law (which holds for all P, Q, R):

$$(P \sqcap Q) \square R = (P \square R) \sqcap (Q \square R)$$

Much more discussion of this issue and related theoretical points can be found in [76].

Informally, we would expect process P to be more nondeterministic than Q if every choice open to Q is also possible for P. It must be free for P to behave exactly like Q. Another way of saying this is that P is indistinguishable from, or equivalent to $P \sqcap Q$. If this holds we say that Q *refines* P. This is written $P \sqsubseteq Q$, and is an extremely important concept, not least since the FDR tool's main function is to decide questions of refinement. There will be further discussion of refinement in Section 1.5.

It is sometimes useful to have generalized versions of the choice operators that can be applied to a nonempty (possibly infinite) collection of processes: if S is a nonempty set of processes then $\square\, S$ offers the choice of all the processes in S. S should be nonempty to ensure that at least one process is offered. Furthermore, $\sqcap\, S$ can choose to act like any member of S. It must choose one of them, which is why S has to be nonempty.

One of the least refined process over a given alphabet A is the following process:

$$Chaos_A = Stop \sqcap ?x : A \rightarrow Chaos_A$$

Like $Stop$ and RUN_A, this is a pretty useless program in itself, but is used in many ways in building and reasoning about systems.

$P \;\square\; Q$ represents choice between P and Q in the hands of the environment that is interacting with the process at run time, while $P \;\sqcap\; Q$ represents choice between P and Q left in the hands of the implementation to make as it wishes. Two other mechanisms for making this choice are supported by CSP. The first is *time*: $P \overset{t}{\triangleright} Q$ represents a process that makes whatever offers P makes for t time units and if nothing is chosen reverts to Q. Obviously $P \overset{t}{\triangleright} Q$ has the same traces as the other two choices (on the assumption that exact times of events are not recorded in traces), but again the choice mechanism is different. It is often a lot easier to ignore exact times in both describing CSP systems and reasoning about them, an issue we will return to in Section 1.6, and in that case we often replace the precise timeout operator with the abstraction $P \triangleright Q$, which offers the initial choices of P until some nondeterministically chosen time, and then behaves like Q.

The final choice mechanism is that of explicit decisions based on the internal state parameters of the process. We have already seen how useful it is to give processes like our coding machine models some parameters representing data. This same data is often the basis of decisions about how a process should behave, and so we need a conditional (*if–then–else*) construct similar to the ones found in just about every other programming language ever devised. Since this is an operator of a rather different flavour to the others in our language – less connected with the particular nature of concurrency and communication than it is with ordinary programming – different presentations of CSP have dealt with it in different notations and with different levels of formality. In this book we will employ two different notations: the straightforward *if–then–else* and definition by cases, as in the following simple model of an unidirectional firewall process:

$$FW(s) = in?x \rightarrow (if\ valid(x, s)\ then\ out!x \rightarrow FW(newstate(s, x))$$
$$else\ FW(newstate(s, x))$$

All this process has to decide is whether to let each input through or not. We are assuming the relatively sophisticated structure where the state (and hence future decisions) is affected by each successive input. There are obvious similarities between this process and the coding machine processes, but the most interesting comparison is with the nondeterministic medium process NDM. The only difference is that the decision-making mechanisms have been turned from a nondeterministic choice into one based on conditionals (even though we don't give the details of the functions and state that make the latter work). To an observer with no knowledge of the state s or perhaps of the two functions used in $FW(s)$, this process does in fact behave like NDM: if he does not know how a decision is made, it appears to be nondeterministic.

We will not be using the elegant alternative notation proposed by Hoare (and used in [76]) in which $P \triangleleft b \triangleright Q$ is an infix operator way of writing *if b then P else Q*, because that often turns out to be hard to read in practical programs and is remote from the machine-readable version of CSP (which uses if--then--else). It does, of course, show the similarity of this form of choice to the others a lot more clearly than the more ordinary forms of conditionals we use.

There is a further conditional construct allowed in machine-readable CSP_M, which is enormously helpful in clarifying programs: we will therefore use it too. If b is any boolean condition and P any process, $b\&P$ is an abbreviation for

$$\textit{if b then P else Stop}$$

This is so useful because it allows the creation of tail-recursive programs where the set of communication options available varies with some parameter values. For example, the following process describes a token moving in single horizontal and vertical steps round a finite (N by M) board:

$$
\begin{aligned}
Counter(i,j) = (i > 0) \& & \quad left \rightarrow Counter(i-1,j) \\
\square \ (i < N-1) \& & \ right \rightarrow Counter(i+1,j) \\
\square \ (j > 0) \& & \quad down \rightarrow Counter(i,j-1) \\
\square \ (j < M-1) \& & up \rightarrow Counter(i,j+1)
\end{aligned}
$$

1.2 Parallel operators

The syntax seen in the previous section is enough to describe the communications of any sequential process, and in particular the actions of any single participant in a protocol. These components are relatively easy to understand as we can see the sequences of actions and states that they go through: at any time a component is simply in one of the states we have defined.

Things become far more interesting when we put a number of these in parallel, as it is usually far harder to understand what happens when they interact with each other. A state of the entire system is composed of one state of each component, so the number of possible states increases exponentially with the size of the network – this quickly gets beyond what we can understand. Usually we would not expect all these states to be reachable, for example if two of the nodes are running a protocol with each other it is reasonable to expect a close relationship between them. In most cases we do not want the network to be able to reach a deadlock state, where no communication is possible. How are we to know and prove this sort of thing and the ways in which the complete network communicates with the outside world?

It is therefore vital that a language like CSP provides a clear understanding of how processes behave when put together into parallel networks. It should also allow us to be able to check formally whether such a network satisfies a specification we hold of it.

CSP does not regard a parallel combination as anything special: it is just another process to which we can apply any of the operators seen so far, like prefixing and □. In fact, formally speaking, every parallel process is equivalent to a sequential one that could have been written using the operators seen in the last section. This demystifies parallelism, but only goes part of the way towards solving the problems discussed above, since for a practical network it is likely that any equivalent sequential process will have an infeasibly large number of states; so we are left with determining what these are and how they behave.

Running in parallel, CSP processes influence each other by affecting what communications they can perform. The simplest operator is the one that forces *all* visible actions to be synchronized: $P \parallel Q$ can perform $a \in \Sigma$ only when both P and Q can. Thus

$$(?x : A \rightarrow P(x)) \parallel (?x : B \rightarrow Q(x)) = ?x : A \cap B \rightarrow (P(x) \parallel Q(x))$$

Notice how this law reflects the idea that each parallel process is equivalent to a sequential one: here the two prefixes in parallel are turned into a single one outside the parallel. As an example of how this operator works, consider a process that will always communicate a but will only communicate b if the number of as to date is divisible by N: $Mult(N, 0)$ where

$$
\begin{aligned}
Mult(N, m) &= a \rightarrow Mult(N, N) \\
&\quad \square\, b \rightarrow Mult(N, m) \quad \text{if } m = 0 \\
&= a \rightarrow Mult(N, m - 1) \quad \text{otherwise}
\end{aligned}
$$

The effect of putting $Mult(N, 0)$ and $Mult(M, 0)$ in parallel using $\parallel$ is equivalent to $Mult(lcm(M, N), 0)$, where $lcm(M, N)$ is the lowest common multiple of M and N. This example shows the concept of *handshaken* communication in a pure form: b can only happen when both sides agree on it, but there is no direction to the communication. The same mechanism can have the effect of an output from one process to another; so we have:

$$(c!x \rightarrow P) \parallel (c?y \rightarrow Q(y)) = c!x \rightarrow (P \parallel Q(x))$$

By forcing the two processes to agree on their first communication, all but one of the options open to the right-hand process are cut off, leaving open only the one corresponding to the data value x that the left-hand process is outputting. It is important to realize, however, that the output event $c!x$ cannot happen until the other process lets it: CSP communication is completely unbuffered (unless, of course, buffer processes are included as separate components in the network).

We can, of course, put as many processes as we like in parallel using $\parallel$, but this is not really a very realistic mode of composition as all the processes have to agree on all events. There is no sensible way in which we can either arrange for a channel from one of a large network of processes to another, or have communications that belong *only* to one process (and represent the interface between itself and the outside world). The solution is, when putting a pair of processes in parallel, to specify which events have to be handshaken/synchronized on and which the processes can do without reference to the other. The easy way to do this for a pair of processes is using the *interfaced* parallel operator: $P \parallel_X Q$ forces P and Q to synchronize on all events in X, but they are allowed to perform events outside X freely. If $P = ?x : A \to P'(x)$ and $Q = ?x : B \to Q'(x)$ then

$$P \parallel_X Q = ?x : X \cap A \cap B \to (P'(x) \parallel Q'(x))$$
$$\Box \; ?x : A \setminus X \to (P'(x) \parallel_X Q)$$
$$\Box \; ?x : B \setminus X \to (P \parallel_X Q'(x))$$

As a simple example, consider a pair of buffer processes:

$$BA = left?x \to mid!x \to BA$$
$$BB = mid?x \to right!x \to BB$$

The obvious interface between these two processes is the channel *mid*, and the combination $B2 = BA \parallel_{\{|mid|\}} BB$ behaves just as one would expect: BA accepts a value on channel left, which is then passed across on channel *mid* to BB (just as in the example of one process outputting to another above) and then output to the world on *right*. The next input on *left* may or may not come before that last output. All of this can be deduced from the step law quoted above, since it quickly proves (abbreviating $mid!x \to BA$ and $right!x \to BB$ by $BA'(x)$ and $BB'(x)$ respectively) all of the following equations:

$$BA \parallel_{\{|mid|\}} BB = left?x \to (BA'(x) \parallel_{\{|mid|\}} BB)$$
$$BA'(x) \parallel_{\{|mid|\}} BB = mid!x \to (BA \parallel_{\{|mid|\}} BB'(x))$$
$$BA \parallel_{\{|mid|\}} BB'(x) = left?y \to (BA'(x) \parallel_{\{|mid|\}} BB'(x))$$
$$\Box \; right!x \to (BA \parallel_{\{|mid|\}} BB)$$
$$BA'(x) \parallel_{\{|mid|\}} BB'(y) = right!y \to (BA'(x) \parallel_{\{|mid|\}} BB)$$

What we have in fact done here is to reduce the parallel program $BA \parallel_{\{|mid|\}} BB$ to a sequential one, since if we simply replace each of the four different parallel expressions above by a suitably parameterized simple name for the state, the above becomes a mutual recursion which, as we will discuss in Section 1.5, gives an equivalent process.

It is obviously possible to build a network consisting of as many processes as we like, using the interface parallel operator. One way of doing this is to add one process at a time, in each case making the interface set the union of all the interfaces between this process and the ones already there. This is usually very easy if the network we are building is something like a chain or a ring, as these interfaces are then simple. In more complex networks there is a real risk of this interface definition becoming a mess if left to the programmer. The solution provided by CSP is the concept of the process *alphabet*: each process is given control of a particular set of events (usually, but not always, the set of all events the process ever communicates). The parallel composition is then formed in which no process is ever permitted to communicate outside its own alphabet, and no event is permitted unless all the processes, to whose alphabet it belongs, agree. Since the interface between two processes is just the intersection of their alphabets, there is no need to specify all the interface sets separately. Pragmatically, in most cases where there are more than two or three processes in a network, alphabets give the clearest and cleanest way of defining how processes interact.

Hoare's book gives process alphabets a very prominent role indeed, and every process has one whether it is to be put in parallel or not. We prefer to make the alphabets explicit in the parallel operator. There is a binary operator $P \, _X\|_Y \, Q$ which places P in parallel with Q, giving them alphabets X and Y respectively. Thus P must agree to all communications in X, and Q to all those in Y. But as discussed above, it is not the binary but the general form in which this form of parallel comes into its own:

$$\|_{i=1}^{n} (P_i, A_i)$$

is the parallel composition of the processes P_i in which each has the given alphabet. This can easily be defined in terms of the binary form: for $n \geq 2$ we have

$$\|_{i=1}^{n+1} (P_i, A_i) = (\|_{i=1}^{n} (P_i, A_i)) \, _{A_n^*}\|_{A_{n+1}} (P_{n+1}, A_{n+a})$$

where $A_n^* = \bigcup_{i=1}^{n} A_i$. This definition of A_n^* begins to show why the general form in which we can leave the process alphabets separate is nicer to use.

When we want to define a large network in future, all we will usually have to do is to define the component processes and their alphabets.

Alphabetized parallel makes one big assumption that the interface parallel operator does not make, namely that if two processes are both allowed to communicate a particular event a then the only way this event can happen is synchronized. In $P \, \|_X \, Q$, if $a \notin X$, either P or Q can do a independently, and if they can both perform it in their current states then it is nondeterministic which (as the step law given above) then yields the nondeterministic case of $\square$.

This assumption usually holds in practical network models, since ambiguity over the source of a communication is often hard to deal with elegantly in programs, and the ambiguity can always be avoided by appropriate naming of events. However, where it is wanted for any reason, it is necessary to use either $\|$ or the operator $\|\|$ (interleaving parallel), which is an abbreviation for $\|_\varnothing$. Most uses of $P \, \|\| \, Q$ in practical examples are in cases where P and Q use disjoint sets of events, and so the same effect could have been achieved with alphabetized parallel, only it is less work to use $|||$. There is also a general version of interleaving: $|||$ S executes concurrent runs of all the processes in the set S. At any stage during the execution, only finitely many of them can have performed some event.

Computer security, as it turns out, provides most of the main applications we know about for interleaving that could not be reduced to $_X\|_Y$.

Recursion through parallel operators can build a dynamically expanding network of processes: if we have a definition like

$$P = a \rightarrow P \parallel P$$

then the longer it runs, the more copies of P will be running in parallel. This particular definition does not produce a very interesting result, but the use of interleaving, and some of the other forms of parallel/hiding constructs we will see later, can build networks where the parallelism serves interesting functions. For example, we can achieve the same effect as $Count_0$ without the infinite parameterization:

$$CT = up \rightarrow (CT \parallel\parallel down \rightarrow Stop)$$

The more ups have happened, the more interleaved $down$s are left available to balance them. This sort of behaviour is more interesting and complex than happens with tail recursions, where recursive calls are made without leaving other baggage around.

It is, of course, possible to use $P \parallel Q$ to synchronize some but not all of the events
P and Q have in common. One possible use of this would be in the broadcast of a global signal to two processes that are otherwise interleaved, but it is not a common feature in programs that give realistic representations of networks.

Unexpected uses of parallel operators

The CSP parallel operators are essentially combinatorial or logical operators on the communications that their arguments perform. The obvious use to put them to is in calculating the patterns of communications that appear when we put the processes forming a realistic network together. There are, however, two interesting common uses that put the combinatorial properties to work in other ways. In each case the objective is not to build a model that is intended to reflect any real parallelism in an implementation, but rather to achieve a particular overall behaviour.

The first is building up a series of constraints on traces. Suppose P is any process and Q is one whose events all belong to the set X. Then all communications of $P \parallel Q$
come from P, but it is only allowed to do those things in X that Q lets it. Suppose we want to build a process that has as many traces drawn from the alphabet A as possible, subject to a series of restriction processes R_i, each of which says something about what our process is allowed to do in a subset A_i of A. Then we can build up the behaviour we want by starting with $Q_0 = Run(A)$ and adding the constraints one

at a time: $Q_{j+1} = Q_j \underset{A_{j+1}}{\parallel} R_{j+1}$.

For example, suppose we have a building with rooms indexed $\{1, \ldots, N\}$, each of which has a door and a light switch. We might then have events *open.i*, *close.i*, *on.i*, *off.i* for each room. If A is the set of all these events (for all rooms), then each of the following properties is easily expressed as a simple process:

- $AltDoor_i = open.i \rightarrow close.i \rightarrow AltDoor_i$, with alphabet $\{open.i, close\}$, says that door i is initially closed and that the open and close events alternate appropriately.

- $AltLight_i = on.i \rightarrow off.i \rightarrow AltLight_i$, with alphabet $\{on.i, off.i\}$, says that light i is initially off and that the on and off events alternate appropriately.

- The process $OnOpenC_i$, with alphabet $\{open.i, close.i, on.i\}$, defined

$$OnOpenC_i = open.i \rightarrow OnOpenO_i$$
$$\square \; close.i \rightarrow OnOpenC_i$$

$$OnOpenO_i = open.i \rightarrow OnOpenO_i$$
$$\square \; close.i \rightarrow OnOpenC_i$$
$$\square \; on.i \rightarrow OnOpenO_i$$

says that the event *on.i* can only occur when the door to room i has been opened more recently than it has been closed. (In other words, this light may only be turned on if the door is open.)

- Finally, we can express properties covering more than one room, such as the following that says that only one door may be open at a time, with alphabet $\{| open, close |\}$:

$$AllClosed = open?i \rightarrow close.i \rightarrow AllClosed$$
$$\square \; close?i \rightarrow AllClosed$$

If we add each of these processes in parallel with $Run(\{| open, close, on, off |\})$ we get a single process whose traces are just those satisfying all of the individual constraints. Even though we would presumably never contemplate actually building a parallel implementation looking like this, we might very well use a process defined like this as a specification – we will find in later sections that the usual way to test the correctness of a CSP process is to check that all its behaviours (e.g. traces) are contained in those of some specification process.

We may also want – either as our whole implementation or part of it – a process that is essentially combinatorial in nature, whose state is naturally expressed as a mapping from one smallish set, A, to another, B. Even if there is no expectation that we will want to create a real parallel process representing it, there can be advantages both of clarity and efficiency on tools (especially FDR) from representing such a system as a parallel combination of $|A|$ processes, each of which has a state for each member of A.

Let us suppose we want a process that represents a varying subset of the finite nonempty set A. It should have events *add.i*, *delete.i* and *member.i* for each i in A, and global events *empty* and *nonempty*. We could build our set process as a single recursion:

$$Set1(X) = add?i \to Set1(X \cup \{i\})$$
$$\square \; delete?i \to Set1(X \setminus \{i\})$$
$$\square \; member?i : X \to Set1(X)$$
$$\square \; (if \; X = \varnothing \; then \; empty \to Set1(X)$$
$$else \; nonempty \to Set1(X))$$

Alternatively, we could build a separate process $S(i, b)$ for each $i \in A$ where b is either true or false:

$$S(i, b) = add.i \to S(i, true)$$
$$\square \; delete.i \to S(i, false)$$
$$\square \; (if \; b \; then \; (member.i \to S(i, b) \; \square \; nonempty \to S(i, b))$$
$$else \; empty \to S(i, b))$$

We can then combine them together into a process equivalent to $Set1(X)$ by synchronizing appropriately initialized $S(i, b)$s on the event *empty* (but not *nonempty* since the set is nonempty if *any* rather than *all* of the components have something in). Thus our ability to synchronize using $\underset{\{empty\}}{\|}$ on selected rather than all shared events proved useful in achieving the desired behaviour.

In this example there are relatively few interactions between the component processes. In other examples they are more interesting: we might model some board game, with the processes representing individual squares and events the moves of the game. The rules of the game – which moves are allowed – can often then be implemented using parallel composition. Further rules can be imposed via extra parallel processes (much as in the example of building a specification incrementally given above), and of course you can experiment with the effects of adding or changing rules very easily. You can find a variety of puzzles, including peg solitaire, the towers of Hanoi and the knight's tour problem implemented for FDR, on this book's website.

Perhaps the most interesting process definition in this book, namely that of the intruder who tries to break cryptographic protocols, will have the shape of our set process, but with much more interesting rules and interactions.

1.3   Hiding and renaming

One normally expects the internal details of how a program runs to be invisible to a user, who only gets to see the program's defined external interface (e.g. a procedure's parameters, or the externally available operations on an object). It is natural to want the same degree of abstraction in CSP, but this is something the language we have seen so far, lacks when it comes to building parallel networks. Consider the process *B2* defined on page 51. In this case we can divide the set of events used into two parts: the natural external interface $\{| \ \textit{left}, \textit{right} \ |\}$ and the rest, which represent internal communications between the processes making up the system. Thus two systems with different internal communications will not be equivalent even if everything they do with the outside world is the same. Furthermore, since the internal communications remain visible it is possible to synchronize further parallel processes with these events: e.g. *B2* $\underset{\{|mid|\}}{\|}$ *Stop* would prevent the internal actions of *B2* happening at all.

The natural thing to do is to remove the details of internal behaviour from view. CSP has a *hiding* operator to do this: if *P* is any process and *X* a set of events, $P \setminus X$ behaves like *P* except that all events in *X* are turned into the invisible action τ. Thus $B2 \setminus \{| \ mid \ |\}$ leaves only the external communications visible, which is what is appropriate for most purposes.

You should think of the CSP parallel and hiding operators as being two different phases of the most common natural mode of putting processes in parallel with each other: connecting the channels over which they are to communicate and removing these channels from view. In many languages the parallel operator incorporates hiding rather than leaving it separate, but the CSP approach has its advantages:

- It becomes easy to vary the way processes are put in parallel, for example by synchronizing a single outputting process with many inputs to achieve a broadcast, or synchronizing all processes on a global clock signal (as we will do in Section 1.6), without the need for more specially defined operators.

- Hiding is a valuable form of abstraction in its own right: there is no reason why events should *only* be hidden on parallel composition.

- The CSP parallel operator can be used to construct many useful processes representing combinatorial systems, one of the best examples of which is the parallel intruder process we will see in Chapter 6, which would be impossible with point-to-point parallel-with-hiding.

- It is useful to have the *option* of seeing, and making specifications about, internal actions. This is something else we will be making much use of in this book: when what we are studying is the operation of a protocol, it would be a shame not to be able to build a version of the network in which the protocol messages were visible.

- It is in any case straightforward to combine parallel, hiding, and the concept of *renaming* that we will see below, into user-friendly operators for plugging processes together in the sense described above. These are discussed at the end of this section.

Hiding turns visible actions into invisible ones. It does not make sense in CSP to do the reverse, since there would then be many processes with equivalent observable behaviour that would become different, creating huge theoretical problems. What we can do safely is to change one visible action into another, or on a grander scale to apply a renaming scheme under which many of the events a process performs are turned into other ones. Different presentations of CSP offer a number of forms of *renaming* operator, but they all apply some sort of alphabet transformation to a single process. The most general one, essentially the one used in the machine-readable version CSP$_M$, is to apply a *relation* to the events.

A relation between two sets A and B is a subset of the Cartesian product $A \times B$. In other words it is a set of pairs (a, b) with $a \in A$ and $b \in B$. Mathematics and computer science are littered with relations: equality on set A (the set of pairs $\{(a, a) \mid a \in A\}$), equivalence relations, and functions (under which the function f is identified with the set $\{(a, f(a)) \mid a \in dom(f)\}$) are just three examples. In renaming the process, $P[\![R]\!]$ behaves like P, except that all visible events a from P are relabelled by whatever R associates a with. It is the custom only to use relations that associate every event of P with at least one event. This procedure is easiest to visualize when R is a function, because it then maps each event to exactly one image. As a simple example of this, consider the processes BA and BB defined on page 51. Obviously these two processes have essentially the same behaviour but use different channels: we ought to be able to apply an alphabet transformation to one to get the other. The appropriate transformation to BA is most conveniently written $[\![mid, right/left, mid]\!]$: in other words the channels *left* and *mid* are respectively mapped to (or substituted by) *mid* and *right* respectively.

This is typical of one common use of renaming: to produce many copies of simple component processes that have the different alphabets required for the parts they have to play in some overall parallel composition. In such cases we usually have a choice of using renaming, or defining the component processes with appropriate parameters that allow the multiple copies to be created by varying the parameters. Thus we could define

$$B1(in, out) = in?x \rightarrow out!x \rightarrow B1(in, out)$$

and define BA and BB in terms of it.

The renaming used to convert BA to BB was doubly simple because not only was each event only mapped to one thing, but also all events get mapped to different things. Renamings of this type really do just create copies of the original except for the names of events. Obviously if we map a pair of events to a single target via a renaming then we introduce confusion: we cannot be sure which event P is performing when we see $P[\![a, a/b, c]\!]$ (in which both b and c are mapped to a) perform a. This is a potential source of nondeterminism: many-to-one renaming like this is used in situations where we deliberately want to lose information about a process, but is rarely used in programs close to realistic implementations.

If a given event a is mapped to both b and c, then whenever P performs a, $P[\![R]\!]$ offers the choice of b and c to the environment, but the state after either of these choices is the same. This might seem a strange operation on processes, but it proves to be extremely useful, not least (as we will see in the next chapter) in modelling security protocols. As a simple example, the process $(a \rightarrow P)[\![b, c/a, a]\!]$ (meaning that a gets mapped to b and c, and all other events of the process are unchanged) is equivalent to

$$(b \to P[\![^{b,c}/a,a]\!]) \;\square\; (c \to P[\![^{b,c}/a,a]\!])$$

A typical application of this one-to-many type of renaming is where there is a set of events in the wider world that a process P needs to regard as equivalent. It is both clearer and safer to define P with a single event representing this class and rename later.

While it is possible in principle to have a renaming that both maps an event a to several, and also introduces nondeterminism through one or more of these images also being the images of other events, this is not something one meets in practice. In other words, the renamings that are used are one-to-one (the simple case), or many-to-one, or one-to-many, but not both of the last two.

In general, renaming is a useful tool to bear in mind when you are having difficulty obtaining a particular effect in CSP. Let's suppose we want to hide the first event (and only the first event) of process P. This cannot be achieved using the hiding operator alone, since it only hides by the name of the event rather than position in a trace. However, if we give each event of P two separate identities using renaming, we can use a suitable parallel composition to distinguish between the first and subsequent events, and then hide only the first event. If the events of P are drawn from set A, we create a unique 'shadow' a' for each $a \in A$, such that the set A' of all these shadows is disjoint from A. The hiding we want is then achieved by

$$(P[\![R]\!] \underset{A \cup A'}{\|} ?x : A' \to Run(A)) \setminus A'$$

where R is the relation that maps each a to both a and a'.

Joining channels together

As discussed above, the CSP parallel and hiding operators complement each other because they each represent half of the natural *point-to-point* parallelism in which the common events of a pair of processes are synchronized and then hidden so that nothing else can interfere with them. It certainly is not hard to create systems of this form using the operators we have already seen: two processes can be joined together $(P \underset{X}{\|} Q) \setminus X$ or a whole network:

$$(\|_{i=1}^{n}(P_i, A_i)) \setminus Z, \quad \text{where } Z = \bigcup \{A_i \cap A_j \mid i \neq j\}$$

(in which point-to-point communication occurs when $A_i \cap A_j \cap A_k = \varnothing$ whenever i, j and k are all different). However, it can be useful to have operators that do the parallel composition and hiding all at once, particularly when they solve another problem that can – in a significant minority of cases – make CSP parallelism more trouble to use. That is the need to have the same name in both of a pair of processes for any event on which they are to synchronize.

For example, if we want to connect a series of N processes in parallel, the outputs of each (except the last) being linked to the inputs of the next, it is a little inconvenient to have to invent separate names for all the $N + 1$ channels ($N - 1$ of them internal) and to have to build each of the component processes to use the right pair of them. This shows up clearly in the example $B2$ seen earlier, of putting two one-place buffers together. While this can be solved by either parameterization or renaming, it would be friendlier to have an operator that did the work for us.

Hoare's book introduced two special-purpose operators that combined parallel, hiding and renaming. These were the *chaining* or *piping* operator $P \gg Q$ and the *enslavement* operator $(P /\!/ a{:}Q)$. Chaining assumes that both the processes it combines have just two channels: an input channel (usually called *left*) and an output channel (usually *right*). $P \gg Q$ is then the result of connecting the output of P to the input of Q (by renaming to some other channel name) and hiding the internal communications. The resulting process has the same two visible channels, namely the input of P and the output of Q, so can itself be combined using $\gg$. For example, we can combine any finite number of $Copy$ ($= \ left?x \ : \ T \ \to \ right!x \ \to \ Copy$) processes using this operator

$$Copy \gg Copy \gg \ldots \gg Copy$$

The enslavement operator takes a 'master' process P and a (usually) named slave $a{:}Q$ whose alphabet is entirely contained within that of P, puts them in parallel (all communications of Q being given the additional label a), hiding the alphabet of $a{:}Q$ (namely all events with label a). It is a useful operator for modelling situations where one process provides a service to another, and for creating recursively parallel networks.

You will find both these operators discussed in [76], and also the reasons why neither of them fit comfortably with the principles of machine-readable CSP_M (in particular the way it handles types). The essential problem with chaining, for example, is the special role given to two channel names: what are their types, particularly in situations where we may want to use $\gg$ on a process whose outputs are of a different type from its inputs?

CSP_M introduces an alternative operator that readily generalizes the other two: it is called the *link* parallel operator: $P[a \leftrightarrow b, c \leftrightarrow c]Q$ means P and Q in parallel, with the a channel of P connected to the b one of Q, and the c channels of the two connected, with all these internal communications hidden. In general this operator can link any list of pairs of channels, where the type of the first and second components of each pair has the same type and no channel is used twice as a first or twice as a second component. Like $\gg$, it can be written as an appropriate combination of parallel, hiding and renaming. The $\gg$ operator then simply becomes $[right \leftrightarrow left]$ in cases where the types of these channels match.

The link parallel operator is a very useful one for programming CSP models of distributed systems where (as one usually does) we want the internal communications to be hidden. We will be using it relatively rarely in this book simply because we need to keep the 'internal' communications of the security protocol models we build visible so we can specify things about them.

1.4 Further operators

Many programming languages have the concept of *sequential composition*. $P;Q$ does whatever P does until it terminates, and then does what Q does. This makes sense in the world of CSP – what the process 'does' is to communicate with its environment – provided we understand what 'terminates' means. CSP programs can stop communicating for a variety of reasons, such as reaching the state *Stop*, deadlocking some other way, or getting into some race condition. All of these really correspond to the process getting stuck in some way rather than terminating gracefully, and while you can imagine wanting some operator that handles errors in a process P by passing control on to a second one Q, it would not be an ordinary sequential composition.

The solution is to represent the act of a process terminating successfully by a special event $\checkmark$, which is only introduced via the process *Skip* (i.e., it is not permitted to write things like $\checkmark \rightarrow Stop$, even though this particular example would be equivalent to *Skip* if we could). Thus termination is something that a process does positively, rather than arising negatively out of the failure to make any sort of progress.

For example, $a \rightarrow b \rightarrow Skip$ is a process that terminates successfully after the events a and b, and $(a \rightarrow Skip);P$ has the same externally observable behaviour as $a \rightarrow P$. Each time that a $\checkmark$ event triggers a sequential composition, the $\checkmark$ gets hidden, since it no longer represents termination of the entire process. In other words $P;Q$ does not terminate until P has and then Q has, but only Q's $\checkmark$ is externally visible. $\checkmark$, when it occurs, is always the final event the process performs: it is never followed by anything else.

Skip and $P;Q$ are easy to understand, and by far most often used, in situations where:

1 They are used to build the sequential components of networks, rather than being used to compose two parallel networks in sequence;

2 You never write a process that attempts to give the environment the choice of terminating or not, as in $P \,\square\, Skip$.

Dealing properly with the general case, particularly when rule (1) above is violated, presents a real challenge, and it would be wrong to get too involved here in these issues since they are irrelevant to the use of CSP in this book and are in any case treated in [76] and [87].[3]

All we do here, therefore, is give an outline of how termination is treated by the other operators. $\checkmark$ may not be hidden or renamed, or be the target of another action under renaming. It never appears explicitly in any set used as a process alphabet or interface in a parallel operator, but is always implicitly there, since we adopt the principle of *distributed termination*: every type of parallel composition only

---

[3] It must be noted here that these two books deal with problem (2) in subtly different ways, each of which has its own advantages and disadvantages.

Stop	the process that does nothing
$a \rightarrow P$	event prefix
$?x : A \rightarrow P$	event prefix choice
$c?x : A \rightarrow P$	input prefix choice
$P \,\Box\, Q$	choice between two processes
$\Box\, S$	general choice
$P \sqcap Q$	nondeterministic choice
$\sqcap\, S$	general nondeterministic choice
$P \parallel Q$	lockstep parallel
$P \,_X\!\parallel_Y Q$	synchronizing parallel
$P \parallel_X Q$	interface parallel
$\vert\vert\vert\, S$	general interleaving
$P \setminus X$	event hiding
$P[\![R]\!]$	process relational renaming
Skip	successful termination
$P;Q$	sequential composition
$P = F(P)$	recursive definition
$\mu\, p.F(p)$	recursive process

Figure 1.1 CSP operators

terminates when all its component processes have terminated. The effect of this is that $P \vert\vert\vert$ *Skip* is equivalent to P, since the right-hand process terminates immediately and waits for P to do so.

The way sequential composition interacts with process parameters makes it a far less universally used operator than it is in most imperative programming languages. The problem is that $P;Q$ provides no mechanism for transferring the parameter values that P has built up at the end of its run over to Q. The second x in

$$(c?x \rightarrow P); (d!x \rightarrow Skip)$$

does not get bound to the value input in the first process, rather it means whatever x means in the world that encloses the entire process. This means that $P;Q$ tends to get used at a very low level on components without data to pass on, or at a high level between components that provide rather independent services to the environment in sequence, rather than as a way of putting together stages of a typical computation.

Recursion through the left-hand argument of ';' can create effects rather like the *CT* definitions above based on recursion through $\vert\vert\vert$. For example, we can create an unbounded *stack* via the definition:

$$Empty = in?x \rightarrow S_x; Empty$$

$$S_x = out!x \rightarrow Skip$$
$$\Box\ in?y \rightarrow (S_y; S_x)$$

The process $Chaos_A$ described earlier never terminates, and therefore is not refined by *Skip*. We can remedy this via an extended version:

$$Chaos_A^{\checkmark} = Stop \sqcap Skip \sqcap ?x : A \rightarrow Chaos_A^{\checkmark}$$

which can perform any trace of events from A, after which it can decide to carry on, terminate successfully, or deadlock.

A summary of all of the operators introduced so far is given in Figure 1.1.

1.5 Process behaviour

Concurrent systems seem to be inherently more difficult to understand than sequential ones. Rather than having a single process that works through its program in a linear fashion a step at a time, we may have many that interact in ways that are less predictable and create the potential for

- *deadlock*, in which, though each individual node may well be willing to do something, the system as a whole cannot agree on any action;

- *livelock*, in which an infinite sequence of hidden internal communications occur between components, so that the external appearance is much like a deadlocked system;

- *nondeterminism*, which though it appears in CSP from various angles, arises most naturally – and unavoidably – in the situation where two processes P_1 and P_2 are each willing to talk to a third, Q, which has to make the choice. These internal communications will often be most naturally hidden, but obviously the subsequent external behaviour may well be affected by which way Q jumps.

Indeed, just thinking about the different states (each a combination of states of the component processes) a network can get into can be very challenging. For example, can process *Anne* ever get into the state where she thinks she has run a protocol with *Bob*, when he does not think he has run it with her? Trying to understand and specify processes in these terms is complex, and perhaps leads one to think at the wrong level of abstraction: how the process is built rather than what it is doing.

While we cannot eliminate potential misbehaviours simply by choice of notation or the models used to specify and reason about CSP, we can use these things to make the problems clearer and less frightening, and to give us a language for specifying how we want systems to behave. We need models that clearly represent aspects of process behaviour that are relevant to correctness – both behaviours that we might positively want our processes to have and ones that we definitely want to exclude, and are not cluttered by irrelevant detail.

The traces model

The finite *traces* of a process provide a strikingly simple model of behaviour: we simply record the sequences of visible events that our process can communicate up to an arbitrary finite time. For example:

- *traces*(*Stop*) = {⟨⟩}, where ⟨⟩ is the empty sequence: however long you watch *Stop*, it will not do anything.
- $traces(\mu P.a \rightarrow P \square b \rightarrow Skip) = \{\langle a \rangle^n, \langle a \rangle^{n}\hat{\ }\langle b \rangle, \langle a \rangle^{n}\hat{\ }\langle b, \checkmark \rangle \mid n \in \mathbb{N}\}$ where $s\hat{\ }t$ is the concatenation of s and t, and s^n is the concatenation of n copies of s. As you would expect, when the event $\checkmark$ that signals termination appears in a trace, it is the last element of the trace.

In the *traces model* of CSP each process P is represented by its set of traces, which is always

- (T1) nonempty, because every process can perform the empty trace;
- (T2) prefix-closed, in the sense that if $s\hat{\ }t$ is a trace then so is s.

The individual traces range over the set of finite sequences of Σ with perhaps a $\checkmark$ added at the end. If X is any set, X^* is the set of finite sequences of members of X (including the empty sequence ⟨⟩, and then:

$$traces(P) \subseteq \Sigma^{*\checkmark}, \quad \text{where}$$
$$\Sigma^{*\checkmark} = \Sigma^* \cup \{s\hat{\ }\langle\checkmark\rangle \mid s \in \Sigma^*\}$$

The traces model itself, which is written $\mathcal{T}$, is the set of all subsets of $\Sigma^{*\checkmark}$ that satisfy (T1) and (T2).

A straightforward set of rules allow us to calculate *traces*(P) for any CSP term P: there is one rule for each construct in the language that shows the effect of that construct on traces. The following clauses describe the effect of the CSP operators we have seen:

- $traces(Stop) = \{\langle\rangle\}$.
- $traces(a \rightarrow P) = \{\langle\rangle\} \cup \{\langle a \rangle\hat{\ }s \mid s \in traces(P)\}$ – this process has either done nothing, or its first event was a followed by a trace of P.
- $traces(?x : A \rightarrow P) = \{\langle\rangle\} \cup \{\langle a \rangle\hat{\ }s \mid a \in A \wedge s \in traces(P[a/x])\}$ – this is similar except that the initial event is now chosen from the set A and the subsequent behaviour depends on which is picked: $P[a/x]$ means the substitution of the value a for all free occurrences of the identifier x.
- $traces(c?x : A \rightarrow P) = \{\langle\rangle\} \cup \{\langle c.a \rangle\hat{\ }s \mid a \in A \wedge s \in traces(P[a/x])\}$ – the same except for the use of the channel name.
- $traces(P \square Q) = traces(P) \cup traces(Q)$ – this process offers the traces of P and those of Q.
- $traces(\square S) = \bigcup\{traces(P) \mid P \in S\}$ for any non-empty set S of processes.
- $traces(P \sqcap Q) = traces(P) \cup traces(Q)$ – since this process can behave like either P or Q, its traces are those of P and those of Q.
- $traces(\sqcap S) = \bigcup\{traces(P) \mid P \in S\}$ for any non-empty set S of processes.

■ $traces(P \parallel Q) = traces(P) \cap traces(Q)$ – when P and Q have to synchronize on everything, every trace of the combination has to be a trace of both P and Q.

■ $traces(P \ {}_X\|_Y\ Q) = \{s \in (X \cup Y)^{*\checkmark} \mid s \upharpoonright X^\checkmark \in traces(P) \wedge s \upharpoonright Y^\checkmark \in traces(Q)\}$ – P must perform all events in X, and Q all in Y, and the combination only terminates when they both have. $X^\checkmark$ is an abbreviation for $X \cup \{\checkmark\}$, and $s \upharpoonright Z$ means s restricted to Z, or in other words s with all members outside Z thrown away. Note that with this parallel operator, once we are told a trace of $P \ {}_X\|_Y\ Q$, we know exactly what traces P and Q must have done to create it. The situation with $P \underset{X}{\parallel} Q$ (and its special case $P \parallel\!\parallel\!\parallel Q$) is not so simple, since, for example, if P and Q can both perform the same initial event a, and it is not one being synchronized, then $\langle a \rangle$ could have happened in either of two ways. Thus the rule for calculating the effects of $\underset{X}{\parallel}$ is a little more complex:

■ $traces(P \underset{X}{\parallel} Q) = \bigcup\{s \underset{X}{\parallel} t \mid s \in traces(P) \wedge t \in traces(Q)\}$, where $s \underset{X}{\parallel} t$ is the set of traces that can result from P and Q respectively performing s and t. This set is empty unless $s \upharpoonright X^\checkmark = t \upharpoonright X^\checkmark$. For further details of this calculation see either [76] or [87].

■ $traces(\big|\big|\big|_{i \in I} P_i) = \bigcup_{F \subseteq_{fin} I} traces(\big|\big|\big|_{i \in F} P_i)$. Since traces are finite sequences of events, any trace of the interleaving indexed over I will arise from only finitely many of the processes. Thus the interleavings of all finite subsets F of indexes from I will generate all the traces required. For a finite collection of processes, $\big|\big|\big| P_1, \ldots, P_n$ can be defined in terms of the binary operator, to be $(\ldots (P_1 \parallel\!\parallel\!\parallel P_2) \parallel\!\parallel\!\parallel \ldots \parallel\!\parallel\!\parallel P_n)$.

■ $traces(P \setminus X) = \{s \setminus X \mid s \in traces(P)\}$, where $s \setminus X = s \upharpoonright (\Sigma^\checkmark \setminus X)$.

■ $traces(P[\![R]\!]) = \{t \mid \exists s \in traces(P) \bullet s\, R^* \, t\}$, where R^* is the relation on traces that relates two traces just when they have the same length, with each element of s being related to the corresponding one in t by $R \cup \{(\checkmark, \checkmark)\}$.

■ $traces(Skip) = \{\langle\rangle, \langle\checkmark\rangle\}$, since all $Skip$ does is terminate successfully.

■ $traces(P; Q) = (traces(P) \cap \Sigma^*) \cup \{s\hat{\ }t \mid s\hat{\ }\langle\checkmark\rangle \in traces(P) \wedge t \in traces(Q)\}$. In other words a trace of $P; Q$ is either a trace of P without a $\checkmark$, or is the combination of a trace after which P can terminate and a trace of Q. Note that the effect of this is to hide the $\checkmark$ produced by P: we only want $P; Q$ to terminate when Q does.

The only construct that leaves is recursion. A recursive definition

$$P = F(P)$$

says that the name P has the same behaviour – and in particular the same traces – as the process $F(P)$, namely the body $F(\cdot)$ of the recursion in which all recursive calls behave as P. In terms of traces, $F(\cdot)$ will always represent a mapping from $\mathcal{T}$ to itself which is *monotone*, namely if $traces(Q_1) \subseteq traces(Q_2)$ then $traces(F(Q_1)) \subseteq traces(F(Q_2))$. It follows that $traces(P) \supseteq traces(F(Stop))$ (the last set are the traces the body of the recursion can do without making any recursive calls). Applying $F(\cdot)$ and monotonicity over and over again tells us that $traces(P) \supseteq traces(F^n(Stop))$ for any n, where $F^n(Stop)$ just means the result of applying F n times to $Stop$.

$traces(F^n(Stop))$ are the traces the process P can produce using no more than n nested levels of recursion. Since we are only considering finite traces and any finite trace must appear in a finite time, it is clear that any such trace must only take a finite number of recursive unfoldings to produce. It follows that

$$traces(P) = \bigcup \{traces(F^n(Stop)) \mid n \in \mathbb{N}\})$$

and indeed it is possible to show that this value is always a fixed point of the $\mathcal{T} \to \mathcal{T}$ mapping derived from $F(\cdot)$ (i.e., it is mapped to itself by this map). For further discussion of how fixed points arise and correspond to recursions, see either [76] or [87].

The above rules give a *denotational semantics* to CSP in terms of traces: an inductive recipe for computing the value in $\mathcal{T}$ for any process. There are other ways to work out the traces as well, such as simply observing the process P in operation: the FDR tool effectively does this by running an abstract implementation of P (its *operational semantics*) through all possible routes.

Traces are a powerful tool for understanding how processes behave, and can be used to specify just about any property that says that our process never communicates anything we don't want it to. Examples of such properties are:

■ The outputs (the sequence of values appearing on channel *right*, say) are always a prefix (initial subsequence of) the inputs (values on channel *left*), and the process performs no other actions. This is the traces specification of a *buffer*, or reliable communication medium.

■ Each occurrence of event *commit* is preceded by *starting* then *running*, both of which have occurred since the last *commit*.

■ The event *error* never happens.

All of these little specifications are relevant to the world of security protocols, since we often want to create a reliable communication service; we may well expect one event in a cryptographic protocol to occur without some other sequence of messages having happened first; and we may add events into our models that signal the occurrence of some insecure state, and then want to specify that such states never actually appear.

There are two distinct ways of expressing trace specifications like the above. The first is to write down a logical expression that explicitly defines a property of traces. The three above might be written (where tr represents a typical trace):

(a) $tr = tr \upharpoonright \{left, right\} \wedge tr \downarrow right \leq tr \downarrow left$, where $tr \downarrow a$ is the sequence of values communicated along channel a in tr.

(b) $tr = tr'^\smallfrown \langle commit \rangle \to \exists tr_1, tr_2 \bullet tr' = tr_1^\smallfrown tr_2 \wedge$
$\langle start, running \rangle \leq tr_2 \upharpoonright \{start, running\} \wedge tr_2 \upharpoonright \{commit\} = \langle\rangle$

(c) $tr \upharpoonright \{error\} = \langle\rangle$

Here (a) is notably simple because the specification is so close to the prefix relation on traces that we have already discussed; (b) is rather involved; and (c) is extremely simple, as befits the concept it is expressing.

When all of the traces of a process P are claimed to satisfy a logical property $S(tr)$ on traces, then we write P **sat** $S(tr)$ as shorthand for $\forall\, tr \in traces(P) \bullet S(tr)$.

Three immediate consequences of this definition are:

- P **sat** $true(tr)$ for any process P. This simply says that every process meets the weakest specification that does not disallow any behaviours.
- $(P$ **sat** $S(tr) \wedge P$ **sat** $T(tr)) \Rightarrow (P$ **sat** $S(tr) \wedge T(tr))$. If a process meets two specifications, then it must also meet their conjunction. This is useful when a specification with a number of conjuncts is to be established: each of the conjuncts can be established separately.
- $(P$ **sat** $S(tr) \wedge (S(tr) \Rightarrow T(tr))) \Rightarrow P$ **sat** $T(tr)$. This states that if P satisfies a specification then it must also satisfy any weaker specification.

It is possible to check that P **sat** $S(tr)$ by calculating the traces of P directly from the definitions, and then establishing that each of them meets the predicate $S(tr)$. Another way of doing this is to make use of a set of compositional proof rules, which allow specifications of a process to be deduced from specifications of their components. These make use of *inference rules*, which have the following form:

$$
\begin{array}{c}
premiss_1 \\
\cdots \\
premiss_n \\
\hline
conclusion
\end{array} \quad [\,side-condition\,]
$$

This states that if we have already established all of the premisses $premiss_1$ to $premiss_n$, and also the side condition, then we may also obtain the conclusion. The side condition is optional, and indeed a rule might have no premisses – in this case, the conclusion is obtained immediately. For example:

$$
\overline{Stop\ \mathbf{sat}\ tr = \langle\,\rangle}
$$

Proof rules for **sat** specifications will typically use statements about **sat** relations as premisses and conclusions, reserving other information for the side condition. For example:

$$
\begin{array}{c}
P\ \mathbf{sat}\ S(tr) \\
Q\ \mathbf{sat}\ T(tr) \\
\hline
P \,{}_X\|_Y\, Q\ \mathbf{sat}\ S(tr \restriction X) \wedge T(tr \restriction Y) \wedge tr \in (X \cup Y)^*
\end{array}
$$

This rule states that if we already have trace specifications $S(tr)$ and $T(tr)$ for P and Q respectively, then any trace of their parallel combination can perform only events in their joint alphabets, and must have its projection to X (which is P's contribution) meeting S, and similarly its projection to Y must meet T.

Rule `sat.stop`

$$Stop \textbf{ sat } tr = \langle\rangle$$

Rule `sat.prefix`

$$\frac{P \textbf{ sat } S(tr)}{a \rightarrow P \textbf{ sat } tr = \langle\rangle \vee (tr = \langle a\rangle \frown tr' \wedge S(tr'))}$$

Rule `sat.extchoice`

$$\frac{\forall i \bullet P(i) \textbf{ sat } S(tr)}{\square_i P(i) \textbf{ sat } S(tr)}$$

Rule `sat.parallel`

$$\frac{\begin{array}{l} P \textbf{ sat } S(tr) \\ Q \textbf{ sat } T(tr) \end{array}}{P \parallel Q \textbf{ sat } S \wedge T(tr)}$$

Rule `sat.interleave`

$$\frac{\begin{array}{l} P \textbf{ sat } S(tr) \\ Q \textbf{ sat } T(tr) \end{array}}{P \mathbin{\vert\vert\vert} Q \textbf{ sat } S(tr \upharpoonright \sigma(P)) \wedge T(tr \upharpoonright \sigma(Q))} \quad [\sigma(P) \cap \sigma(Q) = \varnothing]$$

Figure 1.2 CSP satisfaction rules

For example, suppose we know that

$$P \textbf{ sat } tr = tr \upharpoonright \{left, mid\} \wedge tr \upharpoonright mid \leq tr \upharpoonright left$$
$$Q \textbf{ sat } tr = tr \upharpoonright \{mid, right\} \wedge tr \upharpoonright right \leq tr \upharpoonright mid$$

Applying the rule for parallel combination yields that

$$P \ _{\{\vert left, mid\vert\}}\parallel_{\{\vert mid, right\vert\}} Q \textbf{ sat } tr \upharpoonright right \leq tr \upharpoonright mid \wedge tr \upharpoonright mid \leq tr \upharpoonright left$$

If we are only concerned with the *left* and *right* channels, this may be weakened to obtain

$$P \ _{\{\vert left, mid\vert\}}\parallel_{\{\vert mid, right\vert\}} Q \textbf{ sat } tr \upharpoonright right \leq tr \upharpoonright left$$

There is a complete set of proof rules for trace specifications, whose soundness is based upon the trace definitions for all of the process operators. Some of them are given in Figure 1.2. Recursion is a special case that uses the technique of 'fixed point induction', covered later in this chapter.

It is also possible to identify proof rules for particular kinds of specification, and some examples of this are given in Chapter 7.

The other way of expressing trace specifications is to create the process that has the maximum possible number of traces satisfying the specification, and test for *trace refinement* between this specification process *Spec* and the proposed implementation *Impl*. *Impl* trace-refines *Spec*, written $Spec \sqsubseteq_T Impl$, when

$$traces(Impl) \subseteq traces(Spec)$$

Note that a process becomes *more* refined by having *fewer* traces. That is because the fewer behaviours a process has, the *fewer* ways it has to violate a specification that says each behaviour is right. It follows from this that $Stop \sqsupseteq_T P$ for all processes P. We will discuss this rather curious fact later.

These *characteristic* processes for our three specifications are as follows. In each case a P satisfies the corresponding specification if and only if it trace-refines this process.

(a) The infinite buffer process $B_{\langle\rangle}^{\infty}$, where

$$B_{\langle\rangle}^{\infty} = left?x \rightarrow B_{\langle x \rangle}^{\infty}$$
$$B_{s^{\smallfrown}\langle x \rangle}^{\infty} = left?y \rightarrow B_{\langle y \rangle^{\smallfrown}s^{\smallfrown}\langle x \rangle}^{\infty}$$
$$\square\ right!x \rightarrow B_{s}^{\infty}$$

(b) The process P_0, where

$$P_0 = ?x : \Sigma \setminus \{start, commit\} \rightarrow P_0$$
$$\square\ start \rightarrow P_1$$

$$P_1 = ?x : \Sigma \setminus \{running, commit\} \rightarrow P_1$$
$$\square\ running \rightarrow P_2$$

$$P_2 = ?x : \Sigma \setminus \{commit\} \rightarrow P_2$$
$$\square\ commit \rightarrow P_0$$

This specification moves on from one state to the next when the next event in the cycle $\langle start, running, commit \rangle$ occurs. The first two of these events are always allowed (but at other times do not change the state), but *commit* is only permitted at the designated point in the cycle.

(c) $Run_{\Sigma \setminus \{error\}}$

This correspondence between refinement and the satisfaction of specifications is of enormous practical importance, since, as we will see in Chapter 4, it lies at the heart of how FDR works.

Refinement has other useful properties: it is *transitive*, in that

$$P \sqsubseteq_T Q \wedge Q \sqsubseteq_T R \Rightarrow P \sqsubseteq_T R$$

and is *compositional*: preserved by all the operations of the language, in the sense that if $F(\cdot)$ is any CSP construct with a slot for placing a process, then

$$P \sqsubseteq_T Q \Rightarrow F(P) \sqsubseteq_T F(Q)$$

This last property is, of course, just a re-statement of the idea of monotonicity mentioned above when discussing recursions.

These principles can be used to demonstrate that complex systems meet their specifications by stepwise, compositional development. For example, if we have a system with a number of components

$$C(P_1, P_2, \ldots, P_n)$$

and we can show that if each P_i is replaced by its specification S_i, then the overall system would meet its specification

$$Spec \sqsubseteq_T C(S_1, S_2, \ldots, S_n)$$

Then if we can prove that $S_i \sqsubseteq_T P_i$ for all i, the transitivity and compositionality of refinement prove

$$Spec \sqsubseteq_T C(P_1, P_2, \ldots, P_n)$$

Beyond traces

Traces only tell part of the story about how processes behave. It is a very important part, and indeed most of the formal analysis of protocols we will be doing in this book will be done with traces alone, but there are important things we cannot tell from traces. To put it simply, we can tell from traces that a process will not communicate things we don't want it to, but we cannot tell whether it will definitely accept events that we think it must. For example, for any process P,

$$P \quad P \sqcap Stop \quad P \parallel_\Sigma Chaos_\Sigma^\checkmark$$

have the same traces, but the second of them can deadlock immediately by picking *Stop*, and the synchronization with $Chaos_\Sigma^\checkmark$ in the third can always prevent further communications.

The problem we are facing here is that of nondeterminism: where a process can make internal decisions that can affect subsequent behaviour it may very well be free either to pick a route that will lead to deadlock or one that will not, and there is no way of detecting this type of possibility via traces. The simplest addition to traces that copes with this is the concept of a *failure*: the coupling (s, X) of a trace s and a set of events $X \subseteq \Sigma^\checkmark$ that the process can refuse after s. Here, 'refuse' means permanent refusal: we do not record the failure $(\langle\rangle, X)$ just because nothing happens when our process is offered X for a short time, during which it may still be performing internal computations. *failures*(P) is the set of all P's failures: we can immediately tell the difference between P and $P \sqcap Stop$ since the latter has the failure $(\langle\rangle, \Sigma^\checkmark)$ even when P does not.

Just as with traces, it is possible to compute *failures*(P) either via a rule for each operator or by observing the operational behaviour of P. Since the rules are more complex than those for traces, we do not list them in this book, but they can be found in any of [41], [76] or [87]. For the second option, a state of P refuses X just when it can neither perform any member of X nor any τ actions, since the latter represent internal progress that might lead to states that can accept X.

One of the most obvious deficiencies of $\mathcal{T}$ is that it cannot distinguish between internal choice $P \sqcap Q$ and external choice $P \;\square\; Q$ (a fact that is apparent when you look at the rules for calculating traces quoted above). This problem is solved by failures, since for example

$$(a \rightarrow Stop) \sqcap (b \rightarrow Stop)$$

has the failures $(\langle\rangle, \{a\})$ and $(\langle\rangle, \{b\})$, neither of which occurs in

$$(a \rightarrow Stop) \;\square\; (b \rightarrow Stop)$$

We can now make specifications that demand progress of a process, for example:

(d) Deadlock freedom: a process is deadlock free if for no trace $s \in \Sigma^*$ is $(s, \Sigma^\checkmark) \in failures(P)$. (Note that this does not prevent failures of the form $(s^\frown\langle\checkmark\rangle, \Sigma^\checkmark)$, since it is probably not right to think of a successfully terminated process as deadlocked.)

(e) We can extend the buffer specification quoted earlier to make it insist that the process must definitely accept inputs and give outputs in appropriate circumstances. The usual thing to say here is that an empty buffer must accept any input and that a nonempty buffer cannot refuse to output, so that in addition to the traces specification already quoted we require

$$(s, X) \in failures(B) \land s \downarrow right = s \downarrow left \Rightarrow X \cap \{| \; left \; |\} = \varnothing$$
$$(s, X) \in failures(B) \land s \downarrow right < s \downarrow left \Rightarrow \{| \; right \; |\} \not\subseteq X$$

The idea of trace refinement extends easily to *failures refinement*: $P \sqsubseteq_F Q$ if and only if

$$failures(P) \supseteq failures(Q) \quad \text{and} \quad traces(P) \supseteq traces(Q)$$

A question that might come to mind when studying this definition is 'Since surely all traces of a process P are associated with a failure, why does this definition still have the explicit trace clause in it?' The answer is perhaps surprising: there may in fact be traces without any failures, and we have to take account of them in the modelling of processes.

To discover how this happens we need to think about what a process might do after communicating a trace s. It might already be in a stable state, and therefore refuse at least $\varnothing$, so that would not create a problem. Alternatively it might go through some finite sequence of τ actions and reach a stable state, which would also be fine for the same basic reason. The final possibility is that it goes on doing τs for ever – which we call *diverging* – and that is where things go wrong. Though there is clearly a strong sense in which a diverging process is in fact refusing all visible actions, it does not fit in with the idea that an unstable process is not yet in a state where it can refuse anything. Basically, something like refusal is happening in a quite different way. Perhaps the simplest definition of a process that does nothing but diverge is

$$\mathsf{div} = (\mu p.a \rightarrow p) \setminus \{a\}$$

– a process that has only the empty trace and no failures at all.

In fact, $\mathsf{div} \sqsupseteq_F P$ for all processes P, just as $Stop \sqsupseteq_T P$. It is, when you think about it, rather unlikely that you are going to have the greatest process under refinement in any model that gives a complete description of how processes behave, particularly ones as useless as div and $Stop$, since there is the general expectation that refinement produces in some sense a better process.

The solution, of course, is to incorporate the concept of divergence into our models. The phenomenon of divergence is almost always considered an error, and that provides an excuse for a simplifying assumption that CSP makes, namely once a process has had the possibility of diverging, we are not interested in the details of how it behaves. This assumption lies behind the definition of $divergences(P)$ as all extensions of traces s after which P can diverge. In other words, if $s \in divergences(P)$ and $s\hat{\ }t \in \Sigma^{*\checkmark}$ then $s\hat{\ }t \in divergences(P)$.

The reasons behind this assumption are subtle, and can be found, for example, in [76] and [87]. In order to implement the assumption fully we have to extend the sets of traces and failures by anything that might have happened after divergence:

$$traces_\perp(P) = traces(P) \cup divergences(P)$$
$$failures_\perp(P) = failures(P) \cup \{(s, X) \mid s \in divergences(P) \wedge X \subseteq \Sigma^\checkmark\}$$

In the *failures/divergences* model of CSP, we identify a process with the pair $(failures_\perp(P), divergences(P))$. This plugs the remaining hole we discovered when considering failures by themselves: if a process has performed the trace s, $s \notin divergences(P)$ and $(s, X) \notin failures_\perp(P)$ then we know that P will *certainly* accept a member of X if offered it for long enough.

Failures/divergences refinement is defined in the way we have come to expect: $P \sqsubseteq_{FD} Q$ if, and only if

$$failures_\perp(P) \supseteq failures_\perp(Q) \quad \text{and} \quad divergences(P) \supseteq divergences(Q)$$

The buffer specification quoted earlier should certainly be extended to the failures/divergences model in the obvious way: divergence is not permitted. We can thus be sure that an empty buffer will certainly, if offered, accept any input, and that a nonempty one will output given the chance: they cannot escape from these obligations by diverging.

One can do the same for the deadlock freedom specification quoted above, but should realize that a process can then fail the specification without actually deadlocking. The failures/divergences version of the deadlock freedom specification is really freedom from *both* deadlock and divergence. In most cases, this is an entirely reasonable extension, but there is one important situation in which it is undesirable: it is sometimes beneficial[4] not to check a proposed implementation

---

[4] The reasons for this, which are mainly concerned with efficiency, can be discovered in [76].

Impl for deadlock, but rather *Impl* \ Σ. Intuitively this should not matter: hiding (or, indeed, renaming) cannot affect whether a process can deadlock, but obviously it can introduce divergence. In fact, for a process that never terminates ($\checkmark$), deadlock freedom of *Impl* is equivalent to the statement that *Impl* \ Σ *must* diverge. It is thus reasonable to say that, just as the natural model for assessing the buffer specification is failures/divergences, the natural one for deadlock freedom is failures alone. The deadlock freedom of any process P is equivalent to the truth of the refinement

$$Skip \sqsubseteq_F P \setminus \Sigma$$

In the same way the natural model for the traces specifications (b) and (c) quoted earlier is the traces model. Though it is possible to lift them to the more elaborate models, nothing is gained, and there is again the possibility that a process might fail the failures/divergences version by diverging rather than actually communicating wrongly.

Despite these observations about specifications, it is generally agreed that failures/divergences are the 'standard' model for CSP, and that this model gives the best notion of what it means for two CSP processes to be equivalent.

For most of this book we will, however, be concerned mainly with properties that can successfully be stated in the traces model. The subtleties of failures and divergences will, most of the time at least, not be things we have to worry about.

Unique fixed points

Recursive processes can be defined equationally, by giving an equation $P = F(P)$ that the required process must satisfy. The process P defined in this way is a *fixed point* of $F(X)$, in that applying F to P results in the same process P. If a differently defined process Q is also shown to satisfy the equation $Q = F(Q)$, then it can be useful to know if P and Q actually have the same behaviour – if they are actually the same fixed point of F or not. It turns out that a wide variety of functions, including most of those that are written in practical situations, have precisely one fixed point. For any such function F, any two processes that turn out to be fixed points of F must actually be the same process.

The most useful condition (but by no means the only one) that is sufficient to ensure that $F(X)$ has a unique fixed point is that all occurrences of X are *guarded* in $F(X)$ by some visible event. This means that:

- every occurrence of X appears within the scope of an event prefix, an event prefix choice, or an input, or in a sequential composition following a process that must perform at least one event before terminating;

- $F(X)$ should not contain the hiding operator (since this may make visible guards internal).

For example, the functions $a \rightarrow X$, $c?x : T \rightarrow (X ||| d!x \rightarrow Stop)$, and $(a \rightarrow Skip); X$ meet these two conditions. By contrast, $X \square a \rightarrow Stop$ does not, and neither does $(a \rightarrow X) \setminus a$. Both of these functions have multiple fixed points.

If a function $F(X)$ has a unique fixed point, then *all* process descriptions that satisfy the equation $P = F(P)$ must describe the same process. This can be useful for obtaining a better understanding of a process description.

Section 1.2 discussed one example, and we will consider another one here. Consider the system

$$Prot = (S \underset{\{|mid|\} \cup \{ack\}}{\|} R) \setminus \{| \, mid \, |\} \cup \{ack\}$$

which is intended to act as a one place buffer. It is made up of the following components:

$$S = left?x : T \to mid!x \to ack \to S$$
$$R = mid?y : T \to right!y \to ack \to R$$

It is straightforward to establish that

$$S \underset{\{|mid|\} \cup \{ack\}}{\|} R = left?x : T \to mid!x \to right!x \to ack \to S \underset{\{|mid|\} \cup \{ack\}}{\|} R$$

and hence that

$$(S \underset{\{|mid|\} \cup \{ack\}}{\|} R) \setminus \{| \, mid \, |\} \cup \{ack\}$$
$$= left?x : T \to right!x \to (S \underset{\{|mid|\} \cup \{ack\}}{\|} R) \setminus \{| \, mid \, |\} \cup \{ack\}$$

Thus $(S \underset{\{|mid|\} \cup \{ack\}}{\|} R) \setminus \{| \, mid \, |\} \cup \{ack\}$ is a fixed point of the function

$$F(X) = left?x : T \to right!x \to X$$

The process *Copy* is defined by this equation. Since $F(X)$ meets the conditions above, it has a unique fixed point. That means that *Prot* is the same process as *Copy*, and hence that it does indeed behave as a one-place buffer.

Fixed point induction

If $P = F(P)$ is a recursively defined process, then we require a proof rule that allows us to establish when P **sat** $S(tr)$. Since $traces(P) = \bigcup_{n \in \mathbb{N}} traces(F^n(Stop))$ it is enough to show that $F^n(Stop)$ **sat** $S(tr)$ for each $n \in \mathbb{N}$. This suggests an inductive approach. If we can establish the following, which give a base case and an inductive step:

- ∎ *Stop* **sat** $S(tr)$
- ∎ $\forall X \bullet X$ **sat** $S(tr) \Rightarrow F(X)$ **sat** $S(tr)$

then we can conclude that P **sat** $S(tr)$. The inference rule is given as follows:

$$\frac{\forall X \bullet X \text{ \textbf{sat} } S(tr) \Rightarrow F(X) \text{ \textbf{sat} } S(tr)}{\mu P.F(P) \text{ \textbf{sat} } S(tr)} \quad [\, S(\langle \rangle) \,]$$

The side condition is equivalent to checking that *Stop* **sat** $S(tr)$, since there is only the empty trace to check.

As an example, consider $Copy = left?x : T \rightarrow right!x \rightarrow Copy$. To show that this satisfies the buffer specification

$$B(tr) = tr \downarrow right \leq tr \downarrow left$$

we consider the following two assertions:

- ■ *Stop* **sat** $tr \downarrow right \leq tr \downarrow left$, which is true because the predicate is true for $\langle \rangle$, the only trace of *Stop*;

- ■ X **sat** $tr \downarrow right \leq tr \downarrow left \Rightarrow left?x : T \rightarrow right!x \rightarrow X$ **sat** $tr \downarrow right \leq tr \downarrow left$. To see that this is true, consider a trace of $left?x : T \rightarrow right!x \rightarrow X$. This is either $\langle \rangle$, or $\langle left.v \rangle$, or $\langle left.v, right.v \rangle \frown tr'$ where tr' is a trace of X. The first two cases meet $B(tr)$. In the last case, $tr' \downarrow right \leq tr' \downarrow left$ since X **sat** $B(tr)$, and so $\langle v \rangle \frown (tr' \downarrow right) \leq \langle v \rangle \frown (tr' \downarrow left)$. But this is exactly $tr \downarrow right \leq tr \downarrow left$, and so in the last case $B(tr)$ holds as well.

We see that the function $left?x : T \rightarrow right!x \rightarrow X$ preserves the specification $B(tr)$, and it follows that *Copy* **sat** $B(tr)$.

A form of this rule can be applied when using CSP processes as specifications. In this case, $Spec \sqsubseteq Stop$ is true for any specification process *Spec*, and so the first condition is always trivially true. The second condition turns out to be equivalent to the single refinement requirement $Spec \sqsubseteq F(Spec)$. The inference rule in this case is as follows:

$$\frac{Spec \sqsubseteq_T F(Spec)}{Spec \sqsubseteq_T \mu P.F(P)}$$

If we consider the example of *Copy* again, in order to show that $B_{\langle \rangle}^{\infty} \sqsubseteq Copy$, we have only to show that $B_{\langle \rangle}^{\infty} \sqsubseteq_T left?x : T \rightarrow right!x \rightarrow B_{\langle \rangle}^{\infty}$. But this is true because one of the possibilities allowed by the left-hand process $B_{\langle \rangle}^{\infty}$ is to permit input of some value followed immediately by its output – this is acceptable behaviour for a buffer – followed by some subsequent behaviour of $B_{\langle \rangle}^{\infty}$. And all of the behaviour of the right-hand process is of this form, so the refinement relation holds, and the proof rule supports the conclusion that $B_{\langle \rangle}^{\infty} \sqsubseteq_T Copy$.

1.6 Discrete time

Time is often important in concurrent systems, since we may well want a system to perform its tasks within timing constraints, and many systems use time-outs to avoid deadlocks and related conditions. Time also has a significant role in security since many protocols *timestamp* some or all messages in an effort to avoid attacks in which an old message is replayed.

CSP, of the sort we have so far, does not handle time other than by remembering which order communication events have occurred. The notions of equivalence, refinement and satisfaction that we have created pay no attention to how long processes take to do things.

There are two approaches to building time into CSP. 'Timed CSP' (which is described extensively in [87]) attaches a non-negative real number time to each event in the traces, so that we can record *exactly when* each event occurs. This simple addition leads to what at first sight are larger changes to the theory than might have been expected, and certainly the presence of the continuous time creates substantial problems in building automated tools for reasoning about Timed CSP.

The other approach, and the one we will summarize here, is comparatively simple. We add an extra event into the alphabet Σ, which is assumed to happen at regular time intervals. The usual name for this event is *tock*. You write a CSP program involving this event to define just how the occurrence of other events relates to the passage of time: thus any event that happens between the third and fourth *tock*s is one that happened between three and four time units from the moment the process was started. These time units can be any length appropriate for the system being studied, but for convenience we will assume from here on that there is a *tock* every second. Then for example, the processes

$$T_1 = a \to tock \to T_1$$

$$T_2 = a \to tock \to T_2$$
$$\square \; tock \to T_2$$

both allow a single a every second, but there is a difference since T_1 insists on an a per second, while T_2 is happy to wait.

T_1 illustrates a major difference in how events are sometimes interpreted in the timed world, since in standard CSP there is no obligation on a process's environment to accept any event. In other words, the timing regime implied by T_1 is inconsistent with our earlier generalization about how events are accepted: the inevitable march of time through the regular *tock*s is halted. In a timed framework there is far more need to distinguish between events that a process can rely on being accepted immediately (often outputs) and ones that it might have to wait for (often inputs). Thus it might be reasonable to create a timed buffer process

$$Tcopy = left?x \to tock \to right!x \to tock \to Tcopy$$
$$\square \; tock \to Tcopy$$

but it would be much more surprising to find one that would wait indefinitely for output but insist on immediate input.

A network can contain both timed and untimed processes, the latter placing no restriction on when events happen and not using the event *tock*. All the timed processes should, of course, synchronize on *tock*. If you put processes together that disagree about when events that they share occur, the result may well be deadlock: imagine, for example, the process *Tcopy* above feeding its outputs into a process that insists on at least three *tock*s occurring between inputs. If whatever is giving *Tcopy* its inputs is in a hurry and feeds it data as quickly as possible, this will quickly lead to a state where one process is insisting on output *now*, but the other one is not yet ready. Such a situation is called a *time stop* and represents an inconsistency in the timing requirements of one's model. For obvious reasons these inconsistencies must be avoided: some simple checks for establishing their absence are discussed in [76].

When building a process description in this style of CSP it is often helpful to put process states into one of three categories:

- An *idling* state is one that is happy for time to pass, but this will not change its state (i.e. it can perform the event *tock*, though the latter simply leads back to the same state); examples of idling states are the initial ones of *Tcopy* and T_2.

- An *evolving* state is one that allows time to pass (it has the event *tock*) but this leads to a different state from the original one; all the states the processes T_1, T_2 and *Tcopy* get into immediately after a non-*tock* event are in this category since in each case *tock* is the only possible event, but this leads to states where other events are possible.

- An *urgent* state is one in which no *tock* is possible, and which therefore requires some other event to happen immediately. Examples of these are the states in which T_1 and *Tcopy* respectively insist on *a* and an output. Evidently a time stop is an urgent state with no other event possible, which is therefore paradoxical.

Far more about this approach to describing timed systems in CSP can be found in [76].

2 Modelling security protocols in CSP

Security protocols work through the interaction of a number of processes in parallel that send each other messages. CSP is therefore an obvious notation for describing both the participants in the network and the composition that puts them together. In this chapter we describe how this is done, concentrating specifically on how protocol models can be built that allow us to probe for security flaws.

2.1 Trustworthy processes

The typical security protocol involves several agents (often two: an initiator and a responder) and perhaps a server that performs some service such as key generation, translation or certification. We will see how to program processes that faithfully run the functions of a protocol in an entirely correct and trustworthy way, before worrying about how we are going to look for security flaws.

If we look at the Yahalom protocol:

$$\text{Message 1} \quad a \rightarrow b \ : \ a.n_a$$
$$\text{Message 2} \quad b \rightarrow s \ : \ b.\{a.n_a.n_b\}_{ServerKey(b)}$$
$$\text{Message 3} \quad s \rightarrow a \ : \ \{b.k_{ab}.n_a.n_b\}_{ServerKey(a)}.\{a.k_{ab}\}_{ServerKey(b)}$$
$$\text{Message 4} \quad a \rightarrow b \ : \ \{a.k_{ab}\}_{ServerKey(b)}.\{n_b\}_{k_{ab}}$$

it is clear that a trustworthy agent can take one of two roles, namely as initiator (the sender of message 1, designated a above), or responder (the sender of message 2, designated b). It would seem wise to suppose that all agents can take either of these roles, and it may well be the case that we allow an agent to be able to run several different instances of the protocol at once. For the time being, however, we will see how to build agents for single runs of the initiator and responder roles (separately), as well as the server process s, whose role is to generate a session key k_{ab} when suitably prompted and issue it to a (and indirectly to b).

An agent process has two essentially different communication domains: on the one hand there are the messages it sends and receives over whatever medium it uses to talk to other agents (and servers if any), and on the other it may have interactions with its user through quite separate channels. Imagine a workstation connected to the Ethernet via a secure card implementing our protocol (and in no other way). The first communication domain would then be the Ethernet traffic, and the second would be the messages sent to and fro between the card and the rest of the workstation. For simplicity, let us assume that each process has channels *receive* and *send* that it uses for *all* communications with other nodes via the medium: inputs and outputs take the forms *receive.a.b.m* and *send.a.b.m*, in each case with *a* and *b* being the names of the sender and addressee (each of which is either an agent or a server) and *m* the message content.

All the protocol messages are transacted via *receive* and *send*, and we assume that security threats come from that direction too. It follows that we have to be careful to ensure that these communications faithfully reflect what actually goes on in our implementation. Generally speaking, however, we will be economical with the other, *external* communications, and where we do have them they often are present to help us *assess the security* of systems rather than being things one would expect to see in a real implementation.

Each of the four messages set out above are sent by one process and received by another. It is unrealistic to assume that the two of them always handshake on the message in the sense of the CSP parallel operator seen in the last chapter. It is better to think of a sent message being posted into the communication medium and a received message arriving from it. It would be wrong to build into our model any certainty that a sent message was delivered to its destination or that a received one has really come from where it *seems* to have come from. That sort of thing, after all, is what our protocols are designed to achieve.

The view that each process has of the running protocol is the series of sent or received messages that it sees. The three participants (*A*, *B* and *J*) respectively perform:

A's view (as initiator)
Message 1 *A* sends to *b* : $A.n_A$
Message 3 *A* gets from '*j*' : $\{b.k_{ab}.n_A.n_b\}_{ServerKey(A)}.\{A.k_{ab}\}_{ServerKey(b)}$
Message 4 *A* sends to *b* : $\{A.k_{ab}\}_{ServerKey(b)}, \{n_b\}_{k_{ab}}$

B's view (as responder)
Message 1 *B* gets from '*a*' : $a.n_a$
Message 2 *B* sends to *j* : $B.\{a.n_a.n_B\}_{ServerKey(B)}$
Message 4 *B* gets from '*a*' : $\{a.k_{ab}\}_{ServerKey(B)}.\{n_B\}_{k_{ab}}$

J's view (as server)
Message 2 *J* gets from '*b*' : $b.\{a.n_a.n_b\}_{ServerKey(b)}$
Message 3 *J* sends to *a* : $\{b.k_{ab}.n_a.n_b\}_{ServerKey(a)}.\{a.k_{ab}\}_{ServerKey(b)}$

The quotes '*x*' around the apparent senders of messages are just to emphasize that there is no way at present in which any of these processes can be certain about where the messages came from, just as they cannot be certain that the messages they send will be delivered.

What we need to do is to develop CSP programs for each of these three roles (initiator, responder, server), which in each case take the process through the appropriate series of messages. In this protocol each process alternates between sending and receiving messages, and the programs that implement them simply perform each send when all preceding messages have occurred correctly. Evidently nothing of this type is required as a precondition for the sender a to set the protocol running, though in practice this will be caused by an external communication from a's user (presumably telling it who to run the protocol with).

Each process has to do important things with data. They have to generate keys and nonces, perform encryptions and decryptions, and decide when a message that has been received is correct so as to allow the protocol to continue.

In practice, things like keys and nonces are probably chosen by something like a random number generator and contain many (hundreds or thousands) bits of information. There may very well be no mechanism that ensures all separately created values are different, but the extreme unlikelihood of equality means that we can assume that they are. This assumption does not translate well into CSP, not least because in any practically analyzable file we need to use types of keys and nonces than are vastly smaller than in real implementations. Therefore CSP models always ensure that each key the server generates and each nonce an agent generates is really different from all others in existence. This can either be done by equipping the processes with appropriate lists of values (or a single nonce in the case of an agent that is only intended to run the protocol once), or by adding a process into the parallel composition (in no sense representing a member of the real network) that monitors and distributes values.

The structure of the data type from which messages are drawn is, of course, of great importance, and is the subject of the next section. It is obviously reasonable to assume the existence of an encryption function over it: if k is a key and m a member of the type, then $encrypt(k, m)$ is the encryption of m under k. Clearly if there were several different forms of encryption in use, then a separate function would be required for each.

A process that has to encrypt a message will simply use this function. In our protocol there are two different modes in which processes receive encrypted messages: ones they ought to be able to understand, and ones they do not. An example of the first sort is the message the server receives, because $ServerKey(b)$ is a shared symmetric key between b and the server, meaning that the server ought to be able to look $ServerKey(b)$ up and decrypt the messages. The same thing applies to all other encryptions except the second half of message 3: a gets this from the server but cannot understand it because it is encrypted under a key not known to her. It follows that a cannot check whether what she inputs as this part of message 3 is reasonable, or even has the basic form implied by the protocol.

The best and easiest way to program a CSP process only to accept messages of the right form that it *can* understand is to form an external choice over all acceptable messages. For example, when b receives message 4 he already knows n_B and the name a, but does not yet know k_{ab}. Therefore he offers a choice of the form

$$\square_{k_{ab} \in Key} \; receive.a.B.(\{a.k_{ab}\}_{ServerKey(B)} . \{n_B\}_{k_{ab}}) \rightarrow P(B, a, n_B, k_{ab})$$

and can of course use the key k_{ab} that is thereby input in the process that follows. The effect of a choice like this is to all intents and purposes the same as the CSP input form $a?x$, but the latter cannot cope with the complex data operations used here. If we send the process an incorrect message (say one with the wrong value of n_B) the fact that the real implementation will abandon the protocol run is captured by the non-acceptance of the message by this CSP model. Of course, if we want a process to do something other than deadlock when it fails to get the message it is expecting, this will have to be programmed in as an alternative:

$$\Box_{k_{ab} \in Key} receive.a.B.(\{a.k_{ab}\}_{ServerKey(b)}.\{n_B\}_{k_{ab}}) \rightarrow P(B, a, n_B, k_{ab})$$
$$\Box \ AbortRun(B)$$

This allows conveniently both for the node timing out and abandoning for other reasons.

It ought to be said at this point that in programming our models of protocols we do not usually pay much attention to CSP models beyond traces. That is because the protocols themselves do not generally attempt to say how connection is to be *guaranteed* in the presence of an aggressive intruder, and things become a lot more difficult if we try to invent this detail. Therefore the precise way in which the choice between continuing and aborting the run above is made is not that important; all that matters is that we do not continue the run unless the right message is received, and allow for any traces that might occur following an abort.

We are now in a position to build programs representing the roles of initiator, responder and server. An initiator process equipped with only one nonce (and therefore only able to run the protocol once) and using server J is

$$Initiator(a, n_a) =$$
$$env?b : Agent \rightarrow send.a.b.a.n_a \rightarrow$$
$$\Box_{\substack{k_{ab} \in Key \\ n_b \in Nonce \\ m \in T}} \left(\begin{array}{l} receive.J.a.\{b.k_{ab}.n_a.n_b\}_{ServerKey(a)}.m \rightarrow \\ send.a.b.m.\{n_b\}_{k_{ab}} \rightarrow Session(a, b, k_{ab}, n_a, n_b) \end{array} \right)$$

where T is the set of all objects that our node can accept as something it is willing to pass on to b (remembering that it cannot understand or properly check this object, though clearly it might know how many bits to expect here, for example). Compound objects have been formed by forming sequences $\langle u.v.w \rangle$. For the time being at least, we are not going to try to specify what the agents do once they get into the *Session* state. The key $ServerKey(a)$ is the key that a shares with the server J. Obviously we would expect a only to know her own such key, but the server should know them all.

The initial communication $env?b : Agent$ is a representation of how the process's local environment might tell it to open a session with agent b. The precise way in which this happens is irrelevant to security, provided it is unambiguous and none of the communications involved are over the medium. Notice that there is nothing in this program to stop an agent asking to talk to himself (as $a \in Agent$ and so the communication $env.a$ is allowed). Asking to talk to yourself sounds rather schizophrenic, and indeed, if there is only one process with each identity, it would be as bizarre as it looks. However, there are certainly cases where a given identity for security purposes may well have a number of processes active, quite possibly in different locations, and in that case it would not seem so silly. In building a relatively abstract model of a protocol it therefore seems wise to allow this possibility, though of course if it were part of the protocol definition that a and b must be different, we could replace this communication by $env?b : Agent \setminus \{a\}$.

The most interesting piece of this program, however, relates to the packet of information that a receives from the server and passes on to b. You might have noticed that this was recorded as $\{a.k_{ab}\}_{ServerKey(b)}$ in the original protocol, but all this structure has disappeared from the way in which the CSP above handles it: it has become the arbitrary input m, which is simply relayed to b. There is a general expectation that processes participating in a cryptographic protocol will check that each message as it comes in has the correct form and that all fields have the right value or are in the right type (in the case of an input value). Thus our node, when expecting a message 3, will only accept a first part that is encrypted under her own key $ServerKey(a)$, which has the right values for b and n_a in, and where the other values k_{ab} and n_b are a key and a nonce. The difficulty with the second part of the message, however, is that our node cannot understand it: it is encrypted under the key that b shares with the server. Thus she cannot check to see if it is in the right format or has plausible values in it: it seems reasonable to suppose that she will treat a wide class of values as though they were encryptions under $ServerKey(b)$ and pass them on to B unchecked.

The responder role has a similar program. Again, assuming it has just one nonce to use, we get:

$$
\begin{aligned}
&Responder(b, n_b) = \\
&\quad \underset{\substack{k_{ab} \in Key \\ a \in Agent \\ n_a \in Nonce}}{\square}
\left(
\begin{array}{l}
receive.a.b.a.n_a \rightarrow \\
send.b.J.b.\{a.n_a.n_b\}_{ServerKey(b)} \rightarrow \\
receive.a.b.\{a.k_{ab}\}_{ServerKey(b)}.\{n_b\}_{k_{ab}} \rightarrow \\
Session(b, a, k_{ab}, n_a, n_b)
\end{array}
\right)
\end{aligned}
$$

Obviously in this case it is not the agent process's own local environment that instigates the protocol, but rather it is started when it receives a message from an initiator who hopes to run the protocol with it. Note that in this case the process ought to be in a position to understand everything it receives, and therefore rejects any communication that is not in the 'official' form described in the protocol definition.

The server has to generate a key when appropriately stimulated by receiving a message 2, and send the key back to a in the two-part message 3. Just as with nonces, we must expect all the keys a server generates to be unique, and this gives rise to just the same sort of programming decisions. On the assumption that we want the server to handle more than one protocol run, we cannot simply give our model a single key. The easiest solution is to build into our server the set of keys $KEYS_{Server}$ that it can generate. The server operation is then to permit a single run $Serv(k_{ab})$

involving each of these keys. This can be achieved with a general interleaving:

$$Server(J) = \underset{k_{ab} \,\in\, KEYS_{Server}}{\vert\vert\vert} Serv(J, k_{ab})$$

where

$$Serv(J, k_{ab}) =$$
$$\underset{\substack{a,b \,\in\, Agent \\ n_a, n_b \,\in\, Nonce}}{\Box} \left(\begin{array}{c} receive.b.J.b.\{a.n_a.n_b\}_{ServerKey(b)} \rightarrow \\ send.J.a.\{b.k_{ab}.n_a.n_b\}_{ServerKey(a)} \\ \{a.k_{ab}\}_{ServerKey(b)} \rightarrow Server(J, ks) \end{array} \right)$$

Obviously we could give the agent processes the possibility of a larger or even infinite number of runs by handling nonces in the same way, but it would of course be necessary to give them the ability to start further protocol runs. In the most general case, agents can be modelled as being able to engage in arbitrarily many concurrent protocol runs in both sender and receiver roles. This can be described within CSP using the generalized interleave operator $\vert\vert\vert_{i \in I} P_i$, with each single protocol run represented by one of the P_i.

To ensure that the protocol runs all use different nonces, we use pairwise disjoint sets $Nonce\_I_a$ and $Nonce\_R_a$ to represent all of the nonces that agent a might use in a protocol run in the role of initiator, and in the role of responder, respectively. A particular agent a will then be described as

$$User_a = \underset{n \in Nonce\_I_a}{\vert\vert\vert} Initiator(a, n)$$
$$\underset{n \in Nonce\_R_a}{\vert\vert\vert} Responder(a, n)$$

For example, $Anne = User_{Anne}$ and $Bob = User_{Bob}$. The requirement that the nonce sets are disjoint models the expectation that any nonce can be generated only once.

When we come to use theorem-proving to establish that protocols are correct in the most general sense in Chapter 7, we will use these descriptions of agent protocol behaviour. However, when first analyzing a protocol and searching for attacks on it as described in Chapters 5 and 6, we are concerned with feasibility of model-checking, and so care must be taken to keep the number of possibilities to a minimum. In this case the number of runs involved in the agent descriptions will be chosen with care to be large enough to make such analysis useful, but no larger.

2.2 Data types for protocol models

Real implementations of cryptographic protocols use data that is composed of blocks of bits, and encryption algorithms are computed over the same type of structures and might have properties that are open to exploitation by an intruder. The nature of this data, and the form of the encryption used, are both extremely important when it comes to analyzing a system for security. After all, an intruder is quite free to play around with data at its lowest level, and to try to break or otherwise disturb the encryption.

For example, if *a* knows that a certain message contains an amount of money that is to be paid to her, encrypted by adding some private numeric key to it, she might feel that it is to her advantage to add a modest amount to the message in transit, even though she cannot decrypt it.

But this book is not about breaking codes or analyzing particular encryption methods for subtle weaknesses like the simple example in the last paragraph. Rather, it is about how codes are used in building protocols, and whether the protocols are themselves vulnerable. Pragmatically, the analysis of either a cipher or a protocol is quite complex enough without having to look at them together. What we therefore do is to build CSP models that operate over abstract data types, rather than looking at the representation in bits, and model all the constants like agent names, nonces and keys as symbolic constants, and constructions like encryption, hashing and tupling as formal symbolic operations over the type. For example, instead of the object $\{a.n_a\}_k$ being a list of bits, we might think of it as the construct

$$Encrypt.k.(Sq.\langle a, n_a \rangle)$$

drawn from the syntax

$$
\begin{aligned}
fact := {} & Encrypt.fact.fact \mid \\
& Hash.fact.fact \mid \\
& Sq.fact^* \mid \\
& Key.k \mid Nonce.n \mid Text.t
\end{aligned}
$$

in which *k* ranges over a set of keys, *n* over a set of nonces, and *t* over a type representing message contents (which can include agent names). Thus *Encrypt* is a formal constructor creating an object that we will make sure our programs treat like an encryption.

For the time being we will assume that all *fact*s with different constructions in this syntax are different: there are no equalities between them. Obviously this may not be true of the real data this abstract structure represents, but in a great many cases it is reasonable to assume that coincidences are so rare and unstructured as not to be of serious concern.

The way we have built the type *fact* will be familiar to anyone who has studied programming language design: it is simply an abstract syntax for a little language, where the base objects are things like nonces and keys, rather than numbers and characters, and the constructors are encryption, hashing, and sequencing, rather than addition and division.

Throughout this book we use the notation introduced in the Introduction of writing $\{k\}_m$ for *Encrypt.k.m*. We also use $g(\!|m|\!)$ for *Hash.g.m*. We will abbreviate the other constructs by dropping the formal constructors, so *Key.k*, *Nonce.n*, *Text.t*, and $Sq.\langle m_1, \ldots, m_n \rangle$ will be abbreviated to k, n, t, and $\langle m_1, \ldots, m_n \rangle$ respectively. Furthermore, it is often useful to use pairs instead of sequences, and we will use $m_1.m_2$ to denote the fact consisting of the pair of facts m_1 and m_2. This notation generalizes to arbitrary tuples. In this book we use either pair notation or sequence notation to denote concatenations of facts, depending on convenience – the expressive power in each case is the same.

The CSP models we build operate over this abstract type, which makes operations such as encryption and decryption exceptionally easy to implement, though of course we have to make sure that no agent *does* decrypt a message unless it has the right key.

There are two main consequences of using symbolic objects as data in our models of protocols. The first is that (as we shall see) it becomes possible to handle the models in tools such as FDR; something that would have been quite impossible without this step. The second is that the symbolic type provides a clean interface between the cipher designer and the protocol designer: they have to agree on a set of rules about what inferences and equivalences are potentially exploitable by an intruder, and describe these symbolically. The cipher designer is then obliged to provide a code that has no further weaknesses, and the protocol designer must produce a protocol that is immune from attack by an intruder who can exploit the agreed features.

2.3 Modelling an intruder

If the agent and server processes we created in Section 2.1 were in a world where their messages were transmitted reliably and where there is no other entity generating messages to put into the communication medium, then it seems most unlikely that anything could go wrong. That is not, of course, the world that cryptographic protocols are designed to face. Aside, hopefully, from a different probability of delivery, a better analogy is to imagine Anne and Bob each living on their own desert island, sending messages to each other by putting them in bottles and throwing them into the sea; there is no guarantee of delivery: anyone else might find the bottle and use its contents in any way he can, including putting further bottles in the ocean that purport to be from Anne and Bob or adding his own content to what is already there.

The way in which this risky world of communication is modelled is by adding an *intruder* process into the network, who is given special powers to tamper with the messages that pass around. The only limitations to what the intruder can do are that his only source of knowledge (aside from things he knows initially or invents for himself) is what he observes being communicated, and that he is constrained by the rules of encryption. In other words, he cannot read the mind of another agent to know some secret, and can only decrypt an encrypted message if he has the appropriate key.

On first encountering the idea of an intruder process, it is natural to imagine that we have to program it with the cunning strategies it is going to employ to try to break the security of the protocol under examination. There are two great drawbacks with this idea:

■ This programming exercise is likely to be very complex.

■ By construction, we are only likely to find attacks that follow one of the routes anticipated in the intruder definition, whereas we would really like to test for all cryptographically possible intruder behaviours.

The solution is amazingly simple: just build a process that can, at any stage, perform any action that is cryptographically justifiable:

(a) Overhear and/or block messages that one agent sends to another (including servers).

(b) Generate any message that can be built on the basis of what the intruder has heard, knew initially, or might legitimately have made up (such as nonces and keys), all under the assumptions of what is cryptographically feasible.

(c) Act as agents other than those we explicitly build into our network as trustworthy: in other words the intruder will have all the keys etc. that such agents would have. The point here is that we want runs between Anne and Bob to be secure even if there are other agents around who are corrupt.

So whatever traces the most cunning strategic intruder might have, they will all be traces of this process. Therefore if we can prove that a network with the above intruder in place is secure, we can be sure it is secure against any intruder (within the framework we are using).

Provided we can calculate what messages our intruder can legitimately generate at each stage, it is very easy to achieve all these effects. Most of them, as we shall see, are by-products of the way the network is ultimately connected together. All we have to do in building the intruder process that resides in a typical CSP protocol model is to create a process that has an initial knowledge *IK* of members of *fact* (including things like all agent names, the keys that belong to other agents as discussed in (c) above, and things like nonces and keys that such agents might generate), can at all times hear messages, and can generate any message generable on the basis of *IK* and the messages heard to date.

At a CSP level this is very easy: it is *Intruder*(*IK*), where

$$Intruder(X) = learn?m : messages \rightarrow Intruder(close(X \cup \{m\}))$$
$$\Box \; say?m : X \cap messages \rightarrow Intruder(X)$$

Here, the parameter X ranges over subsets of *fact* and represents all the things the intruder can reasonably create. *messages* is the subset of *fact* that represents all messages that might be generated or accepted over the communication medium by a trustworthy agent or server process. The function *close*(X) calculates all *fact*s that are buildable from X under the rules of encryption.

close(X) is best defined in terms of a set of possible *deductions*, each of which is a pair (X, f) for X a finite set of *fact*s and f a single *fact*. The meaning of (X, f) is that if an intruder can construct every member of X, then it can also construct f. This will be written $X \vdash f$. Since they are evidently useless, and because their presence can complicate some of the codings of intruders we will used later, we conventionally exclude all pairs (X, f) in which $f \in X$ (i.e. vacuous deductions). For the example type *fact* quoted above, under the assumption that only the obvious deductions are possible, a few simple rules cover all possible pairs:

1 $(\{k, m\}, encrypt(k, m))$ for all k and m.

2 $(\{encrypt(k, m), k^{-1}\}, m)$ for all k and m.

3 $(\{Sq.\langle \ldots, x, \ldots \rangle\}, x)$ for all x and sequences that contain it.

4 $(\{x_1, \ldots, x_n\}, Sq.\langle x_1, \ldots, x_n \rangle)$ for all $x_1, \ldots, x_n$.

These simply say that we can form an encryption when we know both the contents and the key, we can decipher an encryption for which we know the inverse of the key, and can both break up and form sequences.

For example, suppose the intruder picks up the following message 4 from the Yahalom protocol:

$$Sq.\langle encrypt(ServerKey(b), Sq.\langle A, k \rangle), encrypt(k, nb) \rangle$$

and happens to know $ServerKey(b)$. Then he can apply rule 3 twice to deduce the two halves of this message, and then rule 2 to the first half and $ServerKey(b)$ to obtain $Sq.\langle A, k \rangle$. Rule 3 again gives him k, and rule 2 on the second half $(encrypt(k, n_b))$ and k gives nb. He could then take some other k' he happened to know and use all these rules in reverse to create

$$Sq.\langle encrypt(ServerKey(b), Sq.\langle A, k' \rangle), encrypt(k', nb) \rangle$$

which could then be sent on to b. Such a possibility would obviously destroy the security of the protocol, so we have to hope that the intruder never does get hold of $ServerKey(b)$ for any trustworthy b. On the other hand, we would expect the intruder definitely to be able to perform similar deductions for messages built using the key $ServerKey(c))$ of an agent whose capabilities he incorporates (as discussed above): he will need them simply to be able to perform the normal role of c.

The FDR tool, as we shall see, deals only with processes that have finite alphabets and finite state spaces. Both of these are still in danger when it comes to modelling *Intruder(IK)*, because the type *fact* is infinite (containing, as it does, arbitrarily deep nestings of the encryption and sequencing constructs). This means that the parameter X of *Intruder(X)* ranges over a potentially infinite set, and that since the initiator accepts an arbitrary second component of message 3 (since it does not seek to understand this object) before passing it on, the set of messages that could be accepted on message 3 might himself be expected to be infinite, even when there are only a few agent names, nonces and keys. What we in fact do in practical models is carefully pick an adequate finite subset of the complete type *fact* and restrict the communications of the agents and the intruder, and the deductions of the intruder, to this set.

In most cases this set consists of all the genuine protocol messages that it is possible to build using the ingredients from finite sets of agent names, keys, nonces and similar, plus all the constituent parts of these messages (namely, the members of these finite types and all the members of *fact* that are created from these on the way to building the messages). While, of course, an intruder who had all these things could build complex objects outside this set, it is generally possible to argue that these would do him no good.

For a typical protocol model in FDR this results in a set *KnowableFacts* that might eventually be learned by the intruder, of size anywhere between a few tens and a few thousand. This creates problems of its own when it comes to building an FDR model, since the potential state space of $Intruder(X)$ is then very large indeed (X varies over subsets of *KnowableFacts* and so the number of such sets grows exponentially.) Fortunately, however, there is an elegant solution to this problem, as we shall see in Chapter 6.

2.4 Putting the network together

We now have a good idea of how reliable agents, the server, and even the intruder operate. In this final section of the chapter we will see how these are all put together into a network that can be used to test the resilience of the protocol.

You might expect to see a network consisting of many reliable agents, together with a server and the intruder. After all, the fact that Anne has run the protocol with other people first may well have a bearing on whether the run she starts with Bob is secure. However, the fact that our intruder is designed to be able to act like other agents mean that Carol, Duncan etc. do not actually have to be present as processes in our network in order for Anne to have done everything she would have done in talking to them. Furthermore, the effect of having the intruder run these other identities is that these 'third party' agents are assumed to be corrupt: they pass all their knowledge on to whoever is trying to break the security of Anne and Bob. Thus, by setting up a network consisting only of Anne, Bob, the server and the intruder we are in fact giving the protocol a particularly stern test: that it keeps connections between our two trusty agents secure, even though (with the exception of the server) the rest of the world may be corrupt.

In fact, in almost all circumstances, there is nothing to be gained from giving the intruder any more than one extra identity to play with. In other words, he has all he needs to act like Carol (say), but no others, and indeed the type of agent processes used consists of just the three names {*Anne, Bob, Carol*}. This is justified by the argument (usually valid, but not invariably) that any attack on Anne and Bob that could ever arise through the intruder using any number of third party identities could equally arise if all of these were replaced in the trace by a single identity other than *Anne* or *Bob*. This topic will be discussed further in Chapter 5.

Therefore we end up with a network consisting of just four processes: Anne, Bob, the server, and the intruder (who also possesses the ability to act like Carol). Two different models of interconnection may be used in putting these together, the choice being whether we think of the intruder as actually being the communication medium, or have a separate communication medium that the intruder can tamper with. The second of these is probably closer to the real world situations we are trying to model, but the first is simpler to code in CSP. We can argue that the second model is good enough for most purposes since (i) the intruder is at liberty to trap every message that is ever sent by another agent, and (ii) he can always choose to pass one of these unaltered on to its original intended recipient. Thus the intruder can emulate a correctly functioning communication medium if he wants to. In particular, any trace that could occur in a network with a real communication medium can be emulated by one in which the only means of communication is via the intruder. Conceptually, if we fear that our communication medium can be manipulated by the intruder process, we might as well identify the two.

This network is connected together via renamings that match up the *receive.a.b.m* and *send.a.b.m* events performed by agent and server processes with the *say.m* and *learn.m* events of the intruder. The *send* and *learn* channels are connected by renaming them both to a *take* channel, and the *receive* and *say* channels are connected by renaming them to a *fake* channel.

The first thing to note is that the sender and receiver fields of the *receive* and *send* messages are missing in the intruder ones. This is because these fields convey no useful information to the intruder: we will generally assume that all agent names are already known to intruder. Since our intruder is programmed to try out *all* possibilities open to it, the fact that a particular message came with sender/address information *a.b* (which would doubtless be very useful to an intruder programmed to follow a particular strategy) is actually irrelevant to it. The event *learn.m* is thus mapped to every event of the form *take.a.b.m* (i.e. for all legitimate choices of *a* and *b*). This event *take.a.b.m* models a communication from *a* to *b* that is trapped by the intruder.

Similarly, we can model the fact that the intruder can offer any message he can make up to any one who will accept it, pretending it is from anybody, by the renaming that maps each *say.m* event to every corresponding *fake.a.b.m*, which is the action that represents the intruder sending *m* to *b*, pretending it is from *a*. Internally, of course, the server and agent processes send and receive communications via *receive* and *send*, rather than *take* and *fake*, and have no way of knowing that the messages they transact are being routed via the intruder. This illusion can be achieved by another renaming: when process *a* performs an output *send.a.b.m* it is renamed to *take.a.b.m*, and whenever it performs an input *receive.b.a.m* this is renamed to *fake.b.a.m*. Clearly we could get by with a single level of renaming rather than having one renaming on the intruder and one on the agents, but putting the network together as just described:[1]

---

[1] Since these details are irrelevant to how the network is wired together, the parameters representing nonces, keys, and knowledge have been omitted here.

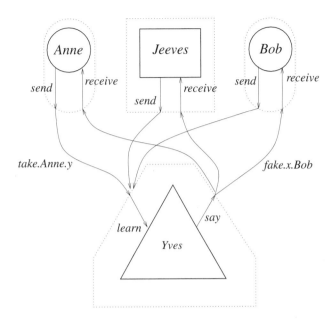

Figure 2.1 Network with all communication routed through the intruder

$$(Agent(Anne)[\![^{fake,\,take}/receive,\,send]\!]$$
$$|\!|\!|\ Agent(Bob)[\![^{fake,\,take}/receive,\,send]\!]$$
$$|\!|\!|\ Jeeves[\![^{fake,\,take}/receive,\,send]\!])$$
$$\underset{\{|take,fake|\}}{|\!|}\qquad Yves[\![^{take.x.y,\,fake.x.y}/learn,\,say\ |\ x,y \in Agents \cup \{Jeeves\}]\!]$$

has two advantages: firstly the communications we see in traces more accurately suggest what is going on, and, as we will see shortly, this model extends smoothly to the case where the medium and intruder are separate.

A picture of this network is shown in Figure 2.1: the dotted lines represent renamings, though in order to avoid clutter only a subset of the channel names are actually included in the picture.

An example trace that can occur in the Yahalom protocol is shown in Figure 2.2: it represents a run between Anne (represented by an actual process) and Carol (whose activities are contained within the intruder). We see both the top-level trace (consisting of *take* and *fake* events), and the events that the four component processes see inside their renamings, plus the deductions performed by the intruder. Only those inferences that the intruder needs to perform this particular trace are shown, even though there are others he does *enabled* by what he hears here. In each of the entries for a non-*infer* event (i.e. a *take* or *fake*) the message body *m* in the external and agent view of the event is the same as in the intruder view.

Externally	agent	which sees	Intruder
$take.A.C.m$	A	$send.A.C.m$	$learn.Sq.\langle A, N_A \rangle$
			$infer.(\{Sq.\langle A, N_A \rangle\}, N_A)$
			$infer.(\{A, N_A, N_C\}, Sq.\langle A, N_A, N_C \rangle)$
			$infer.(\{Sq.\langle A, N_A, N_C \rangle, ServerKey(C)\},$ $\{Sq.\langle A, N_A, N_C \rangle\}_{ServerKey(C)})$
			$infer.(\{C, \{Sq.\langle A, N_A, N_C \rangle\}_{ServerKey(C)}\},$ $Sq.\langle C, \{Sq.\langle A, N_A, N_C \rangle\}_{ServerKey(C)} \rangle)$
$fake.C.J.m$	J	$receive.C.J.m$	$say.Sq.\langle C, \{Sq.\langle A, N_A, N_C \rangle\}_{ServerKey(C)} \rangle$
$take.J.A.m$	J	$send.J.A.m$	$say.Sq.\langle \{Sq.\langle C, K, N_A, N_C \rangle\}_{ServerKey(A)},$ $\{\langle A, K \rangle\}_{ServerKey(C)} \rangle$
$fake.J.A.m$	A	$receive.J.A.m$	$learn.Sq.\langle \{Sq.\langle C, K, N_A, N_C \rangle ServerKey(A)\},$ $\{\langle A, K \rangle\}_{ServerKey(C)} \rangle$
$take.A.C.m$	A	$receive.J.A.m$	$learn.\langle \{\langle A, K \rangle\}_{ServerKey(C)}, \{N_C\}_K \rangle$

Figure 2.2 Run between Anne and the intruder

Having built this model it is relatively simple to modify it to allow agents direct communication as an alternative to using the intruder as a medium: we make *take* and *fake* alternatives to the original communications rather than replacing them completely. The process

$$RenAgent(A) = Agent(A)[\![fake, comm, take, comm / receive, receive, send, send]\!]$$

which has alphabet

$$\alpha RenAgent(A) = \{comm.x.A, comm.A.x \mid x \in \{Anne, Bob, Jeeves\} \setminus \{A\}\}$$
$$\cup \{take.A.x, fake.x.A \mid x \in Agents \cup \{Jeeves\}\}$$

represents A in which *comm* provides an alternative route to other trustworthy processes, in such a way that the process inside has no way of knowing which of the two options has actually occurred for those communications where there is a choice. We can carry out exactly the same transformation on the server, and use alphabetized parallel to put these three processes together (so that pairs of them synchronize on *comm* actions), to get a process *Network*. The intruder is then added:

$$Network$$
$$\|$$
$$\{|take, fake, comm|\}$$
$$(Yves[\![comm.x.y, take.x.y, fake.x.y / learn, learn, say \mid x, y \in Agents \cup \{Jeeves\}]\!]$$

so that he can hear the direct communications without getting in their way.

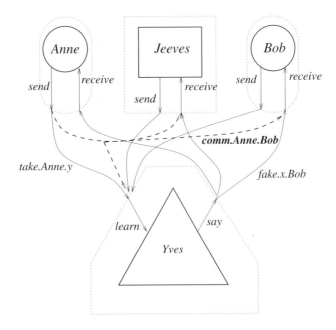

Figure 2.3 Network with alternative of direct communication

By using this coding we avoid the need to build a medium process,[2] and observe that any security breaches that any conceivable medium process might allow could still appear in a trace where all messages pass through the intruder.

A picture of the resulting network appears in Figure 2.3, though only those extra channels that emerge from Anne are shown, again to avoid clutter in the picture.

The main advantage of this slightly more complex network comes when we look at its traces: where a message passes from one agent to another, or between an agent and the server, this now appears as a single event that indicates what has happened, rather than as two in which it looks as though the intruder is doing something interesting. This is helpful both to human readers and to FDR, since the tool will tend to find more straightforward attacks. As we will see in later chapters, it always finds counterexamples with the least possible number of actions, so it will be pushed towards the use of direct communication between agents because this is more efficient in the number of communications.

---

[2] One thing that this direct wiring of *comm* channels does not allow for properly is an agent who wants to send messages to herself: *comm.Anne.Anne* creates problems and is not allowed for in the coding of *Network* above. It could be got right, where agents had internal parallel structure, by appropriate connections between these different processes making up a given identity. Pragmatically, however, it is usually better to rely on the intruder as a medium between an agent and himself (via *take* and *fake*), just as we did between all processes when there was no *comm* channel.

3 Expressing protocol goals

Protocols are designed to achieve particular security properties in the presence of particular kinds and levels of threat. It should thus be part of the specification of the protocol to make explicit the kind of threat that it is designed to counter. For example, protocols for communication over satellite links might assume that a message can be overheard, that spoof messages can be generated, but that messages cannot be blocked. Alternatively, protocols might be designed for protection against an external intruder, but might rely on the assumption that all principals are honest. The threat models we have discussed are fairly generic, and for secrecy and authentication we will implicitly assume (unless stated explicitly) the threat model encapsulated by the *intruder* process introduced in the previous chapter: that attacks can be mounted by principals as well as external agents, and that messages can be intercepted, redirected, duplicated, altered and created by the intruder. Whether or not a protocol meets its goals may well be dependent on the threat model. Alternative threat models will be discussed throughout the chapter. These can usually be described simply by changing the intruder's initial knowledge *IK*, or his capabilities through adjusting the ⊢ relation, or by restricting what can be provided to the agents on the *receive* channels.

This chapter concentrates much of its attention on secrecy and authentication properties. These are safety properties, in the sense that they require that bad things should not happen – that a data item is not leaked and that an agent does not incorrectly accept the identity of another agent. Liveness issues, such as the concern that the protocol might not terminate, will not be addressed explicitly. Other properties – anonymity and non-repudiation – will also be discussed.

The emphasis in this chapter is on explicitness. Security properties will be defined by introducing additional information into protocol descriptions to enable a description of what is expected of the system at particular points during a run of the protocol. This information, in the form of messages, might be thought of as capturing the intention of the designers of the protocol.

- *Secrecy* – If a particular data item *m* is intended to be secret at the end of the protocol run, then a message *Claim_secret* will be inserted at the end of the description of the protocol run. The secrecy property will state that the intruder cannot obtain *m* during a run of the protocol whenever its secrecy is claimed. This is illustrated in Figure 3.1.

- *Authentication* – An authentication protocol should establish particular guarantees when it has completed, concerning the party it has apparently been running with. These are often of the form that if the run has completed then

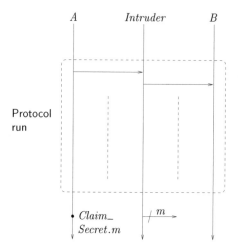

Figure 3.1 Adding a secrecy claim

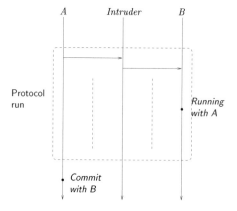

Figure 3.2 Adding an authentication claim

the other party has also been involved in the protocol run. The completion of a run of the protocol will be marked by a *Commit* event, and authentication will require that the occurrence of such an event must mean that a corresponding *Running* event must previously have been performed by the other party. The way in which these events must match will characterize the authentication property. This is illustrated in Figure 3.2.

Specification events, or *signals*, simply make understanding the requirements on the system easier. Any specification that can be expressed in terms of such events can also be expressed on the bare system without them, but perhaps in a less transparent way.

This means that additional signal channels are added to the model of the system. These do not reflect what the agents do, but rather enable the expression of particular properties by identifying points in the protocol run to which we wish to refer in specifying properties. Hence signals are not facts. We will use *Signal* to denote the set of all possible signals that can be introduced in the model of the system. This set is disjoint from the set of facts: $Signal \cap Fact = \varnothing$.

The information that appears on the *signal* channels will be a claim, a sequence of users, and a fact. The claim will correspond to a stage that the signalling agent is currently at; the sequence of users will describe the agents that the signalling agent associates the protocol run with; and the fact will contain some information that the claim is about, usually including facts used in that protocol run. Note that since concatenation of facts yields another fact, so the fact component of a signal can comprise a sequence of atomic facts.

The introduction of these additional messages aids clarity, but at the cost of introducing some complexity into the automated and machine-assisted analysis of protocols. Later chapters will consider equivalent but more concise versions of the properties, optimizing protocol descriptions for model-checking at the expense of explicitness by reducing the number of messages. These optimizations are justified by the theory of CSP, and analysis of the resulting descriptions gives results about the original protocol descriptions. The different ways of expressing protocol goals depend on different motivations:

- we want to be as explicit as possible, so we can be confident that the descriptions capture what we intend;

- we want them to be as simple as possible (in CSP terms) since this makes verification easier;

- we want them to be expressed as processes with as few states as possible, to make model-checking more feasible.

In fact, we will need to ensure that different expressions of the property should be equivalent for the system under analysis, so that two specifications ($S(tr)$ and $T(tr)$, say) have that $(System \; \textbf{sat} \; S(tr)) \Leftrightarrow (System \; \textbf{sat} \; T(tr))$. This can be the case even if $S(tr)$ and $T(tr)$ are not equivalent on all processes.

3.1 The Yahalom protocol

Recall the Yahalom protocol:

$$
\begin{array}{llll}
\text{Message 1} & a \rightarrow b & : & a.n_a \\
\text{Message 2} & b \rightarrow s & : & b.\{a.n_a.n_b\}_{ServerKey(b)} \\
\text{Message 3} & s \rightarrow a & : & \{b.k_{ab}.n_a.n_b\}_{ServerKey(a)} \cdot \{a.k_{ab}\}_{ServerKey(b)} \\
\text{Message 4} & a \rightarrow b & : & \{a.k_{ab}\}_{ServerKey(b)} \cdot \{n_b\}_{k_{ab}}
\end{array}
$$

In itself, this description does not state what the protocol aims to achieve. The expectation that it provides authentication of each of its participants to the other must be made explicit, as must the requirement that the key k_{ab} distributed to the participants must be secret. The property that the nonce n_b should be secret at the end of the protocol can also be expressed. This may or may not be a requirement of the protocol, depending on its intended use.

The CSP description of the protocol was given in Chapter 2. The individual runs of the initiator and responder are:

$$Initiator(a, n_a) =$$
$$env?b : Agent \rightarrow send.a.b.a.n_a \rightarrow$$

$$\underset{\substack{k_{ab} \in Key \\ n_b \in Nonce \\ m \in T}}{\square} \left(\begin{array}{l} receive.J.a.\{b.k_{ab}.n_a.n_b\}_{ServerKey(a)}.m \rightarrow \\ send.a.b.m.\{n_b\}_{k_{ab}} \rightarrow Session(a, b, k_{ab}, n_a, n_b) \end{array} \right)$$

$$Responder(b, n_b) =$$

$$\underset{\substack{k_{ab} \in Key \\ a \in Agent \\ n_a \in Nonce}}{\square} \left(\begin{array}{l} receive.a.b.a.n_a \rightarrow \\ send.b.J.b.\{a.n_a.n_b\}_{ServerKey(b)} \rightarrow \\ receive.a.b.\{a.k_{ab}\}_{ServerKey(b)}.\{n_b\}_{k_{ab}} \rightarrow \\ Session(b, a, k_{ab}, n_a, n_b) \end{array} \right)$$

The Yahalom protocol can then be described as the combination of the users and the server. This is expressed as the *Yahalom* process:

$$Yahalom = User_{Anne} \;|||\; User_{Bob} \;|||\; Jeeves$$

and the system that is to be investigated runs the protocol in the environment provided by the intruder:

$$System = Yahalom \;\|\; Intruder$$

Explicit events reflecting specific claims about the system will be inserted at particular stages in the protocol. These amended protocol descriptions will be expressed as primed versions of the original, so for example the amended *Yahalom* will be *Yahalom'*.

Although claims are often expressed in anthropomorphic terms, concerning the state of mind of the protocol agent, or particular beliefs of the agent, we will express protocol requirements purely in terms of relationships between these events.

Properties can be expressed either as trace specifications $S(tr)$ or as CSP processes *Spec*. However, the property is also dependent on the description of *Intruder*, which encapsulates the threat model. The protocol as described by *Yahalom'* is correct with respect to threat *Intruder* and specification $S(tr)$ if

$$Yahalom' \;\|\; Intruder \; \textbf{sat} \; S(tr)$$

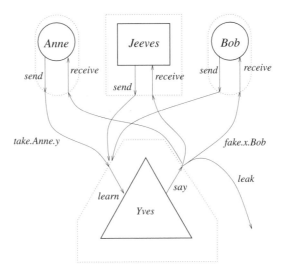

Figure 3.3 Introducing a *leak* channel

Secrecy

In order to formalize secrecy properties, it is natural to use an event

$$signal.Claim\_Secret.a.b.s$$

at the point in a's run of the protocol with b where we believe the protocol guarantees that *Yves* cannot obtain the secret value s. It expresses that expectation that the intruder cannot be in possession of s. It may be understood to mean: 'The value s used in the run apparently between a and b initiated by a should be secret for the entire protocol run'. For example, the Yahalom protocol aims to ensure that the key k_{ab} received by a in the third message is secret. This expectation is expressed by introducing the signal message into the description of the general initiator run *Initiator*(a, n) as follows:

$$
\begin{aligned}
&Initiator(a, n_a) = \\
&env?b : Agent \rightarrow send.a.b.a.n_a \rightarrow \\
&\quad \underset{\substack{k_{ab} \in Key \\ n_b \in Nonce \\ m \in T}}{\Box} \left(\begin{array}{l} receive.J.a.\{b.k_{ab}.n_a.n_b\}_{ServerKey(a)}.m \rightarrow \\ send.a.b.m.\{n_b\}_{k_{ab}} \rightarrow \\ signal.Claim\_Secret.a.b.k_{ab} \rightarrow Session(a, b, k_{ab}, n_a, n_b) \end{array} \right)
\end{aligned}
$$

The property will require that the intruder cannot know k_{ab} in any run in which this signal is emitted. In order to express this, we can observe whether or not k_{ab} can ever appear on the *say* channel.

This extra use of the *say* channel has no impact on the attacks that *Intruder* can mount, since its use does not change the state S of the intruder. It is used purely to provide information about whether the intruder is in possession of particular messages. To separate this specification use of the *say* channel from its more common use of providing messages to protocol agents, we introduce a new *leak* channel to accept outputs from the *say* channel. The resulting network is illustrated in Figure 3.3.

Secrecy will be expressed as the requirement that if an agent claims that a message is secret, then the intruder should not be able to leak it. Naïvely this might be expressed as

$$signal.Claim\_Secret.a.b.m \text{ in } tr \Rightarrow \neg(leak.m \text{ in } tr) \qquad (3.1)$$

However, the characterization of secrecy as protection from *Intruder* means that some care must be taken in the expression of this property. In order to express the secrecy requirement, we can in fact only require the value m to be secret in cases where a runs the protocol with another honest agent, since it is inappropriate to send a secret message to *Yves* and then expect the intruder not to know it.

In fact, the secrecy property we require is that: 'm is secret provided a's communication partner is honest and uncompromised'.

If the set *Honest* is the set of agents that are honest and uncompromised (in the sense that the intruder does not have their secret keys), then we can express the property that the intruder should not be in possession of m provided it is claimed to be a secret as a result of a run with an honest user. The event is introduced into the CSP description, and the property will require that if $j \in$ *Honest* then m should not be able to appear on *leak* when it is claimed to be secret.

The responder is treated in an entirely similar way, with the same possibilities for introducing the signal event into the model. There is no particular need to distinguish between initiator and responder of the protocol, so exactly the same events $signal.Claim\_Secret.i.j.k_{ab}$ can be used to indicate that at the end of a run the key k_{ab} that j has accepted is intended to be secret. These events can be introduced into the protocol in exactly the same way, as follows:

$$Responder(b, n_b) = $$
$$\underset{\substack{k_{ab} \in Key \\ a \in Agent \\ n_a \in Nonce}}{\square} \left(\begin{array}{l} receive.a.b.a.n_a \rightarrow \\ send.b.J.b.\{a.n_a.n_b\}_{ServerKey(b)} \rightarrow \\ receive.a.b.\{a.k_{ab}\}_{ServerKey(b)}, \{n_b\}_{k_{ab}} \rightarrow Session(b, a, k_{ab}, n_a, n_b) \end{array} \right)$$

The resulting system, consisting of the enhanced initiator and responder descriptions, will be denoted *System'*.

Trace specification

The specification therefore requires only that *Yves* should not obtain the secret s in cases where the run is with an agent outside his control. This may be expressed as the following trace specification:

$$Secret_{a,b}(tr) = \tag{3.2}$$
$$\forall m \bullet signal.Claim\_Secret.a.b.m \text{ in } tr \wedge a \in Honest \wedge b \in Honest$$
$$\Rightarrow \neg(leak.m \text{ in } tr)$$

The system with the initiator above meets this specification $Secret_{a,b}(tr)$.

It is now possible to express the complete secrecy property in terms of the signals that have been added to the protocol:

If a has completed a protocol run apparently with b, and b is honest and uncompromised, then the key accepted during that run by a is not known to anyone other than b. Similarly, if b has completed a run with honest and uncompromised a then the key accepted by b is not known to anyone other than a.

This covers the secrecy requirements of both initiator and responder, since either of them can claim that a key is secret. There is no reason in the Yahalom protocol to distinguish between initiator and responder claims of secrecy.

Alternative approach

The discussion above was concerned with secrecy with respect to our default threat model including dishonest agents. It is clear that in such cases secrecy can only be obtained if the other party is not going to compromise the intended secret – the protocol has no control over how the intended secret is to be used afterwards. In order to capture the property as one that can be verified of the protocol, it is important to make this assumption explicit. We chose above to do this within the trace property. However, an alternative approach was available to us: the introduction of the *Claim_Secret* event could have been more restricted, so that it is signalled only in cases where the protocol has been run with an honest party. Since the event *signal.Claim_Secret.a.b.s* is introduced into the protocol purely for specification and verification purposes, we can restrict when it can be performed. We can simply ensure that *Claim_Secret* signals are only performed on protocol runs that are not with compromised agents from the set *CS*. This will embody the caveat that 's is secret provided a's communication partner is honest'. The Yahalom protocol initiator's description would then be described as follows:

$$Initiator(a, n_a) =$$
$$env?b : Agent \rightarrow send.a.b.a.n_a \rightarrow$$

$$\underset{\substack{k_{ab} \in Key \\ n_b \in Nonce \\ m \in T}}{\Box} \left(\begin{array}{l} receive.J.a.\{b.k_{ab}.n_a.n_b\}_{ServerKey(a)}.m \rightarrow \\[4pt] send.a.b.m.\{n_b\}_{k_{ab}} \rightarrow \\ if\ b \in Honest \\ then\ signal.Claim\_Secret.a.b.k_{ab} \rightarrow Session(a, b, k_{ab}, n_a, n_b) \\ else\ Session(a, b, k_{ab}, n_a, n_b) \end{array} \right)$$

The requirement will then be as it was in line 3.1: simply that if a secret is claimed, then the intruder should not be able to leak it. The honesty of the parties is now folded into the introduction of the signal event.

External threat

In the case where the only threat is external, the secrecy property is much easier to capture. It is automatic in this threat model that all agents are honest and uncompromised, and hence the requirement that s should not appear on *leak* does not need to be qualified. The trace property in this case is again simply that in line 3.1:

$$Secret'_{a,b}(tr) = \forall s \bullet signal.Claim\_Secret.a.b.s \text{ in } tr \Rightarrow \neg(leak.s \text{ in } tr)$$

In fact this is a special case of the general threat model, in which the intruder has no keys or any identity of his own: so *Yves* is not a name, and the initial knowledge of the intruder *IK* does not contain any private keys of any agent. In this case the set of honest agents *Honest* is the set of all users. The specification *Secret'* here is simply a special case of the specification given in line 3.2, since $b \in Honest$ will always be true.

Observe that employing this threat model is equivalent to modelling protocol agents who are only prepared to initiate and respond to runs with honest users. However, this is different from (and strictly weaker than) the analysis for the internal threat model above, in which we are only concerned with secrecy in cases where an agent has engaged in a run with an honest agent. The internal threat model is concerned with Anne's claim of secrecy after a run with honest Bob, but allows for the possibility that Bob might be involved in a run with Yves: Anne can interact with agents who are honest but lack judgement. The external threat model, and the requirement that all agents only run with honest agents, do not allow for this possibility: Anne can only interact with agents who are both honest and have good judgement.

Process-oriented specification

The secrecy properties *Secret*(tr) expressed as a property on traces can also be captured as CSP specification processes.

We can use the following specification to capture the requirement that a's state of mind is correct (for all a) concerning s:

$$
\begin{aligned}
Secret\_Spec_0(s) \; &\widehat{=} \\
&signal.Claim\_Secret?a?b.s \rightarrow \\
&(\text{if } b \notin Honest \text{ then } Secret\_Spec_0(s) \text{ else } Secret\_Spec_1(s)) \\
&\square \\
&leak.s \rightarrow Secret\_Spec_0(s) \\
Secret\_Spec_1(s) \; &\widehat{=} \\
&signal.Claim\_Secret?a?b.s \rightarrow Secret\_Spec_1(s)
\end{aligned}
$$

The intruder Yves should only be able to perform the event *leak.s* if no honest agent has previously signalled that they believe that s is a secret shared with an honest agent (via an event *signal.Claim_Secret.a.b.s* for $b \in Honest$).

Of course, there may be several potential secrets; we will write ALL_SECRETS for the set of all these secrets. We can write a single specification testing whether all these secrets really do remain secret as expected:

$$Secret\_Spec \; \widehat{=} \; \big|\big|\big|_{s:ALL\_SECRETS} Secret\_Spec_0(s)$$

This specification is in terms of only *leak* and *signal* events, so if we hide all other events:

$$System_S \; \widehat{=} \; System \setminus (Events \setminus \{\!| \; leak, signal.Claim\_Secret \; |\!\})$$

we can test whether the protocol guarantees secrecy by testing the refinement:

$$Secret\_Spec \sqsubseteq_{tr} System_S$$

There is one point we have not yet considered, as it does not arise in the Yahalom protocol: at what point in the protocol should the honest agents perform the signal events? We can identify two scenarios:

- The secret in question might have significance outside of the protocol itself; for example, the secret is provided as input to the protocol, and one goal of the protocol is to transfer the secret from an agent a to another agent b. In this case, the secret should not be leaked to the intruder under any circumstances, so the signal event should occur as soon as it makes sense: the process representing a would presumably have s in its state initially, so should perform the signal immediately; the process representing b should perform its signal as soon as it actually receives the secret. We will call this *strong secrecy*.

- Alternatively, the secret might be created within the protocol run and only used if the run is successfully completed; for example, a session key would be freshly invented, but if the run does not complete successfully then presumably the key would be discarded, and so a leak of this key would not matter. In this case, the signal event can be placed at the end of the protocol run.

The sooner the *Claim_Secret* event appears in the run, the stronger the requirement.

3.3 Authentication

Entity authentication is concerned with verification of an entity's claimed identity. An authentication protocol provides an agent b with a mechanism to achieve this: an exchange of messages that establishes that the other party a has also been involved in the protocol run. This provides authentication of a to b: an assurance is provided to b that some communication has occurred with a.

Signal *Commit.b.a* events will be introduced into the description of b's run of the protocol to mark the point at which authentication of a to b is taken to have been achieved. Occurrence of *Commit.b.a* in b's protocol run means simply that

Agent b has completed a protocol run apparently with a.

Events of the form *Running.a.b* in a's run of the protocol are introduced to mark the point that should have been reached by the time b performs the *Commit.b.a* event. Occurrence of *Running.a.b* in a's protocol run means simply that

Agent a is following a protocol run apparently with b.

If a *Running.a.b* event must always have occurred by the time the *Commit.b.a* event is performed, then authentication is achieved. Further information ds associated with the protocol run, such as the values of nonces or keys, is also included as components of the *Commit* and *Running* events. For example, in the Yahalom protocol, there are two nonces and a key associated with any particular run. An event *Commit.b.a.n_a.n_b.k_{ab}* in b's run would be appropriate to mean that

Agent b has completed a protocol run apparently with a, and with nonces n_b, n_a, and with key k_{ab}.

A corresponding event *Running.a.b.n_a.n_b.k_{ab}* would be used to denote that

Agent a is following a protocol run with b, with nonces n_a, n_b, and with key k_{ab}.

The details to include will depend on the protocol (in terms of what data will be associated with particular protocol runs) and also on the point at which the events are introduced (since only some of the information might be available at particular points during the protocol).

This pattern is a scheme for authentication properties, but it allows the different flavours of authentication to be expressed by introducing different requirements on the correspondence between the *Commit* and *Running* events within this scheme:

1 One agent b might require simply that the other agent a is alive and has not failed. This is ensured if *Commit.b.a.ds* provides evidence simply that a has participated in some recent communication: an occurrence of *Running.a.c.ds'* with any c and any data ds' will suffice.

2 Agent b might require authentication that a participated in a run in which a took b to be the other participant. In this case, occurrence of the event *Commit.b.a.ds* will guarantee that *Running.a.b.ds'* occurred previously, though the information ds and ds' need not be the same.

3 Agents a and b might further be required to agree on the additional information ds specific to the particular run. This will authenticate to b that a was involved in that particular run.

Some protocols aim to provide authentication for each of the parties: that each party receives an assurance about the identity of the other. The Yahalom protocol is one such example: it aims to provide to each of the parties involved some assurance about the identity of the other. In this case, two properties will need to be specified: authentication of the initiator to the responder, and authentication of the responder

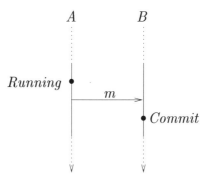

Figure 3.4 Placing signals into a protocol

to the initiator. Thus each party will introduce a *Commit* event to indicate when it has reached the point where authentication is claimed, and a *Running* signal to correspond to the other party's *Commit* signal. The *Commit* signal will usually be inserted at the end of the protocol run, since authentication is generally considered to have been achieved when the run is completed. The corresponding *Running* signal will usually be inserted either right at the beginning of the corresponding protocol to verify that the other party began a corresponding run; or just before the last message sent out by the agent that precedes the *Commit*, which is the latest possible point that can potentially be guaranteed by the protocol. Within the context of the protocol, this provides the strongest possible information about the progress that has been made.

Figure 3.4 illustrates the general situation where B commits to the run with A after receipt of message m which should be sent by A. In this case the *Running* signal should be inserted into the description of A's run at some point before m is transmitted, and it can be at the point immediately before. If the occurrence of *Commit* really does guarantee that the corresponding *Running* signal must previously have occurred, then B's receipt of message m must guarantee that A transmitted it. To see this, consider the contrapositive: if B can receive m without A having sent it (perhaps because an attack on the protocol is possible), then B can receive m without A having performed the *Running* signal (since the performance of that signal affects nothing that B can do), and so B can then perform *Commit* without A having performed the corresponding *Running* signal.

In general, when there are more than two parties involved in the protocol, one of the parties other than A might have been involved in the transmission of m. In this case, the *Running* signal will need to be inserted at a point in A's run at a point causally prior to the *Commit* signal. Figure 3.5 illustrates a situation in which B's receipt of message m_2 is intended to provide an assurance that A transmitted m_1 earlier in the protocol.

Authentication for the initiator of a protocol run will establish that the responder has reached a particular point in his run of the protocol. Conversely,

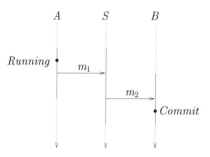

Figure 3.5 Placing signals into a protocol

authentication for the responder will establish that the initiator has reached a (different) particular point in his run. It is therefore appropriate to distinguish commitment of the initiator from commitment of the responder by introducing the events *signal.Commit_Initiator.a.b* and *signal.Commit_Responder.b.a*, and the *Running* events *signal.Running_Responder.b.a* and *signal.Running_Initiator.a.b* which correspond. Authentication (of type (2) above) for the initiator will then be expressed by the requirement that whenever *signal.Commit_Initiator.a.b* is performed for honest agent *b*, then *b* must previously have performed *signal.Running_Responder.b.a*, signalling that he is engaged in a run of the protocol with *a*, in the role of responder, and that he has reached the particular point specified.

Authentication for the responder is described in a similar way: that the signal *signal.Commit_Responder.b.a* must be preceded by *signal.Running_Initiator.a.b*.

Trace specification

The requirement that one kind of event *e* should precede another *d* is easy to express as a trace specification: that whenever *d* appears in the trace then *e* must appear beforehand:

$$tr'^\frown \langle d \rangle \leqslant tr \Rightarrow e \text{ in } tr'$$

This states that if $tr'^\frown \langle d \rangle$ is a prefix of the trace tr, then e should appear in tr' – the part of the trace before d. To make its relationship to authentication explicit, we will abbreviate this specification as

$$e \text{ precedes } d$$

to state that the occurrence of d in tr guarantees that e has previously appeared in tr.

In fact this specification is equivalent on processes to the specification

$$d \text{ in } tr \Rightarrow e \text{ in } tr$$

because the set of traces corresponding to any system must be prefix closed: if a sequence of events is a trace, then so too are all of its prefixes. This means that the prefix ending in d must be a trace, and hence must also contain e; and so e must appear before d in the trace.

In the context of authentication, we require that if *Commit* appears in the trace, then a corresponding *Running* event must also be present: authentication has the general form *Running* precedes *Commit*.

Yahalom: authentication of initiator by responder

A run of the Yahalom protocol between a and b involves two nonces n_a and n_b, and a key k_{ab} that is obtained by each party. We will first consider the protocol from the point of view of the responder. If agreement is required on some or all of this information, (as in authentication of type (3) above) then the signal event at the end of the responder's run should be *signal.Commit_Responder.b.a.n_a.n_b.k_{ab}* and it should follow an event *signal.Running_ Initiator.a.b.n_a.n_b.k_{ab}* in the initiator's run.

The authentication property of initiator by responder will require that

$$a \in Honest \Rightarrow signal.Running\_Initiator.a.b.n_a.n_b.k_{ab}$$
$$\text{precedes } signal.Commit\_Responder.b.a.n_a.n_b.k_{ab}$$

Since the intruder does not provide signals (even when following the protocol), we can only guarantee that the corresponding *Running* signal has occurred provided we assume that the initiator is honest: that $a \in Honest$.

We must decide where to place these authenticating signals in the CSP descriptions of the protocol. Figure 3.6 contains a message sequence chart of the protocol. It shows that the responder is not even in possession of all the information (and in particular k_{ab}) until receipt of the last message, so the only possible place for the commit message is right at the end of the protocol. Similarly, the initiator is not in possession of all the information until just before its final message, so the *Running* signal should either precede or follow that message. However, it must causally precede the responder's *Commit* message, and so it must be inserted before transmission of the final message. Thus we obtain the following enhanced descriptions of the protocol:

$$Initiator(a, n_a) =$$
$$env?b : Agent \rightarrow send.a.b.a.n_a \rightarrow$$

$$\underset{\substack{k_{ab} \in Key \\ n_b \in Nonce \\ m \in T}}{\square} \left(\begin{array}{l} receive.J.a.\{b.k_{ab}.n_a.n_b\}_{ServerKey(a)}.m \rightarrow \\ signal.Running\_Initiator.a.b.n_a.n_b.k_{ab} \rightarrow \\ send.a.b.m.\{n_b\}_{k_{ab}} \rightarrow Session(a, b, k_{ab}, n_a, n_b) \end{array} \right)$$

$$Responder(b, n_b) =$$

$$\underset{\substack{k_{ab} \in Key \\ a \in Agent \\ n_a \in Nonce}}{\square} \left(\begin{array}{l} receive.a.b.a.n_a \rightarrow \\ send.b.J.b.\{a.n_a.n_b\}_{ServerKey(b)} \rightarrow \\ receive.a.b.\{a.k_{ab}\}_{ServerKey(b)}.\{n_b\}_{k_{ab}} \rightarrow \\ signal.Commit\_Responder.b.a.n_a.n_b.k_{ab} \rightarrow \\ Session(b, a, k_{ab}, n_a, n_b) \end{array} \right)$$

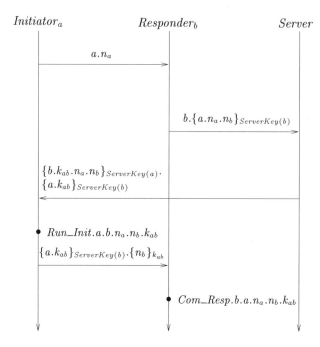

$Initiator_a$ $Responder_b$ $Server$

$a.n_a$

$b.\{a.n_a.n_b\}_{ServerKey(b)}$

$\{b.k_{ab}.n_a.n_b\}_{ServerKey(a)}\cdot$
$\{a.k_{ab}\}_{ServerKey(b)}$

$Run\_Init.a.b.n_a.n_b.k_{ab}$
$\{a.k_{ab}\}_{ServerKey(b)}\cdot\{n_b\}_{k_{ab}}$

$Com\_Resp.b.a.n_a.n_b.k_{ab}$

Figure 3.6 Authentication for the responder in the Yahalom protocol

Yahalom: authentication of responder by initiator

Since the Yahalom protocol aims to establish authentication in both directions, we must also introduce signals to describe the initiator authenticating the responder. The first attempt at this will insert the event *signal.Commit_ Initiator.a.b.n_a.n_b.k_{ab}* at the end of the initiator's run. Then authentication will require that the occurrence of such an event confirms earlier performance of the corresponding responder *Running* event with the same information. However, there is a local difficulty with this. Examination of the protocol in Figure 3.7 reveals that the last message sent by b is the second message of the protocol, so the *Running* signal must be inserted before that. By this stage, the two nonces have been provided to b, but the key to be issued in message 3 cannot be known at that time to agent b. Thus the signal to introduce can be at most *Running_Responder.b.a.n_a.n_b*, with no mention of the key.

On reflection this situation is expected. The protocol does not provide any guarantees to a that b ever obtains the key. The last message between a and b could be intercepted after a has finished the protocol run, and no earlier messages to b contain the key. The protocol does ensure that if b accepts a key, then it must be the same key that a has accepted (since the key in b's *Commit* matches the key in a's *Running*); but a has a weaker authentication than b, since a can never confirm that b did indeed accept the key.

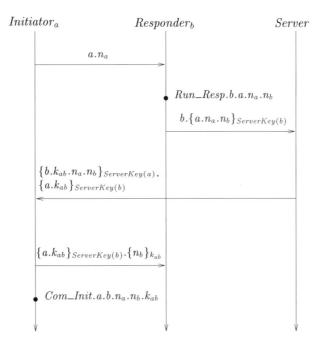

Figure 3.7 Authentication of the responder by the initiator in the Yahalom protocol

The strongest authentication property for authenticating the responder to the initiator is the following:

$$b \in Honest \;\Rightarrow\; signal.Running\_Responder.b.a.n_a.n_b$$
$$\text{\textbf{precedes} } signal.Commit\_Initiator.a.b.n_a.n_b.k_{ab}$$

Provided the other agent b is honest, any commitment should establish that a corresponding *Running* event has previously occurred.   This assurance is independent of the key that the initiator has committed to, but it does require agreement on the nonces.

This requirement can be expressed and the points at which the *Commit* event is inserted into the protocol specifies the stage at which a is provided with a guarantee about the fact that b has reached the corresponding stage.

The CSP description of the protocol is decorated as follows:

$$Initiator(a, n_a) =$$
$$env?b : Agent \rightarrow send.a.b.a.n_a \rightarrow$$

$$\underset{\substack{k_{ab} \in Key \\ n_b \in Nonce \\ m \in T}}{\square} \left(\begin{array}{l} receive.J.a.\{b.k_{ab}.n_a.n_b\}_{ServerKey(a)}.m \rightarrow \\[4pt] send.a.b.m.\{n_b\}_{k_{ab}} \rightarrow \\[4pt] signal.Commit\_Initiator.a.b.n_a.n_b.k_{ab} \rightarrow Session(a, b, k_{ab}, n_a, n_b) \end{array} \right)$$

$$Responder(b, n_b) \; = $$

$$\square \atop {k_{ab} \in Key \atop {a \in Agent \atop n_a \in Nonce}}} \left(\begin{array}{l} receive.a.b.a.n_a \; \rightarrow \\ signal.Running\_Responder.b.a.n_a.n_b \; \rightarrow \\ send.b.J.b.\{a.n_a.n_b\}_{ServerKey(b)} \; \rightarrow \\ receive.a.b.\{a.k_{ab}\}_{ServerKey(b)}.\{n_b\}_{k_{ab}} \; \rightarrow \\ Session(b, a, k_{ab}, n_a, n_b) \end{array} \right)$$

Weaker authentication

In fact weaker authentication requirements can be expressed by relaxing the correspondence between *Commit* and *Running* signals, so that they do not need to agree on all of their information. For example, if b only requires evidence that a has been running the protocol with him and that they agree on the key k_{ab}, then $signal.Commit\_Responder.b.a.n_a.n_b.k_{ab}$ simply needs to authenticate that there are some nonces n and n' such that $signal.Running\_$ $Initiator.a.b.n.n'.k_{ab}$ must previously have occurred. Alternatively, this expresses that some element of

$$signal.Running\_Initiator.a.b.NONCE.NONCE.k_{ab}$$

must have occurred.

This leads to a generalization of the authentication trace property: that if some element of a set D of events has appeared in a trace tr, then this provides a guarantee that some element of some other set E has previously appeared in tr. In this case we say that E **precedes** D, defined as follows:

$$E \; \textbf{precedes} \; D = d \in D \wedge tr'^\frown \langle d \rangle \leqslant tr \Rightarrow tr' \upharpoonright E \neq \langle \rangle$$

This states that if some prefix of tr finishes with some event from D, then there must be some event from E already in that prefix (i.e. the projection of tr' on to E is not empty). When D and E are singleton sets then the set brackets may be elided to obtain the notation introduced earlier for authentication between events.

If b requires authentication with regard to the key but not the nonces, then the requirement is captured as the trace specification

$$a \in Honest \Rightarrow signal.Running\_Initiator.a.b.NONCE.NONCE.k_{ab}$$
$$\textbf{precedes} \; signal.Commit\_Responder.b.a.NONCE.NONCE.k_{ab}$$

The requirement authenticating the responder to the initiator, where the value of the key k_{ab} is ignored, can also be expressed as follows:

$$b \in Honest \Rightarrow signal.Running\_Responder.b.a.n_a.n_b$$
$$\textbf{precedes} \; signal.Commit\_Initiator.a.b.n_a.n_b.KEY$$

Process-oriented specification

Signal events can also be used to specify authentication requirements in a process-oriented way.

We can capture the requirement that d authenticates e by providing a specification process in which d can occur only if the e has previously occurred:

$$Precedes(e, d) \ = \ e \rightarrow Run(\{d, e\})$$

More generally, if the set D authenticates the set E, then we require that some element from E must occur before any element of D. This generalizes the process *Precedes* as follows:

$$Precedes(E, D) \ = \ e : E \rightarrow Run(D \cup E)$$

Then the various flavours of authentication can be given as particular instances of these processes:

■ If a as initiator is to authenticate b as responder, where a has particular data ds_a in its *Commit* signal, and b has corresponding data ds_b in its running signal, then we can define

$$Init\_Auth\_Spec_0(a, b, ds_a, ds_b) =$$
$$Precedes(signal.Running\_Responder.b.a.ds_b, signal.Commit\_Initiator.a.b.ds_a)$$

We will write $ds_a \leftrightarrow ds_b$ to state that the information in the signals ds_a and ds_b correspond.

■ Similarly, a definition can be given for b as responder authenticating a as initiator:

$$Resp\_Auth\_Spec_0(b, a, ds_b, ds_a) =$$
$$Precedes(signal.Running\_Initiator.a.b.ds_a, signal.Commit\_Responder.b.a.ds_b)$$

If we want to specify that all initiators are correctly authenticating honest responders, we can combine several copies of the above specification together:

$$Init\_Auth\_Spec \ \widehat{=} \ \left|\left|\left|\right._{a:Agent, b:Honest, ds_a \leftrightarrow ds_b} \ Init\_Auth\_Spec_0(a, b, ds_a, ds_b)\right.\right.$$

And similarly for the responders:

$$Resp\_Auth\_Spec \ \widehat{=} \ \left|\left|\left|\right._{b:Agent, a:Honest, ds_b \leftrightarrow ds_a} \ Resp\_Auth\_Spec_0(b, a, ds_b, ds_a)\right.\right.$$

And we can test whether the appropriate restriction of the system refines this specification:

$$Init\_Auth\_Spec \ ||| \ Resp\_Auth\_Spec \ \sqsubseteq \ System_S$$

where

$$System_S \ \widehat{=} \ System \setminus (Events \setminus \{| \ signal.Honest.Honest \ |\})$$

We focus attention only on authentication of honest users to and by each other, in the same way as the conditions that $a \in Honest$ and $b \in Honest$ restricted the specification only to honest users. The intruder does not perform signal events (and could not be relied upon to, even if they were available to him) and so it is inappropriate to try to authenticate that these have occurred.

Duplicate runs

The above specifications allow b to complete several runs of the protocol for only a single run of a. In some instances (for example, financial transactions) a stronger requirement might be appropriate, that different occurrences of *Commit* events correspond to different occurrences of *Running* events. One can specify a one-one correspondence between the runs with the additional requirement that

$$tr \downarrow signal.Commit\_Responder.b.a.ds_a.ds_b$$
$$\leqslant tr \downarrow signal.Running\_Initiator.a.b.ds_a.ds_b$$

This states that the number of responder *Commit* signals with respect to the information in any run must be no greater than the number of initiator *Running* signals – in other words, that there cannot be more protocol runs completing than starting. This additional requirement is called *injective authentication*, in contrast to *non-injective authentication* which requires only that completion of a run indicates that there is some corresponding start to the run.

Injective authentication can also be captured as a process-oriented specification as follows:

$$Init\_Auth\_Spec_0(a, b, ds_a, ds_b) \,\hat{=}$$
$$signal.Running\_Initiator.a.b.ds_a.ds_b \rightarrow$$
$$(signal.Commit\_Responder.b.a.ds_a.ds_b \rightarrow Stop$$
$$||| \ Init\_Auth\_Spec_0(a, b, ds_a, ds_b))$$

However, the above process is infinite state, so would be impractical for model-checking purposes. In this case, if there is some bound n on the number of runs a can perform, then one can use a specification like the following:

$$Init\_Auth\_Spec_0(a, b, ds_a, ds_b) \,\hat{=}$$
$$signal.Running\_Initiator.a.b.ds_a.ds_b \rightarrow$$
$$signal.Commit\_Responder.b.a.ds_a.ds_b \rightarrow Stop$$
$$Init\_Auth\_Spec_1(a, b, ds_a, ds_b) \,\hat{=}$$
$$\underbrace{Auth\_Spec_0(a, b, ds_a, ds_b) ||| \ldots ||| Auth\_Spec_0(a, b, ds_a, ds_b)}_{n}$$

The data ds_a or ds_b often contains nonces, and so typically the bound n will be 1, since different runs of the protocol should make use of different nonces.

3.4 Non-repudiation

Non-repudiation protocols are used to enable agents to send and receive messages, and provide them each with *evidence* so that neither of them can successfully deny at a later time that the message was transmitted or received. Participants aim to collect evidence to prove that the other party did send or receive the message (as appropriate). Non-repudiation evidence can be generated for one party or for both parties. A protocol designed to achieve this is generally required to provide the property of correctness of the evidence: that the evidence really is strong enough to guarantee what the holder requires of it. Evidence is often in the form of signed messages, which provide guarantees concerning their originator.

In some cases where evidence is provided to both parties, the protocol might also aim to provide fairness: that no party should be able to reach a point where they have the evidence or the message that they require without the other party also having their required evidence. Fairness is not required for non-repudiation, but it may be desirable in some cases from the point of view of the participants.

In contrast to authentication and key-exchange protocols, non-repudiation protocols are not concerned with communication in the presence of an intruder between two parties who trust each other. Instead they are used when a communication is required between two agents who require protection from each other and who do not entirely trust each other to behave honourably in the future. They are typically proposed in the context of a passive communication medium that cannot be manipulated by either party or by other agents, but which may nevertheless have some unreliable behaviour.

In analysis, the system must be modelled from the point of view of the environment of the system that would be used to arbitrate in the case of a dispute. Correctness is concerned with whether the environment, which cannot know *a priori* which agents are honest, must accept evidence as guaranteeing that the message was sent. This concerns the nature of *evidence*: an agent might himself know that a message was sent, and yet not be in a position to prove this to anyone else.

This means that for the modelling and analysis of non-repudiation protocols, a different threat model must be used. In deciding whether a particular message has been sent, neither of the participants can be trusted to behave according to the protocol, and the possibility that either or both of them do not behave honestly must be allowed. However, it will generally have to be assumed that trusted third parties (which are sometimes used in non-repudiation protocols) do behave according to the protocol.

Although the threat model is different, non-repudiation properties are expressed in a similar way to authentication: that the occurrence of some event guarantees that some previous message was sent. The provision of a certain piece of evidence should guarantee that a particular message was previously sent by a particular party.

A non-repudiation protocol is thus concerned with the creation of evidence for the parties involved. Correctness will be concerned with the suitability of the evidence, and the analysis (given the altered threat model) will have to take into account the fact that the participants might not behave in accordance with the protocol. These parties are therefore modelled almost as the intruder is for secrecy and authentication analysis: that they can behave in any way in line with their capabilities, apart from some elementary security requirements, for example that they do not give away their private keys. Their capabilities with these assumptions built in will be encapsulated into a relation $\vdash_a$, which is essentially the same as $\vdash$ except that a's private keys cannot appear as part of any fact on the right-hand side: we assume that the agent will never give out his own private key in any form.

The behaviour of an arbitrary user of the network is therefore described by the CSP process description $Agent_a$:

$$Agent_a(S) =$$
$$\square_{b\in Agent, m\in S} \; send.a.b.m \rightarrow Agent_a(S)$$
$$\square \; receive?b.a?m \rightarrow Agent_a(close_{\vdash_a}(S \cup \{m\}))$$
$$\square \; \square_{m\in S} \; evidence.a.m \rightarrow Agent_a(S)$$

An agent with information S is able to send any data in S, and can also present any such information as evidence. He can also receive any message m (which will increase S) from the medium.

Depending on the context of the protocol, the medium might be considered to be under the control of an intruder, or it may be considered simply to be an unreliable medium. Which of these models to use depends on the threat model that is deemed to be realistic: whether we will be concerned with the possibility that evidence is correct in the presence of an external intruder who might have interfered with the protocol, or whether the medium is not considered to be so actively hostile but simply unreliable. Furthermore, the unreliability of the medium (or the power of participating agents over the medium) might conceivably make a difference, particularly on issues such as whether messages can be delivered to the wrong address.

The system is then described in the usual way, as follows:

$$System = \left(\|\|_{a\in Agent} Agent_i(IK_a) \right) \| \; Medium(IK_m)$$

The initial knowledge of the agents IK_a will include their own private keys, and possibly keys shared with other agents. The initial knowledge of the medium will depend on the model of the medium. If it is simply an unreliable medium then it will simply hold messages that are passed to it, and hence its initial knowledge will be empty. However, if the medium can behave as a more active intruder then there may be some specific initial information, such as the private keys of compromised agents.

The non-repudiation property can require that occurrence of $evidence.a.m$ (presented to the environment) provides a guarantee that some other message m' must previously have been produced by b. This may be expressed as follows:

$$evidence.a.m \text{ in } tr \Rightarrow b \text{ sent } m'$$

Since b cannot be relied upon to behave in accordance with the protocol, the message m' might not have been issued by b directly as a complete message. However, m should still provide evidence that m' was somehow issued by b, even if it was in a different form than the protocol expects.

For example, if a has the message $\{m\}_{Private\_Key(b)}$ which has been signed by b using a private key unavailable to any agent other than b, then a is in possession of evidence that b issued m in some sense. However, it may have been sent as a component of a larger message or under further encryption, so the fact $\{m\}_{Private\_Key(b)}$ might not have been transmitted as a message itself. The notation b sent m' will be used to mean that m' was transmitted by b, possibly as a component of a larger message (and not necessarily to the agent presenting the evidence):

$$a \text{ sent } m = \exists M : Fact;\ b : Agent \bullet (send.a.b.M \text{ in } tr \wedge M \text{ contains } m)$$

where the contains relation is defined as follows: For all messages m, m', and m'', and keys k:

- ▨ m contains m
- ▨ m' contains $m \Rightarrow m''.m'$ contains m
- ▨ m' contains $m \Rightarrow m'.m''$ contains m
- ▨ m' contains $m \Rightarrow k(m')$ contains m

In the face of the threat model we are considering, this appears to be the strongest property that can be expressed for a non-repudiation protocol. In some sense if the message sent by b is going to be taken as evidence then it is incumbent upon b to issue it with care, and it would be unusual in practice for b to transmit it in any other form (though he should take care to ensure this does not occur by accident).

Example: the Zhou-Gollmann protocol

We will consider the modelling of a particular non-repudiation protocol. In fact this makes use of some additional features that require extensions to the model described above. The aim is for a to send a message m to b, and for the parties to obtain evidence that the message was sent and received. This protocol also aims to achieve fairness.

The message m is transferred in two stages: an encrypted form is first sent directly to b under some key k, and after a has received evidence of receipt from b the key k itself is sent via a trusted server. The server makes the key available via *ftp*, and both a and b have the responsibility to retrieve the key and the evidence that it was deposited by a.

Agent b should not be able to extract m until both of these messages have been received.

A cut-down version of the protocol, with the unsigned parts of the message omitted, is described as follows:

$$
\begin{aligned}
&\text{Message 1} &a \rightarrow b &\ :\ \{f_{NRO}.b.l.c\}_{SK_a} \\
&\text{Message 2} &b \rightarrow a &\ :\ \{f_{NRR}.a.l.c\}_{SK_b} \\
&\text{Message 3} &a \rightarrow j &\ :\ \{f_{SUB}.b.l.k\}_{SK_a} \\
&\text{Message 4} &b \leftrightarrow j &\ :\ \{f_{CON}.a.b.l.k\}_{SK_j} \\
&\text{Message 5} &a \leftrightarrow j &\ :\ \{f_{CON}.a.b.l.k\}_{SK_j}
\end{aligned}
$$

Zhou and Gollmann explain the elements of the protocol as follows:

- ▨ a: originator of the non-repudiation exchange.
- ▨ b: recipient of the non-repudiation exchange.

■ *j*: on-line trusted server providing network services accessible to the public.

■ *m*: message that is to be sent from *a* to *b*.

■ *c*: commitment (ciphertext) for message *m*, e.g. *m* encrypted under a key *k*. The point is that *c* in itself is not enough to identify the message *m*, but that *c* together with *k* is.

■ *k*: message key defined by *a*.

■ *l* is a label used to identify a particular protocol run. It should be unique to a single protocol run.

■ f_{NRO}, f_{NRR}, f_{SUB} and f_{CON} are flags used to identify the step of the protocol in which a particular message was generated.

■ SK_i is a private signature key known only to its owner *i*; and SK_j is the server's private signature key.

The steps of the protocol are explained as follows:

1 With the first message, *a* sends a signed combination of $c = k(m)$, a label *l*, and the recipient's name *b*. *b* will use this as evidence that $k(m)$ was sent in a run identified with *l*.

2 *b* responds with a signed record that *c* has been received in run *l*. This will provide evidence for *a* that $k(m)$ was received.

3 *a* then sends the key *k* to the trusted server together with the label *l*. If *a* tries to cheat by sending the wrong key, then he will not obtain the evidence he requires, since $k(m)$ and k' will not provide evidence that *m* was sent.

4 & 5 Each of *a* and *b* can retrieve, by means of an *ftp-get*, a signed record from *s* that the key *k* associated with protocol run *l* has been deposited. Responsibility for retrieving this information rests with the agents themselves, to nullify a possible future claim that 'the message was never received'. Thus both *a* and *b* can obtain evidence that the key *k* was made available to *b*.

The server only needs to handle relatively small messages, and make them available by *ftp*, so this protocol is appropriate even if the messages themselves are extremely large, since the server never has to handle them directly.

At the end of the protocol run, if *a* wishes to prove that the message has been received, he presents $\{f_{NRR}.a.l.c\}_{SK_b}$ and $\{f_{CON}.a.b.l.k\}_{SK_j}$: the first piece of evidence confirms that *b* received *c*, and the second piece confirms that the key was deposited with the server, which means that *b* has access to it, and hence to the message. The label *l* in both pieces of evidence connects the two items *k* and *c* as being associated with the same protocol run. This reasoning is really concerned with two pieces of evidence, and is thus captured as two requirements on the system:

$$evidence.a.\{f_{NRR}.a.l.c\}_{SK_b} \text{ in } tr \Rightarrow b \text{ sent } (f_{NRR}.a.l.c)$$
$$evidence.a.\{f_{CON}.a.b.l.k\}_{SK_j} \text{ in } tr \Rightarrow receive.a.j.\{f_{SUB}.b.l.k\}_{SK_a} \text{ in } tr$$

The *non-repudiation of receipt* property $NRR(tr)$ is taken as the conjunction of these two implications. If the system provides both of these properties, then a has only to present his evidence to prove that b did indeed have access to the message m. The honest operation of the server means that a need only present evidence that the server received the correct message. The system then guarantees that this information is also available to b.

If b wishes to prove that the message was sent by a, he presents both pieces of evidence $SK_a(f_{NRO}.b.l.c)$ and $SK_j(f_{CON}.a.b.l.k)$: the first provides evidence that c was sent, and the second provides evidence that k was also sent, to the server. This treatment of evidence is again expressed as two trace requirements:

$$evidence.b.\{f_{NRO}.b.l.c\}_{SK_a} \text{ in } tr \Rightarrow a \text{ sent } f_{NRO}.a.l.c$$
$$evidence.b.\{(f_{CON}.a.b.l.k)\}_{SK_j} \text{ in } tr \Rightarrow a \text{ sent } f_{SUB}.b.l.k$$

The *non-repudiation of origin* property $NRO(tr)$ is defined as the conjunction of these two trace properties.

The CSP model of the system will have to include at least the two participants in the protocol and the server. It is also reasonable to allow the presence of other agents who are potential protocol participants, since the protocol is expected to be correct even in the presence of other users of the network. The *ftp* connection can be modelled as another channel *ftp* directly between the server and the participants. In fact this does not make any difference to correctness with respect to the properties above, but it justifies the informal argument that messages are available to the agents once they have arrived at the server, and underpins the claim that the properties above are appropriate.

The entire network is the parallel combination of these components:

$$Network =$$
$$(\|_{a \in Agent} Agent_a(IK_a)) \underset{\{|ftp|\}}{\|} Server) \underset{\{|send|\} \cup \{|receive|\}}{\|} Medium(\varnothing)$$

This is illustrated in Figure 3.8.

The description of the participating agents is extended to permit receipt of facts along the *ftp* channel from *Jeeves*:

$$Agent_a(S) =$$
$$\square_{b \in Agent, m \in S} send.a.b.m \rightarrow Agent_i(S)$$
$$\square\ receive.a?b?m \rightarrow Agent_a(close_{\vdash_a}(S \cup \{m\}))$$
$$\square\ ftp.a.Jeeves?m \rightarrow Agent_a(close_{\vdash_a}(S \cup \{m\}))$$
$$\square\ \square_{m \in S} evidence.a.m \rightarrow Agent_i(S)$$

The server described by process *Server* accepts signed messages of the form of step 3 of the protocol, and makes them available via *ftp*. It is assumed that the server acts in accordance with its role in the protocol. It is therefore modelled as follows:

$$Server(S) = receive?a.Jeeves?SK_a(f_{SUB}.b.l.k) \rightarrow Server(S \cup \{SK_j(f_{CON}.j.b.l.k)\}$$
$$\square$$
$$\square_{a \in Agent, m \in S} ftp.a.Jeeves.m \rightarrow Server(S)$$

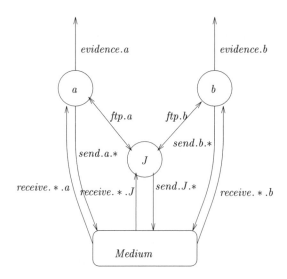

Figure 3.8 Network for the Zhou-Gollmann non-repudiation protocol

The server guarantees that any messages retrieved from it via *ftp* correspond to receipt of an appropriately signed f_{SUB} message in accordance with the protocol.

The correctness requirements on the entire system are then

$$System \textbf{ sat } NRO(tr)$$

and

$$System \textbf{ sat } NRR(tr)$$

The protocol itself is not modelled explicitly within CSP. The descriptions of the agents allow correct execution of the protocol as possible behaviour. If the system meets these properties, then it proves that the evidence is sufficient to provide the guarantees we require, in the context of the server. The protocol can be seen as a pragmatic suggestion for how the participants might obtain the evidence they require, but the security property of the protocol rests more on the nature of the evidence than on the participants following the protocol itself.

3.5 Anonymity

Anonymity is concerned with protecting the identity of agents with respect to particular events or messages. In this case, unlike secrecy, the messages themselves need not be protected, only their association with particular agents. Hence it is natural to model events in the system as consisting of two components: the identity of the agent performing that event, and the content itself. For anonymity, we consider events of the form $a.x$, where a is the identity of the agent and x is the content of the event.

An anonymity protocol will be designed to achieve some kind of transaction or exchange of messages without revealing the identity of some or all of the participants. This means not only that the name of the participants should not appear directly, but also that the identities of the participants should not be deducible from the information that is available. The threat is often considered to be more passive than for secrecy and authentication: that agents are not actively working to subvert the protocol, but are simply observing the occurrence of events and making deductions about the participants. Thus an anonymity protocol will generally be over a fairly reliable medium. However, such protocols can also be analyzed in the presence of stronger threats or a more unreliable medium (which might misdeliver messages for example) to see if their anonymity properties still hold.

The principle of anonymity is that a data item that could have originated from one agent could equally have originated from any other (perhaps any other from some given set of users). Hence we wish our definition to capture the notion that any message of the form $i.x$ could equally well have been of the form $j.x$. If the set *Anonusers* consists of the set of all users whose identities should be masked by the system in providing anonymity, then the set of messages we wish to confuse for a given piece of information x is given by the set A:

$$A = \{a.x \mid a \in Anonusers\}$$

Rather than deal directly with the identity of users, we can capture anonymity by requiring that whenever any event from the set A occurs, it could equally well have been any other event. In terms of agent identity and content, this means that if an observer has access only to the content of the message then it is not possible to deduce the identity of the agent associated with it.

A protocol described as a CSP system P will provide anonymity on the set A if any arbitrary permutation p_A of the events in A, applied pointwise to all of the traces of the system, does not alter the set of possible traces of the system. This means that the other events from A that can appear in the trace are independent of the identity of the agent performing events from A. If A is of the form above (a set of possible users associated with a piece of information) then permutations will correspond to permutations on agents.

Anonymity is often relative to particular observers or particular viewpoints. In other words, anonymity is provided in cases where an observer has access only to certain kinds of information, and might not be provided in cases where more information is available. For example, a donation to a charity or a political party would be anonymous if the only information available is details of the amounts of money passing through particular accounts, but might not be anonymous if all details of particular transactions are available.

In general, an observer does not have complete access to all the events occurring in a system, but has only limited or no direct access to some events. The events that an observer has access to could be captured as another set B.

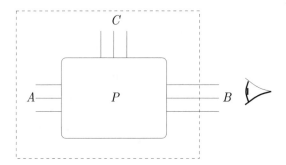

Figure 3.9 Analyzing *P* for anonymity

It is an immediate requirement for anonymity that $A \cap B = \emptyset$. If an observer has direct access to the very events that we wish to mask, then it will always be possible to tell some events in A (in particular, those also in B) from some others.

The events that are not in B are those events that the observer does not have direct access to. From the point of view of modelling the system in order to analyze for anonymity, the events other than A and B should be *abstracted*, since the system to be analyzed for anonymity should encapsulate the information available to the observer.

If C is the set of events that are to be abstracted from P, then the system to be analyzed is $Abs_C(P)$, where Abs_C is an abstraction mechanism such as hiding, masking, or renaming. This situation is pictured in Figure 3.9. In each case the requirement will be to check for any arbitrary permutation on A, lifted to apply to events and thus to traces, that

$$p_A(Abs_C(P)) = Abs_C(P)$$

The dining cryptographers

We will consider the toy example of the dining cryptographers protocol. This is concerned with a situation in which three cryptographers share a meal. At the end of the meal, each of them is secretly informed by their organization whether or not she is paying. Either at most one is paying, or else the organization is itself picking up the bill.

The cryptographers would like to know whether it is one of them who is paying, or whether it is their organization that is paying; but they also wish to retain anonymity concerning the identity of the payer if it is one of them. They will use the following protocol to achieve this.

They each toss a coin, which is made visible to them and their right-hand neighbour. Each cryptographer then examines the two coins that they can see. There are two possible announcements that can be made by each cryptographer: that the coins agree, or that they disagree. If a cryptographer is not paying then she will say that they agree if the results on the coins are the same, and that they disagree if the

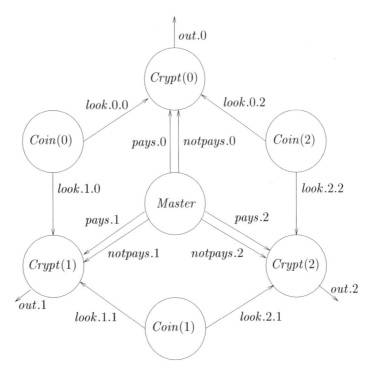

Figure 3.10 Components of the protocol

results differ; a paying cryptographer will say the opposite.

If the number of 'disagree' announcements is even, then the organization is paying. If the number is odd, then one of the cryptographers is paying. The two cryptographers not paying will not be able to identify the payer from the information they have available.

The protocol is modelled in CSP as the parallel combination of cryptographers and coins, and a master process dictating who pays, as illustrated in Figure 3.10. The events of the form *pays.i* and *notpays.i* are the instructions from the organization concerning payment. Events of the form *look.i.j.x* model cryptographer *i* reading value *x* from coin *j*. The channels *out.i* are used for the cryptographers to make their declaration.

The *Master* process nondeterministically chooses either to pay, or one of the cryptographers to pay.

$$Master = (\sqcap_{i:Cryptnames} pays.i \to notpays.((i+1) \bmod 3)$$
$$\to notpays.((i+2) \bmod 3) \to Stop)$$
$$\sqcap notpays.0 \to notpays.1 \to notpays.2 \to Stop$$

Each cryptographer process follows the protocol. This is described in CSP as follows:

$$Crypt(i) = notpays.i \rightarrow look.i.i?x \rightarrow look.i.((i+1) \bmod 3)?y \rightarrow$$
$$(\textbf{if } (x = y) \textbf{ then } (out.i.agree \rightarrow STOP)$$
$$\textbf{else } (out.i.disagree \rightarrow STOP))$$
$$\Box \ (pays.i \rightarrow look.i.i?x \rightarrow look.i.((i+1) \bmod 3)?y \rightarrow$$
$$(\textbf{if } (x = y) \textbf{ then } out.i.disagree \rightarrow STOP$$
$$\textbf{else } out.i.agree \rightarrow STOP))$$

Each coin is modelled as a choice between reading heads and reading tails:

$$Coin(i) = Heads(i) \sqcap Tails(i)$$
$$Heads(i) = look.i.i.heads \rightarrow Heads(i)$$
$$\Box \ look.((i-1) \bmod 3).i.heads \rightarrow Heads(i)$$

$$Tails(i) = look.i.i.tails \rightarrow Tails(i)$$
$$\Box \ look.((i-1) \bmod 3).i.tails \rightarrow Tails(i)$$

The *master* either sends a pay message to one of the cryptographers and a do-not-pay to the other two or a do-not-pay message to all of them.

The system is constructed from the cryptographers and coins, which are two collections of independent processes.

$$Crypts = Crypt(0) \ ||| \ Crypt(1) \ ||| \ Crypt(2)$$
$$Coins = Coin(0) \ ||| \ Coin(1) \ ||| \ Coin(2)$$

They must synchronize on the events representing the examination of coins and the *Master* decides who is paying.

$$Meal = ((Crypts \underset{\{|look|\}}{||} Coins) \underset{\{|pays|\} \cup \{|notpays|\}}{||} Master)$$

It is also possible to provide a parametric description of the system for an arbitrary number n of cryptographers; but automatic verification via model-checking will be possible only once a particular n is chosen.

Analysis

There are a number of parameters that dictate the precise form of anonymity available to the dining cryptographers:

- the events A for which anonymity is provided;
- the events B of the system that can be observed;
- the way the remaining events $\Sigma \setminus (A \cup B)$ are abstracted.

If anonymity is to be provided with respect to the environment of *Meal* (for example, an observer on another table), then the set A for anonymity to be provided is simply

$\{pays.i \mid 0 \leqslant i \leqslant 2\}$: the observer should not be able to distinguish the paying cryptographer from the others. Such an observer should only see the publicly announced values on *out*: occurrences of the *notpays* and *look* events should be abstracted. In this situation, the parameters are as follows:

- ▨ $A = \{\mid pays \mid\}$
- ▨ $B = \{\mid out \mid\}$
- ▨ the remaining events will be hidden: this means that the observer does not even know whether and how often these events occur.

The system under consideration will be

$$Meal \setminus \{\mid look, notpays \mid\}$$

and the question of anonymity will be whether or not

$$p_A(Meal \setminus \{\mid look, notpays \mid\}) = Meal \setminus \{\mid look, notpays \mid\}$$

for an arbitrary permutation p_A.

It might be plausible to expect that *look* events can be observed, simply requiring that the particular values associated with them are abstracted. In this case a renaming abstraction is more appropriate, using the following alphabet renaming:

$$f_{look}(look.i.j.v) = look.i.j$$

The system $f_{look}(Meal)$ allows the occurrence of user i inspecting coin j to be observed, but abstracts the information given by the coin. If this form of abstraction is instead used (with *notpays* events remaining completely hidden) then the equivalence to be checked for anonymity is

$$p_A(f_{look}(Meal) \setminus \{\mid notpays \mid\}) = f_{look}(Meal) \setminus \{\mid notpays \mid\}$$

The cryptographers themselves are privy to more information than an outsider watching the protocol running. They have access to the values of coins, and also they know whether they themselves are paying or not. In principle this additional information might be enough to break anonymity, and indeed anonymity on the set A is trivially not provided, since cryptographer i can distinguish *pays.i* from *pays.j* for some other j: *pays.i* is in both A and B.

In this case, the requirement is that anonymity is provided for each cryptographer against the other two. In other words, if a particular cryptographer is paying then each of the other two should not know whether it is her or the third cryptographer. From the point of view of each cryptographer, this means that the other two *pays* events should be indistinguishable.

Since the situation is symmetric, we will consider anonymity with respect to cryptographer 0. In this case we have the following parameters defining the anonymity property. A is the set of events that must be indistinguishable, and B is the set of events that are available to cryptographer 0:

- ▨ $A = \{pays.1, pays.2\}$

◼ $B = \{pays.0, notpays.0\} \cup \{| \ look.0 \ |\} \cup \{| \ out \ |\}$

◼ $C = \Sigma \setminus (A \cup B)$

There is in fact only one permutation p_A to consider: swapping $pays.1$ and $pays.2$. The equivalence to check is that

$$p_A(Meal \setminus C) = Meal \setminus C$$

This equivalence holds, and hence the protocol is correct.

The threat model considered above is benign: the participants all behave as they should, and we consider whether this allows any information to leak out. However, we may also consider situations where attempts are made to subvert the protocol. For example, a cryptographer might have access to the value on the third coin. This can be captured by allowing the cryptographer access to one of the *look* events at that third coin. For example the set B that cryptographer 0 has access to might include events of the form $look.2.2$.

In this case anonymity is lost. In the configuration

◼ $A = \{pays.1, pays.2\}$

◼ $B = \{pays.0, notpays.0\} \cup \{| \ look.0, look.2.2 \ |\} \cup \{| \ out \ |\}$

◼ $C = \Sigma \setminus (A \cup B)$

we find that

$$\langle pays.2, notpays.0, look.0.0.heads, look.0.1.heads, look.2.2.heads, out.2.disagree \rangle$$

is a trace of $Meal \setminus C$ but that it is not a trace of $p_A(Meal \setminus C)$. In other words, heads on all three coins are observed and so $out.2.disagree$ is consistent with $pays.2$. However, it is not consistent with $pays.1$: if $pays.2$ is replaced by $pays.1$ then the rest of the trace is not consistent with that change. This means that the rest of the trace contains enough information to distinguish $pays.1$ from $pays.2$, and hence break the anonymity required for cryptographers 1 and 2.

It is instructive to consider this example when $look.2.2$ is not available. In this case we have

$$\langle pays.2, notpays.0, look.0.0.heads, look.0.1.heads, out.2.disagree \rangle$$

as the equivalent trace of $Meal \setminus C$. But now this is also a trace of $p_A(Meal \setminus C)$: the rest of the trace is consistent with $pays.1$, since the value of $Coin(2)$ could be *tails*, leading to $out.2.disagree$. If the value of $Coin(2)$ is not available then anonymity is again obtained.

3.6 Summary

This chapter has considered how authentication and secrecy properties can be captured by enhancing CSP descriptions of protocols with the introduction of 'specification events' into the descriptions of honest agents. These events do not affect the interactions between the components of the protocol, and so they do not change the attacks that are possible on a protocol. They allow the intentions of the protocol designer or specifier to be expressed explicitly in terms of what should have been achieved when a protocol participant reaches a particular state. Requirements on protocols are captured by the introduction of appropriate specification events at particular points of the CSP protocol description, and then by describing the requirements on these events.

If *Claim_Secret* signals are introduced into the CSP description only for runs with honest protocols, then secrecy requirements on protocols tend to take the form

$$signal.Claim\_Secret.a.b.s \in tr \Rightarrow \neg(leak.s \text{ in } tr)$$

so that when an honest agent *a* claims that *s* is a secret value, then the intruder should not be in possession of it – *leak.s* can occur only when the intruder has *s*.

Alternatively, the assumption that the agents are honest might be captured more explicitly within the property, as the fact that $a \in Honest\, b \in Honest$.

$$signal.Claim\_Secret.a.b.s \text{ in } tr \wedge a \in Honest\, b \in Honest \Rightarrow \neg(leak.s \text{ in } tr)$$

In this case, the signal event is always possible at the end of the protocol run, and the requirement is that only in the appropriate cases should this be taken to indicate secrecy of *s*.

These secrecy properties can also both be expressed as process-oriented specifications, enabling model-checking.

Authentication properties are expressed in terms of the relationship between a *Commit* signal and a *Running* signal: that the performance of a *Commit* signal by one agent must guarantee that the other agent has already performed a corresponding *Running* signal, such as in the following property:

$$signal.Commit.b.a.ds \text{ in } tr \Rightarrow signal.Running.a.b.ds \text{ in } tr$$

The *Commit* signal is introduced into the protocol description at the point where the protocol designer expects the protocol to have achieved authentication for that agent of the other party. It is required to correspond to the other party having reached a particular stage in their part of the protocol. Although the other party need not have committed, they should at least have done something, and so the *Running* signal is introduced to mark the point they must have reached. Early approaches to authentication and secrecy [84, 61, 86, 57] expressed properties on the bare protocols without the introduction of signal events. The approach favoured in this book prefers signal events to enable clearer expression of the properties required.

We have also considered non-repudiation properties [44], where evidence is introduced; and anonymity, where we require that permutations of the agents requiring anonymity does not affect the visible parts of the system. These approaches were first presented in [88] and [85]. The full Zhou-Gollmann non-repudiation protocol is described in [102]. The dining cryptographers example was first described in [21].

4 Overview of FDR

FDR is a commercial tool[1] designed to establish results about concurrent and reactive systems described in CSP. (In fact, the same underlying 'engine' can be applied to a range of other notations that admit similar semantic interpretations; but CSP will suffice for this discussion.)

With one or two exceptions,[2] FDR obtains its results by comparing two descriptions in a common universe of discourse: a *specification* and an *implementation*; in order to determine if the latter is a *refinement* of the former. If a check is successful, it means that the implementation is a reasonable candidate for substitution into the role of the specification: no observation of any single run of the implementation can tell that it is not, in fact, the specification resolving any nondeterministic choices it may have in some particular way.

The most obvious use for such a checking capability is when the specification is an abstract description of a system, perhaps 'obviously correct' by construction or relatively easily established to meet the (probably informal) requirements on the system, while the implementation is a (typically more complex) process with some desired efficiencies or structural properties (such as parallel composition with a 'narrow' interface, making it suitable for realization on distributed hardware). This turns out not to be the most common case, however.

A second, closely related way of using refinement is when the specification describes some interface protocol, and the implementation is an appropriate view of a component that should obey that protocol. In fact, with appropriate choices of specification and viewpoint, perhaps augmented by judicious instrumentation of the implementation process, a wide range of properties of the implementation can be encoded in this way; FDR can be used as a 'theorem prover' to establish that the implementation satisfies the logical specification captured in the specification process.

The other paradigm of use turns this neatly on its head; instead of describing some desirable property of the implementation in the specification, you can challenge it by denying that some desirable outcome can be achieved. For example, if the implementation describes a puzzle, with events marking the moves or manipulation of pieces and with constraints so that it can perform the event *done* only when the solution has been reached (see, e.g., [76] and [15.1]), then specify that *done* cannot occur. If this is true, then the puzzle is insoluble; but if it is not, FDR will exhibit a counterexample. This counterexample contains precisely the directions for

---

[1] A product of Formal Systems (Europe) Ltd: visit www.formal.demon.co.uk for details.
[2] For example, determinism checking.

reaching the solution from the given starting position, and so tells you how to solve the problem for real.

The use we make in the crypto-protocol work lies somewhere between these last two: we might hope that the protocol works, and that we can extend the absence of counterexample on the small, fixed system analyzed to a proof that there are no vulnerabilities within the powers of the intruder we have modelled, using data-independence techniques discussed in Chapter 10.

But in many cases we will find that there are apparent vulnerabilities: the counterexample gives the sequence of events the intruder must arrange to occur (or take advantage of, when they are outside his control) in order to breach the specified security property. This can be related back to the real-world messages that are being modelled, to decide if it is something serious that needs to be fixed.

We will return to the specifically crypto-protocol-related modelling in the next chapter, but here we look in more detail at the mechanics of performing the refinement check in general. Besides its intrinsic interest, this may give insights into why the CSP that Casper generates does things one way rather than another, and why some superficially innocuous scripts behave rather badly, in performance terms. Anyone interested only in interaction with Casper may skip this chapter, at least at first reading.

4.1 Comparing processes

The relationships between processes that FDR calculates are denotational properties: what is of interest is a comparison of their observable behaviours (in particular, for refinement, that every observation possible of the implementation should also be possibly observed of the specification), not the internal evolution that gives rise to them. What constitutes an observable behaviour depends on the kind of property one is interested in:

- *Traces*, the finite sequences of visible events a process may engage in, give the coarsest useful comparison; refinement in the traces model corresponds to language inclusion in automata theory, and to Hennessy's 'may' testing [40]. Assuming that the specification describes what is 'good' behaviour, traces refinement means 'nothing bad happens' in the implementation.

- *Failures* and *divergences* give further information about a process,[3] if we allow ourselves to observe them: this can be, after each trace, which choices can be made by its environment and which are at the whim of the process; and when the process may engage in unbounded internal activity (*livelock*), and so not provide any further observation of it doing (or choosing not to do) anything. This has been regarded as the standard model since the early 1980s, since in addition to the pure safety conditions expressible in traces it allows one to specify that a process will eventually be prepared to engage in some set of

---

[3] And the name to the tool: FDR stands for *F*ailures-*D*ivergences *R*efinement.

events after a given trace: the only ways it could fail to do so being to reach a stable state where it is (perhaps nondeterministically) unwilling to (which is a property of its failures), or never to reach a stable state at all (which is to say that the trace is a divergence). Divergence is treated as catastrophic in this model: once a process might diverge, we assume nothing about its subsequent behaviour.

■ *Failures* from stable states alone, together with traces, give a model that treats divergence as rather benign, and so allows further investigation of a process that reaches a stable state despite the potential for divergence. This has interesting applications in its own right, but also proves (as we shall discuss below) to be a relation more efficiently tested than the failures/divergence one. The models agree, of course, on divergence-free processes; and so if a process can once be checked for livelock-freedom (or is known to be so, by construction or otherwise), then failures-model checks give the same results as in the failures/divergences model, but faster and smaller.

For crypto-protocol analysis the traces model generally suffices, but testing resilience to denial-of-service attacks requires the richer models, as does the CSP characterization of information flow [80] and related topics.[4]

The relationships and properties, then, are described in terms of the denotational models. The mathematical values associated with processes are quite complex structures (pairs of sets of pairs of sequences and sets of events with sets of sequences, in the case of failures/divergences), however; and worse, for mechanical treatment, in general they are infinite. FDR therefore does not manipulate the denotational values directly; rather it exploits the congruences between the denotational and operational semantics of CSP [76] to calculate the properties based on an operational realization of the processes in question.

In order for this to be practical we require that any process P we consider be *finite state*: the set of distinct P/s (the state reached by P after performing trace s) as s ranges over *traces*(P) must be finite,[5] and moreover we must be able to find a finite operational representation of P. Once we have this we can complete a check in finite time, provided we can recognize states – or rather, in general, pairs of states – we have visited before.

---

[4] In fact, recent research [59] suggests the need for models making finer discrimination than these: denying information flow while allowing nondeterminism in the interface to the potential recipient requires notions of correlation and consistent refinement of nondeterministic choices; but an underlying design decision for the CSP models is that when nondeterminism is resolved should not matter to the observer

[5] This condition is actually excessively restrictive: all that we require is that there is no need to *explore* more than a finite set of states in any given check and that there is some finite representation of the system. The exploration strategy and infrastructure of FDR are in principle quite capable of checking that any finite capacity buffer is a refinement of the (infinite-state) most general buffer of that type, for example; and such specifications have been experimentally hand-coded in terms of internal data structures. It is another matter, however, to make a compiler capable of generating efficient recipes of this sort in the general case.

This problem is one shared by all state exploration tools, and the various solutions employed distinguish them as much as the more obvious issues of language and specification style. Intimately related with state storage are exploration strategies and performance goals. The primary dichotomy is between implicit and explicit state storage: on the one hand we have 'symbolic' model-checking systems based on (Ordered) Binary Decision Diagrams (BDD), which can represent large sets of states by, hopefully, relatively small logical formulæ. These have met with considerable success, particularly in hardware verification [62, 17], where the regularity in the designs tends to allow a substantially compacted representation; they have also been applied to CSP refinement checking [101]. The transition relation of the system in question is encoded as some kind of predicate transformation, and can be applied to find all the possible next (or previous) states connected with a given set. This lends itself to analyzing whether an identified set of 'bad' states is reachable from the 'good' initial states, searching either forwards or backwards or from both ends towards the middle.

The alternative is explicit-state exploration, where each individual state visited is recorded in some way. This has the advantage that it is not necessary to calculate the entire transition relation in advance: it can be evolved piecemeal, 'on-the-fly'. It is not enough to record states that have been seen; it is important to be able to consult those records efficiently: a brute-force search yields an overall exploration that is at best quadratic in the number of states, which itself has to be measurable in millions, at least, to address most real-world problems at even a minimal level of detail. Most tools use some form of sorting or hashing to address this problem.

Hashing has the advantage of near constant-time lookup, as long as the table is relatively empty. As the table fills, depending on the precise mechanism employed for resolving clashes, there may be a logarithmic or linear penalty on both insertions and lookups. But when the size of the data structures exceeds available physical memory, the constant factors grow to dominate, and effectively bring the exploration to a halt: a good hash function, by its very nature, will produce essentially random indirections, and random access into paged virtual memory places an intolerable load on to disk subsystems and kernel paging strategies. Hashing can accommodate both depth-first and breadth-first searching, but is particularly well suited to the former: a separate list of states on the current path both eliminates the need to record back-links in order to be able to report the trace to an error, and facilitates the detection of loops (and so, in particular, divergences in the CSP context).

Using a separate listing of the current path, a variation on hashing is possible: rather than recording the states visited in the hash table, one can simply mark whether the hash value has been encountered; this allows a single bit to be used in place of the bit vector that naturally represents the state – which has length logarithmic in the *a priori* bound on the number of states, rather than the number actually reachable – and eliminates any overhead associated with the data structures used to represent the contents of hash buckets. The relatively small improvement this *bitstate* hashing offers has a dramatic impact when it brings a problem within the capabilities of the machine it is run on; but at a cost. Now, any clash in hash values has the potential to excise substantial sections of the transition graph, as all entry points may be believed, incorrectly, to have been visited already. Worse, there is no way to detect when such a fault may have given rise to a false positive result. The supertrace algorithm [42] improves slightly on this approach: by using two independent hash functions (and a bit for each value) one is able to make a better estimate of the likelihood of hash clashes, since a clash in only one hash is detectable. Nonetheless, these approaches cannot guarantee more than a randomized partial search; this may uncover flaws, but can give only limited statistical value to the failure to find any.

FDR prefers to try and complete the exploration, using secondary storage when necessary, based on sorting rather than hashing. Maintaining sorted structures has essentially logarithmic complexity for at least one of insertion or lookup; and a depth-first search runs into similar performance difficulties when the size of the data exceeds physical memory. But breadth-first search offers scope for more storage-friendly strategies: we do not need to know immediately whether a successor state has been seen before. We can therefore maintain a separate collection of successors of the current ply in the search, sort them at the end of the ply,[6] and then merge them into the seen set, determining in the process which were new and so require exploration. Early versions of FDR used linked lists of sorted blocks of virtual memory for the main state storage, but recent versions have used B-trees [7] with filestore backing; advances in processor speed and disk capacities, combined with reductions in memory and disk-cost, mean that virtual-address space limitations had become a significant consideration, which the new architecture circumvents.

Breadth-first exploration is undoubtedly preferable from an engineering point of view, too. In particular, the fact that the shortest path to a fault is returned as a counterexample is a significant advantage for human comprehension and debugging compared with the corresponding trace from a depth-first exploration. The one thing breadth-first exploration is not good at, however, is loop detection; so FDR in fact uses a hybrid search strategy in failures/divergences checks. The main exploration is breadth-first, as described; but we maintain a separate hash-based cache of divergence information for all unstable states (of a single process, *not* pairs of states) encountered during the check, which allows a depth-first scan of the space of states connected by internal transitions to be executed incrementally. This does add an overhead, in space as well as time, to the exploration of checks in this model – which explains why failures-model checks are to be preferred when the system is known to be free of divergence, or trace checks when that model suffices.

4.2 Labelled Transition Systems

The classic operational representation of a CSP process is as a Labelled Transition System (LTS) [75]: a set of nodes representing the states of the process are connected

---

6 Or whenever convenient: FDR mixes random-access sorting of reasonable-size pools with merges of the resulting sorted arrays.

by directed arcs, labelled with either a visible event or the internal action τ, which describe how one state can evolve into another. There is a structured operational semantics for CSP [14] and more particularly for CSP_M [83], which allow these arcs to be deduced between nodes representing process terms – or rather closures, terms together with bindings for their free identifiers – and this operational semantics forms the basis of the compilation strategy for purely sequential or recursive terms. One of the components of the FDR tool is a compiler that takes the CSP_M script supplied by the user (or written by Casper) and a number of process terms in the vocabulary this establishes. Unless the provisions of the next section apply, an LTS labelled with closures on the vertices is calculated from the inference rules of the operational semantics; nodes are identified when they are evidently equal (with functions and processes, for instance, compared by closure, not value). This LTS is transferred to the refinement engine with a simple numbering of the nodes, together with the initial node number corresponding to each term.

Each LTS comes with a distinguished initial node. The initial nodes of the specification and implementation processes are used to seed an explorer object that provides four abstract operations:

$$complete() \;:\; bool$$
$$take() \;:\; Pair\langle Node, Node\rangle$$
$$add(Node) \;:\; unit$$
$$path(Pair\langle Node, Node\rangle) \;:\; Seq\langle Pair\langle Node, Node\rangle\rangle$$

Hidden behind this interface are all the mechanisms necessary to implement the efficient breadth-first search. Alternative search strategies and implementations could be slotted in instead, if desired, provided only that they support this interface.

In terms of these operations the core of the refinement-checking algorithm is very straightforward:

```
initialise explorer with pair of initial nodes;
while explorer is not complete
    take a (fresh) pair of nodes from the explorer
    if nodes are compatible in appropriate model
        then add mutually reachable successor pairs to explorer
        else return counterexample with explorer path to this pair
```

In the traces model, the local test to see if an implementation node is compatible with the corresponding specification node is simply to check whether the visible events that can be performed by that state of the implementation are a subset of those that can happen in the specification at that point.

As an example of this procedure in practice, let us consider the process S

$$S = a \rightarrow S1$$
$$S1 = b \rightarrow S \,\square\, c \rightarrow S \,\square\, a \rightarrow S2$$
$$S2 = b \rightarrow S1 \,\square\, c \rightarrow S1$$

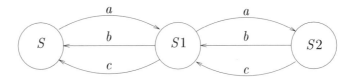

Figure 4.1 Labelled Transition System for S

as a specification: informally, each a event enables either a b or a c, but at most two can be outstanding. The LTS is pictured in Figure 4.1. As a putative implementation, consider $AB \,|||\, AC$, where $AB = a \rightarrow b \rightarrow AB$ and $AC = a \rightarrow c \rightarrow AC$. As an LTS, this has four states:

$$\mathcal{AA} \text{ corresponding to } AB \,|||\, AC$$
$$\mathcal{BA} \text{ corresponding to } b \rightarrow AB \,|||\, AC$$
$$\mathcal{AC} \text{ corresponding to } AB \,|||\, c \rightarrow AC$$
$$\mathcal{BC} \text{ corresponding to } b \rightarrow AB \,|||\, c \rightarrow AC$$

The LTS for $\mathcal{AA}$ is illustrated in Figure 4.2. We seed the explorer with the pair $(S, \mathcal{AA})$ and proceed

? $S \sqsubseteq_T AB \,|||\, AC$?				
Checking	Spec inits	Impl inits	Successors	To check
				$(S, \mathcal{AA})$
$(S, \mathcal{AA})$	$\{a\}$	$\{a\}$	$(S1, \mathcal{BA}), (S1, \mathcal{AC})$	
$(S1, \mathcal{BA})$	$\{a, b, c\}$	$\{a, b\}$	$(S2, \mathcal{BC}), (S, \mathcal{AA})$	$(S1, \mathcal{AC})$
$(S1, \mathcal{AC})$	$\{a, b, c\}$	$\{a, c\}$	$(S2, \mathcal{BC}), (S, \mathcal{AA})$	$(S2, \mathcal{BC})$
$(S2, \mathcal{BC})$	$\{b, c\}$	$\{b, c\}$	$(S1, \mathcal{AC}), (S1, \mathcal{BA})$	

where the underlined successor pairs are those that have not been encountered before; these are appended (in some arbitrary order) to the list of pairs to check, by the breadth-first search. After the four pairs listed have been checked, there are no new ones to consider; the refinement holds.

If we prevent S from performing c events (for instance, by making it synchronize on c with $Stop$), this will no longer be the case; the first two state-pairs continue to match but $\mathcal{AC}$ is not compatible with $S1 \,\|_{\{c\}}\, Stop$. The events possible for the specification state are $\{a, b\}$, while the implementation can perform c (as well as a). The refinement does not hold, and this state pair gives rise to a counterexample as described in Section 4.4.

If we hide c on the implementation side, we have the same four states, but now two of the transitions are labelled with the internal event τ. This is pictured in Figure 4.3. The difference that this makes is to the 'mutually reachable' successor state pair:

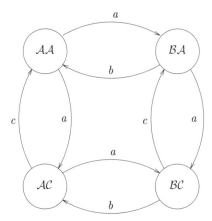

Figure 4.2 Labelled Transition System for $AB \parallel\parallel AC$

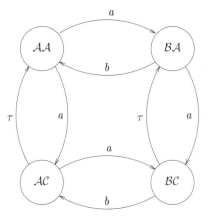

Figure 4.3 Labelled Transition System for $AB \parallel\parallel AC \setminus \{c\}$

there is no event on the specification side corresponding to the τ, so the specification state remains unchanged. This results in the following exploration

? $S \sqsubseteq_T AB \parallel\parallel AC \setminus \{c\}$?				
Checking	Spec inits	Impl inits	Successors	To check
				$(S, \mathcal{AA})$
$(S, \mathcal{AA})$	$\{a\}$	$\{a\}$	$(S1, \mathcal{BA}), (S1, \mathcal{AC})$	
$(S1, \mathcal{BA})$	$\{a, b, c\}$	$\{a, b\}$	$\overline{(S2, \mathcal{BC})}, \overline{(S, \mathcal{AA})}$	$(S1, \mathcal{AC})$
$(S1, \mathcal{AC})$	$\{a, b, c\}$	$\{a, \tau\}$	$\overline{(S2, \mathcal{BC})}, \overline{(S1, \mathcal{AA})}$	$(S2, \mathcal{BC})$
$(S2, \mathcal{BC})$	$\{b, c\}$	$\{b, \tau\}$	$\overline{(S1, \mathcal{AC})}, \overline{(S2, \mathcal{BA})}$	$(S1, \mathcal{AA})$
$(S1, \mathcal{AA})$	$\{a, b, c\}$	$\{a\}$	$\overline{(S2, \mathcal{BA})}, \overline{(S2, \mathcal{AC})}$	$(S2, \mathcal{BA})$
$(S2, \mathcal{BA})$	$\{b, c\}$	$\{a, b\}$	—mismatch—	$(S2, \mathcal{AC})$

Again, the refinement fails to hold. But note that in order to discover this we have had to check states of the implementation against more than one state of the specification; it really is, in general, the Cartesian product of the two state spaces that needs to be explored!

This exploration strategy works nicely as long as the specification is operationally deterministic: if it has no τ transitions and there is no more than one arc with any given label from any node. But that is a necessary condition: let us try to perform our original refinement check the other way round. When we come to check the pair $(\mathcal{BA}, S1)$ we find that the implementation can perform a c that the specification cannot, and we are inclined to declare a mismatch. But $\mathcal{AC}$ is a state of the specification, reachable on the same trace, which can do that event; it is impossible to form an accurate judgement looking at only one of them.

This is obviously unsatisfactory; but fortunately, there is a way around the problem by transforming the specification – a procedure called *normalization*. We need to make the specification exhibit that operational determinacy, while preserving the information about its nondeterminacy that is important for checks in the richer models. The construction of a deterministic state machine with the same traces is well known from automata theory, and adapts to this context: we need to work in the powerspace of the original machines states.

1 The initial state of the normalized machine is the τ-*closure* of the original initial state; that is, the set of all states reachable from it by a finite sequence of internal transitions.

2 The events a superstate can perform are the union of the visible events its elements can perform.

3 The successor superstate after any event is the union of the τ-closures of all the possible successors of that event from any of its elements.

This gives rise to an LTS that is potentially exponentially larger than the original, but that in practice is typically of comparable size, often smaller. But such an LTS does not preserve the refusal and divergence information of the original, so we add a labelling that records this to the nodes of the LTS:

4 The refusals of a superstate are the union of the refusals calculated from its elements; a state that can perform τ contributes none, while one that cannot contributes (any subset of) the visible events it cannot do. The label is an efficient encoding of the resulting set.[7]

5 A superstate is marked as divergent if and only if there is an unbounded sequence of τ transitions (in the original machine) from any of its elements.

---

[7] In fact, we calculate the dual attribute, acceptances, since (empirically) processes tend to have to do less than they may refuse to; in either case it suffices to record only extremal sets (maximal refusals or minimal acceptances).

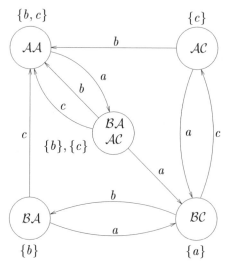

Figure 4.4 Generalized Labelled Transition System for normal (*AB* ||| *AC*) (states labelled with maximal refusals)

As a final step in the normalization procedure, the resulting Generalized Labelled Transition System (GLTS) is factored by a maximal bisimulation: nodes are identified unless they differ in their labellings or possible events, or the corresponding successor nodes after each event can (recursively) so be distinguished. This is not strictly necessary, but it is clear that any exploration from bisimilar states will yield the same results and so all but the first will be redundant.

To return to our example, the normalization of *AB* ||| *AC* turns out to have five states: $\{\mathcal{AA}\}$, $\{\mathcal{BA}, \mathcal{AC}\}$, $\{\mathcal{BC}\}$, $\{\mathcal{BA}\}$ and $\{\mathcal{AC}\}$ shown in Figure 4.4. Now, when we seed the exploration with $(\{\mathcal{AA}\}, S)$ it proceeds:

? *AB* ||| *AC* $\sqsubseteq_T$ *S* ?				
Checking	Spec inits	Impl inits	Successors	To check
				$(\{\mathcal{AA}\}, S)$
$(\{\mathcal{AA}\}, S)$	$\{a\}$	$\{a\}$	$(\{\mathcal{BA}, \mathcal{AC}\}, S1)$	
$(\{\mathcal{BA}, \mathcal{AC}\}, S1)$	$\{a, b, c\}$	$\{a, b, c\}$	$(\{\mathcal{BC}\}, S2), (S, \{\mathcal{AA}\})$	
$(\{\mathcal{BC}\}, S2)$	$\{b, c\}$	$\{b, c\}$	$(\{\mathcal{AC}\}, S1), (\{\mathcal{BA}\}.S1)$	
$(\{\mathcal{AC}\}, S1)$	$\{a, c\}$	$\{a, b, c\}$	—mismatch—	$(\{\mathcal{BA}\}, S1)$

So we would have been correct to deny the refinement, but not at the point we first suspected; it is only after both *b* and *c* have been available at the same time that we can tell that whichever just happened cannot immediately happen again.

For the traces model, it is sufficient to look only at the initial events of each component of a state pair. In the failures model, if the implementation state is stable (has no τ-arcs) then, in addition, the visible events it cannot do must be contained within a refusal of the specification state. Thus $(S1, \mathcal{BA})$ in our original example would be a cause for complaint in this model: the implementation refuses c, while the specification cannot. When we come to explore more complex machines than simple LTSs on the right-hand side of a refinement, this condition must be generalized to any maximal refusal of the implementation being contained within a maximal refusal of the specification.

In the failures-divergences model, we first check whether either state is divergent for its process. If the specification node is, then since $\mathsf{div} \sqsubseteq P$ for any process P, we can, in fact, take a short-cut in the check at this point and ignore any part of the state-space reachable only through such nodes. But if the specification is not divergent at this point and the implementation is, then this is an unwanted livelock that needs to be reported. We will discuss the counterexamples further below, in Section 4.4.

Rather than code separate checking procedures for each of the three models, FDR instead makes the processes tell white lies about their behaviour in order effectively to change the model, by applying a wrapper to the objects that implement them. For the failures model, any enquiry whether a state of the process is divergent is answered in the negative; for the traces model, every set of maximal refusals (or minimal acceptances) is empty. Careful use of this mechanism means that none of the algorithms in the tool that manipulate process representations need be aware in the context of which model they are being exercised.

4.3 Exploiting compositional structure

The classic problem in analyzing the behaviour of concurrent systems is the way the states of component processes combine to form the state of the whole. The best general bound on the number of states in the parallel composition of an M-state process with an N-state process is $M \times N$, although this is not always achieved: the requirement for synchronization may make parts of the component state-spaces unreachable, and synchronization may also impose a large degree of correlation between their states. Nonetheless, systems that we want to analyze, including those arising in the present context, tend to be large; to the extent that keeping track of the visited states is the principal limiting factor on the complexity of problem that can be tackled.

If storing the states is a problem, then storing the transition relation as an explicit GLTS is unthinkable: its size would be, in general, quadratic in the number of states and multiplied by a factor reflecting the size of the alphabet; in the worst case, complex nondeterminism can require an exponential number of minimal acceptances. Worse, the exploration strategy described above requires reasonably efficient random access to the operational semantics, which precludes the storage-friendly tricks used for state-pair storage.

The solution is to take advantage of the structure of the composition that gave rise to the complexity in the first place, in order to generate the full transition relation 'on-the-fly,' as and when required. The existence of this structure also enables a number of other techniques for combating the combinatorial explosion, both representational and algorithmic.

The basic idea is very simple: rather than calculate the transition relation for the whole system at one go, use the rules governing the operational semantics of the various language constructs to infer the behaviour local to a particular configuration of the system when needed. In practice, a compromise approach is used: calculate it for simple subcomponents, and remember how these are to be combined to give the overall behaviour.

This is precisely what the output of the CSP_M compiler is: when the user asks FDR to check an assertion its first task is to obtain such a representation for the process terms involved. The script describing the problem has already been loaded and parsed, and the compiler is ready to handle requests for the operational semantics of a process term. On receiving such a request, it calculates[8] an LTS for any recursive subprocess – during this it reports in the status window the number of transitions added or the terms under consideration, according to option settings – and constructs a tree reflecting the operators by which they are combined, suitably parametrized by synchronization sets, renaming relations, and the like, with references to the LTSs at the leaves. (Early versions of FDR imposed a strict division between low-level constructs – basically sequential, which were flattened into an LTS – and high-level ones – parallel, hiding and renaming, which went into the tree – but the modern compiler determines from context when it is desirable to shift an operator from one role to the other, so the sequential composition of two parallels will generally be represented in the tree.) This is the raw material on which the refinement engine operates.

It is possible to use this representation directly, with states represented by structures dictated by the shape of the operator tree and their place in any high-level sequential constructs. To determine what the possible initial events or the minimal acceptances are for such a state, the same question is asked, recursively, of the component states of the immediate subprocesses and an encoding of the operational semantic rule for the appropriate operator is applied to combine the results. To determine the successor states after a given event, a similar recursive calculation is required, with the added complication that it may correspond to a different event or a set of events in the subprocess, if renaming or hiding is involved.

The disadvantage of this approach is that essentially the same combination of operations is applied repeatedly, while the decomposition and recombination of substates carries its own costs, to the extent that the inefficiency of simply running the machine has a significant impact on overall performance. To combat this, FDR by default applies a procedure called *supercompilation*, which flattens the tree of natural-deduction inferences in the structured operational semantics into a single super-rule for each way that each 'shape' of structured state can evolve. This allows

---

[8] Incrementally; where a process evolves into or depends on one that has already been compiled, the earlier work is re-used.

a state to be represented by a configuration number[9] and a vector of leaf-process states. The effect of each leaf process on the overall behaviour can be tabulated. For each leaf we generate a bit-mask for each state which records (as zeros) which of the ways the full process can possibly perform an event is inhibited by this leaf being in that state (i.e. where the leaf has to be an active participant and this state cannot perform the requisite component action). Now calculating the initial events of a state in the full process can be accomplished by a simple bit-wise conjunction of the masks corresponding to its component leaves, resulting in greatly improved performance. The calculation of minimal acceptances requires the exact same inference from the leaf minimal acceptances (another reason to prefer them to maximal refusals!). Each way in which an event can occur yields a set of successors, formed by the cross-product of, on the one hand, the sets of successors of each leaf actively involved in that rule after its component action and, on the other, singleton sets of the (stationary) states of the leaves not involved. The complete set of successors after an event is the union of these products across all rules giving rise to it. In practice, it is not necessary to form the set of all successors as a whole; it suffices to hand them off to the explorer as they are calculated.

This representation is quite efficient and very general, but it is not as good as the explicit tabulation of an LTS when that is sufficiently small to be tractable. This is particularly the case where complex renamings may result in a large number of different ways of an event arising (and these multiply, too, under parallel composition), giving rise to very wide bit-masks; or where a large number of components synchronize to a small number of states (if $P(i) = c.0 \rightarrow d.0 \rightarrow P(i) \,\square\, c.i \rightarrow d.i \rightarrow P(i)$, then the fully synchronized composition $\left\|\right._{i=0}^{999} P(i)$ is equal to $P(0)$, but it takes a thousand bits to represent each state of the supercompiled machine, not one).

The user can direct the system to tabulate a particular subprocess[10] by declaring a *transparent* (semantics preserving) function *explicate* in the script and applying it where desired. The compiler leaves such calls in the operator tree, and as the refinement engine receives its output it applies a function that calculates a tabulation of the argument process, which is used in place of the argument in subsequent operations. The argument to be tabulated is itself supercompiled, so we get the best of both worlds.

This change of representation is an example of a more general form of manipulation of the process tree, but it is somewhat different from most of the other examples in that its result has exactly the same number of states as its argument. In most cases, one expects the result of applying such a *transparent* function to have the same denotational behaviour, but a representation with fewer states; for this reason they are usually called *compression* operators.

---

[9] If there are more than one; the classic high-low dichotomy yields systems with a single 'shape' and this component is optimized away.

[10] It can rarely if ever be sensible to apply this procedure at the top level, since it will usually require as much work and storage, or more, to do the tabulation as to operate on the original representation.

Commonly used examples of such functions are strong bisimulation (*sbisim*), the same normalization as is applied to specifications (*normal*), and a manipulation (*diamond*) that has a similar effect in eliminating τ-transitions but is guaranteed not to expand the state space (unlike *normal*, which in pathological circumstances can actually increase the number of states exponentially). Further details of the algorithms involved can be found in [76].

Strong bisimulation is, in fact, routinely applied to each LTS at the leaf of an operator tree, unless the appropriate option is deselected. This does not prevent further compressions being applied to larger subtrees of the process composition; indeed, the compressions may be applied hierarchically and, as the operator tree is in fact a graph respecting shared subterms in the original process, more or less arbitrarily complex descriptions of simple processes can, in favourable circumstances, be reduced to tractable forms [79].

We remarked earlier that it is only in exceptional circumstances that it can pay to apply a compression to the whole process; it is sometimes undesirable even to calculate all of its result on a subprocess, if its context means that a substantial part of that space is unreachable. In some circumstances, it is unavoidable: strong bisimulation, for example, needs to know the entire transition graph in order to decide whether to distinguish two nodes that are n-step similar (in a graph of diameter $n+1$). There are, however, some operators that can be calculated lazily; rather than calculating a tabulated machine which is referred to by a pruned operator tree, they insert a recipe that builds up the table gradually, as entries are demanded. This has the disadvantage that the bit-masks for the supercompiled machine cannot be precomputed, and that the size of the subcomponent (and so the number of bits to reserve for it in the vector representation) is not known in advance; but in the right situation the benefits more than outweigh these problems.

A classic example is the specification that a given set of events must have occurred before another particular event. This has the unfortunate property that it has an (irreducible) number of states exponential in the size of the set it is looking for. If this set is even moderately large, then both compilation and normalization become infeasible, by the obvious routes. The compilation problem can be solved by well-known techniques, recasting the process as a parallel composition of recognizers for each element of the set followed by (and synchronized on) the target event, but allowing FDR to use its usual normalization strategy will still typically exceed resources. The solution is to apply the *lazynorm* 'compression' to produce the annotated determinized transition system that the first phase of *normal* (before the strong bisimulation) generates, on demand. (The resulting state machine is marked by its place in the class hierarchy as being in prenormal form in this way; so FDR 'knows' not to normalize it any further.) We may expect the implementation to be restricted as to the order in which it can perform the guarding events; in this case, since the state of the specification is a function of the trace performed, if the implementation can be handled at all then only a relatively small part of the specification need be explored.

There is another operator that uses similar lazy explication of a transformed state machine: *chase*, which resolves and collapses sequences of internal events. Unlike the other functions, which preserve the denotational value of their argument (which is why they are called 'transparent'), this *external* function may not; in general, its result may be a strict refinement of its argument. In some circumstances (for instance, when its argument is denotationally deterministic and so is maximal in the refinement order) this is not possible, and *chase* can be used in the same way as other compressions, often to dramatic effect. We will see more of this operator when we come to implement the model of the intruder (Section 6.2).

4.4 Counterexamples

When the exploration encounters a pair of states that are not compatible in the model of the check, this is a witness that the refinement does not hold. It remains to cast this into a counterexample that is informative to the user.

The first step is to determine how we got to this point. Each pair is stored with a reference to the pair (or the first of possibly many) from which it was reached during the exploration. Thus it is possible to build up (backwards) a path through the plies of the breadth-first search leading from the initial pair of start states up to the witness. Because this steps forward a ply at a time, it is guaranteed to be minimal in length among such paths, leading to a counterexample with no unnecessary noise.

The path of states is not itself presentable as the counterexample; in general, states have no designation that the user would recognize. But we know that they arise through a possible evolution of the two processes, synchronizing on all visible events. We can always find an explanation for the next state pair: a visible event that allows each machine to make its corresponding transition, or a τ-transition that moves one forward while the other remains stationary. (Because of the normalization of the specification, τ-transitions invariably belong to the implementation side.) This augmented trace (in $(\Sigma \cup \{\tau\})^*$) is enough to tell the user the trace that is part of the denotational behaviour present in the implementation but not the specification. The other part depends on the type of mismatch detected.

If the initials of the implementation state are not contained within those of the specification, a trace is all that is required: all but its last element is the possible evolution of both processes just described, but an additional event, taken from the difference, is appended to give the illicit trace it performs. If the implementation is too nondeterministic, it has a minimal acceptance that does not wholly include any of those of the specification; the complement of this, paired with the trace, is an unwanted refusal. If the implementation diverges while the specification does not, then the trace is an unwanted divergence, on its own. The FDR debugger is able to present each of these kinds of counterexample. An example of a trace possible for the implementation S but not the specification $AB \ ||| \ AC$, provided by the debugger, is $\langle a, a, c, c \rangle$.

These top-level behaviours may be enough to diagnose the problem (or to extract the solution, in puzzle mode); but it often helps to be able to examine the contribution of the component processes. To this end the debugger also offers a folding view on to a tree of subprocesses: in fact, the very operator tree that the compiler produces prior to supercompilation. Clicking on a node in this tree displays a projection of the top-level behaviour on to that subprocess.

This projection is not always trivial: in passing through renaming or hiding the events may change (but not their number or relative position; this is a reason for leaving the τs visible in the debugger traces). There are also three new kinds of behaviour that need to be presented. It is possible that a subprocess plays no part at all in the unwanted evolution: the right-hand-side of a sequential composition whose left-hand-side misbehaves, for example. (This non-behaviour is also what appears at top level if a successful check is debugged.) Alternatively, a subprocess may not actively contribute to the unwanted feature at the end of the trace, yet still be complicit in arriving at that state; this too is simply a trace, which the process allows. Finally, if the implementation diverges there is a loop of τ-transitions; this typically corresponds to a repeated sequence of hidden events that become visible – and reported – when we look inside the hiding operator.

The situation becomes more complicated when there are compressions involved. These do not appear explicitly in the debugger's view of the operator tree; rather the node corresponding to the argument is coloured red and does not automatically unfold when the *unfold-all* action is invoked. This is because there is potentially a significant amount of work involved in finding a behaviour of the uncompressed machine that corresponds to the compressed behaviour to hand: there are typically changes in representation to cope with, a many-one relationship between uncompressed and compressed states, and possibly a number of intermediate states that the compression had eliminated to reinvent. Fortunately, these problems are not insurmountable, and some compressions admit a clever inversion; in the worst case, we can frame a specification for the uncompressed machine to which the behaviour we are looking for is the only minimal counterexample, and run a subsidiary refinement check.

FDR allows the user to request multiple counterexamples to an assertion, but care must be taken to avoid confusion as what it does and does not find as additional cases. The request is passed to the refinement engine, which accumulates a counterexample behaviour for each noncompliant state-pair it encounters, while not attempting to search downstream of such pairs. This means that it will not report multiple traces leading to essentially the same discrepancy and will not discover errors masked by preceding ones: $Stop \sqsubseteq a \rightarrow Stop \,\square\, b \rightarrow Stop$ generates only one counterexample, as does $a \rightarrow Stop \sqsubseteq b \rightarrow Stop \,\square\, a \rightarrow b \rightarrow Stop$.

5 Casper

In previous chapters we have seen how to produce CSP descriptions of security protocols, and how to analyze them using FDR. However, producing the CSP by hand is a rather time-consuming and error-prone process. We have therefore produced a compiler, called Casper, to help produce the CSP description. The user produces an input script – typically only about one page long – describing the protocol, in an abstract notation similar to that used to describe protocols earlier; Casper compiles this into CSP code, suitable for checking using FDR.

In this chapter, we give an overview of Casper, and how to use it to model protocols and different protocol features. The intricacies of the FDR encoding will be discussed in more detail in Chapter 6.

The reader is recommended to download a copy of Casper, and to experiment with it while reading this chapter. Casper is available from the book's website, as are all the Casper scripts that appear in this chapter.

5.1 An example input file

In this section, we give a gentle introduction to the Casper syntax by explaining an example input script, and showing how to use Casper to compile the script into CSP, and then interpret the output from FDR.

Overview of input file

As we have seen in Chapter 4, FDR operates by explicitly enumerating and then exploring the state space of the system in question, and so this method can only be used to check a *particular* (typically fairly small) system running the protocol, for example, with a single initiator and a single responder, rather than being able to check an *arbitrary* system with an arbitrary number of initiators and responders; similarly, FDR can only deal with systems where the underlying atomic datatypes – for example, the types of nonces or keys – are themselves finite. For these reasons, the Casper input file must define not only the operation of the protocol, but also the particular system to be checked. Therefore, the input file contains two distinct parts:

- A definition of the way in which the protocol operates, describing the messages passed between the agents, the tests performed by the agents, the types of the data items used, the initial knowledge of the agents, a specification of what the protocol is supposed to achieve, and a definition of any algebraic equivalences over the types used.

■ A definition of the actual system to be checked, defining the agents taking part in the actual system and the roles they play, the actual datatypes to be used, and the intruder's abilities.

The first part can be thought of as a function that returns a model of a system running the protocol; the second part can then be thought of as defining a particular image of that function, by instantiating the parameters of the protocol.

We will illustrate how one produces a Casper description of a protocol by considering the following example protocol, a slight adaptation of the Yahalom protocol:

$$\text{Message 1} \quad a \rightarrow b \ : \ n_a$$
$$\text{Message 2} \quad b \rightarrow s \ : \ \{a.n_a.n_b\}_{ServerKey(b)}$$
$$\text{Message 3}a \quad s \rightarrow a \ : \ \{b.k_{ab}.n_a.n_b\}_{ServerKey(a)}$$
$$\text{Message 3}b \quad s \rightarrow b \ : \ \{a.k_{ab}\}_{ServerKey(b)}$$
$$\text{Message 4} \quad a \rightarrow b \ : \ \{n_b\}_{k_{ab}}$$

User b's key delivery message is sent directly to him, rather than being forwarded via a as in the original Yahalom protocol; we will consider the standard version of the protocol in the next section, but this adaptation will simplify our explanation.

Casper scripts are split into a number of sections; each section is headed by a line beginning with #. Comments may be added to the file by beginning the relevant lines with --. Any logical line may be split across two or more physical lines by preceding any non-logical linebreak by a backslash (\).

Defining the protocol

The protocol description

The protocol description section of a Casper script describes the sequence of messages making up a protocol run. The entire Casper input script and output CSP is included in Appendix B. Here is that section for the version of the Yahalom protocol, above:

```
#Protocol description
0.    -> a : b
1. a -> b : na
2. b -> s : {a, na, nb}{ServerKey(b)}
3a. s -> a : {b, kab, na, nb}{ServerKey(a)}
3b. s -> b : {a, kab}{ServerKey(b)}
4. a -> b : {nb}{kab}
```

Each step of the protocol is defined using an ASCII representation of the normal notation. We write {m}{k} for m encrypted with k, i.e. $\{m\}_k$.

The message 0 is included to start the protocol run, informing a of the identity of the agent b with whom he should run the protocol. One can think of this as a message from a user, or the environment, including *b*'s identity. The absence of a sender field in the above line represents that this message is sent by the environment. We assume that such messages cannot be overheard by the intruder; neither can they be faked.

Free variables

The types of the variables and functions that are used in the protocol definition are defined under the heading '#Free variables'; for the example protocol, this definition takes the following form:

```
#Free variables
a, b : Agent
s : Server
na, nb : Nonce
kab : SessionKey
ServerKey : Agent -> ServerKeys
InverseKeys = (kab, kab), (ServerKey, ServerKey)
```

The first four lines simply declare the types of the free variables. When modelling a protocol in Casper, one can choose any names for the types – Casper has no notion of what a nonce is, for example; however, we will adopt standard names.

The fifth line declares the type of the function *ServerKey*, which takes an agent's identity, and returns a key of type *ServerKeys*.

The final line is a definition of which keys are inverses of one another. *kab* is its own inverse; and the function *ServerKey* returns keys that are self-inverse (i.e. *ServerKey*(*a*) is self-inverse, for every agent's identity *a*).

Processes

The #Processes section gives various information about the agents running in the protocol. The names of the CSP processes representing the agents are defined as below:

```
#Processes
INITIATOR(a,na) knows ServerKey(a)
RESPONDER(b,s,nb) knows ServerKey(b)
SERVER(s,kab) knows ServerKey
```

These lines have several tasks:

■ They give names to the roles played by the different agents (here *Initiator*, *Responder* and *Server*). These names are also used as the names of the CSP processes that represent the agents. In each case, the first argument represents the identity of the agent, as used in the protocol description. For example, the agent represented by *a* in the protocol description will be represented by a CSP process *Initiator*(*a*, *na*), in the style described in Chapter 2.

■ The parameters in parentheses, and the variables following the keyword 'knows', define the knowledge that the agent in question is expected to have at the beginning of the protocol run. For example, the initiator a is expected to know his own identity a, the nonce na, and the key $ServerKey(a)$ that he shares with the server. Similarly, the server s knows the key function $ServerKey$, which means he can obtain all the server keys (in an implementation, he would probably look up the keys in some table).

This information is used to check that the protocol definition is feasible, in the sense that agents only send messages that they could be expected to create and only receive messages that they can decrypt (we make this precise below).

■ Later (under the #System heading, below) we will define a system by instantiating the parenthesized parameters with actual values, so as to define the data values that each agent should use in their runs. Thus the parenthesized parameters should be ones that can be instantiated in this way, whereas those parameters in the 'knows' list will be ones for which the same value (possibly depending on the identity of the agent) will be used in every run.

For example, suppose we define a system with a particular initiator Anne performing several runs: that is, the system contains several instances of the *Initiator* process, with the variable a instantiated with the value *Anne*. Then we would expect that Anne would use different nonces in each run: that is na would be instantiated with different values in each run. On the other hand, the data item $ServerKey(a)$ does not appear as a parameter, because we would expect the same value to be used in every run ($ServerKey(a)$, depending upon the identity a).

Whenever an agent sends a message, it should be the case that the agent knows the recipient's identity and possesses all the components necessary to produce it; for example, b is able to send message 2 because he knows a and na (learnt from message 1), s and nb (from his parameter list), and $ServerKey(b)$ (from his 'knows' list). Similarly, if it is the intention that an agent should decrypt an encrypted component that he receives, then he should possess the decrypting key; for example, b is able to decrypt message 4, because he has learnt the key kab from message 3b. (We consider the case where an agent is not expected to be able to decrypt a message he receives in the next section.)

An agent will accept a message he receives if all fields represented by variables already in the agent's knowledge contain the expected values; for example, in message 3a above, a will accept any values for kab and nb, but will only accept the values for b and na that match the values in his current state (that is, the same values that a sent in message 1), and will only accept a message that is encrypted with $ServerKey(a)$ (the key he shares with the server).

Specifications

The '#Specification' section is used to specify the requirements of the protocol. There are two sorts of specifications dealt with by Casper: secrecy and authentication. Specifications may be declared as below:

```
#Specification
Secret(a, kab, [b,s])
Secret(b, kab, [a,s])
Agreement(b, a, [na,nb])
Agreement(a, b, [kab])
```

The lines starting `Secret` specify that certain data items should be secret. The first secret specification above may be paraphrased as: '*a* thinks that *kab* is a secret that can be known to only himself, *b* and *s*'. Of course, if *b* or *s* happens to be the intruder then there is nothing to prevent him passing the secret on to others. However, this line will cause a CSP specification to be generated with the meaning: if *a* completes a run of the protocol, apparently with *b* and *s*, and *b* and *s* are not the intruder, then the intruder will never learn the value of *kab*.

This is the secrecy specification $Secret_{a,b}$ given in Section 3.2 of Chapter 3, with the *Claim_Secret* signal inserted at the end of the protocol run.   It is also possible to make strong secret specifications, for example writing `StrongSecret(a,kab,[b,s])`. The specification $Secret_{a,b}$ is used in both cases, but for strong secrecy Casper places the *Claim_Secret* signal earlier in the run, yielding a stronger requirement on the protocol.

The lines starting `Agreement` are agreement authentication specifications; the first one specifies that *b* is authenticated to *a* in the following (injective) sense:

> If *a* completes a run of the protocol, apparently with *b*, then *b* has been running the protocol, apparently with *a*; further, the two agents agree upon the roles each took and upon the values of the nonces *na* and *nb*; and there is a one-one relationship between such runs of *a* and those of *b*.

As we have observed, in this particular protocol *a* cannot be assured that *b* agrees upon the value of the key *k*, or even that *b* received a key, because *b* does not send any message after receiving the key in message 3b. If one were to include a specification line

```
Agreement(b, a, [kab])
```

in the script, then Casper would detect, by static analysis, that there is no way this specification could be met, and would report this fact.

The system definition

The second part of the input file deals with the actual system to be checked.

Type definitions

The datatypes used in the actual system to be checked are defined in a similar way to the types of the free variables, for example:

```
#Actual variables
Anne, Bob, Yves : Agent
Jeeves : Server
Kab : SessionKey
Na, Nb : Nonce
InverseKeys = (Kab, Kab)
```

Thus we will be dealing with a system with three agents (*Yves* will be the intruder), one server, two nonces, and one session key. The session key is declared to be self inverse. The server keys of these agents are defined in the #Functions section, as below.

Functions

Any functions used by the agents in the protocol description, and declared in the free variables section, have to be defined under the #Functions heading:

```
#Functions
symbolic ServerKey
```

The above defines the function *ServerKey* to be *symbolic*: this means that Casper produces its own values to represent the results of function applications.

It is also possible to give explicit definitions of functions, but this technique is now largely deprecated.

The system

The most important part of the system definition covers which agents should be present in the system to be checked. This is done by listing the agents, with the parameters suitably instantiated, as follows:

```
#System
INITIATOR(Anne, Na)
RESPONDER(Bob, Jeeves, Nb)
SERVER(Jeeves, Kab)
```

Here we consider a system with a single initiator, Anne (taking the role of *a* in the protocol description), a single responder, Bob, and a single server, Jeeves, who can each run the protocol once. Anne uses nonce *Na* (taking the place of *na* in the protocol description); Bob uses Jeeves as the server, and uses nonce *Nb*; Jeeves uses key *Kab*. The types of the parameters of the processes should match the types of the parameters of the corresponding processes defined under the #Processes heading.

The intruder

Finally, the operation of the intruder is specified by giving his identity, and the set of data values that he knows initially:

```
#Intruder Information
Intruder = Yves
IntruderKnowledge = {Anne, Bob, Yves, Jeeves, ServerKey(Yves)}
```

The above defines the intruder's identity to be *Yves*, and defines that the intruder initially knows all the agents' identities, and his own key *ServerKey(Yves)*.

Using Casper

For details about obtaining Casper, see the notes at the end of this chapter.

Casper is written in the functional programming language Haskell. It is distributed with a shell script that starts up the Haskell interpreter and loads in the Casper files. If the input script is stored in a file Yahalom.spl, typing

```
compile "Yahalom"
```

at the prompt will cause Casper to read in the file, check it, and if correct write the CSP description of the system to the file Yahalom.csp. This CSP script can then be checked using FDR; in this case FDR finds no attack.

Consider, now, the following adaptation of the Yahalom protocol discussed in [20]:

$$
\begin{aligned}
\text{Message 1} \quad & a \rightarrow b \ : \ n_a \\
\text{Message 2} \quad & b \rightarrow s \ : \ n_b.\{a.n_a\}_{ServerKey(b)} \\
\text{Message 3}a \quad & s \rightarrow a \ : \ n_b.\{b.k_{ab}.n_a\}_{ServerKey(a)} \\
\text{Message 3}b \quad & s \rightarrow b \ : \ \{a.k_{ab}.n_b\}_{ServerKey(b)} \\
\text{Message 4} \quad & a \rightarrow b \ : \ \{n_b\}_{k_{ab}}
\end{aligned}
$$

where we have again redirected some messages, so that *s* sends the key delivery message direct to *b*. In this version, n_b is sent in the clear in the second message, and is returned to *b* once it has been encrypted by *S*. This protocol can be modelled by changing the #Protocol description section of the script to:

```
#Protocol description
0.      -> a : b
1.   a -> b : na
2.   b -> s : nb, {a, na}{ServerKey(b)}
3a.  s -> a : nb, {b, kab, na}{ServerKey(a)}
3b.  s -> b : {a, kab, nb}{ServerKey(b)}
4.   a -> b : {nb}{kab}
```

Note that this is the only change necessary to model the new protocol.

If we model a system with a single initiator Anne and a single responder Bob, then no attack is found. However, if we change the #System section to the following:

```
#System
INITIATOR(Anne, Na1)
RESPONDER(Anne, Jeeves, Na2)
SERVER(Jeeves, Kab)
```

so that Anne can run the protocol as both initiator and responder, then FDR finds an
attack, showing that the responder Bob is not correctly authenticated to the initiator
Anne. At the top level of the system definition, only those events necessary to capture
the specification are included. To obtain the actual sequence of messages performed,
the FDR debugger should be used to descend two levels, as discussed in Chapter 6,
where the following trace is found:

```
env.Anne.(Env0,Bob,<>)
send.Anne.Bob.(Msg1,Na1,<>)
receive.Bob.Anne.(Msg1,Na1,<>)
send.Anne.Jeeves.
   (Msg2,Sq.<Na2,Encrypt.(ServerKey.Anne,<Bob,Na1>)>,<>)
receive.Anne.Jeeves.
   (Msg2,Sq.<Na1,Encrypt.(ServerKey.Anne,<Bob,Na1>)>,<>)
send.Jeeves.Bob.
   (Msg3a,Sq.<Na1,Encrypt.(ServerKey.Bob,<Anne,Kab,Na1>)>,<>)
send.Jeeves.Anne.
   (Msg3b,Encrypt.(ServerKey.Anne,<Bob,Kab,Na1>),<>)
receive.Jeeves.Anne.
   (Msg3a,Sq.<Na2,Encrypt.(ServerKey.Anne,<Bob,Kab,Na1>)>,<>)
send.Anne.Bob.(Msg4,Encrypt.(Kab,<Na2>),<Na1,Jeeves>)
```

To make the output from FDR easier to understand, Casper includes a function
interpret that takes the raw trace and converts it into the standard style for
describing attacks:

```
0.                -> Anne      : Bob
1.   Anne    ->  I_Bob     : Na1
1.   I_Bob   ->  Anne      : Na1
2.   Anne    ->  I_Jeeves  : Na2, {Bob, Na1}{ServerKey(Anne)}
2.  I_Anne   ->   Jeeves   : Na1, {Bob, Na1}{ServerKey(Anne)}
3a. Jeeves   ->  I_Bob     : Na1, {Anne, Kab, Na1}{ServerKey(Bob)}
3b. Jeeves   -> I_Anne     : {Bob, Kab, Na1}{ServerKey(Anne)}
3a. I_Jeeves ->  Anne      : Na2, {Bob, Kab, Na1}{ServerKey(Anne)}
4.   Anne    ->  I_Bob     : {Na2}{Kab}
```

The notation I_Bob on the right-hand side of the arrow (->) represents the intruder
intercepting a message intended for Bob; the notation I_Bob on the left-hand side
of the arrow represents the intruder faking a message, making it appear to come
from Bob. In this attack, the intruder uses the responder run of Anne to create an
appropriate message 2 to send to the server; the intruder then uses the message 3b
produced by the server in order to create a message 3a to send to the initiator run of
Anne, so as to make Anne falsely believe that she has completed a run with Bob.

5.2 The %-notation

It will often be the case that the sender and receiver of a message treat that message somewhat differently. For example, in many protocols an agent receives an encrypted message that it does not decrypt; instead the agent simply forwards the message to a third party. This is the case in the standard Yahalom protocol:

$$\text{Message 1} \quad a \rightarrow b \;:\; a.n_a$$
$$\text{Message 2} \quad b \rightarrow s \;:\; b.\{a.n_a.n_b\}_{ServerKey(b)}$$
$$\text{Message 3} \quad s \rightarrow a \;:\; \{b.k_{ab}.n_a.n_b\}_{ServerKey(a)}.\{a.k_{ab}\}_{ServerKey(b)}$$
$$\text{Message 4} \quad a \rightarrow b \;:\; \{a.k_{ab}\}_{ServerKey(b)}.\{n_b\}_{k_{ab}}$$

a does not decrypt the second component of message 3, but simply forwards it to b in message 4.

As a default, Casper treats agents receiving messages as if they are able to decrypt them (this helps to trap many user errors); hence when this is not possible we need some way of indicating to Casper that messages really are not intended to be decrypted: this is the role of the %-notation. We write $m\%v$, where m is a message and v is a variable, to denote that the recipient of the message should not attempt to decrypt the message m, but should instead store it in the variable v. Similarly, we write $v\%m$ to indicate that the sender should send the message stored in the variable v, but the recipient should expect a message of the form given by m.

For example, we would model the standard Yahalom protocol using a script with Protocol description section as follows (the rest of the script would be as in the previous section):

```
#Protocol description
0.      -> a : b
1.  a -> b : a, na
2.  b -> s : b,{a, na, nb}{ServerKey(b)}
3 . s -> a : {b, kab, na, nb}{ServerKey(a)}, \
               {a, kab}{ServerKey(b)} % v
4.  a -> b : v % {a, kab}{ServerKey(b)}, {nb}{kab}
```

(Recall that a backslash – as in message 3 – is used to split a single logical line across two physical lines.) a stores the second component of message 3 in the variable v and forwards it to b in message 4.

In an implementation, the agents would not be able to tell whether the message they receive is of the expected form, without some further information such as typing information. The Casper model of the agents therefore allows agents to be described so that they accept an arbitrary message of the expected type, or a special value Garbage representing a random sequence of bits invented by the intruder.

The %-notation and public keys

The %-notation can be used not only for the case where a message is simply forwarded without decryption, but, more generally, wherever the sender and receiver treat the message differently. For example, consider the seven-message version of the Needham-Schroeder-Lowe Public-Key protocol:

$$\text{Message 1} \quad a \rightarrow s \; : \; b$$
$$\text{Message 2} \quad s \rightarrow a \; : \; \{b.PK(b)\}_{SK(s)}$$
$$\text{Message 3} \quad a \rightarrow b \; : \; a.b.\{na.a\}_{PK(b)}$$
$$\text{Message 4} \quad b \rightarrow s \; : \; a$$
$$\text{Message 5} \quad s \rightarrow b \; : \; \{a.PK(a)\}_{SK(a)}$$
$$\text{Message 6} \quad b \rightarrow a \; : \; b.a.\{na.nb.b\}_{PK(a)}$$
$$\text{Message 7} \quad a \rightarrow b \; : \; a.b.\{nb\}_{PK(b)}$$

The purpose of message 2 is for a to obtain b's public key. However, writing $PK(b)$ in the protocol description is rather misleading: a should be willing to accept any key, call it pkb, in this message, and then use that key pkb for the rest of the protocol. We hope that the form of message 2 ensures that the key that a receives really is $PK(b)$, but this is something we need to check in our analysis; for example, this would not be the case if b's identity were removed from the encrypted component of this message.

The following Casper protocol description treats $PK(b)$ (and $PK(a)$) as required:

```
#Protocol description
0.      -> a : b
1.   a -> s : b
2.   s -> a : {b, PK(b) % pkb}{SK(s)}
3.   a -> b : {na, a}{pkb % PK(b)}
4.   b -> s : a
5.   s -> b : {a, PK(a) % pka}{SK(s)}
6.   b -> a : {na, nb, b}{pka % PK(a)}
7.   a -> b : {nb}{pkb % PK(b)}
```

The server s sends the correct value $PK(b)$ in message 2; a is willing to accept an arbitrary value pkb, which it uses in messages 3 and 7; b is only willing to accept messages 3 and 7 if they are indeed encrypted with $PK(b)$.

Tickets and key certificates

Some protocols are designed to establish a shared key that can be reused in subsequent exchanges; therefore one agent, say a, should end up with some evidence that it can send to the other agent, b, so as to re-establish the key; this evidence is known as a *ticket*.

For example, the Kehne-Langendörfer-Schönwälder protocol has two phases:

- an initial exchange between *a* and *b*, which establishes a ticket of the form $\{a.kab\}_{Private(b)}$ where *kab* is a session key, and *Private*(*b*) is a key known only to *b*;[1]

- a re-authentication phase, where the ticket is re-used to re-establish authentication.

The %-notation can be combined with environment messages to model an agent retrieving a ticket from wherever it is stored. For example, the re-authentication phase of the Kehne-Langendörfer-Schönwälder protocol can be modelled as follows:

```
#Protocol description
0.    -> a : b, Shared(a,b) % kab, \
              {a, Shared(a,b)}{Private(b)} % tickb
1.  a -> b : na, tickb % {a, kab}{Private(b)}
2.  b -> a : nb, {na}{kab}
3.  a -> b : {nb}{kab}
```

The agent *a* receives three things in message 0:

- the identity of the agent *b* with whom *a* will run the protocol, as normal;

- the key *kab* to be used in the exchange, which we model as the result of a function application *Shared*(*a*, *b*);

- a ticket of the form $\{a.Shared(a, b)\}_{Private(b)}$ which *a* stores in the variable *tickb*.

One can think of an environmental message such as this as representing an agent retrieving information from wherever it is stored.

Some protocols make use of a *public-key certificate*: an electronic certificate linking an agent with his public key, normally signed[2] by a trusted third party or a certification authority. A typical certificate might be of the form $\{a.PK(a).t\}_{CASK(ca)}$, where *CASK*(*ca*) is the private key of certification authority *ca*, and *t* is a timestamp giving the expiry date of the public key. Such key certificates can be handled similarly to tickets, for example, using an environment message of the form:

```
0. -> a : b, {a, PK(a), t}{CASK(ca)} % certA.
```

5.3 Case study: the Wide-Mouthed-Frog protocol

In this section we consider the example of the Wide-Mouthed-Frog protocol:

$$\text{Message 1} \quad a \to s \ : \ \{ts1.b.kab\}_{ServerKey(a)}$$
$$\text{Message 2} \quad s \to b \ : \ \{ts2.a.kab\}_{ServerKey(b)}$$

---

[1] In the original version of the protocol, the ticket included a timestamp, which we omit here for simplicity.
[2] Signatures and private keys are identified here.

Here the server shares keys *ServerKey*(*a*) and *ServerKey*(*b*) with *a* and *b*, respectively; the protocol aims to establish a session key *kab* between *a* and *b*, and to authenticate *a* to *b*. The agent *a* invents a session key and sends it to *s* along with a timestamp *ts*1; *s* then forwards the key to *b* along with a new timestamp *ts*2.

Timestamps are used so that agents receive evidence that the messages they receive were created recently. We note in passing that for this mechanism to work it is necessary for the different agents' clocks to be synchronized; each agent's clock has become critical to the security of the protocol.

By considering this protocol, we will explain how time can be modelled in Casper. We also introduce a couple of other features of the Casper syntax.

Further, we discuss the pragmatics of choosing the system to check. We will consider four different systems running the protocol. FDR finds that there is no attack upon the first system, but finds three different attacks on the other systems. Larger systems require considerably more time to check, so a pragmatic approach is to start with a small system, and work up, which is what we do here. The fourth system we check has, admittedly, been tailored slightly to enable a particular attack; however, the first three systems are examples of systems that one should always consider.

Modelling the protocol

Most of the modelling of the protocol is straightforward; we discuss a few points below.

```
#Free variables
a, b : Agent
s : Server
ServerKey : Agent -> ServerKeys
kab : SessionKey
ts1, ts2 : TimeStamp
InverseKeys = (ServerKey, ServerKey)
```

The distinguished type `TimeStamp` represents timestamps; most names of types in Casper scripts can be chosen by the user, but this is an exception.

Timestamps are modelled in Casper by natural numbers. The modelling of time in the CSP description follows the approach described in Section 1.6. In order to be as general as possible, we make no assumptions about the size of a time unit compared with the time taken to send a message: several messages may occur within the same time unit, or several time units may elapse between consecutive messages.

```
#Processes
INITIATOR(a,s,kab) knows ServerKey(a)
RESPONDER(b) knows ServerKey(b)
SERVER(s) knows ServerKey
```

```
#Protocol description
0.     -> a : b
1.  a -> s : {b, ts1, kab}{ServerKey(a)}
[ts1==now or ts1+1==now]
2.  s -> b : {a, ts2, kab}{ServerKey(b)}
[ts2==now or ts2+1==now]
```

We assume that when the agents in the Wide-Mouthed-Frog protocol receive a message, they check that the timestamps they receive are recent. Checks such as these are represented in Casper scripts by lines within square brackets; they are performed by the agent who receives the preceding message; if the check fails (evaluates to false), the agent aborts the run. In this particular case, the agents compare the timestamps they receive with the distinguished variable now, which represents the current time; they abort the run if the timestamp is more than one time unit old.

The specification we use is a timed version of the agreement specifications.

```
#Specification
TimedAgreement(a,b,2,[kab])
```

The specification is that if a responder b completes a run of the protocol, apparently with a, then a should have been running the protocol within the previous two time units; further, the two agents should agree on the value of kab, and there should be a one-one relationship between the runs of a and the runs of b. The tests performed on the timestamps each allow for a delay of one time unit, apparently making for a maximum possible delay of two time units.

In order for this specification to have any chance of holding, there needs to be a negligible delay between s checking message 1 and sending message 2; we will formalize this assumption below, where we will specify that each agent's run lasts for a negligible amount of time.

First system

We now consider the modelling of the system. There are many (in fact infinitely many) systems that one could model, but it is normally a good idea to start off by checking a small system, because more often than not this will uncover any attacks. We therefore consider a system with a single initiator, Anne, and a single responder, Bob, each of whom can run the protocol once; we take all the datatypes to be as small as possible, consistent with this system.

Most of the definition of the actual variables is straightforward; the only new feature here is how we model time:

```
#Actual variables
Anne, Bob, Yves : Agent
Jeeves : Server
Kab : SessionKey
```

```
TimeStamp = 0 .. 0
MaxRunTime = 0
```

The line 'TimeStamp = 0 .. 0' defines the set of timestamps used to be the singleton set $\{0\}$; choosing a small set like this will speed up the model checking, but risks missing attacks that require more time; we will consider a larger time domain later.

The line 'MaxRunTime = 0' means that the maximum time any agent spends running the protocol will be 0 time units; if any run lasts for longer than this time, then the agent involved will timeout and abort the run. Again, we choose a small value so as to speed up the model checking. One point to note is that if we chose a larger value, we would have to adapt the time parameter in the authentication specification, appropriately; if we did not include any limit on the running time, then no timed authentication specification would be satisfied.

The rest of the system definition is straightforward:

```
#System
INITIATOR(Anne, Jeeves, Kab)
RESPONDER(Bob)
SERVER(Jeeves)

#Functions
symbolic ServerKey

#Intruder Information
Intruder = Yves
IntruderKnowledge = {Anne, Bob, Yves, Jeeves, ServerKey(Yves)}
```

We implicitly assume that the intruder can produce all timestamps; they do not have to be included in the intruder's initial knowledge.

When the above file is compiled using Casper, FDR fails to find any attack upon the resulting small system.

Second system

We now consider a slightly different system, where the agent Anne can run the protocol once as initiator and once as responder, possibly concurrently. We suppose that Bob is absent, so doesn't run the protocol. Many protocols can be attacked when one agent is able to adopt both roles, so it is normally a good idea to consider a system such as this one:

```
#System
INITIATOR(Anne, Jeeves, Kab)
RESPONDER(Anne)
SERVER(Jeeves)
```

Note that this change to the system involves changing precisely one line of the input file.

When we check either system, FDR discovers that the protocol does not correctly authenticate the initiator Bob to responder Anne. Using the FDR debugger and the `interpret` function, we find that the attack takes the following form:

$$\text{Message } \alpha.1 \quad Anne \rightarrow Jeeves \ : \ \{Bob.0.Kab\}_{ServerKey(Anne)}$$
$$\text{Message } \beta.2 \quad I_{Jeeves} \rightarrow Anne \quad : \ \{Bob.0.Kab\}_{ServerKey(Anne)}$$

The intruder simply replays Anne's first message back at her, which she interprets as being message 2 of a run initiated by Bob. This attack can be prevented by including some directional information in the messages, so a message from *Anne* cannot be passed off as a message to her.

Third system

We will now consider a slightly different system, where the responder Bob can run the protocol twice, sequentially:

```
#System
INITIATOR(Anne, Jeeves, Kab)
RESPONDER(Bob) ; RESPONDER(Bob)
SERVER(Jeeves)
```

Again, many protocols can be attacked if an agent can run the protocol more than once; often the intruder can use information from the first run in order to fake a second run. In the above system the runs are sequential; one could similarly allow the runs to be concurrent, by writing the instances on different lines:

```
#System
INITIATOR(Anne, Jeeves, Kab)
RESPONDER(Bob)
RESPONDER(Bob)
SERVER(Jeeves)
```

The latter is more general than the former (i.e. any attack found by the former system will also be found by the latter system), but the state space of the latter will be larger, because there are more ways of interleaving the runs.

When we check either system, FDR tells us that Anne is not correctly authenticated. The debugger and `interpret` can be used to exhibit the following attack, which violates the injective authentication property:

$$\text{Message } \alpha.1 \quad Anne \rightarrow Jeeves \ : \ \{Bob.0.Kab\}_{ServerKey(Anne)}$$
$$\text{Message } \alpha.2 \quad Jeeves \rightarrow Bob \quad : \ \{Anne.0.Kab\}_{ServerKey(Bob)}$$
$$\text{Message } \beta.2 \quad I_{Jeeves} \rightarrow Bob \quad : \ \{Anne.0.Kab\}_{ServerKey(Bob)}$$

The problem is that Bob thinks he has completed two runs of the protocol, while Anne only wanted to perform a single run. The intruder simply replays the message from Jeeves to Bob, so that Bob thinks that Anne is trying to establish a second session.

Fourth system

We now seek an attack that breaks the two-time-unit limit, i.e. an attack where Bob completes a run more than two time units after the corresponding run of Anne. To do this, we clearly need to consider a larger time domain:

```
TimeStamp = 0 .. 3
```

We will consider a system where initiator Anne and responder Bob each run the protocol once, but where the server can run the protocol three times:

```
#System
INITIATOR(Anne, Jeeves, Kab)
RESPONDER(Bob)
SERVER(Jeeves) ; SERVER(Jeeves) ; SERVER(Jeeves)
```

When this system is checked, FDR finds that initiator Anne is not authenticated according to the above timed specification. Using the debugger and interpret, we can find that the attack takes the following form:

$$
\begin{aligned}
&\text{Message } \alpha.1 \quad Anne \rightarrow Jeeves \;:\; \{Bob.0.Kab\}_{ServerKey(Anne)} \\
&\text{Message } \alpha.2 \quad Jeeves \rightarrow I_{Bob} \quad\;:\; \{Anne.0.Kab\}_{ServerKey(Bob)} \\
&\qquad\qquad\qquad\qquad\qquad\qquad tock \\
&\text{Message } \beta.1 \quad I_{Bob} \rightarrow Jeeves \;:\; \{Anne.0.Kab\}_{ServerKey(Bob)} \\
&\text{Message } \beta.2 \quad Jeeves \rightarrow I_{Anne} \;:\; \{Bob.1.Kab\}_{ServerKey(Anne)} \\
&\qquad\qquad\qquad\qquad\qquad\qquad tock \\
&\text{Message } \gamma.1 \quad I_{Anne} \rightarrow Jeeves \;:\; \{Bob.1.Kab\}_{ServerKey(Anne)} \\
&\text{Message } \gamma.2 \quad Jeeves \rightarrow I_{Bob} \quad\;:\; \{Anne.2.Kab\}_{ServerKey(Bob)} \\
&\qquad\qquad\qquad\qquad\qquad\qquad tock \\
&\text{Message } \delta.1 \quad I_{Jeeves} \rightarrow Bob \quad\;:\; \{Anne.2.Kab\}_{ServerKey(Bob)}
\end{aligned}
$$

Each *tock* represents one unit of time passing. The intruder repeatedly replays instances of message 2 at the server, and has them interpreted as instances of message 1. The effect of this is that the timestamp is updated each time, and so remains recent enough to be accepted. Eventually, the intruder allows a message to reach Bob, but only after the two-time-unit limit has been passed. It should be obvious how the intruder could continue such an exchange for longer, so as to break a timed specification with a weaker time constraint. This attack could also be prevented by including directional information in the messages.

Discussion

We have considered several different systems running the protocol. More generally, when analyzing a protocol, the following scenarios are a reasonably complete list of the checks that are worth making:

- an initiator Anne, and a responder Bob;

- an initiator Anne, and a responder Anne;

- an initiator Anne, a responder Anne, and an initiator Bob;

- an initiator Anne, a responder Anne, and a responder Bob;

- an initiator Anne, and two responders Bob;

- two initiators Anne, and a responder Bob.

In each case the check is made with either one or two servers (subject to the limitations imposed by the hardware on which the checks are performed). Our experience is that these checks will find nearly all attacks.

5.4 Protocol specifications

Casper supports a number of different forms of specification for protocols, some of which we have seen before. The complete list is as follows:

- `Secret(A, s, [B₁, ... ,Bₙ])` specifies that in any completed run A can expect the value of the variable s to be a secret; $B_1, \ldots , B_n$ are the variables representing the roles with whom the secret is shared. This specification fails if A can complete a run, where none of the roles $B_1, \ldots , B_n$ is legitimately taken by the intruder, but the intruder learns the value A gives to s.

- `StrongSecret(A, s, [B₁, ... ,Bₙ])` is similar to `Secret(A, s, [B₁, ... ,Bₙ])`, except it also includes incomplete runs. Thus, this specification fails if A can take part in a run – complete or not – where none of the roles $B_1, \ldots , B_n$ is taken by the intruder, but the intruder learns the value A gives to s. This form of secrecy is appropriate when the secret is significant outside of the protocol.

These specifications are both similar in form to *Secret*$_{ab}$ of Chapter 3, though here a secret can be shared by more than two parties. Both of these properties require that if *signal.Claim_Secret.s* occurs then *leak.s* should not. The difference between them is that in the former the *Claim_Secret* signal occurs at the end of the protocol run, and in the latter it occurs at the start.

- `Agreement(A, B, [v₁, ... ,vₙ])` specifies that A is correctly authenticated to B, and the agents agree upon $v_1, \ldots , v_n$; more precisely, if B thinks he has successfully completed a run of the protocol with *A*, then *A* has previously been running the protocol, apparently with *B*, and both agents agreed as to which roles they took, and both agents agreed as to the values of the variables $v_1, \dots, v_n$, and there is a one-one relationship between the runs of *B* and the runs of *A*.

■ The specification NonInjectiveAgreement(A, B, [v₁, ... ,vₙ]) means that if *B* thinks he has successfully completed a run of the protocol with *A*, then *A* has previously been running the protocol, apparently with *B*, and both agents agreed as to which roles they took, and both agents agreed as to the values of the variables $v_1, \dots, v_n$. In this case several runs of *B* may correspond to the same run of *A*.

■ The specification WeakAgreement(A, B) means that if *B* thinks he has successfully completed a run of the protocol with *A*, then *A* has previously been running the protocol, apparently with *B*. Note that *A* and *B* may disagree as to which role each was taking.

■ The specification Aliveness(A, B) means that if *B* thinks he has successfully completed a run of the protocol with *A*, then *A* has previously been running the protocol. Note that *A* may have thought she was running the protocol with someone other than *B*.

■ The specification TimedAgreement(A, B, t, [v₁, ... ,vₙ]) is a timed version of Agreement(A, B, [v₁, ... ,vₙ]) where, in addition, *A*'s run was within the previous *t* time units of *B* completing his run; by contrast, the Agreement specification macro places no constraints on the amount of time between the runs.

■ Similarly, the specifications
TimedNonInjectiveAgreement(A, B, t, [v₁, ... ,vₙ]),
TimedWeakAgreement(A, B, t) and
TimedAliveness(A, B, t) are timed versions of
NonInjectiveAgreement(A, B, [v₁, ... ,vₙ]),
WeakAgreement(A, B) and Aliveness(A, B).

All of the authentication properties are concerned with the requirement that *Commit* signals should follow *Running* signals. The difference between them is the degree to which the information on the signals should agree. In the case of Agreement, there is also a required relationship between the number of occurrences of each of these signals. When time is introduced, relationships between the times on the signals are also incorporated into the properties.

We include several different forms of authentication specification because different protocols satisfy different specifications. When a protocol claims to provide authentication, it is not always clear precisely what is meant; by experimenting with these different specifications, it is possible to find out.

5.5 Hash functions and Vernam encryption

Hash functions can be used in a Casper script by declaring them as having the type
HashFunction in the #Free variables section. If f is declared in this way, then
$f(m)$ represents the application of f to message m. For example:

```
3.  a -> b : {f(nb)}{PK(b)}
```

In such cases, both the sender and the recipient should be able to create $f(m)$; the
recipient will only accept a value for this message if the value received matches the
value he calculates for himself. It is assumed that all hash functions are known to all
agents.

For example, consider the following, somewhat simplified, version of the
Needham-Schroeder Signature protocol:

$$\text{Message 1} \quad a \rightarrow b \; : \; m$$
$$\text{Message 2} \quad a \rightarrow s \; : \; b.\{f(m)\}_{ServerKey(a)}$$
$$\text{Message 3} \quad s \rightarrow b \; : \; \{a.f(m)\}_{ServerKey(b)}$$

a wants to transmit a message m to b in an authenticated manner; it sends a hash of
the message to server s, encrypted with a key shared between a and s (message 2); s
forwards the hash to b (message 3), thus acting as a key translation service.

The protocol can be modelled as follows:

```
#Protocol description
0.    -> a : b
1. a -> b : m
2. a -> s : b, {f(m) % v}{ServerKey(a)}
3. s -> b : {a, v % f(m)}{ServerKey(b)}
```

Note that s does not know m and so should be willing to accept any value
for $f(m)$; we use the %-notation to specify this. Note, though, that b will only accept
the expected value in message 3, namely the hash of the message he received in
message 1.

Recall from Chapter 0 that the Vernam encryption of two messages $m1$ and $m2$,
written $m1 \oplus m2$, is their bit-wise exclusive-or; it can be produced by an agent who
knows both $m1$ and $m2$; and an agent who sees this message and who knows $m1$ can
extract $m2$ (or vice versa).

In Casper, this Vernam encryption is written $m1$ (+) $m2$. The receiver of a message
containing a Vernam encryption should be able to create at least one of $m1$ and $m2$
so as to obtain the other.

For example, consider the TMN protocol:

$$\text{Message 1} \quad a \rightarrow s \; : \; b.\{ka\}_{pks}$$
$$\text{Message 2} \quad s \rightarrow b \; : \; a$$
$$\text{Message 3} \quad b \rightarrow s \; : \; a.\{kb\}_{pks}$$
$$\text{Message 4} \quad s \rightarrow a \; : \; ka \oplus kb$$

where *pks* is the public key of server *s*, *ka* and *kb* are session keys, and the intention is to establish a new session key *kb* shared between *a* and *b*. This protocol can be modelled using Casper as follows:

```
#Protocol description
0.      -> a : b
1.  a -> s : b, {ka}{pks}
2.  s -> b : a
3.  b -> s : a, {kb}{pks}
4.  s -> a : kb (+) ka
```

There are a number of attacks on this protocol with respect to different properties; the reader might like to use Casper and FDR to discover them, and then consider how they can be prevented.

5.6 Summary

This chapter has introduced the protocol compiler Casper, and shown how it can be used to model security protocols and produce scripts for analysis in FDR with respect to a variety of secrecy and authentication properties.

Casper, and all the scripts used in this chapter, can be obtained from this book's web page.

Casper was first described in [56] and in [58], although the Casper input language has evolved since those papers. A report on a number of case studies carried out using Casper and FDR appears in [26]. A recent extension to Casper, to include support for the data independence techniques discussed in Chapter 10, appears in [13].

The Kehne-Langendörfer-Schönwälder protocol of Section 5.2 first appeared in [46]; attacks upon this protocol have appeared in [43] and [55]. The Wide-Mouthed-Frog protocol of Section 5.3 was first described in [20], and the ping-pong attack from Section 5.3 was described by Anderson and Needham in [5]. The Needham-Schroeder Signature protocol of Section 5.5 first appeared in [68]. The TMN protocol of Section 5.5 is from [99]; an attack upon this protocol was first reported in [93]; this protocol was the subject of a case study using CSP and FDR – in which ten different attacks were found – in [61].

The different authentication specifications supported by Casper are discussed in more detail in [57].

6 Encoding protocols and intruders for FDR

We have seen in Chapter 5 how protocols are described to Casper, and in Chapter 2 we have given an abstract overview of how the systems described can be realized in CSP. This chapter examines the result of the translation in rather more detail, discusses some of the features of the implementation designed to achieve a model that can be explored in reasonable time, and looks at some alternative design choices.

Small excerpts from the result of translating the Yahalom protocol through Casper illustrate the text. The complete script that results can be found in Appendix B.

6.1 CSP from Casper

As we have seen in Chapter 2, it is reasonably straightforward to encode the trustworthy principals involved in an execution of a crypto-protocol. Leaving aside the intruder until Section 6.2, the more complicated issues arise in keeping the data involved both finite and manageably sized.

The recursive datatype *fact*[1] described in Chapter 2 is naturally infinite. FDR is quite happy to accept such definitions, and even channels that can carry any value of the type; but it does require that inputs be constrained to offer finite choices and equally that synchronization sets be finite. In practice, typically, both the time to explore the system and the fixed space needed to hold the representation of the transition system increase linearly with the number of events; the compilation time also increases. So it pays to minimize the size of these sets.

The datatype used by Casper draws from two sources: the constants introduced in the 'actual variables' section of the input script, which are particular to the protocol being studied; and a generic arsenal of constructions, which cover the range of protocol features supported by the tool. This may include constructions that are not used in the script in question, but it allows the supporting functions to be defined unconditionally and a large part of the CSP programming to be independent of the protocol. This not only simplifies the task for the implementor, but also reduces the potential for a coding error to manifest in one protocol model and not the others.

For the Yahalom protocol, the resulting definition is:

```
datatype Encryption =
  Anne | Bob | Yves | Jeeves | Na | Nb | Kab | Garbage |ServerKey.Agent|
  Sq.Seq(Encryption) | Encrypt.(ALL_KEYS,Seq(Encryption)) |
  Hash.(HashFunction, Seq(Encryption)) | Xor.(Encryption, Encryption)
```

---

[1] Casper calls this `Encryption`.

Here the first line is the protocol-specific values, the second the part of the generic framework relevant to the protocol (Garbage models all data that is recognizably not in any form, for example the result of decrypting with the wrong key), and the third line supports features not used in the protocol.

The Sq branch provides for compound messages, such as message 3 and message 4 in Yahalom, where there is no cryptographic glue holding the parts together. It is arguably redundant, since we could always recast the protocol with the parts of these messages sent separately, as discussed in Chapter 5:

$$\text{Message } 3a \quad s \rightarrow a \; : \; \{b.k_{ab}.n_a.n_b\}_{ServerKey(a)}$$
$$\text{Message } 3b \quad s \rightarrow b \; : \; \{a.k_{ab}\}_{ServerKey(b)}$$

and so on. This reduces the number of different messages that need be modelled (it becomes the sum, rather than the product, of the number of possible submessages that this message contributes to the total) at the expense of some extra states in the implementation of the agents due to the additional communication. This optimization could be implemented automatically, but the choice is currently left to the user.

The sets Agent, ALL_KEYS and HashFunction which appear in the definition are in fact subsets of the main type; again, the particular subset depends on the protocol. For Yahalom, we have:

```
Agent = {Anne, Bob, Yves}
ALL_KEYS = Union({SessionKey, ServerKeys})
SessionKey = {Kab}
ServerKeys = {ServerKey(arg_1) | arg_1 <- Agent}
HashFunction = {}
```

Other relevant subsets are also defined:

```
Server = {Jeeves}
Nonce = {Na, Nb}
```

This datatype provides the carrier set from which the payload of the messages between the principals is built. The set of message bodies that a trustworthy principal is willing to accept or can be persuaded to generate, under any circumstances, is quite constrained at each stage of the protocol. Even when some component of a message is opaque to its recipient, as in the second half of message 3, it is straightforward to establish that unless it is a value that some other participant may accept at some point, it may as well be Garbage.

Thus, for each message in the protocol, we can define the set of payloads it is worth considering in the analysis; and we might expect to declare the channels that the principals use for input and output to carry the union of these sets. There are two reasons why this is not precisely the case: one an implementation issue, and one a matter of design. First, for technical reasons, the CSP compiler requires that the (CSP) protocols on channels be 'rectangular'; that is, that the set it carries must be expressible as the Cartesian product (under the '.' constructor). One is not allowed to constrain correlation between dotted components in the channel declaration itself. The way in which this restriction is circumvented is to tuple together the body of a message with a tag describing to which message it belongs; such tuples are atomic from the point of view of the dotted construction.

This coding trick also simplifies capturing desired properties in the specifications. As well as the tag and the message payload, we can include a component reflecting the 'state of mind' of the participant: the believed identity of its correspondent, values of nonces and keys, and so on, as far as they are not immediately obvious from the message data itself. This information is not made available to the other players, but can be renamed to indicate beliefs of secrecy or commitments of the kind required by authentication specifications. The resulting set of triples is now suitable for forming the message bodies on the channels used by the models of the principals.

For Yahalom, this is also appropriate for the channels between components, but there is another layer of complexity required for some protocols, where values that are distinct in the free datatype need to be identified. This may either be to reflect the extra power the intruder acquires through being able to reinterpret combinations of data, or even to allow the protocol to work properly at all. A case in point is Diffie-Hellman key exchange, which relies on algebraic properties of exponentiation and multiplication to succeed: one participant uses $(g^a)^b$ as part of his key; the other $(g^b)^a$. The fact that these are equal is essential.

The user instructs Casper on the laws that need to be taken into account; the result is a set of equivalent pairs, axiomatizing the algebra. When equivalent values are compounded, equivalent composites arise; and equivalence is transitive. Extending the supplied atomic equivalences to the entire domain of interesting messages proved to be a bottleneck in early experiments, when expressed in the functional language of CSP_M. The solution is to push the manipulation of these equivalences into *external* operators – essentially new language primitives – of CSP_M. The operator *mtransclose* takes a set of pairs and a set of values, and returns the partitioning of the latter induced by the former, each component paired with a canonical representative (chosen by some undisclosed mechanism). The return value is conceptually used in a renaming comprehension, so that only the canonical representatives are used in global communications; in fact, this is mediated by functions defined in terms of the *external* operators *relational_image* and *reverse_relational_image* (which are carried, to take the relation and return a function mapping element to the sets they are related to). This accounts for the prevalence of the *rmb* function (for renaming message bodies) in the CSP output by Casper; but for Yahalom it is the trivial identity. We return to consider more examples of algebraic equivalence in Section 6.5.

6.2   Modelling the intruder: the perfect spy

Recall from Section 2.3 that we need to model a malicious intruder, bent on acquiring information that should be maintained secret among the agents, or on sowing confusion among them so as to undermine their trust in one another.

The intruder has two major tasks: information gathering, by overhearing or destructively capturing messages; and misinformation, by faking messages from data in his possession. The only restriction we usually impose is that he should not be able to manipulate cryptographically protected message components without access to the appropriate keys. These two tasks have to be connected by an information repository, storing data items that have either been learnt directly, or are deduced (possibly recursively) by analysis or synthesis from knowledge gained earlier.

It is this component that makes the most substantial demand on state-space storage, since there are typically hundreds or thousands of potentially relevant 'facts' that must be recorded. The implementation of the function *close*, which takes a set of facts and returns all facts deducible from them, and even of the parameter to the *Intruder* process, which models the set of all its current knowledge, becomes a significant challenge.

Modelling issues

One of the perennial problems with model-checking approaches, especially those using primarily explicit state-exploration algorithms, is state-space growth. Earlier work sought to keep this within bounds by limiting the intruder's 'memory' to only a few data items, but even very tight limits typically left this as a limiting factor on the complexity of problem that could practically be addressed. Simple experiments verified the intuition that significant performance benefits could be gained by exploring only those possible behaviours of an intruder that are reachable given the specific history of values observed in a sequence of protocol runs, rather than compiling the whole of the intruder's possible behaviour. Indeed, exploiting such a 'lazy intruder' implemented as an extension to FDR allowed (and positively benefited from) relaxing the limitations on the intruder's memory.

An intellectually attractive decomposition might provide a two-state process for each possible 'fact', essentially representing the boolean value, whether it is available to the intruder or not. This would then need some mechanism added to implement the inferences. Our initial intuition was that this was perhaps beyond the point of sensible decomposition, but it has turned out to be the case that in most of the classes of example we are considering it is not only practical but highly desirable to decompose the system in this manner.

First, we can observe that there is no advantage to keeping track of all possible data items. Messages and their larger subcomponents that are constructed from simpler pieces of information essentially by catenation are known if and only if all the subcomponents are. This purely structural deduction can be encoded by making the communication of the compound message equivalent to the communication of all its atomic components (that is, plaintext atoms and all encrypted subcomponents). This generally reduces the number of facts that must be tracked to be the sum, rather than the product, of the size of the atomic types involved. This makes practical the following construction.

Given the set *Messages* of possibly interesting message payloads described above (essentially, those with the form of messages that are sent in the protocol, but not necessarily respecting any internal or external invariants), and a function *components*, mapping the elements of this set to their immediately accessible subcomponents, we can form the converse function, yielding all messages involving a given fact f:

```
messages(f) = { m | m <- Messages, member(f,components(m)) }
```

Similarly, given a set *Deductions* of *(conclusion,antecedents)* pairs that axiomatize the inference system, we can identify those yielding or requiring a given fact:

```
inferences(f)   = { (c,a) | (c,a) <- Deductions, f == c }
implications(f) = { (c,a) | (c,a) <- Deductions, member(f,a) }
```

Casper actually calculates all three of these sets and caches them as extra parameters of the processes below, for efficiency.

Essentially, the intruder's knowledge within a given domain (of, say, N facts) is represented by N two-state processes, called *Knows* and *Ignorant*, each of which represents a given fact that is known or unknown. Transitions from unknown to known are possible by one of two events for each fact f. One possibility is that the fact is a component in 'clear' of a message that can be overheard; the other that it is the consequent of an inference from other facts known to the intruder:

```
IGNORANT(f) =
  hear?_:messages(f) -> KNOWS(f)
  []
  infer?_:inferences(f) -> KNOWS(f)
```

Once a fact f is known, the process will permit further events representing any inferences that use f as an antecedent, as well as allowing messages containing f to be synthesized. In addition, if f has been said to be a secret, its disclosure can be signalled:

```
KNOWS(f) =
  hear?_:messages(f) -> KNOWS(f)
  []
  say?_:messages(f) -> KNOWS(f)
  []
  infer?_:implications(f) -> KNOWS(f)
  []
  member(f,ALL_SECRETS) & leak.f -> KNOWS(f)
```

The activity of an intruder performing deductions is thus represented by the occurrence of these *infer* events, and no additional process is required. The deductions thus make no additional contribution to the state space of the intruder. The two ways of learning the event are treated differently once it is known: the inference events naturally want to be concealed from the rest of the system, so if they could be repeated this would lead to the possibility of infinite chatter; in contrast, the *hear* events must not be inhibited, as further messages involving *f* can quite legitimately form part of the protocol. The requirement for non-repetition of *infer* events can be met by blocking those deductions that involve the conclusion among the antecedents of the axiom, which are in any case tautological.

Synchronizing parallel composition is used to combine these two-state processes in such a way that an inference event can only occur when all of its antecedents are known and its conclusion is not already known, and that hearing and saying compound messages involves the participation of all their components:

```
INTRUDER =
  ( || f : ATOMIC_FACTS @
     [ Union {
         { hear.m, say.m | m <- messages(f) },
         { infer.d | d <- diff(inferences(f),implications(f)) },
         { infer.d | d <- diff(implications(f),inferences(f)) },
         { leak.f | member(f,SECRETS) }
       }
     ]
       if member(f,INTRUDER_INITIAL_KNOWLEDGE)
         then KNOWS(f)
         else IGNORANT(f)
  ) \ {|infer|}
```

There is a further slight optimization possible by separating out the facts that are known at the start, since there is no point in working out what might allow them to be inferred; equally, they can be trimmed from the antecedents of all the other deductions. So the Casper implementation composes a process for each fact in the difference with a single *Say_Known* that acts like the composition of all the *Knows* for facts deducible from the intruder's initial knowledge.

Managing the deduction system

Although this structure of intruder model does have significant advantages, it does have a crucial practical drawback if implemented directly as described. Because of the way the CSP semantic models treat internal τ-actions, in order to establish the normal refinement properties of a protocol composed with an intruder it is necessary to consider all possible combinations of reachable states. For example, if two deductions may occur that do not depend on one another, there are four configurations of the intruder's memory that need to be tested, even though in our application the exact order of deductions will make no difference to the final outcome. This combinatorial explosion is clearly undesirable, and is made worse if the trustworthy principals can engage in some events without the co-operation of the intruder: each such event further increases the number of interleaved paths by which the intruder can complete the deductive process.

In the case of crypto-protocol analysis, however, intruders of the type described above have specific properties of which we may make use. Since the deduction system is, in semantic fact, deterministic despite the internal actions, we can use a kind of partial-order technique to optimize the exploration. Each state of the intruder has a unique final τ-successor; our approach to simplifying the exploration of systems containing an intruder is thus to consider not the parallel process described in the previous section, but the state machine that results from replacing any intruder state by its ultimate τ successor; and eliminate the internal actions of the intruder from our representation of the process altogether. In effect we evaluate the effect of internal actions of the intruder before considering the intruder's interaction with the environment. This eager evaluation of transitions out of a single state does not, of course, prevent our exploring the actual state space itself in a lazy fashion.

FDR provides a highly flexible interface for adding transformations on state machines, and the τ-removal scheme described above has been implemented using this facility. The resulting transformation is available as an external function *chase* in the FDR input language. As we remarked in the previous chapter, *chase* differs from the regular *transparent* compression functions, in that in general its result may be a strict refinement of its argument. When its argument is, as here, denotationally deterministic and so maximal in the refinement ordering, the resulting machine must indeed be denotationally equivalent, but its operational representation is dramatically smaller.

6.3 Wiring the network together

The legitimate principals of the system are coded so that all of their interactions with the rest of the system are programmed using channels *input* and *output*:

```
ALL_PRINCIPALS = Union({Agent, Server})

channel input  : ALL_PRINCIPALS.ALL_PRINCIPALS.INPUT_INT_MSG_BODY
channel output : ALL_PRINCIPALS.ALL_PRINCIPALS.OUTPUT_INT_MSG_BODY
```

The first index represents the purported sender of the message, and the second the intended receiver, and the data components are the union of the unfactored message-body tuples discussed above.

Rather than simply wire these channels point-to-point between the principals, the parallel composition of the system needs to allow for the potential actions of the intruder. This is mediated by two or three additional channels of the same type, *take* and *fake*:

```
channel take: ALL_PRINCIPALS.ALL_PRINCIPALS.OUTPUT_MSG_BODY
channel fake: ALL_PRINCIPALS.ALL_PRINCIPALS.INPUT_MSG_BODY
```

These carry the message bodies factored by equivalence, and a single renaming both brings the events into this network view and identifies equivalent values. Thus, for example, the initiator ends up being coded:

```
INITIATOR_0(a, na) =
  [] b : Agent @ env.a.(Env0, b,<>) ->
  output.a.b.(Msg1, na,<>) ->
  [] kab : SessionKey @ [] nb : Nonce @ [] s : Server @
    [] v : addGarbage({ Encrypt.(ServerKey(b), <a,kab>)
                        | a <- Agent, b <- Agent, kab <- SessionKey}) @
    input.s.a.(Msg3, Sq.<Encrypt.(ServerKey(a), <b,kab,na,nb>), v>,<>) ->
    output.a.b.(Msg4, Sq.<v, Encrypt.(kab, <nb>)>,<na, s>) ->
    SKIP

INITIATOR(a, na) =
  INITIATOR_0(a, na)
    [[input.s.a.m  <- fake.s.a.rmb(m) |
        s <- Server, m <- INPUT_INT_MSG3_BODY]]
    [[output.a.b.m <- take.a.b.rmb(m) |
        b <- Agent, m <- OUTPUT_INT_MSG1_BODY]]
    [[output.a.b.m <- take.a.b.rmb(m) |
        b <- Agent, m <- OUTPUT_INT_MSG4_BODY]]
```

The intruder's *hear* and *say* channels are also renamed to this network view:

```
INTRUDER_1 =
  chase(INTRUDER_0)
    [[hear.(second(m)) <- take.A.B.m |
        m <- OUTPUT_MSG_BODY, A <- SenderType(m), B <- ReceiverType(m)]]
    [[say.(second(m)) <- fake.A.B.m |
        m <- INPUT_MSG_BODY, A <- SenderType(m), B <- ReceiverType(m)]]
```

and, in the currently implemented solution, the interleaving of the legitimate agents is synchronized with the intruder, who also acts as the medium. That is, messages are correctly delivered by the accident of the intruder choosing to fake the same message he has just intercepted on the *take* channel. All the dastardly cunning possible to the intruder is captured by the simple expedient of exploring the effect of every random sequence of communications available to him by which he might try to inject a spanner into the works!

It is unproblematic to implement the alternative wiring scheme discussed at the end of Chapter 2, where the legitimate principals also have a direct connection. We would declare:

`channel comm: ALL_PRINCIPALS.ALL_PRINCIPALS.MSG_BODY`

and use renaming to present a choice of external event when a principal engages in an *input* or *output*.

At the intruder's end, *hear* events are renamed to give a choice between the *comm* between two principals (modelling simple overhearing) and the corresponding *take* event (modelling complete capture).[2] This requires more complex synchronizations,

---

[2] In both cases, we must take care that a legitimate principal is involved as the sender; otherwise the intruder could learn facts from overhearing himself!

along the lines of:

```
SYSTEM =
  INTRUDER_1 [[ take<-take, take<-comm ]]
  [| {| comm, take, fake |} |]
  || id : LEGITIMATE_PRINCIPALS
    [ {| comm.id, take.id, comm.a.id, fake.a.id |
          a <- ALL_PRINCIPALS |} ]
      AGENT(id) [[ take.id<-comm.id, take.id<-take.id,
                   fake.a.id<-comm.a.id, fake.a.id<-fake.a.id |
                   a <- ALL_PRINCIPALS ]]
```

The renaming of one event to several means that which happens is at the choice of the environment, while the process within the renaming has no way of telling which way this has been resolved. If we now hide the *comm*, *take* and *fake* channels, the choice becomes nondeterministic.

As well as the perhaps more natural presentation, with shorter counterexample traces, that this alternative offers there is also greater scope for modifying the potency of the intruder. It would be straightforward, for instance, to model an intruder without the power to prevent message delivery (which is certainly an unreasonably pessimistic assumption for some media); all we need do is block (top-level) *take* events, by making them synchronize with *Stop*. Equally, the direct connection is necessary if any analysis of liveness is desired: if the intruder is responsible for *all* delivery of messages, then it is hardly possible to preclude a denial-of-service attack!

The advantage of the scheme currently implemented is the greater simplicity of treatment of the 'extra' information in the third component of the message-body tuples, where the clear distinction between transmission and reception simplifies the recognition and signalling of significant milestones in the running of the protocol.

6.4 Example deduction system

Recall that *Messages* is the finite subset of the *Encryption* datatype that includes all the bodies of messages of the forms used in the protocol that are type-correct (have nonces in the right place, use keys as the key in encryptions, and so on). We can decompose these using the *components* function discussed above, to give the set *Fact* (of which the set *KnowableFact* over which we replicate the intruder's knowledge cells is a subset).

There are standard axioms concerning encryption that will apply whenever the relevant type of encryption is part of the protocol:

```
EncryptionDeductions =
  {(Encrypt.(k,fs), unknown(union({k}, set(fs)))) |
     Encrypt.(k,fs) <- Fact}
```

```
DecryptionDeductions =
  {(f, unknown({Encrypt.(k,fs), inverse(k)})) |
      Encrypt.(k,fs) <- Fact, f <- unknown(set(fs))}
```

These sets represent the ways in which the intruder can deduce new facts by performing encryptions and decryptions. They contain pairs of the form (f, S) to represent that f can be deduced from S, together with the intruder's initial knowledge. The function unknown_(T) simply removes the intruder's initial knowledge from T, to make the implementation more efficient. The function *inverse* returns the inverse of a key: for symmetric encryption, it is the identity function; for public-key encryption, it maps public keys to the corresponding private key, and vice versa. For many systems these will be all the deductions that we need to model.

CSP is not an appropriate vehicle either for describing encryption algorithms or for devising methods of deciphering coded messages. That involves a lot of sophisticated mathematics in number theory, algebra, etc. It is often the case that a use of encryption fails not because of vulnerability of the cipher in use, but because of the way it is used, which is the scenario we have been addressing so far. All too frequently it is possible to defeat protocols using and supporting encryption even under the assumption that the encryption method used is unbreakable. In other cases, however, the combination of weaknesses in the precise encryption method and the shape of messages in the protocol allow additional attacks; if these weaknesses are made known as axioms in the inference system, then FDR can search out the attacks.

Examples of the kind of weakness that are straightforward to model include schemes such as block ciphers where (subject to alignment of the data items) knowing the encryption of a sequence of data items is tantamount to knowing their encryptions under the same key individually, without needing to know the key! Cipher-block chaining exhibits a similar if less fatal property, in that the encryption of prefixes of a sequence can be inferred from the encryption of the whole.

Algebraic attacks on low-exponent RSA have been exhibited by Franklin, Reiter and others ([34], for example). If this is the form of public-key encryption used, then we can add deductions to reflect the additional fragility:

```
LowRSAdeductions =
  Union (
    {
     { (x,{Encrypt.(PublicKey.k,<a,x>),Encrypt.(PublicKey.k,<x>),a})
      | Encrypt.(PublicKey.k,<a,x>) <- Fact,
member(Encrypt.(PublicKey.k,<x>),Fact) },
     { (x,{Encrypt.(PublicKey.k,<x,a>),Encrypt.(PublicKey.k,<x>),a})
      | Encrypt.(PublicKey.k,<a,x>) <- Fact,
member(Encrypt.(PublicKey.k,<x>),Fact) },
     { (x,{Encrypt.(PublicKey.k,<a,x>),Encrypt.(PublicKey.k,<b,x>),a,b})
      | Encrypt.(PublicKey.k,<a,x>) <- Fact, b <- Fact, b != a
member(Encrypt.(PublicKey.k,<b,x>),Fact) },
     { (x,{Encrypt.(PublicKey.k,<a,x>),Encrypt.(PublicKey.k,<x,b>),a,b})
      | Encrypt.(PublicKey.k,<a,x>) <- Fact, b <- Fact,
member(Encrypt.(PublicKey.k,<x,b>),Fact) },
```

```
      { (x,{Encrypt.(PublicKey.k,<x,a>),Encrypt.(PublicKey.k,<b,x>),a,b})
      | Encrypt.(PublicKey.k,<x,a>) <- Fact, b <- Fact,
member(Encrypt.(PublicKey.k,<b,x>),Fact) },
      { (x,{Encrypt.(PublicKey.k,<x,a>),Encrypt.(PublicKey.k,<x,b>),a,b})
      | Encrypt.(PublicKey.k,<x,a>) <- Fact, b <- Fact, b != a
member(Encrypt.(PublicKey.k,<x,b>),Fact) }
   } )
```

These deductions capture the simplest linear cases of the identified weaknesses; further axioms could be added to deal with multivariate polynomial relationships between the bodies of messages encrypted with the same key, where this gives rise to feasible attacks.

The CSP generated by Casper uses a set of deductions based on the basic encryption axioms given above; similar ones deal with Vernam encryption and decryption (using exclusive-or) and with the construction of hash values (with no corresponding decryption law!), together with user-defined laws such as those just exhibited.

6.5   Algebraic equivalences

We have already discussed the mechanisms by which Casper allows the resulting CSP to take account of equivalences between terms such that the semantic value that they represent is in fact identical. Further examples include the commutativity and cancellation properties of exclusive-or, and the commutativity of many forms of public-key encryption.

These not only serve positive ends, as in Diffie-Hellman key exchange (where, as well as the arithmetic identities we have discussed, commutativity of the operation used to combine the two resulting half-keys is also a necessary feature), but they also give rise to a range of attacks. Notorious examples include the commutativity and associativity of RSA yielding signing-after-encryption problems

We generally prefer the renaming approach to encoding the equivalence as deductions which can take place even within opaque encrypted terms, and then relying upon the intruder to *take* one principal's view of the value and *fake* the other's. Where the intruder can gain access to additional values by moving outside the normal space of terms used in the protocol – as for instance, exploiting

```
Xor.Xor.a.b.Xor.c.b = Xor.a.c
```

while the protocol never Xor's Xor's together – then there are two equally possible solutions. Either such additional equivalences can be coded in as deductions; or *Fact* can be expanded to give the intruder licence to use a suitable larger language, and the renaming should then take care of it once more.

This technique of modelling algebraic equivalences can also be used to weaken the type system, so that an agent may be fooled into thinking a key is a nonce, for example, and perhaps be persuaded to decrypt it.

6.6 Specifying desired properties

The claims from the 'specification' part of the Casper description of the protocol give rise to assertions in the CSP script. These are in terms of processes over the *signal* and *leak* channels and a view of the system in which all other events have been renamed (to yield the appropriate signals) or hidden. The channel *signal* is defined to carry the types of information needed by the specification processes:

```
datatype Signal =
  Claim_Secret.ALL_PRINCIPALS.ALL_SECRETS.Set(ALL_PRINCIPALS) |
  Running1.ROLE.ALL_PRINCIPALS.ALL_PRINCIPALS.Nonce.Nonce |
  Commit1.ROLE.ALL_PRINCIPALS.ALL_PRINCIPALS.Nonce.Nonce |
  Running2.ROLE.ALL_PRINCIPALS.ALL_PRINCIPALS.SessionKey |
  Commit2.ROLE.ALL_PRINCIPALS.ALL_PRINCIPALS.SessionKey

channel signal : Signal
```

Secrecy

The *Secret* claim generalizes the property given in Chapter 3. It asserts that whenever the principal, which is its first argument, has completed a protocol run with only legitimate principals, its second argument is known only to that principal and those listed in the third argument. In Yahalom, for the initiator, the *ClaimSecret* signal is identified with its reception of message 4; for the responder, with its transmission of that message. The extra information in the message tuple, describing the agents' state of mind, is needed in this case to identify the correct server in the set of those allowed in on the secret (there is, of course, only one candidate in the subtype here, but the mechanism is quite general).

Given that the point at which the secrecy is recognized and the various parameters are correctly computed, the specification itself is quite simple. Once the claim has been made, then any *leak* of the secret should be flagged as an error (unless it has been admitted that the intruder is in on the secret, in which case anything goes).

```
SECRET_SPEC_0(s) =
  signal.Claim_Secret?A!s?Bs ->
    (if member(Yves, Bs) then SECRET_SPEC_0(s) else SECRET_SPEC_1(s))
  []
  leak.s -> SECRET_SPEC_0(s)

SECRET_SPEC_1(s) = signal.Claim_Secret?A!s?Bs -> SECRET_SPEC_1(s)
```

It may seem a little strange to allow the secret to be leaked *before* the claim is made; but if it is genuinely known to the intruder, he can always repeat the leak afterwards, so it does not matter. There is also research into using techniques from data independence to sanction the recycling of short-term secrets (*see* Section 10.8), allowing unbounded multiple sequential runs of the protocol, and this is the appropriate coding in that scenario, too.

Detecting failure of authentication

The implementation of agreement and authentication follows a similar line: simple processes demand that *Commit* signals, indicating a belief that the other principal is indeed running the protocol with a given set of parameters, should not occur before the *Running* signal that indicates this is true:

```
AuthenticateRESPONDERToINITIATORAgreement_na_nb(b) =
  signal.Running1.RESPONDER_role.b?a?na?nb ->
  signal.Commit1.INITIATOR_role.a.b.na.nb -> STOP

AuthenticateINITIATORToRESPONDERAgreement_kab(a) =
  signal.Running2.INITIATOR_role.a?b?kab ->
  signal.Commit2.RESPONDER_role.b.a.kab -> STOP
```

For this example, these four signals correspond (respectively) to

- responder sending message 2
- initiator sending message 4
- initiator sending message 4
- responder receiving message 4.

Counterexamples as attacks

When these assertions fail to hold, the FDR debugger is available to explore why (there is also a utility as part of Casper that can do this for the user, largely mechanically). At the top level, the example will not be very illuminating: for secrecy specifications, a sequence of τs bracketing a solitary *ClaimSecret* signal will be followed by a *leak*; for agreement, a sequence of τs ends in a *Commit* with no preceding *Running*. The interest lies in what is behind the τs.

The process tree in the debugger shows that the root node of the operator tree is a hiding $\boxed{\setminus}$; this is where most of the events are abstracted. Double-clicking on that node reveals that the argument process is a renaming $\boxed{[[\ldots]]}$, which is where the signals are recognized. Double-clicking again, on the newly revealed node, exposes the communicating parallel composition $\boxed{[|\ldots|]}$, which is the SYSTEM before it was manipulated for the purposes of the specification. Clicking on that should show the sequence of *take*s and *fake*s that led to the problem.

Further exploration is possible, to see what each principal contributed to the run, and even to see what sequence of inferences allowed the intruder to generate the fatal message that broke the protocol. All the gory details are available, for those who wish to know, but the quintessential attack is that displayed at the SYSTEM level.

7 Theorem proving

The analysis and verification techniques discussed in previous chapters make use of model-checking methods to analyze protocols. In order to do this they must make various finitary restrictions to enable the model-checking to terminate. Using these restrictions flaws can be quickly identified. Furthermore, data-independence results permit general protocol correctness to be deduced in some cases from correctness of the checked finite system.

This chapter is concerned with the development of a general proof technique built upon the traces model of CSP. Properties of the Yahalom protocol will be verified as a running example. In Chapter 2 we introduced a general CSP model of protocols and intruders, and in Chapter 3 we defined various security properties such as authentication and secrecy, in terms of the CSP trace semantics. It is therefore a well-defined and precise question to ask whether a particular CSP description of a protocol over a network (which has a well-defined semantics) meets a particular property. This is true even when the system can engage in arbitrarily many interleaved runs of the protocol, when the space of facts is infinite, and when the number of users is unbounded.

Secrecy and authentication properties are concerned with the fact that certain messages should not occur, or should occur only under particular circumstances. We are therefore concerned with providing theories for establishing the impossibility of particular combinations of events.

The following two specifications are particularly important:

$$R \text{ precedes } T = tr \upharpoonright R = \langle\rangle \Rightarrow tr \upharpoonright T = \langle\rangle$$
$$\text{no } R = tr \upharpoonright R = \langle\rangle$$

In fact 'no R' can be defined as '$\varnothing$ precedes R', but it is useful to write this special case separately.

A number of proof rules based upon the CSP traces model can be derived for establishing that CSP processes meet these specifications. Such rules are useful for showing that CSP descriptions of protocol runs have particular properties.

For example, if we have a collection of interleaved components such that each of them either satisfies R precedes T or no T, then their combination also satisfies R precedes T:

$$\frac{\forall i \bullet (P_i \text{ sat } R \text{ precedes } T) \vee (P_i \text{ sat no } T)}{\left|\left|\right|\right|_i P_i \text{ sat } R \text{ precedes } T}$$

This rule means that to show that an interleaved composition of protocol runs

175

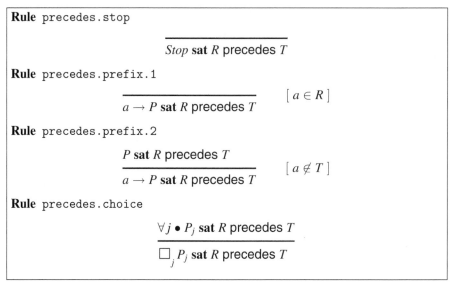

Figure 7.1 Proof rules for `precedes`: prefix and choice

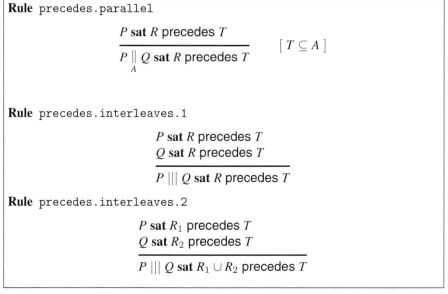

Figure 7.2 Proof rules for `precedes`: parallel

satisfies *R* **precedes** *T*, it is enough to show that each of the runs either satisfies that same specification, or else can never perform *T*. There are proof rules to assist in establishing each of these possibilities. Figures 7.1 and 7.2 provide compositional

Rule `absent.stop`

$$\frac{}{Stop \; \textbf{sat} \; \mathsf{no} \; R}$$

Rule `absent.prefix`

$$\frac{P \; \textbf{sat} \; \mathsf{no} \; R}{a \rightarrow P \; \textbf{sat} \; \mathsf{no} \; R} \qquad [\, a \notin R \,]$$

Rule `absent.choice`

$$\frac{\forall j \bullet P_j \; \textbf{sat} \; \mathsf{no} \; R}{\square_j \, P_j \; \textbf{sat} \; \mathsf{no} \; R}$$

Rule `absent.parallel`

$$\frac{P \; \textbf{sat} \; \mathsf{no} \; R}{P \parallel_A Q \; \textbf{sat} \; \mathsf{no} \; R} \qquad [\, R \subseteq A \,]$$

Rule `absent.interleaves`

$$\frac{P \; \textbf{sat} \; \mathsf{no} \; R \\ Q \; \textbf{sat} \; \mathsf{no} \; R}{P \vertbar\vertbar\vertbar Q \; \textbf{sat} \; \mathsf{no} \; R}$$

Figure 7.3 Proof rules for absence of events

proof rules for `precedes`: they enable results of the form P **sat** R precedes T to be derived from results about the component processes of P. Figure 7.3 provides proof rules for P **sat** no R, and Figure 7.4 provides proof rules for combining the two.

For example, to show that

$$down \rightarrow on \rightarrow \mathit{off} \rightarrow Stop \; \textbf{sat} \; \{on\} \; \text{precedes} \; \{\mathit{off}\}$$

we use Rule `precedes.prefix.1` (since $on \in \{on\}$) to establish directly that

$$on \rightarrow \mathit{off} \rightarrow Stop \; \textbf{sat} \; \{on\} \; \text{precedes} \; \{\mathit{off}\}$$

and then use Rule `precedes.prefix.2` (since $down \notin \{\mathit{off}\}$) to establish that

$$down \rightarrow on \rightarrow \mathit{off} \rightarrow Stop \; \textbf{sat} \; \{on\} \; \text{precedes} \; \{\mathit{off}\}$$

7.1   Rank functions

We will provide a number of results based on CSP traces that can be used in protocol verification of secrecy and authentication properties. These properties are concerned

---

Rule `precedes.absent.1`

$$\frac{\begin{array}{l} P \text{ sat } R \text{ precedes } T \\ P \text{ sat no } R \end{array}}{P \text{ sat no } T}$$

Rule `precedes.absent.2`

$$\frac{\begin{array}{l} P \text{ sat } R \text{ precedes } T \\ Q \text{ sat no } T \end{array}}{P \;|||\; Q \text{ sat } R \text{ precedes } T}$$

$$\frac{\forall\, i \bullet (P_i \text{ sat } R \text{ precedes } T) \vee (P_i \text{ sat no } T)}{|||_i\, P_i \text{ sat } R \text{ precedes } T}$$

Figure 7.4 Precedes and absence

with conditions under which particular facts become available to the intruder. In the case of secrecy, we require that a particular fact is never obtained by the intruder. In the case of authentication, we are concerned that a fact (the authenticating event) should only be possible after some other fact (the authenticated event) has already been provided.

In both cases we are therefore concerned to establish that (in particular circumstances) a fact is not available to the intruder. In order to establish this, we will aim to show that all the facts that can be generated within the network (by the agents running the protocol, by the other agents, and by the intruder) must have a particular characterizing property, and that the facts that the intruder should not be able to obtain do not have that property. The aim of the verification is to identify the property that enables the proof to succeed.

To achieve this, we will assign a value or *rank* to each fact, with the intention that only facts with strictly positive rank can ever circulate within the system. The ranks that are assigned will, of course, depend on the protocol itself, the initial knowledge and the capabilities of the intruder, as well as the facts that we wish to show cannot be obtained by the intruder (which must not have positive rank).

Definition 7.1.1 (Rank function) A rank function ρ is a function $\rho : Fact \cup Signal \to \mathbb{Z}$ which maps facts and signals to integers. □

New facts can be generated by the intruder and by any of the agents in the network. In order to ensure that only facts of positive rank can circulate, and only signals of positive rank produced, it is necessary to ensure that each of these participants cannot introduce anything of non-positive rank.

For the intruder, this means that two checks have to be made:

- that all of the facts initially known by the intruder must be of positive rank;

- that the ⊢ relation respects positive rank – in other words, that only facts of positive rank can be generated from sets of facts of positive rank.

Since the description of the intruder is independent of the protocol under analysis, this is essentially a check on the initial state of the intruder, and a check on the deductions that can be made under the ⊢ relation.

The protocol description will be encapsulated within the CSP descriptions of the protocol participants $User_a$. (Recall from Chapter 2 that $User_a$ is an interleaving of initiator and responder runs.) Any trusted server is also considered as a particular agent following a particular role within the protocol, and can be treated in the same way as the other agents. We will need to show that the steps of the protocol followed by $User_a$ cannot introduce any facts of non-positive rank. In other words, if it has accepted only messages of positive rank on its receive channel, then the messages sent out on its send channel must only be of positive rank.

This requirement can be expressed as a trace specification 'maintains positive rank', which states that if all messages received have positive rank, then all messages sent must also have positive rank. This is more easily expressed as the contrapositive: if some message with non-positive rank is sent, then some message with non-positive rank must have been received.

Definition 7.1.2 (Maintains positive rank) The trace property maintains positive $\rho(tr)$ is defined as follows:

$$\text{maintains positive } \rho(tr) \Leftrightarrow$$
$$(send.a.b.m \text{ in } tr \vee signal.c.a.b.m \text{ in } tr) \wedge \rho(m) \leqslant 0 \Rightarrow$$
$$\exists\, receive.a'.b'.m' \text{ in } tr \bullet \rho(m') \leqslant 0$$

This is a special case of **precedes**: any output message of non-positive rank must be preceded by a received message of non-positive rank.

Observe that the identity of the users does not need to appear in this definition – it is appropriate for all users.   In any particular case $User_a$ **sat** maintains positive $\rho(tr)$, the *send* and *receive* channels used in the construction of $User_a$ means that the only send channel considered here is of the form *send.a.j.m* and the only possible receive channel is of the form *receive.i'.a.m'*.   Thus the correct instantiations for a occur naturally whenever maintains positive $\rho(tr)$ is used.

Clearly the suitability of a rank function will depend crucially on the protocol itself, since whether or not $User_a$ **sat** maintains positive $\rho(tr)$ depends on the match between the description $User_a$ and the rank function ρ.

The key result that provides the basis for the verification method is that if these requirements all hold, then no fact of non-positive rank can ever be introduced into the system. This means that such facts cannot be obtained (and thus leaked) by the intruder.

Rule stop.positive ρ

$$\overline{\rule{6cm}{0pt}}$$

$Stop$ **sat maintains positive** ρ

Rule output.positive ρ

$$\frac{P \text{ sat maintains positive } \rho}{send.a.b.m \rightarrow P \text{ sat maintains positive } \rho}[\rho(m) > 0\,]$$

Rule input.positive ρ

$$\frac{\forall\, b, x \bullet (\,\rho(f(x)) > 0 \Rightarrow}{\qquad\qquad (P(b, x) \text{ sat maintains positive } \rho))}$$

$receive?b.a?.f(x) \rightarrow P(b, x)$ **sat maintains positive** ρ

Figure 7.5 Proof rules for maintains positive ρ: input and output

More formally, if

- ■ $\forall\, m \in IK \bullet \rho(m) > 0$
- ■ $((\forall\, s \in S \bullet \rho(s) > 0) \wedge S \vdash m) \Rightarrow \rho(m) > 0$
- ■ $\forall\, a \in Agent \bullet User_a$ **sat maintains positive** ρ

then it follows that no messages of rank 0 or less can ever appear:

$$\left(\big\|\big\|_{a \in Agent} User_a \,\|\, Intruder(IK)\right) \text{ **sat no** } \{c.m \mid \rho(m) \leqslant 0\}$$

This result enables a proof obligation of this form on the entire system to be reduced to proof obligations on the individual components of the system. The key step in the development of a proof that builds on this result is the identification of a suitable rank function ρ.

There are a number of rules for establishing the **maintains positive** ρ specification. These are given in Figures 7.5 and 7.6. They will be used in establishing that the users maintain positive rank.

Informally, their soundness can be justified as follows. Rule stop is sound because $Stop$ is unable to violate **maintains positive** ρ since to do so requires an output of a message of non-positive rank, and $Stop$ can perform no such output. Rule output states that if the first output provided by a process has positive rank, then the process satisfies **maintains positive** ρ provided the behaviour after this first output does not violate it.

Rule input is concerned with the behaviour of a process subsequent to an input. The requirement to maintain positive rank is concerned that if messages coming in have positive rank, then the messages going out should also have positive rank. For a particular incoming message, there are therefore two cases to consider: if the input message $f(x)$ has rank 0 or less, then the subsequent behaviour is irrelevant since

Rule `choice.positive` ρ

$$\frac{\forall j \bullet P_j \text{ sat maintains positive } \rho}{\square_j P_j \text{ sat maintains positive } \rho}$$

Rule `interleave.positive` ρ

$$\frac{\forall j \bullet P_j \text{ sat maintains positive } \rho}{|||_j P_j \text{ sat maintains positive } \rho}$$

Rule `absence.positive` ρ

$$\frac{U \text{ sat no } (\{send.a.b.m \mid \rho(m) \leqslant 0\} \cup \{signal.c.a.b.m \mid \rho(m) \leqslant 0\}}{U \text{ sat maintains positive } \rho}$$

Figure 7.6 Proof rules for maintains positive ρ: other operators

$$c?m \to P(m) = \square_m c.m \to P(m)$$
$$a \to \square_i Q_i = \square_i (a \to Q_i)$$
$$P \,|||\, \square_i Q_i = \square_i (P \,|||\, Q_i)$$
$$|||_i (\square_j P(i,j)) = \square_{\vec{ji}} (|||_i P(i,j_i))$$

Figure 7.7 CSP algebraic laws for distributing choice

responsibility for maintaining positive rank is no longer required; if the message $f(x)$ input has positive rank, then the subsequent process $P(j, x)$ should maintain positive rank. Hence the rule states that the input process $rec.i?j?f(x) \to P(j, x)$ satisfies maintains positive ρ whenever $P(j, x)$ does so after an input of positive rank. The form of the input $f(x)$ describes the pattern matching implicit in the input process: f describes the input patterns allowed.

Rules `choice` and `interleave` state that if each of its component processes maintains positive rank, then so does the entire process.

Finally, a special case is given by Rule `absence`: if U_a cannot send any message of non-positive rank at all, then it must maintain positive rank.

7.2 Secrecy of the shared key: a rank function

As our example, we will consider the description of the Yahalom protocol discussed in Section 3.1, with the *Claim_Secret* signal inserted. We wish to prove that

$$Yahalom \,\|\, Intruder(IK) \text{ sat } Secrecy(tr)$$

This means that for any two users a and b, $Secret_{ab}(tr)$ must hold. Hence we can consider for arbitrary A and B the requirement

$$Yahalom \parallel Intruder(IK) \textbf{ sat } Secret_{AB}(tr)$$

where $Secrecy$ and $Secret_{AB}$ are defined as in Section 3.2. In other words, if A claims that s is a secret shared with B, and B is honest, then $leak.s$ should not appear in the trace tr.

Thus we aim to show for some arbitrary A, B, and s, that

$$Yahalom \parallel Intruder(IK) \textbf{ sat } signal.Claim\_Secret.A.B.s \text{ in } tr$$
$$\wedge \, A \in Honest \wedge B \in Honest$$
$$\Rightarrow \neg(leak.s \text{ in } tr)$$

If $A \notin Honest$ or $B \notin Honest$ then there is nothing to prove. If they are both honest, then the only secrets that are claimed by honest agents A and B concern the key received during the protocol. So s will be some arbitrary key k_{AB}. We are therefore aiming to prove that

$$Yahalom \parallel Intruder(IK) \textbf{ sat } signal.Claim\_Secret.A.B.k_{AB} \text{ in } tr \Rightarrow \neg(leak.k_{AB} \text{ in } tr)$$

There are essentially two cases to consider: either k_{AB} is not a key issued by the server, or it is. We consider each of these cases in turn – each will make use of a different rank function.

Case $k_{AB} \notin KEYS_{Server}$

If k_{AB} is a key that is not issued by the server ($k_{AB} \notin KEYS_{Server}$), then it must be assumed to be known to the intruder. However, in this case the intruder will not be able to incorporate k_{AB} into a message that will persuade either A or B to believe that it is a secret shared with the other. This is established by use of the rank function given in Figure 7.8. We have to check the following:

- All facts of rank 0 or less are not initially known to the intruder. This is reasonable, since the only such facts are the keys that A and B share with the server, together with the key k_{AB} encrypted within a message by such keys.

- $\vdash$ preserves positive rank. This is easily checked by examining the clauses that define $\vdash$.

- $User_a$ **sat** maintains positive $\rho(tr)$ for all agents a. This is easily checked, since no user ever produces a message of the form of those of rank 0.

- $Serv(k)$ **sat** maintains positive $\rho(tr)$ for all $k \in KEYS_{Server}$. This is immediate, since k_{AB} never appears in a message (encrypted or otherwise) produced by $Serv(k)$.

It follows that neither $User_A$ or $User_B$ will ever issue a signal $Claim\_Secret.A.B.k_{AB}$, since to do so they first have to receive a message of rank 0, and this is not possible (since if they can receive such a message then the intruder must also be in possession

$$\rho(u) = 1$$
$$\rho(n) = 1$$
$$\rho(k) = \begin{cases} 0 & \text{if } k = ServerKey(A) \text{ or } k = ServerKey(B) \\ 1 & \text{otherwise} \end{cases}$$

$$\rho(\{m\}_k) = \begin{cases} 0 & \text{if } \{m\}_k = \{a.k_{AB}.n_a.n_b\}_{ServerKey(A)} \\ & \text{or } \{m\}_k = \{b.k_{AB}\}_{ServerKey(B)} \\ 1 & \text{otherwise} \end{cases}$$
$$\rho(m_1.m_2) = \min\{\rho(m_1), \rho(m_2)\}$$

$$\rho(Claim\_Secret.s) = \begin{cases} 0 & \text{if } s = A.B.k_{AB} \\ 1 & \text{otherwise} \end{cases}$$

Figure 7.8   Rank function for secrecy of k_{AB} in the Yahalom protocol I

of it). Hence in this case:

$$Yahalom \parallel Intruder(IK) \textbf{ sat } \neg(signal.Claim\_Secret.A.B.k_{AB} \text{ in } tr)$$

and the specification can be weakened to obtain

$$Yahalom \parallel Intruder(IK) \textbf{ sat } signal.Claim\_Secret.A.B.k_{AB} \text{ in } tr \Rightarrow \neg(leak.k_{AB} \text{ in } tr)$$

Case $k_{AB} \in KEYS_{Server}$

The other case to consider is when k_{AB} is a key issued by the server (i.e. $k_{AB} \in KEYS_{Server}$). In this case *Server* can be considered as a choice over which agents should be associated with key k_{AB}. It turns out that the other keys do not affect the correctness property we are considering, and so the agents associated with them do not need to be made explicit:

$$Serv'(k, a, b) = receive.b.Jeeves.?(b.\{a.n_a.n_b\}_{ServerKey(b)}) \rightarrow$$
$$send.Jeeves.a.(\{b.k.n_a.n_b\}_{ServerKey(a)}.\{a.k\}_{ServerKey(b)} \rightarrow Stop$$
$$Serv(k) = \square_{a,b:Agent} Serv'(k, a, b)$$

If the server allocates a particular key k_0 to a pair of agents a and b, then the particular description of *Server* that picks out this run will be described by

$$Server(k_0, a, b) = (\||_{k \neq k_0} Serv(k)) \||| Serv'(k_0, a, b)$$

Then for any particular key k_0, the original server can be described as

$$Server = \square_{a,b} Server(k_0, a, b)$$

The description of the *Yahalom* system we need to consider will pick out the key k_{AB}:

$$(User_A \ ||| \ User_B \ ||| \ \square_{a,b:Agent} \ Server(k_{AB}, a, b)) \ || \ Intruder(IK)$$

The choice can be brought out to the front by an application of the last algebraic law in Figure 7.7.

$$\square_{a,b} ((User_A \ ||| \ User_B \ ||| \ Server(k_{AB}, a, b)) \ || \ Intruder(IK))$$

If each branch of the choice satisfies the secrecy requirement, then so too does the entire choice, by Rule `sat.extchoice` of Figure 1.2. This allows each possibility for a and b to be considered separately. In fact there are two subcases to consider: either $a = A$ and $b = B$, in which case k_{AB} should never be disclosed (and hence should have rank 0); or $a \neq A$ or $b \neq B$, in which case k_{AB} might become disclosed, but it is not claimed to be secret. Each subcase will therefore use a different rank function to show that its components maintain the rank, and we will thereby establish that each case meets the required secrecy property.

Case $a = A$ **and** $b = B$

In this case the appropriate rank function is given in Figure 7.9. We have to check the following:

- All facts of rank 0 or less are not initially known to the intruder. This is reasonable, since the only such facts are the keys that A and B share with the server, together with the new key k_{AB}.
- $\vdash$ preserves positive rank. This is easily checked by examining the clauses that define $\vdash$.
- $User_a$ **sat maintains positive** $\rho(tr)$ for all users.
- $Server(k_{AB}, A, B)$ **sat maintains positive** $\rho(tr)$. By Rule `interleave.positive` ρ, it is sufficient to prove the following:
  - $Serv'(k_{AB}, A, B)$ **sat maintains positive** $\rho(tr)$. This is immediate, since the only message that is sent has rank 1.
  - $Serv(k)$ **sat maintains positive** $\rho(tr)$ when $k \neq k_{AB}$. This is immediate, since k_{AB} never appears in a message of $Serv(k)$ (encrypted or otherwise).

The last two items together yield that $Server(k_{AB}, a, b)$ **sat maintains positive** $\rho(tr)$, from Rule `interleave.positive` ρ from Figure 7.6.

Case $a \neq A$ **or** $b \neq B$

In this case the messages that the server dispatches will contain names different to those required by A and B to claim that k_{AB} is a secret shared with the other. The rank function in this case will establish that A and B will never receive such messages. It is given in Figure 7.10. Observe that in this case the key k_{AB} has rank 1: it cannot be expected to remain secret if the server can send it to other users (who might not be

$$\rho(u) = 1$$
$$\rho(n) = 1$$
$$\rho(k) = \begin{cases} 0 \text{ if } k = k_{AB} \text{ or } k = ServerKey(A) \text{ or } k = ServerKey(B) \\ 1 \text{ otherwise} \end{cases}$$

$$\rho(\{m\}_k) = \begin{cases} 1 + \rho(m) \text{ if } k = k_{AB} \text{ or } k = ServerKey(A) \text{ or } k = ServerKey(B) \\ \rho(m) \qquad \text{otherwise} \end{cases}$$
$$\rho(m_1.m_2) = \min\{\rho(m_1), \rho(m_2)\}$$

$$\rho(Claim\_Secret.s) = 1$$

Figure 7.9 Rank function for secrecy of k_{AB} in the Yahalom protocol II

honest). In this case the correctness of the protocol rests on the fact that k_{AB} is never claimed to be a secret between *A* and *B*.

The signal *Claim_Secret.A.B.k_{AB}* can occur only if *User$_A$* as initiator or *User$_B$* as responder perform it.

In the first case, inspection of *Initiator$_A$* reveals that if *signal.Claim_Secret.A.B.k_{AB}* occurs, then previously *receive.Jeeves.A.($\{B.k_{AB}.n_a.n_b\}_{ServerKey(A)}.y$)* must have occurred for some *y*, and hence that $\{B.k_{AB}.n_a.n_b\}_{ServerKey(A)}$ will have been available to the intruder. If there is a rank function that gives this message a rank of 0 then this case is not possible.

In the second case, if *signal.Claim_Secret.A.B.k_{AB}* occurs, then inspection of *Responder$_B$* reveals that previously *receive.A.B.$\{A.k_{AB}\}_{ServerKey(B)}.\{n\}_{k_{AB}}$* must have occurred for some nonce *n*. If there is a rank function that gives a rank of 0 to $\{A.k_{AB}\}_{ServerKey(B)}$ then this case is not possible.

Since these two cases are the only two possibilities to consider, the rank function given in Figure 7.10 establishes that neither *A* nor *B* will claim that k_{AB} is a secret shared between them. We have only to check for this rank function that it meets the conditions required to show that facts of rank 0 cannot appear in the system:

▪ All facts of rank 0 or less are not initially known to the intruder. This is reasonable, since the only such facts are the keys that *A* and *B* share with the server, and some messages encrypted under those keys.

▪ ⊢ preserves positive rank. This is easily checked by examining the clauses that define ⊢.

▪ *User$_a$* **sat** maintains positive $\rho(tr)$ for all users. This is immediate, since the messages sent out by the users do not even have the form of the messages of rank 0.

▪ *Serv′(k_{AB}, a, b)* **sat** maintains positive $\rho(tr)$ when $a \neq A$ or $b \neq B$. This is immediate, since the only message that is sent has rank 1, since its two parts both have rank 1. (They would only have rank 0 if $a = A$ and $b = B$.)

▪ *Serv*(k) **sat** maintains positive $\rho(tr)$ when $k \neq k_{AB}$. This is immediate, since k_{AB} never appears in a message (encrypted or otherwise) and the messages of rank 0 include k_{AB} as a component.

The last two items together yield that *Server*(k_{AB}, i, j) **sat** maintains positive $\rho(tr)$. Hence in the case where $a \neq A$ or $b \neq B$ we have that

$$Yahalom(a, b) \parallel Intruder(IK) \text{ } \textbf{sat}$$
$$\neg(signal.Claim\_Secret.A.B.k_{AB} \text{ in } tr)$$

and so

$$Yahalom(a, b) \parallel Intruder(IK) \text{ } \textbf{sat}$$
$$signal.Claim\_Secret.A.B.k_{AB} \text{ in } tr \Rightarrow \neg(leak.k_{AB} \text{ in } tr)$$

We also have from the case $a = A \wedge b = B$ that

$$Yahalom(A, B) \parallel Intruder(IK) \text{ } \textbf{sat} \text{ } \neg(leak.k_{AB} \text{ in } tr)$$

and hence that

$$Yahalom(A, B) \parallel Intruder(IK) \text{ } \textbf{sat}$$
$$signal.Claim\_Secret.A.B.k_{AB} \text{ in } tr \Rightarrow \neg(leak.k_{AB} \text{ in } tr)$$

In all cases, *Yahalom*(a, b) $\parallel$ *Intruder*(IK) satisfies the desired specification. Hence from Rule `sat.extchoice` it follows that $\square_{a,b}$ *Yahalom*(a, b) $\parallel$ *Intruder*(IK) also satisfies it:

$$Yahalom \parallel Intruder(IK) \text{ } \textbf{sat}$$
$$signal.Claim\_Secret.A.B.k_{AB} \text{ in } tr \Rightarrow \neg(leak.k_{AB} \text{ in } tr)$$

$$\rho(u) = 1$$
$$\rho(n) = 1$$
$$\rho(k) = \begin{cases} 0 \text{ if } k = ServerKey(A) \text{ or } k = ServerKey(B) \\ 1 \text{ otherwise} \end{cases}$$

$$\rho(\{m\}_k) = \begin{cases} 0 \text{ if } \{m\}_k = \{B.k_{AB}.n_a.n_b\}_{ServerKey(A)} \\ \quad \text{or } \{m\}_k = \{A.k_{AB}\}_{ServerKey(B)} \\ 1 \text{ otherwise} \end{cases}$$
$$\rho(m_1.m_2) = \min\{\rho(m_1), \rho(m_2)\}$$

$$\rho(Claim\_Secret.s) = \begin{cases} 0 \text{ if } s = A.B.k_{AB} \\ 1 \text{ otherwise} \end{cases}$$

Figure 7.10 Rank function for secrecy of k_{AB} in the Yahalom protocol III

Observe that secrecy of the nonce n_B is not required to establish secrecy of k_{AB}. The nonce n_B could have been known to the intruder, since it had rank 1 in the rank function of Figure 7.10.

7.3 Secrecy on n_B

We can also consider whether the nonce n_B is kept secret if the intruder does not know it. The specification in this case introduces an arbitrary fixed nonce N_B into the claimed secret. Agents will claim that both the distributed key and the nonce issued by the responder are secrets. The following is the property to check, for honest agents A and B:

$$signal.Claim\_Secret.A.B.k.N_B \text{ in } tr \Rightarrow \neg(leak.N_B \text{ in } tr)$$

If a claims that N_B is a secret, this is in response to receiving it as part of his own run. If b claims it, this is because b issued it.

We separate the protocol runs of the user in order to analyze them separately. We will again use the rules of Figure 7.6 to combine the results of the separate analyses.

Here is an initiator run with a particular value of k_{ab} and n_b, which are both claimed to be secret:

$$Initiator'_a(k_{ab}, n_a, n_b) = \Box_b \; send.a.b.(a.n_a) \rightarrow$$
$$receive.Jeeves.a.(\{b.k_{ab}.n_a.n_b\}_{ServerKey(a)}.y) \rightarrow$$
$$send.a.b.(y.\{n_b\}_{k_{ab}}) \rightarrow$$
$$signal.Claim\_Secret.a.b.k_{ab}.n_b \rightarrow Stop$$

so

$$Initiator'_a(n_a) = \Box_{k_{ab},n_b} Initiator'_a(k_{ab}, n_a, n_b)$$

We also consider a responder run with nonce n_b engaging in a run with a, and the revised declaration of a secret:

$$Responder'_b(a, n_b) = receive.a.b?(a.n_a) \rightarrow$$
$$send.b.Jeeves.(b.\{a.n_a.n_b\}_{ServerKey(b)}) \rightarrow$$
$$receive.a.b?(\{a.k_{ab}\}_{ServerKey(b)}.\{n_b\}_{k_{ab}}) \rightarrow$$
$$signal.Claim\_Secret.a.b.k_{ab}.n_b \rightarrow Stop$$

So

$$Responder'_b(n_b) = \Box_{a \in Agent} Responder'_b(a, n_b)$$

So a user can be described as follows:

$$User'_a = \Big|\Big|\Big|_{n \in Initnonce_a} Initiator'_a(n)$$
$$|||$$
$$\Big|\Big|\Big|_{n \in Responce_a, n \neq n_b} Responder'_a(n)$$
$$|||$$
$$\Box_{b \in Agent} Responder'_a(b, n_b)$$

Thus we separate out B's run with nonce N_B in the following description:

$$Yahalom = User'_A \,|||\, Server \,|||$$
$$Initiator'_B \,|||\, \Big|\Big|\Big|_{n \neq N_B} Responder'_B(n)$$
$$|||$$
$$\Box_{a \in Agent} Responder'_B(a, N_B)$$

Once again, we bring the choice to the head of the process description:

$$Yahalom = \Box_{a \in Agent} \; (User'_A \,|||\, Server \,|||$$
$$Initiator'_B \,|||\, \Big|\Big|\Big|_{n \neq N_B} Responder'_B(n)$$
$$|||\, Responder'_B(a, N_B))$$

We can thus check for each branch of the choice that it satisfies the required secrecy property:

$$signal.Claim\_Secret.A.B.k_{AB}.N_B \text{ in } tr \Rightarrow \neg(leak.N_B \text{ in } tr)$$

The two cases to consider are $a \neq A$ and $a = A$. In the first case the initiator will never claim that N_B is a secret shared between initiator A and responder B, since the initiator of the run involving N_B will be some agent other than A. And A will not claim it either. Furthermore, the responder will not claim this either, since the only claim of the responder involving N_B is that it is shared with a and not with A. In the second case we will show that N_B is actually secret, by exhibiting a suitable rank function that gives it a rank of 0. The CSP verification makes this argument rigorous.

Case $a \neq A$

We firstly consider the network in the case where $a \neq A$. In this case the rank function of Figure 7.11 will establish that the $Claim\_Secret.A.B.N_B$ signal cannot occur. Observe that N_B has a rank of 1, since it may become known to the intruder in this case. We are not concerned with the disclosure of N_B in this case, only with the fact that it is not claimed to be secret.

We must first check that all the parallel components of the resulting network preserve positive rank:

- ◼ The only facts with rank 0 are the two keys shared between A and B and the server, and messages involving the new nonce N_B encrypted with these keys. It is therefore reasonable to expect that none of these appear in IK, and hence that all facts in IK have positive rank.

$$\rho(u) = 1$$
$$\rho(n) = 1$$
$$\rho(k) = \begin{cases} 0 \text{ if } k = ServerKey(A) \\ \text{ or } k = ServerKey(B) \\ 1 \text{ otherwise} \end{cases}$$

$$\rho(\{m\}_k) = \begin{cases} 0 \text{ if } \{m\}_k = \{B.k_0.n.N_B\}_{ServerKey(A)} \text{ for some } k_0 \\ \text{ or } \{m\}_k = \{A.n.N_B\}_{ServerKey(B)} \\ 1 \text{ otherwise} \end{cases}$$
$$\rho(m_1.m_2) = \min\{\rho(m_1), \rho(m_2)\}$$

$$\rho(Claim\_Secret.s) = \begin{cases} 0 \text{ if } s = A.B.N_B \\ 1 \text{ otherwise} \end{cases}$$

Figure 7.11   Rank function for Yahalom secrecy of N_B I

- The $\vdash$ relation preserved positive rank. Messages of rank 0 cannot be generated from messages of purely positive rank.
- $User_A$ does not generate any messages containing N_B (though it may pass one on without changing it).
- $Initiator'_B$ maintains positive rank.
- $Responder'_B(n)$ maintains positive rank when $n \neq N_B$ since it does not generate any message containing N_B.
- $Responder'_B(a, N_B)$ maintains positive rank when $a \neq A$.
- Each $Serv(k)$ maintains positive rank: it can only generate a message of rank 0 if it previously receives one of rank 0. (This is the reason for assigning a rank of 0 to messages of the form $\{A.n.N_B\}_{ServerKey(B)}$ – to capture the fact that $Server$ can never receive them).

B will never claim this secret is shared with A (irrespective of the rank function). This is because each interleaved $Responder'_b(n)$ will not claim that secret: those with $n \neq N_B$ will not claim anything about N_B, and the run with N_B will claim the secret is shared with a and not with A.

The rank function of Figure 7.11 establishes that A will never receive a message of the form $\{B.k.n.N_B\}_{ServerKey(A)}$ for any key k and nonce n, since any such message has rank 0. Examination of the definition of $User_A$ shows that a message of this form is a prerequisite for A to claim that N_B is a secret shared with B – it must appear earlier in the protocol run. Thus A will never signal $Claim\_Secret.A.B.N_B$.

Case $a = A$

In this case we expect the nonce N_B to be secret.

To consider this case we will need to make explicit the agents associated with each key that is distributed by the server. $Serv(k, a, b)$ is the server distributing key k to users a and b.

$$Serv(k, a, b) = receive.b.Jeeves?(b.\{a.n_a.n_b\}_{ServerKey(b)}) \rightarrow$$
$$send.Jeeves.a.(\{b.k.n_a.n_b\}_{ServerKey(a)}.\{a.k\}_{ServerKey(b)} \rightarrow Stop$$

Then $Serv(k) = \square_{a,b} Serv(k, a, b)$.

Then all the choices can be brought outside the interleaving using the algebraic identity in Figure 7.7, with the infinite choice ranging over vectors of users $\vec{a_k}$ and $\vec{b_k}$ indexed by $k \in KEYS_{Server}$:

$$Server = |||_k Serv(k)$$
$$= |||_k \square_{a,b} Serv(k, a, b)$$
$$= \square_{\vec{a_k}, \vec{b_k}} |||_k Serv(k, a_k, b_k)$$

So since we are considering the case where $a = A$ we have

$$
\begin{aligned}
&User'_A \ ||| \ Server \ ||| \\
&Initiator'_B \ ||| \ |||_{n \neq N_B} Responder'_B(n) \\
&||| \ Responder'_B(A, N_B) \\
= \ &User'_A \ ||| \ (\square_{a_k, b_k} |||_k Serv(k, a_k, b_k)) \ ||| \\
&Initiator'_B \ ||| \ |||_{n \neq N_B} Responder'_B(n) \\
&||| \ Responder'_B(A, N_B) \\
= \ &\square_{\vec{a_k}, \vec{b_k}} User'_A \ ||| \ Serv(k, a_k, b_k) \ ||| \\
&Initiator'_B \ ||| \ |||_{n \neq N_B} Responder'_B(n) \\
&||| \ Responder'_B(A, N_B)
\end{aligned}
$$

We will establish the required result for each branch of the choice, corresponding to each possible choice of $\vec{a_k}$, and $\vec{b_k}$.

The rank function of Figure 7.12 will establish that N_B is secret. This rank function assigns a rank of 0 to any message containing N_B or a key to be shared between A and B, apart from those expected in a correct protocol run. Thus it will establish that N_B can occur only where it is expected.

We must check that each of the components of the network maintains positive rank:

- *IK* will only contain items of positive rank: the intruder cannot initially be in possession of N_B or keys in $KEYS_{Server}$ since these are new facts to be generated by B and the server respectively.

- $\vdash$ preserves positive rank.

■ If $n \neq N_B$ then $Responder'_B$ only sends out one message, and it does not contain N_B (or k_{ab}); it thus has positive rank.

■ $Responder'_B(A, N_B)$ sends out one message, and the rank function has been constructed specifically so that this message has rank 1.

■ $Initiator'_B$ maintains positive rank: if it only receives messages of positive rank then it cannot obtain N_B, and so it will never send it out (under any key) as its final protocol message. Hence any message it sends out will have rank 1.

■ $User_A$ as responder (i.e. $Responder_A$) only ever sends out messages in response to receipt of a nonce. If this nonce has positive rank (i.e. it is not N_B), then so too is the response message (since $Responder_A$ will never generate N_B).

■ $User_A$ as initiator (i.e. $Initiator_A$) also preserves positive rank. Whenever a message 3 of positive rank is received encrypted with $ServerKey(A)$, either the contents has positive rank (and so cannot contain either N_B or a key generated for A and B) in which case the response in message 4 must have positive rank; or the contents is a message of the form $B.k.n.N_B$ in which the key k has rank 0, in which case the response in message 4 again has positive rank.

■ $Serv(k, a_k, b_k)$ maintains positive rank: if $a_k = A$ and $b_k = B$ then any message it sends out will have rank 1, both in the case where it contains N_B and in the case where it does not; if $a_k \neq A$ or $b_k \neq B$ then by its definition $Serv(k, a_k, b_k)$ cannot accept a message containing N_B and so the response it gives out must have positive rank.

Thus N_B has rank 0, and so it can never appear on *leak*. Since this is true for every branch of the choice, it must be true for the entire choice, as required.

7.4 Authentication

Authentication can also be established using the rank function approach. We want to establish that R precedes T. This can be achieved by restricting R and showing that T cannot occur in the resulting system. This works because

$$P \text{ sat } R \text{ precedes } T \Leftrightarrow P \parallel_R Stop \text{ sat } tr \upharpoonright T = \langle\rangle$$

Hence we simply have to show that $System \parallel_R Stop \text{ sat } tr \upharpoonright T = \langle\rangle$, which we can do using rank functions: simply find an appropriate rank function for which all facts in T have rank 0.

Furthermore, the restriction of R can be distributed to the various components of $System$. Since R will actually be a set of signal events associated with one particular agent, this means that most of the system description will be unaffected by this restriction.

To establish

$$(\parallel\mid_a User_a) \parallel Intruder(IK) \text{ sat } R \text{ precedes } T$$

$$\rho(u) = 1$$

$$\rho(n) = \begin{cases} 0 & \text{if } n = N_B \\ 1 & \text{otherwise} \end{cases}$$

$$\rho(k) = \begin{cases} 0 & \text{if } k \in KEYS_{Server} \wedge a_k = A \wedge b_k = B \\ & \text{or } k = ServerKey(A) \\ & \text{or } k = ServerKey(B) \\ 1 & \text{otherwise} \end{cases}$$

$$\rho(\{m\}_k) = \begin{cases} 1 & \text{if } m \in A.Nonce.N_B \wedge k = ServerKey(B) \\ & \text{or } m \in B.k_0.Nonce.N_B \wedge a_{k_0} = A \wedge b_{k_0} = B \\ & \quad \wedge k = ServerKey(A) \\ & \text{or } m = A.k_0 \wedge a_{k_0} = A \wedge b_{k_0} = B \wedge k = ServerKey(B) \\ & \text{or } m = N_B \wedge a_k = A \wedge b_k = B \\ \rho(m) & \text{otherwise} \end{cases}$$

$$\rho(m_1.m_2) = \min\{\rho(m_1), \rho(m_2)\}$$

$$\rho(Claim\_Secret.s) = 1$$

Figure 7.12 Rank function for Yahalom secrecy of N_B II

it is therefore enough to find a rank function that is strong enough to establish the following properties of the individual components of this network:

- $\forall m \in IK \bullet \rho(m) > 0$
- $((\forall s \in S \bullet \rho(s) > 0) \wedge S \vdash m) \Rightarrow \rho(m) > 0$
- $\forall m \in T \bullet \rho(m) \leqslant 0$
- $\forall a \in Agent \bullet User_a \parallel_R Stop$ **sat maintains positive** ρ

Process equivalences

The traces model for CSP supports a number of algebraic equivalences on processes, whose soundness follows from the trace semantics. These are often useful in manipulating process descriptions into a form that is easier to reason about. There are many laws expressing useful identities. We will be interested in the effect of restricting particular events of a parallel combination $P \parallel_R Stop$. This process restricts all of P's occurrences of events from R, so it has precisely those traces of P that do not contain any event from R. The equations are given in Figure 7.13.

Rule `restrict.1` states that restricting a process on a set of events R that it cannot perform has no effect. Rule `restrict.2` states that restricting a process on a set of

---

Rule `restrict.1`

If $\sigma(P) \cap R = \varnothing$ then $P \parallel_R Stop = P$

Rule `restrict.2`

$$(P \;|||\; Q) \parallel_R Stop = (P \parallel_R Stop) \;|||\; (Q \parallel_R Stop)$$

Rule `restrict.3`

$$(c?x : T \rightarrow P(x)) \parallel_R Stop = c?x : U \rightarrow (P(x) \parallel_R Stop)$$

where $U = T \setminus \{t \mid c.t \in R\}$.

Rule `restrict.4`

$$(c!v \rightarrow P) \parallel_R Stop = \begin{cases} c!v \rightarrow (P \parallel_R Stop) & \text{if } c.v \notin R \\ Stop & \text{if } c.v \in R \end{cases}$$

Figure 7.13 Equations for restricted parallel combinations

events distributes over interleaving.

Rules `restrict.3` and `restrict.4` are concerned with the effect of a restriction on inputs and outputs.

These equations are used throughout this chapter whenever a process of the form $User_A \parallel_R Stop$ is expanded. They will not be referred to explicitly when used, in order to avoid cluttering proofs.

Yahalom: authentication

Authentication of the initiator to the responder was expressed by introducing the additional signals *Running* and *Commit* into the protocol description, as given on page 105.

In order to verify that

$$A \in Honest \;\Rightarrow\; signal.Running\_Initiator.A.B.N_A.N_B.K_{AB}$$
$$\textsf{precedes } signal.Commit\_Responder.B.A.N_A.N_B.K_{AB}$$

we restrict the system so that no signal $signal.Running\_Initiator.A.B.N_A.N_B.K_{AB}$ can be performed, and then check that the resulting system is unable to perform $signal.Commit\_Responder.B.A.N_A.N_B.K_{AB}$. The restriction on the entire system is achieved by restricting each component of the system. However, only one component ($Initiator_A(N_A)$) will be affected by the restriction, since the remaining components cannot perform the signal being restricted in any case.

$$Initiator_A(N_A) \quad \underset{signal.Running\_Initiator.A.B.N_A.N_B.K_{AB}}{\|} \quad Stop \text{ simplifies to}$$

$$\square_b \ send.A.b.(A.N_A) \rightarrow$$
$$receive.Jeeves.a?(\{b.k.N_A.n\}_{ServerKey(A)}.y) \rightarrow$$
$$if \ b = B \wedge k = K_{AB} \wedge n = N_B$$
$$then \ Stop$$
$$else \ signal.Running\_Initiator.A.b.N_A.n.k \rightarrow$$
$$send.A.b.(y.\{n\}_k) \rightarrow Stop$$

The description of the responder that receives nonce n_a is given by

$$Responder_b(n_b, n_a) = receive?a.b?(a.n_a) \rightarrow$$
$$send.b.Jeeves.(b.\{a.n_a.n_b\}_{ServerKey(b)}) \rightarrow$$
$$receive.a.b?(\{a.k_{ab}\}_{ServerKey(b)}.\{n_b\}_{k_{ab}}) \rightarrow$$
$$signal.Commit\_Responder.b.a.n_a.n_b.k_{ab} \rightarrow Stop$$

In $Initiator_A(N_A)$ there are two cases to consider for possible values of b: that it is the user B, and that it is some other user.

Case $b = B$

If A is using the nonce N_A in a run with B, then there are three possibilities to consider concerning the server's run that distributes the key K_{AB}. It is useful to consider the server as

$$Server = \|\|_{k \neq K_{AB}} Serv(k)$$
$$\|\|$$
$$\square_{a',b',n'_a,n'_b} Serv_0(K_{AB}, a', b', n'_a, n'_b)$$

where $Serv_0$ describes a single run with its parameters:

$$Serv_0(k, a, b, n_a, n_b) =$$
$$receive.b.Jeeves.(b.\{a.n_a.n_b\}_{ServerKey(b)}) \rightarrow$$
$$send.Jeeves.a.\{b.k.n_a.n_b\}_{ServerKey(a)}.\{a.k\}_{ServerKey(b)} \rightarrow Stop$$

The choice can be brought outside the interleaving, to yield

$$Server = \square_{a',b',n'_a,n'_b} \|\|_{k \neq K_{AB}} Serv(k)$$
$$\|\| Serv_0(K_{AB}, a', b', n'_a, n'_b)$$

Each of the branches of the choice can be considered separately. The categories to consider are:

■ a' and b' are A and B, and the nonces n'_a and n'_b are N_A and N_B;

■ $a' \neq A$ or $b' \neq B$;

■ $n'_a \neq N_A$ or $n'_b \neq N_B$

We will consider each of these cases in turn. Each uses a different rank function to establish the authentication requirement.

$$\rho(u) = 1$$
$$\rho(n) = 1$$
$$\rho(k) = \begin{cases} 0 \text{ if } k = K_{AB} \\ \quad \text{or } k = ServerKey(A) \\ \quad \text{or } k = ServerKey(B) \\ 1 \text{ otherwise} \end{cases}$$

$$\rho(\{m\}_k) = \begin{cases} 0 \text{ if } \{m\}_k = \{N_B\}_{K_{AB}} \\ \quad \text{or } \{m\}_k = \{b.K_{AB}.n.N_B\}_{ServerKey(a)} \\ \quad \land (b \neq B \lor n \neq N_A \lor a \neq A) \\ 1 \text{ otherwise} \end{cases}$$
$$\rho(m_1.m_2) = \min\{\rho(m_1), \rho(m_2)\}$$

$$\rho(Running\_Initiator.s) = 1$$
$$\rho(Commit\_Responder.s) = \begin{cases} 0 \text{ if } s = B.A.N_A.N_B.K_{AB} \\ 1 \text{ otherwise} \end{cases}$$

Figure 7.14 Rank function for authentication of the Yahalom protocol I

Subcase $\langle a', b', n'_a, n'_b \rangle = \langle A, B, N_A, N_B \rangle$

Then $\{N_B\}_{K_{AB}}$ is prevented from happening by the restriction. The appropriate rank function is given in Figure 7.14. Each of the components of the network need to be checked:

- *IK* will not contain anything of rank 0.
- ⊢ maintains positive rank.
- $User_A \underset{signal.Running\_Initiator.A.B.N_A.N_B.K_{AB}}{\|} Stop$ maintains positive rank.
- $User_B$ maintains positive rank: it cannot produce the message $\{N_B\}_{K_{AB}}$ without first being provided with a message of rank 0.
- $Serv(k)$ maintains positive rank when $k \neq K_{AB}$.
- $Serv(K_{AB}, A, B, N_A, N_B)$ maintains positive rank, since its only possible output is of rank 1.

Thus in this case nothing of rank 0 can be performed. This means that $User_B$ can never receive $\{N_B\}_{K_{AB}}$, and hence will never commit to a run with those facts.

Subcase $a' \neq A$ or $b' \neq B$

Then $\{A.K_{AB}\}_{ServerKey(B)}$ cannot occur, so the *Commit* signal will not occur. This is established by the rank function of Figure 7.15.

$$\rho(u) = 1$$
$$\rho(n) = 1$$
$$\rho(k) = \begin{cases} 0 \text{ if } k = K_{AB} \\ \quad \text{or } k = ServerKey(A) \\ \quad \text{or } k = ServerKey(B) \\ 1 \text{ otherwise} \end{cases}$$

$$\rho(\{m\}_k) = \begin{cases} 0 \text{ if } \{m\}_k = \{A.K_{AB}\}_{ServerKey(B)} \\ 1 \text{ otherwise} \end{cases}$$
$$\rho(m_1.m_2) = \min\{\rho(m_1), \rho(m_2)\}$$

$$\rho(Running\_Initiator.s) = 1$$
$$\rho(Commit\_Responder.s) = \begin{cases} 0 \text{ if } s = B.A.N_A.N_B.K_{AB} \\ 1 \text{ otherwise} \end{cases}$$

Figure 7.15 Rank function for authentication of the Yahalom protocol II

Subcase $n_a' \neq N_A$ or $n_b' \neq N_B$

If $n_a' \neq N_A$, then the commit signal $Commit\_Responder.B.A.N_A.N_B.K_{AB}$ will not occur. Otherwise $n_a' = N_A$: in this case no message of the form $\{A.n_0.N_B\}_{ServerKey(B)}$ is possible for $n_0 \neq N_A$. Hence no message of the form $\{b.K_{AB}.n_0.N_B\}_{ServerKey(a)}$ will be provided by $Serv_0(K_{AB}, a, b, n_1, n_2)$, for any n_0, a, or b (even if $n_0 = N_A$). Hence no user can produce $\{N_B\}_{K_{AB}}$, a prerequisite for user B to produce his *Commit* signal. This is established by the rank function of Figure 7.16.

Case $b \neq B$.

Only in a run of $Responder_B(N_B, N_A)$ can the $Commit\_Responder.B.A.N_A.N_B.K_{AB}$ signal claim possibly be made. All other $Responder_B$ process runs cannot make that particular claim.

We can also assume that the choice of agents and nonces made in $Serv(K_{AB})$ is of the form $Serv_0(K_{AB}, A, B, n_a, n_b)$, since otherwise $\{A.K_{AB}\}_{ServerKey(B)}$ cannot be produced, which again means that the commit signal will not occur.

Subcase $n_a \neq N_A$: then $Serv(K_{AB}, A, B, n_a, n_b)$ will not give any response, since it cannot be provided with an acceptable input: $\rho(\{A.n_a.N_B\}_{ServerKey(B)}) = 0$. Hence it cannot produce $\{A.K_{AB}\}_{ServerKey(B)}$, which again means that the commit signal will not occur.

Subcase $n_a = N_A$: in the case where $n_b = N_B$, we observe that $Initiator_A(n)$ will never produce $\{N_B\}_{K_{AB}}$ when $n \neq N_A$, since it can never receive $\{b.k_{AB}.n.N_B\}_{ServerKey(A)}$; and neither can $Initiator_A(N_A, b)$. The point is that any other message of the form $\{b.K_{AB}.n_a.N_B\}_{ServerKey(A)}$ must have rank 0. It can only

$$\rho(u) = 1$$
$$\rho(n) = 1$$
$$\rho(k) = \begin{cases} 0 \text{ if } k = K_{AB} \\ \quad \text{or } k = ServerKey(A) \\ \quad \text{or } k = ServerKey(B) \\ 1 \text{ otherwise} \end{cases}$$

$$\rho(\{m\}_k) = \begin{cases} 0 \text{ if } \{m\}_k = \{A.n.N_B\}_{ServerKey(B)} \wedge n \neq N_A \\ \quad \text{or } \{m\}_k = \{b.K_{AB}.n.N_B\}_{ServerKey(a)} \\ \quad \text{or } \{m\}_k = \{N_B\}_{K_{AB}} \\ 1 \text{ otherwise} \end{cases}$$
$$\rho(m_1.m_2) = \min\{\rho(m_1), \rho(m_2)\}$$

$$\rho(Running\_Initiator.s) = 1$$
$$\rho(Commit\_Responder.s) = \begin{cases} 0 \text{ if } s = B.A.N_A.N_B.K_{AB} \\ 1 \text{ otherwise} \end{cases}$$

Figure 7.16 Rank function for authentication of the Yahalom protocol III

have rank 1 when $b = B$ and $n_a = N_A$.

If $n_b \neq N_B$ then the server will not produce $\{B.K_{AB}.n.N_B\}_{ServerKey(A)}$; and so $\rho(\{B.K_{AB}.n.N_B\}_{ServerKey(A)}) = 0$ for any nonce n, and so $\rho(\{N_B\}_{K_{AB}}) = 0$. Yet receipt of this message is a prerequisite for b to produce its commit signal, so we have again established that this cannot occur.

All of this reasoning is encapsulated within the rank function of Figure 7.17. In all cases considered, positive rank is maintained.

7.5 Machine assistance

In practice, the identification of suitable rank functions can be difficult, and (as the previous case study has shown) the verification proofs can generate an almost overwhelming amount of detail to keep track of. Two forms of mechanical support that address this problem are currently available for the rank function verification technique.

The first form of mechanical assistance is provided by the general purpose theorem prover PVS (Prototype Verification System) [91]. This interactive theorem prover allows theories to be constructed and verified in a hierarchical fashion, making use of previously verified theories. A theory for the trace semantics of CSP has been provided, and then more specialized theories about rank functions, maintaining of rank functions, authentication, and secrecy, have been provided on

$$\rho(u) = 1$$
$$\rho(n) = 1$$

$$\rho(k) = \begin{cases} 0 \text{ if } k = K_{AB} \\ \quad \text{or } k = ServerKey(A) \\ \quad \text{or } k = ServerKey(B) \\ 1 \text{ otherwise} \end{cases}$$

$$\rho(\{m\}_k) = \begin{cases} 0 \text{ if } \{m\}_k = \{N_B\}_{K_{AB}} \\ \quad \text{or } \{m\}_k = \{A.n.N_B\}_{ServerKey(b)} \\ \qquad \wedge n \neq N_A \\ \quad \text{or } \{m\}_k = \{b.K_{AB}.n.N_B\}_{ServerKey(a)} \\ \qquad \wedge (b \neq B \vee n \neq N_A \vee a \neq A) \\ 1 \text{ otherwise} \end{cases}$$

$$\rho(m_1.m_2) = \min\{\rho(m_1), \rho(m_2)\}$$

$$\rho(Running\_Initiator.s) = 1$$
$$\rho(Commit\_Responder.s) = \begin{cases} 0 \text{ if } s = B.A.N_A.N_B.K_{AB} \\ 1 \text{ otherwise} \end{cases}$$

Figure 7.17 Rank function for authentication of the Yahalom protocol IV

top of this basic theory, initially in [27], with further developments in [15] and [29]. For example, the proof rules given in Figures 7.1 to 7.6 are included (and their soundness established) within the theory files. The result is a proof environment for proposing rank functions and verifying protocol descriptions. Furthermore, by providing a 'blank' rank function to the theorem prover, it is possible to generate all of the constraints that must be true of any rank function that is to be maintained by the protocol agents. If these are contradictory, then the contradiction may correspond to a protocol flaw (see e.g. [29]). Conversely, the conditions may naturally suggest a rank function.

The second form of mechanical assistance is provided by RankAnalyser, a tool that automatically constructs a rank function for a protocol. It makes use of results [39] that allow the space of facts involved in a protocol to be partitioned into a finite number of equivalence classes. It then constructs a 'minimal' rank function by identifying those facts that must have positive rank, and gives a rank of 0 to all the others – all facts in an equivalence class will have the same rank, so a rank need only be computed once for each class. If the resulting rank function meets all the conditions required for correctness of the protocol, then the verification is complete. However, some message that is deduced to have positive rank might also be required to have rank 0, and this gives a contradiction and establishes that no suitable rank function can exist. In this case, the contradiction might indicate an attack.

One advantage of the rank function approach is that it does not suffer from the state explosion problem. Both forms of mechanical assistance mentioned here are appropriate for verifying networks of arbitrary size, and with arbitrarily many concurrent executions of the protocol.

7.6 Summary

This chapter has introduced the *rank-function* technique, initially given in [86]. This technique is used for establishing that certain events in a protocol execution cannot occur, or can only occur under particular circumstances. The idea is to provide a function that assigns a value or *rank* to facts and to signals, such that only those with positive rank can arise in a protocol execution: if agents only receive facts of positive rank, then they can only ever produce facts and signals of positive rank. Thus verification of the overall protocol is reduced to proof obligations on each of the components separately.

The laws of CSP allow different cases to be considered separately, and hence to be verified with different rank functions. The different cases often reflect the kind of informal reasoning that might be made about the various cases to be considered, and the CSP proof can be seen as making the argument precise. There is also PVS support for the construction of proofs.

Construction of a rank function can provide some insight into why a protocol is correct, and perhaps what might go wrong if aspects of the protocol are changed. Alternatively, it might be possible to construct a rank function automatically. This will be quicker, and also serves as a proof, but it provides less insight as to why the protocol is correct, since the resulting rank function is given simply as an enumeration of the ranks of all of the facts without any further structure. However, it will provide confidence to underpin a search for the simplest rank function if further understanding is required.

8 Simplifying transformations

In previous chapters we have seen how we can analyze small security protocols. However, most commercial protocols are considerably more complicated than those we have seen so far. For example, the CyberCash Main Sequence protocol is as in Figure 8.1; those fields whose names finish with an underscore are abbreviations, defined in Figures 8.2 and 8.3. This is a protocol for carrying out commercial transactions over the internet between a customer and a merchant. It is designed to provide many functions within a single protocol, including secrecy of sensitive information (such as customer card numbers) and authentication for the involved parties. This protocol contains dozens of fields, and in one place, six levels of nested cryptography.

This extra complexity of such protocols makes analysis much more difficult: if we try to use a model checker, the complexity leads to an explosion in the state space and the message space; if we try to do a direct proof, the complexity makes the protocol harder to understand – it is very hard to see how the protocol is supposed to work, let alone verify it.

8.1 Simplifying transformations for protocols

However, it will often appear plausible that much of the complexity of a large protocol, such as that given in Figure 8.1, could be removed without altering its security: some of the fields and some of the nested encryption might appear to be irrelevant to security; for example, in the CyberCash protocol, it appears as though the field representing the customer's postal code is not relevant to the secrecy of the customer's credit card number (we might require that the postal code be authenticated, but that is a different question). If we could prove that this complexity is indeed not needed for the security of the protocol, then it would be enough to analyze the protocol with this complexity removed. This is the question we address in this chapter. We identify a number of *simplifying transformations* on protocols that have the property that if there is an attack upon the original protocol (i.e. it is insecure) then there is also an attack upon the simplified protocol; we call transformations with this property '*safe*' because they do not hide any protocol flaws. They are safe from the point of view of protocol analysis. It means that if we can verify the simplified protocol, we will have verified the original protocol.

Note that the property of being safe is unidirectional: it is possible to apply safe simplifying transformations in such a way as to introduce new attacks, by oversimplifying the protocol. This will depend on the nature of the simplification,

Message 1 $M \rightarrow C$: *Accepts . MerchantAmount . MerchantAmount2Optional .*
                                            MerchantCcId . MerchantOrderId . MerchantDate .
                                            MerchantSwVersion . Note . Payload . PayloadNote . Type .
                                            UrlCancel . UrlFail . UrlPayTo . UrlSuccess .
                                            MD5(Payload) . MerchantSignedHashKey_ .
                                            *MerchantSignedHash_*

Message 2 $C \rightarrow M$: *CyberKey . Date . Id . MerchantCcId . MerchantDate .*
                                            MerchantSignedHashKey_ . OrderId . ServiceCategory .
                                            Transaction . Type . PrHash_ . PrSignedHash_ .
                                            *OpaqPrefixCH1_ . OpaqueCH1_*

Message 3 $M \rightarrow CB$: *CyberKey . MerchantCcId . MerchantCyberKey .*
                                            MerchantDate . MerchantTransaction . ServiceCategory .
                                            OpaqPrefixCH1_ . OpaqueCH1_ .
                                            *MerchantOpaqPrefixCM1_ . MerchantOpaqueCM1_*

Message 4 $CB \rightarrow M$: *MerchantCcId . MerchantTransaction . MerchantDate .*
                                            *ServiceCategory . MerchantOpaqueCM6_ . OpaqueCM6_*

Message 5 $M \rightarrow C$: *Date . MerchantCcId . MerchantDate . MerchantMessage .*
                                            MerchantResponseCode . MerchantSwVersion . Id .
                                            ServiceCategory . Transaction . Type . PrHash_ .
                                            *PrSignedHash_ . OpaqueCM6_*

Figure 8.1 The CyberCash Main Sequence protocol

and on the property we are concerned about. We need to use our experience and intuition to avoid oversimplifying. To quote Albert Einstein: 'Everything should be made as simple as possible, but no simpler.'

The idea will be, starting from the original protocol, to apply as many safe simplifying transformations as possible, trying to avoid introducing new attacks, and then to analyze the simplified protocol. If the simplified protocol is secure, then so is the original; if, however, our analysis discloses an attack upon the simplified protocol, we have to consider whether there is a corresponding attack on the original protocol (by effectively undoing all the simplifying transformations); if there *is* such an attack, then clearly the original protocol is flawed; otherwise, we have oversimplified, so we have to try again.

Our approach is to identify a function f on the facts of the original protocol P, describing how facts are simplified. We then lift this function to traces (i.e. finite sequences of messages), by pointwise application. In order for the transformation to be safe, we require that if tr is a trace representing an attack upon the original protocol, then $f(tr)$ is an attack upon the simplified version. Proving this for a particular simplification f will consist of two things: proving that for every trace tr

$MerchantSignedHashKey\_ \mathrel{\widehat{=}} MD5(PK(M)),$

$MerchantSignedHash\_ \mathrel{\widehat{=}}$
  $\{MD5(Accepts\,.\,MerchantDate\,.\,MerchantAmount\,.\,MerchantCcId\,.$
    $MerchantOrderId\,.\,MerchantSignedHashKey\_\,.\,Note\,.\,Type\,.$
    $UrlCancel\,.\,UrlFail\,.\,UrlPayto\,.\,UrlSuccess)\}_{SK(M)},$

$PrHash\_ \mathrel{\widehat{=}}$
  $MD5(Accepts\,.\,Date\,.\,MerchantAmount\,.\,MerchantCcId\,.$
    $MerchantOrderId\,.\,MerchantSignedHashKey\_\,.\,Note\,.\,Type\,.$
    $UrlCancel\,.\,UrlFail\,.\,UrlPayTo\,.\,UrlSuccess),$

$PrSignedHash\_ \mathrel{\widehat{=}} MerchantSignedHash\_,$

$OpaqPrefixCH1\_ \mathrel{\widehat{=}} \{kcs\}_{PKCyberKey},$

$OpaqueCH1\_ \mathrel{\widehat{=}}$
  $\{Amount\,.\,CardCIdOptional\,.\,CardCityOptional\,.$
  $CardCountryOptional\,.\,CardExpirationDate\,.\,CardName\,.$
  $CardNumber\,.\,CardOtherFieldsOptional\,.\,CardPostalCodeOptional\,.$
  $CardPrefixOptional\,.\,CardSalt\,.\,CardStateOptional\,.$
  $CardStreetOptional\,.\,CardType\,.\,SwVersion\,.\,MD5(PK(C))\,.$
  $SignatureCH1\_\}_{kcs},$

$SignatureCH1\_ \mathrel{\widehat{=}}$
  $\{MD5(Amount\,.\,CardCIdOptional\,.\,CardCityOptional\,.$
    $CardCountryOptional\,.\,CardExpirationDate\,.\,CardName\,.$
    $CardNumber\,.\,CardOtherFieldsOptional\,.$
    $CardPostalCodeOptional\,.\,CardPrefixOptional\,.\,CardSalt\,.$
    $CardStateOptional\,.\,CardStreetOptional\,.\,CardType\,.$
    $CyberKey\,.\,Date\,.\,Id\,.\,MerchantCcId\,.$
    $MerchantSignedHashKey\_\,.\,OrderId\,.\,PrHash\_\,.$
    $PrSignedHash\_\,.\,SwVersion\,.\,Transaction\,.\,Type)\}_{SK(C)},$

$MerchantOpaqPrefixCM1\_ \mathrel{\widehat{=}} \{kms\}_{PKCyberKey(Merchant)},$

$MerchantOpaqueCM1\_ \mathrel{\widehat{=}}$
  $\{Date\,.\,DescriptionListOptional\,.\,Id\,.\,MerchantAmount\,.\,MerchantDba\,.$
  $MerchantLocationOptional\,.\,MerchantMessage\,.$
  $MerchantSignedHashKey\_\,.\,MerchantSwMessageOptional\,.$
  $MerchantSwServerOptional\,.\,MerchantSwVersion\,.$
  $MerchantUrlOptional\,.\,OrderId\,.\,PrHash\_\,.\,PrSignedHash\_\,.$
  $RetrievalReferenceNumberOptional\,.\,ServerDateMerchantOptional\,.$
  $TerminalIdFuture\,.\,Transaction\,.\,TransactionDescriptionOptional\,.$
  $Type\,.\,MD5(PKCyberKey(Merchant))\,.$
  $MerchantSignatureCM1\_\}_{kms},$

Figure 8.2 Abbreviations in the CyberCash protocol

$MerchantSignatureCM1\_ \,\widehat{=}\,$
    $\{MD5(CyberKey \,.\, Date \,.\, Id \,.\, MerchantAmount \,.\, MerchantCcId \,.$
       $MerchantCyberKey \,.\, MerchantDate \,.\, MerchantTransaction \,.$
       $OrderId \,.\, PrHash\_ \,.\, PrSignedHash\_ \,.$
       $ServerDateMerchantOptional \,.\, Transaction \,.\, Type)\}_{SK(M)},$

$MerchantOpaqueCM6\_ \,\widehat{=}\,$
    $\{AcquirerRefDataOptional \,.\, ActionCode \,.$
    $Addn1ResponseDataOptional \,.\, AuthorizationCode \,.\, AvsInfoOptional \,.$
    $CardCIdOptional \,.\, CardCityOptional \,.\, CardCountryOptional \,.$
    $CardExpirationDate \,.\, CardName \,.\, CardNumber \,.$
    $CardPostalCodeOptional \,.\, CardPrefixOptional \,.\, CardStateOptional \,.$
    $CardStreetOptional \,.\, CardType \,.\, Date \,.\, DebuggingInfoOptional \,.\, Id \,.$
    $MerchantMessage \,.\, MerchantSignedHashKey\_ \,.$
    $MerchantSwMessageOptional \,.\, MerchantSwSeverityOptional \,.$
    $OrderId \,.\, ProcessorErrorCodeFuture \,.\, PrHash\_ \,.\, PrSignedHash\_ \,.$
    $MerchantResponseCode \,.\, ResponseDetailCodeFuture \,.$
    $RetrievalReferenceNumberOptional \,.\, ServerDate \,.\, TerminalIdFuture \,.$
    $Transaction \,.\, Type\}_{kms},$

$OpaqueCM6\_ \,\widehat{=}\,$
    $\{Amount \,.\, AuthorizationCode \,.\, CardCIdOptional \,.\, CardCityOptional \,.$
    $CardCountryOptional \,.\, CardExpirationDate \,.\, CardName \,.$
    $CardNumber \,.\, CardOtherFieldsOptional \,.\, CardPostalCodeOptional \,.$
    $CardPrefixOptional \,.\, CardSalt \,.\, CardStateOptional \,.$
    $CardStreetOptional \,.\, CardTypeOptional \,.\, MerchantDba \,.$
    $MerchantLocationOptional \,.\, MerchantUrlOptional \,.$
    $Message \,.\, OrderId \,.\, ResponseCode \,.\, ServerDate \,.\, SwMessageOptional \,.$
    $SwSeverityOptional \,.\, TransactionDescriptionOptional\}_{kcs}.$

Figure 8.3 Abbreviations in the CyberCash protocol

of P, $f(tr)$ is a trace of the simplified version of P; and that if a trace tr constitutes an attack upon P, then $f(tr)$ constitutes an attack upon the simplified version of P.

In the next section we describe a collection of simplifying transformations that we are interested in, and describe *safety conditions* that are sufficient to establish that a transformation is safe. In Section 8.3 we describe a number of simplifying transformations that meet these conditions:

- removal of encryption;
- removal of hash function application;
- removal of some fields in protocol messages;
- renaming of atoms;
- swapping atoms;

■ moving fields out of encryptions.

In Section 8.4 we describe further transformations, to split messages into smaller components, and to redirect them. In Section 8.5 we illustrate our techniques by applying them to the CyberCash protocol, simplifying the protocol to a stage where we can apply standard model checking and rank function analysis techniques.

8.2   Transformations on protocols

In this section we formalize how we represent transformations upon protocols; we then state a result, giving sufficient conditions for a transformation to be safe.

Formalizing transformations

A transformation will be defined via a function

$$f : fact \rightarrow fact$$

which defines how facts in the original protocol are replaced by facts in the simplified protocol. In the following, we will overload f to apply to several different types of arguments.

We lift the function f to events as follows:

$$f(send.a.b.M) \;\widehat{=}\; send.a.b.f(M),$$
$$f(receive.a.b.M) \;\widehat{=}\; receive.a.b.f(M),$$
$$f(signal.c.a.b.M) \;\widehat{=}\; signal.c.a.b.f(M),$$

and lift it to traces by applying it pointwise to each event in the trace.

As in earlier chapters, we can build a CSP representation of a system running the original protocol by modelling each honest agent a by a process $User_a$, modelling the intruder by a process $Intruder(IK)$ where IK is his initial knowledge, and then defining the complete system by:

$$System \;\widehat{=}\; \left(\big|\big|\big|_{a \in Honest} User_a \right) \,\|\, Intruder(IK)$$

We now define the CSP representation of an honest agent a in the transformed system, corresponding to the process $User_a$ in the original system. We need a process that sends or receives the message $f(m)$ whenever the process $User_a$ sends or receives m. We therefore define the new representation to be the process $f(User_a)$ obtained by applying the alphabet renaming f to the description $User_a$. As well as describing honest agents sending and receiving transformed messages, this also captures the appropriate tests that agents might perform on the messages they receive.

Although the protocol agents are transformed in this way, the intruder remains the same, so the transformed protocol must still execute in the original environment. However, we have to transform the initial knowledge of the intruder; we will let IK'

be this transformed initial knowledge. In most cases we will take IK' to be $f(IK)$, but in some cases (where f removes some information from facts that should not be removed from IK) some additional information will need to be included.

The complete transformed system is modelled, therefore, by:

$$System' \mathrel{\widehat{=}} \left(\left|\left|\right|_{a \in Honest} f(User_a) \right) \parallel Intruder(IK')$$

A general result for safe transformations

We now present a general result that gives sufficient conditions under which a transformation is safe. In the next section we give particular examples of such transformations.

In order to show that a particular transformation f is safe, we need any attack upon *System* to correspond to an attack upon *System'*. We firstly require that if $tr \in traces(System)$ then $f(tr) \in traces(System')$. We then require that if tr is an attack on *System*, then $f(tr)$ is a corresponding attack on *System'*.

The trace contributions of the protocol agents are transformed through f by the alphabet renaming, and so will correspond under f. On the other hand, the contribution of the intruder process is still given by the original deduction rules, together with the new initial knowledge IK'. To show that the transformed deductions are possible for the intruder, we need the following conditions to hold:

1 Given any set of facts S and a fact m, if m can be generated from S (what the intruder has seen on the network) together with IK (what the intruder starts with), then $f(m)$ can be generated from $f(S)$ (what the intruder has seen on the network running the simplified protocol) together with IK'. More formally:

$$S \cup IK \vdash m \Rightarrow f(S) \cup IK' \vdash f(m)$$

2 The intruder's initial knowledge in the simplified system should include transformations of all the initial knowledge in the original system:

$$f(IK) \subseteq IK'$$

These two properties are called the *safe transformation conditions*. The second property tells us how to choose the initial knowledge for the intruder in the transformed system, given his initial knowledge in the original system.

It is possible to show that if these two conditions hold, then any trace tr of *System* will be such that $f(tr)$ is a trace of *System'*. This means that every trace of the original system is 'matched' by one in the new system. We want to show that every *attack* on the original system is 'matched' by one on the new system. An attack is simply a violation of a security requirement expressed as a predicate on traces $S(tr)$. For the properties we are interested in – secrecy and authentication – we need to know under what conditions the failure of tr to meet S means that $f(tr)$ also fails to meet S. In other words, when an attack on the protocol corresponds to an attack on the simplified version.

The secrecy property considered in Chapter 3 between agents a and b is defined as follows:

$$Secret_{a,b}(tr) =$$
$$\forall m \bullet signal.Claim\_Secret.a.b.m \text{ in } tr \wedge a \in Honest \wedge b \in Honest$$
$$\Rightarrow \neg(leak.m \text{ in } tr)$$

The full secrecy property for the entire network is given by

$$Secrecy(tr) = \forall a, b \in USER \bullet Secret_{a,b}(tr)$$

This property is violated only when some fact m is claimed to be a secret, and is also leaked within a single trace tr. But then the fact $f(m)$ is both claimed to be a secret and is leaked in the corresponding trace $f(tr)$, and so the attack is preserved by the simplifying transformation f. Thus if the simplified version is free of attacks, then so too is the original version of the protocol. The result is that

$$System' \text{ sat } Secrecy(tr) \Rightarrow System \text{ sat } Secrecy(tr)$$

It is always sufficient to analyze the system transformed under a safe simplifying transformation.

We now consider authentication. An authentication property has the form

$$Auth_{m_1,m_2}(tr) = signal.c_1.a.b.m_1 \text{ precedes } signal.c_2.a.b.m_2$$

which states that some claim c_2 concerning some fact m_2 can occur only after some previous claim c_1 about some fact m_1. The facts m_1 and m_2 often overlap in some of the information they contain, and indeed are often identical.

The transformed protocol will firstly be using $f(m_1)$ and $f(m_2)$ in place of m_1 and m_2, so we should consider a transformed version of the requirement:

$$Auth_{f(m_1),f(m_2)}(tr) = signal.c_1.a.b.f(m_1) \text{ precedes } signal.c_2.a.b.f(m_2)$$

However, if tr fails to meet $Auth_{m_1,m_2}$ then it does not automatically follow that $f(tr)$ will fail to meet $Auth_{f(m_1),f(m_2)}$. The reason is that $signal.c_2.a.b.m_2$ might be preceded by some other event $signal.c_1.a.b.m_3$ in tr, rather than m_1, (so $Auth_{m_1,m_2}$ is violated), yet if $f(m_3) = f(m_1)$ then $f(tr)$ does meet $Auth_{f(m_1),f(m_2)}$ since $f(m_1)$ does precede $f(m_2)$ in $f(tr)$.

The difficulty arises from the fact that f might map many of the facts on which authentication is required on to a single fact, turning an attack into a non-attack by introducing the authenticated signal from elsewhere.

The condition that prevents this requires injectivity on the authenticated fact: that if $f(m) = f(m_1)$ then $m = m_1$ for every fact m. This is called the *safe transformation for authentication* condition. This is of course dependent on the authentication property required. In general, an authentication property will be a conjunction of $Auth_{m_1,m_2}$ properties. In this case, injectivity on each of the authenticated facts is required.

If the simplifying transformation f meets the safe transformation for authentication condition, then attacks on authentication will be preserved by simplifying the protocol. The result is that

$$System' \text{ sat } Auth_{f(m_1),f(m_2)} \Rightarrow System \text{ sat } Auth_{m_1,m_2}$$

The simplified protocol can be analyzed for authentication, and if the verification succeeds then the original protocol is correct with respect to that property.

8.3   Examples of safe simplifying transformations

In this section we present a number of transformations that satisfy the conditions from the previous section, and are hence safe.

Removing encryptions

We begin by defining a transformation that removes some of the encryptions from the protocol. We identify a set *Encs* of encrypted messages such that all encrypted components $\{m\}_k$ from *Encs* that appear in the protocol should be replaced with the body m. The transformation function f is as follows:

$$
\begin{aligned}
f(a) &\cong a && \text{for } a \in Atom,\\
f(m_1.m_2) &\cong m_1.m_2,\\
f(\{m\}_k) &\cong f(m), && \text{if } \{m\}_k \in Encs,\\
& \{f(m)\}_k, \text{ otherwise},\\
f(g(\!|m|\!)) &\cong g(\!|f(m)|\!)
\end{aligned}
$$

The interesting case is the case for $\{m\}_k$ with $\{m\}_k \in Encs$, where the outermost encryption is stripped off; most of the other cases simply apply the function recursively.

We define the intruder's initial knowledge in the transformed protocol as the result of applying the simplifying function to his knowledge in the original protocol:

$$IK' \cong f(IK)$$

It is straightforward to show that f satisfies the safe transformation conditions. Hence, it follows from the previous sections that it is a safe transformation with respect to secrecy. In other words, if s is a secret even with some encryptions removed, then it must be secret in the original protocol.

Further, f is clearly injective on atoms and concatenations of them, so we can use the safe transformation for authentication condition to deduce that this transformation is a safe transformation with respect to agreement on sequences of atoms. For example, in the Yahalom protocol, authentication requires agreement on $n_a.n_b.k_{ab}$. This is a sequence of atoms, so a verification could be attempted in a version of the protocol simplified by using a transformation that removes encryption.

The way this simplifying transformation will be used in practice is to identify a particular encryption in the protocol description that we think is unnecessary, and to take f to be the function that removes this encryption; that is, we take *Encs* to be the set of all instances of the encrypted component in question. Note though, that if messages in *Encs* appear elsewhere in the protocol description – that is, another encrypted component in the protocol has the same form as the one we are simplifying – then they must also be simplified.

Removing some atomic or hashed fields

We now define a transformation that completely removes some fields from the protocol. It turns out that we must restrict these fields to being either atoms that are not keys, or the application of hash functions. Formally, we let

$$M \subseteq \textit{fact}$$

be the set of such messages, and assume that every element in M is either an atomic fact that is not a key, or of the form $g(\!|m|\!)$ for some hash function g.

In order to define this transformation, we need to specify how it acts upon a message that is to be removed, leaving an 'empty message'. The *fact* datatype has no concept of an 'empty fact', so we model such 'empty facts' by a distinguished atomic value nil.

We define the transformation as follows:

$$
\begin{aligned}
f(m) &\mathrel{\hat{=}} \text{nil} && \text{if } m \in M, \\
f(a) &\mathrel{\hat{=}} a && \text{for } a \in \textit{Atom}, \\
f(m_1.m_2) &\mathrel{\hat{=}} f(m_1), && \text{if } f(m_2) = \text{nil}, \\
& \quad\; f(m_2), && \text{if } f(m_1) = \text{nil}, \\
& \quad\; f(m_1).f(m_2) && \text{otherwise}, \\
f(\{m\}_k) &\mathrel{\hat{=}} \text{nil}, && \text{if } f(m) = \text{nil}, \\
& \quad\; \{f(m)\}_k, && \text{otherwise}, \\
f(g(\!|m|\!)) &\mathrel{\hat{=}} \text{nil}, && \text{if } f(m) = \text{nil}, \\
& \quad\; g(\!|f(m)|\!), && \text{otherwise}.
\end{aligned}
$$

We adopt a convention from functional programming languages such as Haskell, namely that the patterns in the definition are matched from top to bottom, so that a definition further down the page will be applied only if no earlier definition applies. Thus for messages $m \in M$ the first line of the definition applies.

For composite messages, the definition gets applied recursively to the subcomponents; if either member of a pair gets removed in this way, then we are left with the other member of the pair; if all of the body of an encryption or a hash function application gets removed, then the encryption or hash function is removed.

We define the intruder's initial knowledge in the transformed protocol by:

$$IK' \mathrel{\hat{=}} f(IK) \cup \{\text{nil}\}$$

Note that we assume the intruder can produce nil, i.e. an empty message.

Our definitions satisfy the safe transformation conditions. It follows that this is a safe transformation with respect to secrecy. Note that the transformation is safe even if we remove a field that we are trying to prove is secret; however, in this case the secret will be renamed to nil, which is in the intruder's initial knowledge, and so this transformation will introduce a new attack: such a transformation is safe but useless.

If all the values upon which agreement is intended are atoms or their concatenations, and none are removed, then the transformation satisfies the safe transformation for authentication condition, and so we deduce that this is a safe transformation with respect to agreement on such values. The above condition simply states that if you want to be sure that the protocol guarantees agreement on a particular field, then your simplification shouldn't remove that field!

In practice, we will use this transformation to remove *all* fields of a particular type: to remove one field we would have to define M to be all values with which that field could be instantiated, i.e. all values of that type; this would have the effect of removing all fields of the type.

For example, all the nonces could be removed from the description of the Yahalom protocol, resulting in the following simplification:

$$\text{Message } 1 \quad a \rightarrow b \ : \ a$$
$$\text{Message } 2 \quad b \rightarrow s \ : \ b.\{a\}_{ServerKey(b)}$$
$$\text{Message } 3 \quad s \rightarrow a \ : \ \{b.k_{ab}\}_{ServerKey(a)}.\{a.k_{ab}\}_{ServerKey(b)}$$
$$\text{Message } 4 \quad a \rightarrow b \ : \ \{a.k_{ab}\}_{ServerKey(b)}$$

This simplified protocol guarantees that the key k_{ab} is secret. Hence this secrecy property is also true for the full Yahalom protocol.

Coalescing atoms

Our next transformation is one that coalesces certain pairs of atoms, replacing them by the first. This is typically used to remove redundancy in the protocol description. We define the transformation with respect to a set of pairs of atomic facts:

$$Pairs \ : \ \mathbb{P}(Atom \times Atom)$$

the idea being that for each $(m_1, m_2) \in Pairs$, any occurrence of the pair $m_1.m_2$ is replaced by m_1.

We need the following condition upon *Pairs*:

$$\forall (m_1, m_2) \in Pairs \bullet IK' \cup \{m_1\} \vdash m_2$$

that is, the atom removed can be deduced from the atom remaining and the intruder's initial knowledge. If we did not have this condition, then removing the atom m_2 would remove a possible source of information for the intruder, perhaps rendering the simplified protocol secure where the original was not. We will therefore tend to use this transformation in two situations: where the atom removed is in the intruder's initial knowledge, and where the atom removed is equal to the one remaining.

We formalize the transformation as follows:

$$
\begin{aligned}
f(a) &\mathrel{\widehat{=}} a && \text{for } a \in Atom \\
f(m_1.m_2) &\mathrel{\widehat{=}} m_1, && \text{if } (m_1, m_2) \in Pairs, \\
& \phantom{\mathrel{\widehat{=}}} f(m_1).f(m_2), && \text{otherwise,} \\
f(\{m\}_k) &\mathrel{\widehat{=}} \{f(m)\}_k, \\
f(g(\!|m|\!)) &\mathrel{\widehat{=}} g(\!|f(m)|\!)
\end{aligned}
$$

We define the intruder's initial knowledge in the transformed system by:

$$ IK' \mathrel{\widehat{=}} f(IK) $$

Our definitions satisfy the safe transformation conditions. Hence we deduce that this is a safe transformation with respect to secrecy. It also meets the safe transformation for authentication condition provided f is injective on the messages upon which agreement is intended.

Other transformations

There are a number of other safe transformations. They all meet the safe transformation condition, and so they are all appropriate for investigating secrecy. Furthermore, they all meet the safe transformation for authentication condition with respect to any authentication requirement concerned only with atomic facts and their concatenations (which is true for almost all authentication requirements in practice). These transformations include the following:

- a transformation that removes some of the hash functions from the protocol: this transformation is very similar to that for removing encryptions;
- a transformation that uniformly renames atoms in protocol messages, and is injective on facts to be authenticated;
- a transformation that moves fields outside the body of encryptions;
- a transformation that swaps particular pairs of atoms when they appear next to one another: this transformation is very similar to that for coalescing atoms.

8.4 Structural transformations

We now consider two classes of transformations that are not formed by simple renaming of messages within the protocol, but instead change the structure of the protocol: we consider a transformation that splits a single message into two, and another that replaces two messages with a single message, redirecting a message that is sent via a third party so that it is sent direct.

We begin by describing message-splitting transformations. The idea is that if we have a fact $m_1.m_2$ that is transmitted in a protocol run, then we replace this with a pair of facts, m_1 and m_2 respectively.

Such a transformation can be advantageous when model checking, because it reduces the size of the message space (the number of distinct messages in the model); however, there is a trade-off, because it increases the size of the state space; our experiences using the model-checker FDR suggests that it is a worthwhile transformation for moderately large messages. It is perhaps more useful when used in combination with a redirecting transformation, defined later in this section.

We define the transformation with respect to a set *Pairs* of pairs of messages, the idea being that *Pairs* represents those messages that should be split.

We can define a process $User'_A$ representing the behaviour of an agent A, corresponding to the process $User_A$ in the original system. Whenever the process $User_A$ sends or receives a message $m_1.m_2$ from *Pairs*, the process $User'_A$ will send or receive the two messages m_1 and m_2 one after the other.

The net effect of this is to split messages in the protocol into a number of smaller messages that are sent one after the other. For example, messages 3 and 4 of the Yahalom protocol could be divided in this way, to yield:

$$\text{Message 1} \quad a \rightarrow b \ : \ a.n_a$$
$$\text{Message 2} \quad b \rightarrow s \ : \ b.\{a.n_a.n_b\}_{ServerKey(b)}$$
$$\text{Message 3}a \quad s \rightarrow a \ : \ \{b.k_{ab}.n_a.n_b\}_{ServerKey(a)}$$
$$\text{Message 3}b \quad s \rightarrow a \ : \ \{a.k_{ab}\}_{ServerKey(b)}$$
$$\text{Message 4}a \quad a \rightarrow b \ : \ \{a.k_{ab}\}_{ServerKey(b)}$$
$$\text{Message 4}b \quad a \rightarrow b \ : \ \{n_b\}_{k_{ab}}$$

We now consider a class of transformations that we call *redirecting transformations*. In many protocols, some information is to be sent from an agent a to another agent b; however, rather than sending this message direct, the message is sent via some third party c; c does nothing with this message except forward it. For example, consider the protocol:

$$\text{Message } ac \quad A \rightarrow C \ : \ M$$
$$\text{Message } cb \quad C \rightarrow B \ : \ M$$

(where ac and cb are message numbers; the names are intended as mnemonics for the sender and receiver). The redirecting simplification will adapt the protocol so that this message is sent direct:

$$\text{Message } ab \quad A \rightarrow B \ : \ M$$

Such a transformation produces very significant gains when model checking, because in the original protocol it is possible to interleave c's events with a's and b's in many different ways; further, c should be willing to accept any message for m, because it performs no checks on this message, which markedly increases the state space. An experiment applying this transformation to the Otway-Rees protocol reduced the time FDR took to analyze a system from 7 minutes to 7 seconds.

For example, in combination with the previous transformation, the Yahalom protocol can be transformed to the following (which we considered in Chapter 5):

Message 1 $a \rightarrow b$: $a.n_a$

Message 2 $b \rightarrow s$: $b.\{a.n_a.n_b\}_{ServerKey(b)}$

Message 3a $s \rightarrow a$: $\{b.k_{ab}.n_a.n_b\}_{ServerKey(a)}$

Message 3b $s \rightarrow b$: $\{a.k_{ab}\}_{ServerKey(b)}$

Message 4b $a \rightarrow b$: $\{n_b\}_{k_{ab}}$

Both these transformations can be formally defined on CSP protocol descriptions. It is then possible to obtain results about the preservation of attacks. Since facts are not renamed by either of these transformations, the signals in the transformed protocol are exactly the same as in the original. It turns out that if *tr* is a trace of the original protocol violating a secrecy or authentication property, then there is a corresponding trace *tr'* in the transformed protocol that violates the same property. The intruder can mount essentially the same attack since he still has access to essentially the same information (though he might obtain it in a different way). Hence both of the above restructuring transformations preserve attacks on both secrecy and authentication specifications.

One point to note is that the placement of the signal events in the transformed protocol should correspond to their placement in the original protocol, although this might not be the natural placement for the signals in the transformed protocol. For instance, consider the case of testing whether *s* is authenticated to *b* in the example protocol above. The normal placement for *s*'s *running* signal would be just before message 3*b* in the transformed protocol; but this does not correspond to the natural placement of the signal in the original protocol, which would be before message 3*a*. We will see a concrete example of this when we consider the CyberCash protocol in the next section.

8.5   Case study: The CyberCash Main Sequence protocol

We illustrate our simplifying transformations by sketching how they can be used to simplify the CyberCash Main Sequence protocol.

The protocol is designed to allow credit-card purchases to take place securely between a customer and merchant, with the aid of CyberCash who acts as a trusted third party. The customer and merchant each generate a session key, which they encrypt with CyberCash's public key; they then use this session key to encrypt data sent to CyberCash, for secrecy. They each sign some data with a secret key, for authentication. CyberCash verifies the transaction, and sends acknowledgements to each, encrypted with the appropriate session key.

The goals of the protocol are not well documented, but it is reasonable to assume that the credit card number is intended to remain secret, that the customer and merchant should agree on the details of the transaction and the amount payable, and that the customer and merchant should be authenticated to CyberCash.

In order to make the simplifying transformations easier to apply (particularly the swapping and coalescing pairs transformations), we have produced tool support as an extension to Casper. The tool takes in a description of the complete protocol and a specification of a sequence of transformations, and applies them in order.

Tool support

The syntax for the protocol description is precisely as in Casper; we describe the syntax for defining the transformations below.

The transformations in Section 8.3 were defined using values; however, protocols are normally described in terms of variables, which can be instantiated with different values (of the appropriate types) in different runs. We want to define transformations that are applied uniformly, independent of the values with which variables are instantiated. Therefore, the tool supports transformations defined in terms of types, and applies these transformations to all variables and values of the appropriate types.

Here are some examples of simplifying transformations as they should appear in the input file:

```
#Simplifications

RemoveFields [Nonce, TimeStamp]
RemoveEncryption {Nonce, Agent}{PublicKey}
RemoveHash f(Nonce, Nonce, TimeStamp)
Coalesce (Agent, Agent)
SwapPairs (Nonce, Agent)
```

The effect of these transformations is as follows:

RemoveFields [Nonce, TimeStamp] This removes every variable of type Nonce or TimeStamp from the protocol description; it corresponds to the transformation of Section 8.3.

RemoveEncryption {Nonce, Agent}{PublicKey} This transformation removes a level of encryption from the protocol description, removing the encryption from all messages of the form $\{N.A\}_K$ for N in Nonce, A in Agent and K in PublicKey (represented by the notation '{Nonce, Agent}{PublicKey}'). This is the transformation of Section 8.3 where *Encs* is taken to be this set.

RemoveHash f(Nonce, Nonce, TimeStamp) This transformation removes some hash functions from the protocol description, replacing every hashed message of the form $f(N.N'.T)$ for N, N' in Nonce, T in TimeStamp by the corresponding unhashed message.

Coalesce (Agent,Agent) This transformation coalesces adjacent pairs of agent identities. This is the transformation described in Section 8.3 where *Pairs* is taken to be the set of all pairs of agent identities.

SwapPairs (Nonce, Agent) This transformation swaps adjacent pairs of nonces and atoms.

Simplifying the protocol

The complete protocol contains dozens of fields, but very few seem directly relevant to the security of the protocol. Many fields are included solely for reasons of functionality (e.g. *CardCityOptional*). Our first simplification is therefore a 'remove fields' simplification, to remove all atomic fields other than those that we believe are necessary: the fields that are retained are the price of the transaction according to each agent (*Amount* and *MerchantAmount*), the customer's credit card number (*CardNumber*), agents' identities, keys, and transaction numbers (which act as a kind of run identifier). (If we were testing whether the protocol guarantees timeliness, we would want to retain the timestamps.)

The protocol description contains many occurrences of the fields *PrSignedHash_* (also known as *MerchantSignedHash_*) and *PrHash_*. These seem to duplicate security already present, and so appear unnecessary. Several hashes of public keys are passed around by the protocol; these similarly seem to be unnecessary for the security of the protocol. Our second transformation is to remove all these fields, using the transformation of Section 8.3.

The next simplification is to remove all applications of the hash function *MD5*, using the transformation of Section 8.3; this hash function is simply used to reduce the size of messages, for efficiency.

This produces the following simplified version of the protocol:

Message 1 $M \rightarrow C$:   *MerchantAmount . MerchantCcId*

Message 2 $C \rightarrow M$:   *Id . MerchantCcID . Transaction . MerchantAmount .*
            *MerchantCcId . {kcs}$_{PKCyberKey}$. OpaqueCH1_*

Message 3 $M \rightarrow CB$:   *MerchantCcId . MerchantTransaction .*
            {kcs}$_{PKCyberKey}$. OpaqueCH1_ .
            *{kms}$_{PKMerchantCyberKey}$. MerchantOpaqueCM1_*

Message 4 $CB \rightarrow M$:   *MerchantCcId . MerchantTransaction .*
            {CardNumber . MerchantAmount .
               MerchantCcId . Id . Transaction}$_{kms}$.
            {CardNumber . Amount}$_{kcs}$

Message 5 $M \rightarrow C$:   *MerchantCcId . Id . Transaction . MerchantAmount .*
            {CardNumber . Amount}$_{kcs}$

where

$$OpaqueCH1_ =$$
$$\{ Amount . CardNumber .$$
$$\{ Amount . CardNumber . Id . MerchantCcId .$$
$$MerchantAmount . MerchantCcId . Transaction$$
$$\}_{SK(C)}$$
$$\}_{kcs}$$

$MerchantOpaqueCM1\_ =$
$\quad \{ \, Id . MerchantAmount . MerchantAmount . MerchantCcId . Transaction .$
$\qquad \{ \, Id . MerchantAmount . MerchantCcId .$
$\qquad\quad MerchantAmount . MerchantCcId . Transaction$
$\qquad \}_{SK(M)}$
$\quad \}_{kms}$

There is still nested encryption within $OpaqueCH1\_$ and $MerchantOpaqueCM1\_$: an encryption with a private, asymmetric key, and an encryption with a symmetric shared key. The encryption with the asymmetric key acts as a signature to provide authentication, whereas the encryption with the symmetric key is to ensure the secrecy of fields such as *CardNumber*. Both these encryptions are essential to the security of the protocol. However, if we consider the two security properties separately, we can perform different simplifications for each, in each case removing one encryption while retaining the other.

Simplifying for secrecy analysis

In order to simplify the protocol for secrecy analysis, we begin by removing the signatures. In the resulting protocol, several fields are repeated within some encryptions. By swapping pairs of atoms around we can bring together like atoms, which can then be coalesced to a single atom. Doing this produces the following protocol:

Message 1 $M \rightarrow C$: $MerchantCcId . MerchantAmount$

Message 2 $C \rightarrow M$: $Id . MerchantAmount . MerchantCcId .$
$\qquad\qquad\qquad\qquad Transaction . \{kcs\}_{PKCyberKey} .$
$\qquad\qquad\qquad\qquad \{Amount . CardNumber . MerchantCcId . Id .$
$\qquad\qquad\qquad\qquad\quad MerchantAmount . Transaction\}_{kcs}$

Message 3 $M \rightarrow CB$: $MerchantCcId . MerchantTransaction . \{kcs\}_{PKCyberKey} .$
$\qquad\qquad\qquad\qquad \{Amount . CardNumber . MerchantCcId . Id .$
$\qquad\qquad\qquad\qquad\quad MerchantAmount . Transaction\}_{kcs} .$
$\qquad\qquad\qquad\qquad \{kms\}_{PKMerchantCyberKey} .$
$\qquad\qquad\qquad\qquad \{Id . MerchantAmount . MerchantCcId .$
$\qquad\qquad\qquad\qquad\quad MerchantTransaction . Transaction\}_{kms}$

Message 4 $CB \rightarrow M$: $MerchantCcId . MerchantTransaction .$
$\qquad\qquad\qquad\qquad \{CardNumber . MerchantAmount . Id .$
$\qquad\qquad\qquad\qquad\quad MerchantCcId . Transaction\}_{kms} .$
$\qquad\qquad\qquad\qquad \{CardNumber . Amount\}_{kcs}$

Message 5 $M \rightarrow C$: $MerchantCcId . MerchantAmount . Transaction . Id .$
$\qquad\qquad\qquad\qquad \{CardNumber . Amount\}_{kcs}$

Note that the term

$\{kcs\}_{PKCyberKey}$.
$\{Amount\,.\,CardNumber\,.\,MerchantCcId\,.\,Id\,.\,MerchantAmount\,.\,Transaction\}_{kcs}$

appears in both messages 2 and 3. We can use the swapping pairs and splitting transformations to transform these messages to:

Message 2a $C \to M$: $Id\,.\,MerchantAmount\,.\,MerchantCcId\,.\,Transaction$

Message 2b $C \to M$: $\{kcs\}_{PKCyberKey}$.
$\qquad\qquad\qquad\qquad\quad \{Amount\,.\,CardNumber\,.\,MerchantCcId\,.\,Id\,.$
$\qquad\qquad\qquad\qquad\qquad\quad MerchantAmount\,.\,Transaction\}_{kcs}$

Message 3a $M \to CB$: $\{kcs\}_{PKCyberKey}$.
$\qquad\qquad\qquad\qquad\quad \{Amount\,.\,CardNumber\,.\,MerchantCcId\,.\,Id\,.$
$\qquad\qquad\qquad\qquad\qquad\quad MerchantAmount\,.\,Transaction\}_{kcs}$

Message 3b $M \to CB$: $MerchantCcId\,.\,MerchantTransaction$.
$\qquad\qquad\qquad\qquad\quad \{kms\}_{PKMerchantCyberKey}$.
$\qquad\qquad\qquad\qquad\quad \{Id\,.\,MerchantAmount\,.\,MerchantCcId$.
$\qquad\qquad\qquad\qquad\qquad\quad MerchantTransaction\,.\,Transaction\}_{kms}$

We can then use a redirecting transformation to replace messages 2b and 3a by a single message from C to CB. Similarly, we can use a combination of swapping, splitting and redirecting so that the term $\{CardNumber\,.\,Amount\}_{kcs}$ is sent directly from CB to C.

This gives the following fully simplified version of the protocol:

Message 1 $M \to C$: $MerchantCcId\,.\,MerchantAmount$

Message 2a $C \to M$: $Id\,.\,MerchantAmount\,.\,MerchantCcId\,.\,Transaction$

Message 2b $C \to CB$: $\{kcs\}_{PKCyberKey}$.
$\qquad\qquad\qquad\qquad\quad \{Amount\,.\,CardNumber\,.\,MerchantCcId\,.\,Id\,.$
$\qquad\qquad\qquad\qquad\qquad\quad MerchantAmount\,.\,Transaction\}_{kcs}$

Message 3 $M \to CB$: $MerchantCcId\,.\,MerchantTransaction$.
$\qquad\qquad\qquad\qquad\quad \{kms\}_{PKMerchantCyberKey}$.
$\qquad\qquad\qquad\qquad\quad \{Id\,.\,MerchantAmount\,.\,MerchantCcId$.
$\qquad\qquad\qquad\qquad\qquad\quad MerchantTransaction\,.\,Transaction\}_{kms}$

Message 4a $CB \to M$: $MerchantCcId\,.\,MerchantTransaction$.
$\qquad\qquad\qquad\qquad\quad \{CardNumber\,.\,MerchantAmount\,.\,Id$.
$\qquad\qquad\qquad\qquad\qquad\quad MerchantCcId\,.\,Transaction\}_{kms}$

Message 4b $CB \to C$: $\{CardNumber\,.\,Amount\}_{kcs}$

Message 5 $M \to C$: $MerchantCcId\,.\,MerchantAmount\,.\,Transaction\,.\,Id$

Simplifying for authentication analysis

In order to simplify the protocol for authentication analysis, we remove the encryptions using the symmetric keys *kcs* and *kms*. We can continue to simplify the protocol as above, using the swapping pairs and coalescing pairs transformations to remove duplicated atoms, and then using the splitting and redirecting transformations to send certain terms direct. This produces the following version of the protocol:

Message 1 $M \rightarrow C$:   *MerchantCcId . MerchantAmount*

Message 2a $C \rightarrow M$:   *Id . MerchantAmount . MerchantCcId .*
                                    Transaction . Amount . CardNumber

Message 2b $C \rightarrow CB$: $\{kcs\}_{PKCyberKey} \cdot$
                                    $\{Amount . CardNumber . MerchantCcId . Id .$
                                        $MerchantAmount . Transaction\}_{SK(C)}$

Message 3 $M \rightarrow CB$:   *MerchantCcId . MerchantTransaction .*
                                    $\{kms\}_{PKMerchantCyberKey} . Id .$
                                    MerchantAmount . Transaction .
                                    $\{Id . MerchantAmount . MerchantCcId .$
                                    $MerchantTransaction . Transaction\}_{SK(M)}$

Message 4a $CB \rightarrow M$:   *MerchantCcId . MerchantTransaction .*
                                    $\{CardNumber . MerchantAmount . Id .$
                                    $MerchantCcId . Transaction\}_{kms}$

Message 4b $CB \rightarrow C$: $\{CardNumber . Amount\}_{kcs}$

Message 5 $M \rightarrow C$:   *MerchantCcId . MerchantAmount . Transaction . Id*

Analysis of the simplified protocol

We analyzed the simplified version of the Main Sequence protocol using Casper and FDR, testing whether the protocol kept the customer's credit card number and the session keys secret, and testing whether the two agents were authenticated to CyberCash and to one another with agreement on the amount of the transaction.

We found a rather weak authentication attack upon the simplified protocol, where the intruder watches a run of the protocol up until message 4b, intercepting message 4a, and then fakes the message 5 from what he has seen in previous messages. This can be traced back to an attack on the full protocol, where the intruder intercepts message 4 and fakes message 5. The customer thinks he has completed the protocol run successfully, but the merchant thinks the run was broken off after message 3. It is arguable whether this should be classified as an attack; however, it is certainly a behaviour of which we should be aware. We are, however, able to verify that whenever the customer completes a protocol run, the merchant has progressed at least as far as message 3.

Our analysis has revealed some hidden assumptions about the operation of the protocol; without these assumptions, the protocol is insecure.

1 The identity numbers – the fields *Id* and *MerchantCdId* – are known to all agents, and so when an agent receives another's identity number, he can tell whether it is the correct number. If certificates were used, these could be used to link the identities to the identity numbers. Without this assumption, there are attacks where the intruder replaces one identity number with another. In one attack the merchant sells to the intruder, and the intruder begins another run impersonating the merchant and selling to the customer; the result is that CyberCash believes the transaction is between the merchant and customer and so debits the customer's account, but the intruder receives the goods. In the other attack the customer tries to buy from the intruder, and the intruder impersonates the customer in a run with the real merchant; CyberCash believes the transaction is between the real merchant and customer, and the merchant will deliver the goods to the customer; it is hard to see what the intruder gains from this attack, but it is a behaviour of which we should be aware.

2 The keys *PKMerchantCyberKey* and *PKCyberKey* are not public keys, known by everyone, but are in fact private, shared, asymmetric keys: CyberCash shares a *PKMerchantCyberKey* with each merchant, and a *PKCyberKey* with each customer. This is important, as these keys are used as part of the authentication mechanism.

Failure to find an attack using a model-checker does not necessarily imply that the protocol is secure: there might be attacks upon systems running the protocol that are larger than those analyzed; however, the model-checking results certainly improve our confidence in the security of the protocol. It is then possible to carry out a rank function analysis of each simplification of the protocol so as to prove the security properties noted above; for example, the rank function appropriate for proving the claimed secrecy property is in Figure 8.4. The full rank function analysis of both simplifications of the protocol is included in Appendix C, establishing that the secrecy and authentication properties indeed hold for the protocol.

The overall effect of these simplifications is to reduce the protocol to versions that can be easily understood with respect to the properties under consideration. The main aspects of the protocol have in each case been retained to ensure that it still meets its original requirement, yet it is simple enough to apply standard analysis techniques.

8.6 Summary

In this chapter we have introduced the notion of *safe simplifying transformations*: transformations that have the property of preserving attacks. We have produced sufficient conditions for a transformation to be safe and used this result to show that

$$\rho_0(u) = 1$$

$$\rho_0(t) = \begin{cases} 0 & \text{if } t = CardNumber_0 \\ 1 & \text{otherwise} \end{cases}$$

$$\rho_0(pk) = \begin{cases} 0 & \text{if } pk = pkCyberKey(mr) \text{ for } mr \in HM \\ 1 & \text{otherwise} \end{cases}$$

$$\rho_0(sk) = \begin{cases} 0 & \text{if } sk = skCyberKey(mr) \text{ for } mr \in HM \text{ or } sk = skCyberKey \\ 1 & \text{otherwise} \end{cases}$$

$$\rho_0(shk) = \begin{cases} 0 & \text{if } shk \in KEYS_{cu_0} \text{ or } shk \in KEYS_{mr} \text{ for } mr \in HM \\ 1 & \text{otherwise} \end{cases}$$

$$\rho(\{m\}_k) = \begin{cases} 1 & \text{if } k = pkCyberKey \\ & \text{or } k = KEYS_{mr} \text{ for some } mr \in HM \\ & \text{or } \rho(m) = \rho(k) \wedge (\rho(k) = 0 \wedge m = am.cn.mci.cu.ma.tr \\ & \qquad\qquad\qquad\qquad \Rightarrow merchant(mci) \in HM) \\ 0 & \text{otherwise} \end{cases}$$

$$\rho(m_1.m_2) = \min\{\rho(m_1), \rho(m_2)\}$$

Figure 8.4 Rank function for verification of Simplified CyberCash Protocol Secrecy property

a number of transformations are indeed safe. We have illustrated these techniques by applying them to a large commercial protocol, simplifying this down to a size that can be modelled and analyzed. Attacks that are found can be traced back to the original protocol to see if they are feasible.

The theory of safe simplifying transformations was originally presented in [60]. In order to make the simplifying transformations easier to apply (particularly the swapping and coalescing pairs transformations), we have produced tool support as an extension to Casper [58]. The tool takes in a description of the complete protocol and a specification of a sequence of transformations, and applies them in order.

The description of the CyberCash main sequence protocol is taken from the description given in [12].

9 Other approaches

9.1 Introduction

That security protocols required careful analysis was recognized very early on. It was also realized that just eyeballing a design until you got bored and had failed to spot an attack does not provide any good assurance that the design is sound. In this chapter we provide an overview of approaches that have been proposed to make the reasoning about security protocols more systematic and in many cases more formal and automated.

We make no claim that this is an exhaustive survey but seek to give what we hope is a representative sampling of techniques and give a flavour of the historical development of the subject. The descriptions will necessarily be rather shallow, but we hope that this will provide the reader with enough of an impression to pursue topics further if any take their fancy.

In recent years the area has seen an explosive growth, with numerous formalisms being brought to bear. Broadly speaking they fall into four main categories:

- logic-based
- model-checking, state enumeration
- proof-based
- cryptographic (provable security).

There has been a trend more recently to try to combine these. For example, bringing together model-checking and proof-based techniques and tools looks to be a very fruitful way to go, not just for security protocols but for the evaluation of critical systems in general. Similarly, some recent work attempts to bring together the strengths of formal and cryptographic techniques.

Security protocols were introduced with the 1978 paper of Needham and Schroeder 'Using encryption for authentication in large networks of computers' [68]. In this paper the authors describe the use of symmetric and asymmetric cryptographic mechanisms to achieve authentication and key distribution over a network and propose a number of protocols, including early versions of their secret and public-key protocols. The paper concludes with the remarkably prescient paragraph:

> Protocols such as those developed here are prone to extremely subtle errors that are unlikely to be detected in normal operation. The need for techniques

to verify the correctness of such protocols is great, and we encourage those interested in such problems to consider this area.

The challenge has been taken up by many researchers and the problems posed by these fascinating objects has stimulated the development of new conceptual frameworks and tools. Even now, after over 20 years of intense study, security protocols still conceal traps for the unwary and present us with open research challenges.

9.2 The Dolev-Yao model

A significant early step in the development of the subject was the 1983 paper of Dolev and Yao [25]. This laid the conceptual foundations of the subject by presenting the basic intruder model that has been used in virtually all the work since, including our own. Here the idea of an intruder with the ability to manipulate messages passing over the system – deleting, replaying, faking, redirecting, and so on, limited only by the cryptographic constraints – was set out. The paper also introduced the idea of viewing the problem as a form of word problem.

9.3 BAN logic and derivatives

The BAN logic of authentication due to Burrows, Abadi and Needham [20] was one of the first attempts to make the reasoning about the properties of security protocols more systematic. The basic idea is to reason about the states of belief of the (legitimate) agents involved. This involves understanding how such beliefs evolve as new information is received. To this end, initial knowledge, assumptions and the steps of the protocol are mapped into formulae in the logic in a process known as idealization. It must be stressed that the BAN logic really is about authentication. This seems obvious, given that the authors clearly describe it as such, but it is a fact that often seemed to have been overlooked. Many researchers seem to have fallen into the trap of ascribing more to the logic than was intended; in particular, to assume that secrecy properties also fall out of a BAN analysis. We should also observe that the BAN authors do not define the term authentication and indeed they quite explicitly state that they are not defining it.

Another important point to stress is that BAN explicitly assumes that all principals are honest. This is clearly not a universally applicable assumption, but a valid one in some contexts. It was certainly appropriate for the client-server type context the authors originally had in mind. It is however less appropriate in the distributed network environments prevalent today. If BAN is applied outside such contexts the results can be seriously misleading, as exemplified by the Lowe attack on NSPK.

In a curious twist of history the authors did not use the term 'belief' in their original writings. However they were urged to suggest a pronunciation of the triple turnstile symbol $\models$, and came up with 'believes'. As a result, there has been a widespread misconception about what the BAN authors had in mind.

The BAN logic provides an elegant and comparatively easy formalism to use. It has proved to be a very useful tool in the design and analysis of protocols and, to borrow a phrase from Roger Needham, 'it has plenty of scalps under its belt'. Here we outline the approach.

Examples of the formulae include:

$$P \models X$$

which is pronounced 'P believes X'. More precisely it should be interpreted as meaning that P has good reason to believe X. Another formula is

$$P \xleftrightarrow{K} Q$$

which is interpreted as: 'the key K is good for communication between P and Q'. This should be interpreted as meaning that K is only and will only be known to P and/or Q (assuming always that P and Q do not compromise K). The formula

$$\sharp(X)$$

is pronounced 'the term X is fresh'. The notion of freshness is delicate and has been hotly debated. It is not really about how old the value is. BAN has a very weak notion of time, with only the past and present epochs being distinguished. The present means from the start of the current run under consideration. Note that some subtleties lurk here: in an asynchronous universe the time at which a run starts is not necessarily globally well-defined. Freshness is really more like the motion of 'uniquely originated' of the Strand Spaces approach (*see* below). That is, $\sharp(X)$ is really asserting, to quote the BAN authors, 'that X has not been sent in a message before the current protocol run'.

$$P \triangleleft X$$

'P sees X'. Roughly P receives X. X might be a term inside a compound term and might require decryption by P, in which case it is assumed that P has the appropriate key.

$$P \hspace{0.2em}\vert\hspace{-0.4em}\sim X$$

'P once said X'. That P has in the past sent a message that contained X and furthermore believed X at the time of sending.

Examples of the inference rules include:

$$\frac{P \models (P \xleftrightarrow{K} Q)}{P \triangleleft \{X\}_K} \\ \overline{P \models (Q \hspace{0.2em}\vert\hspace{-0.4em}\sim X)}$$

This should be interpreted as saying: if P believes that K is good for communication with Q and he sees a message comprising X encrypted under K, then he is entitled to believe that Q at some time uttered X. Note that the logic assumes that principals can identify their own messages.

An example of a rather more obvious, structural rule:

$$\frac{P \models (X, Y)}{P \models X}$$

This simply asserts that if P believes the concatenation of X and Y then he should believe X.

Further rules deal with the notion of jurisdiction, which concern when agents have the authority to make statements.

The protocol goals can also be formulated in the logic. For example, a key establishment protocol would typically aim to achieve:

$$A \models (A \xleftrightarrow{K} B)$$

and

$$B \models (A \xleftrightarrow{K} B)$$

i.e. that A believes that K is good for communication with B and similarly for B. Some protocols will strive to achieve more, for example:

$$A \models (B \models (A \xleftrightarrow{K} B))$$

i.e. that A believes that B believes K is good for communication between them.

A goal such as:

$$A \models (B \models X)$$

can be interpreted as A believes that B recently sent X. In particular it encodes the weak notion of authentication: that B has recently been online. Here 'recently' should be interpreted as since the beginning of the protocol run.

The idea then is to see if the protocol goals can be derived using the inference rules from the formulae representing the initial assumptions and the protocol steps. Failure to reach the required goals can indicate the need to change details of the protocol or the need for further assumptions. Alternatively, the analysis can sometimes identify places where the assumptions are unnecessarily strong or the protocol is over-engineered, for example an unnecessary encryption of a term.

The BAN logic has proved itself highly effective in this sense. However, for high-assurance applications, the precise interpretation of a successful BAN analysis is not so clear. The original semantics justifying the rules were found to be problematic, raising questions like 'can a principal believe something that is false?' Improved semantics have been provided subsequently, but the fact remains that it can still be quite difficult to interpret the results of a BAN analysis.

The difficulties are exemplified by the Lowe attack on the Needham-Schroeder Public-Key protocol. This protocol was given a clean bill of health by a BAN analysis and yet was much later found to harbour a serious vulnerability in the form of the Lowe attack. There has been much debate since about whether this vulnerability is a real attack and what it really tells us about BAN. In fact the protocol does support an, albeit rather weak, form of authentication and it is this that the proof establishes: namely Bob is assured that Anne is online recently, what is often referred to as entity authentication.

It should also be stressed that the authors of the logic are careful to state that they are assuming that protocol participants are honest and that, in particular, they do not leak secrets. Of course in the Lowe scenario one of the players, namely Yves, does not play by the rules, despite being a recognized user. But in fact the same attack will work if the private key of an honest agent is compromised.

In many ways the BAN honesty of principals assumption is very natural and indeed you have to make an assumption rather like this to get anywhere. At the very least, an agent will have to assume that the party with whom he believes that he is interacting will play by the rules. He presumably can determine whether he himself is playing by the rules. Thus Bob, when he receives a message from Anne saying that she wants to communicate with him, will assume that she will not cheat in this. But note that we have to be very careful here: firstly Bob has to be able to authenticate messages purporting to be from Anne. Secondly it should be the case that it is in Anne's interests to play by the rules if she is trying to communicate with Bob.

We see that we have to be very careful how these assumptions are framed: they must be strong enough that we can establish the goals but not so strong that they overlook vulnerabilities. The BAN trust assumption turns out to be too strong for some applications: it is fine in a closed environment, like an operating system, in which it may well be reasonable to assume that all principals will play by the rules. It is not appropriate in an open environment, like the internet, in which principals may well be both capable and motivated to cheat. Note that in Lowe's scenario Anne and Bob are both playing by the rules and it is with Anne (who is honest, but misguided about whom she runs protocols with) that Bob thinks that he is running the protocol. Making clear whom you are assuming to be honest in a situation in which the identities of other remote principals is itself in question is rather delicate. Our assumptions are in danger of getting mixed up with our proofs if we are not careful: we are trying to establish results about the reliability of authentication and yet the assumptions we are relying on depend on correctly establishing identities. We are thus in danger of establishing that 'we have authentication as long as we have authentication'.

There are many subtle issues here and we refer the reader to the excellent papers by Gollmann [35, 36] that discuss them in detail. For the moment it is sufficient to note that there is a danger of misinterpreting the implications of a BAN analysis. In particular there has been a tendency amongst later researchers to read too much into a BAN analysis, for example to assume that the analysis of the NSPK protocol shows that Bob can legitimately assume that the nonces N_a and N_b remain secret to Anne and Bob and go on to use them for re-authentication or key establishment.

Another observation is that the BAN logic takes the viewpoint of the legitimate players: we study how their beliefs evolve as the protocol unfolds. Arguably a healthier mindset from the point of view of trying to probe the protocol for flaws is to take the hostile point of view. What really matters is what Yves can discover, not what Anne and Bob suppose that he can or cannot discover. The situation is analogous to the evaluation of a cryptographic algorithm: you need to adopt the mindset of the cryptanalyst: assume that the algorithm can be broken and set about it, rather than assume that it should be secure and try to construct a proof that it is. Indeed this is reminiscent of the dilemma of being faced with a mathematical conjecture and having to decide whether it is more effective to seek a counterexample or a proof.

A corollary of this observation is to notice that the intruder's capabilities are never explicitly defined in the BAN approach; they are implicit in the choice of inference rules. By assuming that if Bob receives a message X encrypted under a key he believes good for communication with Anne, then he should suppose that Anne said X, you are in effect implicitly assuming that Yves cannot fabricate such a message. This is fine up to a point, but if you want to tailor your model of Yves's capabilities, for example by allowing him to break keys after a certain time or being able to exploit algebraic identities of the crypto algorithm, it becomes rather tricky.

The BAN logic is primarily about authentication. If you need to reason about other properties, for example secrecy, anonymity, non-repudiation and so on, you need to extend the logic or develop a new one. Similarly, if you want to incorporate new cryptographic mechanisms you need to extend the rule set. An example of this is the situation in which a key is formed as a function of a pair of values believed to be secret – quite common in key establishment protocols. The original rules do not allow you to establish formally that the derived key will be secret if the input values are. Indeed such a rule is actually not trivial as it also depends on the nature of the combining function. A constant function, to take an extreme example, would not do.

Various extensions have been proposed to deal with such situations, but clearly you are unlikely ever to get a complete logic able to deal with all possible security properties and mechanisms. Indeed, many of the extensions are found to be too unwieldy for practical use. There are also issues of establishing that the extensions do not introduce contradictions. Technically this requires extensions to the underlying semantics to show consistency and completeness and so on.

In summary, the BAN logic is undoubtedly seminal and has been highly influential in the field. It has scored many successes and continues to be a useful tool in the design and debugging of security protocols. It is, however, rather limited in its range of applicability and for high-assurance applications and for more exotic properties and mechanisms it is inappropriate. Abadi and Tuttle provided an early semantics for the BAN logic in [3]. Notable extensions to the logic and its semantics include the GNY and SVO logics [37, 98]. Automated support for BAN and related logics have been provided by, for example, Brackin's HOL-based tool [11].

9.4   FDM and InaJo

The earliest attempt to apply mainstream formal methods is due to Kemmerer in the early 1980s [47] based on some earlier work of his on testing formal specifications. He applied the formal method FDM with the formal specification language InaJo to the problem. FDM treats the problem as a state machine, with conditional transition rules corresponding to the protocols steps. Axioms can also be incorporated to represent known properties of the encryption algorithms, for example the usual decryption inverse to encryption property. The security properties were encoded as predicates on the states, allowing secrecy properties in particular to be conveniently coded.

The approach had tool support in the form of a symbolic simulator called Inatest, which allowed the user to exercise the specification and potentially find states that violate the security invariants. In principle it is possible to perform inductive style proofs that invariants are preserved under the various transitions of the system though this seems not to have been done, presumably due to poor proof support at the time.

The approach met with rather limited success, mainly due to the immaturity of such formal methods at that time. The tool support available then was not really up to dealing with the subtlety and complexity associated with the analysis of security protocols.

In more recent work, Kemmerer and colleagues apply a model-checker they developed for the real-time concurrent system specification language ASTRAL for the analysis of cryptographic protocols [48].

9.5   NRL Analyser

One approach that has been around for some time and is still going strong is Meadows' NRL Analyser. This, too, breaks away from the logic-based approaches and treats the problem, in the first instance at least, as a form of word problem. The steps of the protocol are represented as conditional rewriting rules, along with various reduction rules that correspond to the usual identities of the data-types (decryption inverse to encryption and so on). The goals of the protocol are formalized as unreachability theorems. This works very nicely for secrecy properties, where the problem can be couched in terms of whether or not the intruder can deduce certain sensitive words.

For more subtle security properties, for example key agreement, the basic re-writing approach has to be enhanced by representations of local state variables that serve to encode the knowledge or beliefs of the principals. Thus the goal of key establishment can be coded in terms of being able to reach a state in which Anne and Bob both know the key. Of course, you also need to show the secrecy property – that the system cannot reach a state in which Yves acquires knowledge of this key.

In essence then, the NRL Analyser is an equational re-writing tool, written in Prolog. It also incorporates automated support to assist the user in proving certain unreachability theorems that serve to prune the search space, typically discarding infinite chunks of potential state space. Running the tool involves backward search from some insecure state to see if the state could be reached from the initial state. The search is partly automatic, but allows for user interaction to guide the search.

Running the tool tends to require quite a high level of user expertise. The rules of the protocol have to be accurately coded, the insecure states from which the search is to be driven have to be identified. The search typically needs a high level of expert user interaction. That said, the tool has been getting increasingly automated over the years and so more accessible.

At the time of writing the tool is not widely available and is restricted to government use. It is nonetheless an important milestone in the development of the subject.

The underlying philosophy is similar to the CSP approach, except that it does use a specially tailored framework and tool rather than the generic formal method of the CSP/FDR approach.

Meadows has used the Analyser to great effect in uncovering flaws in a number of protocols. Another tool-based approach along rather similar principles, called the Interrogator, was developed somewhat earlier by Millen, then at MITRE. This, as well as the NRL tool and Kemmerer's approach, described earlier, can all be found described in [49].

9.6 The B-method approach

In the early 1990s Abrial applied his B-method to an analysis of the Needham-Schroeder Secret-Key protocol. This provides another and more recent example of the application of a main-stream formal method to the problem. The results were promising and indeed this work was inspirational to the authors of this book in that it did show that an established, generic formal method could be used effectively to model and analyze security protocols.

The protocol is formalized in the Abstract Machine Notation (AMN) of the B-method and the security properties represented in terms of invariants.

The main, rather elegant, idea is to perform the proof of the protocol's security properties by a process of step-wise refinement. At the top-most level of abstraction the goal of the protocol is expressed as a single 'magic' step. For the NSSK protocol, for example, we suppose that the system starts in a state in which Anne and Bob share long-term keys with the server but do not share a session key. We then postulate a high-level transition, after which the system has magically ended up in a state in which Anne and Bob both know a fresh key K and furthermore this key is not known to Yves.

We now progressively refine this top-level step towards the actual protocol steps, all the while showing that appropriate invariants are preserved. In this case the invariants assert that the session key never becomes known to Yves.

The approach is developed further by Bieber and others, for example in [10].

9.7 The non-interference approach

In the mid 1990s Gorrieri *et al.* started applying the process algebra CCS (Calculus of Communicating Systems [66]) to information security, first to formalizing notions of secrecy in the form of non-interference [32] and then to the analysis of security protocols [31].

They introduce an extension to the CCS language to allow for action hiding, that they call SPA (Secure Process Algebra). Non-interference can be expressed as the property that a process with high level events hidden is *equivalent* to the process with high level events blocked. In other words, the view at the low level is unable to tell whether or not high level activity has occurred. Different notions of equivalence—traces, may and must testing, flavours of bisimulation—give rise to different strengths of non-interference, and a catalogue of the relationships between them is provided.

Requirements on security protocols are couched in terms of non-interference: that an intruder cannot interfere with the progress of the protocol as far as the legitimate users are concerned. This requires that the protocol running with the intruder active allows no more behaviours than with the intruder blocked. This is expressed via the introduction of various signals, similar to the way that such events are used in this book. For example, an authentication property would use a *Running* and a *Commit* signal. Correct protocol runs always have *Running* preceding *Commit*, so non-interference requires that *Commit* cannot occur before (or without) *Running*. Thus the net result is similar in spirit to our approach.

They have developed an automated tool called CoSec [33] based on the CCS Workbench. More recently they have developed a higher level language and compiler that is analogous to Casper: it takes a description of the protocol and its goals and produces SPA code that can be fed to the CoSec tool. Casting the checks in terms of non-interference allows a whole raft of properties to be checked at once.

9.8 Strand spaces

The strand spaces approach has been developed fairly recently by Guttman *et al.* from MITRE. Roughly speaking, a strand represents the sequence of actions in which a particular protocol principal may participate. For an honest principal this encodes the expected sequence of send and receive messages associated with a particular role of the protocol. Agents can play multiple roles simultaneously. Thus for the (corrected) Needham-Schroeder-Lowe Public-Key protocol the initiator strand is:

$$\langle +\{N_a.a\}_{PK_b}, -\{N_a.N_b.b\}_{PK_a}, +\{N_b\}_{PK_b} \rangle$$

The $+$ and $-$ signs signify whether the term is transmitted or received respectively by the agent in question. Thus the initiator, a in this case, starts by transmitting the nonce N_a along with his identity a, all encrypted under b's public key. The next term of the strand indicates the reception of N_a, N_b and b under a's public key and so on. Similarly the responder strand reads:

$$\langle -\{N_a.a\}_{PK_b}, +\{N_a.N_b.b\}_{PK_a}, -\{N_b\}_{PK_b} \rangle$$

A number of strands represent the intruder's possible interactions. These correspond to the possible intruder actions you will already have seen in our models and so correspond to the usual Dolev-Yao model. Of course, these can be adjusted if we want to tailor the intruder capabilities. We use the strand-space terminology for these types of strand. This differs in places from ours. The intruder strands are parameterized by K_p: the set of keys initially known to him.

Text message: $\langle +t \rangle$ for some term $t \in T$ (the atomic terms)

Concatenation: $\langle -g, -h, +gh \rangle$

Separation: $\langle -gh, +g, +h \rangle$

Key: $\langle +K \rangle$ where $K \in K_p$

Encryption: $\langle -K, -h, +\{h\}_K \rangle$

Decryption: $\langle -K^{-1}, -\{h\}_K, +h \rangle$

The first rule represents the possibility that the intruder may emit a message containing an atomic term. Similarly with the fourth rule he can emit a key that is in the set known to him. The second corresponds to his receiving two terms and emitting a message containing their concatenation and so on. Notice that addressing information is not included in these rules. The intruder can receive from or transmit to whoever he wants. In particular he can transmit back to himself. In this way we see how this framework can mimic the inference system we associate with the intruder. He can thus arrive at all derivable terms by transmitting back to himself all intermediate terms

Strands may, of course, interact or intertwine according to the ways in which nodes can interact by the exchange of messages. Thus a term transmitted by one agent may correspond to that received by another agent. Similarly, the intruder strands can intertwine with other strands.

We introduce a partial order on the space. Two kinds of edge are introduced, indicated by single and double arrows: $\longrightarrow$ and $\Longrightarrow$. These represent the two possible causal relationships between nodes of a bundle. The double arrow connects successive nodes of a strand. Thus a pair of nodes n_i and n_{i+1} on a strand would be linked thus:

$$n_i \Longrightarrow n_{i+1}$$

This corresponds to the causal ordering of actions under the control of the principal in question. In the case of a legitimate agent it corresponds to the order in which he will perform actions in accordance with the protocol. In the case of the intruder it represents the causal constraints on his behaviour. The single arrow indicates the causal ordering that arises from the transmission and subsequent reception of a message. Thus if we have a term $+t$ at the node of one strand and the corresponding reception term $-t$ at the node of another strand, then we link these by a single arrow. Thus, if $n_1 = +t$ and $n_2 = -t$ then we write:

$$n_1 \longrightarrow n_2.$$

Any pair of nodes with an arrow between them will be said to be causally linked.

Analysis in a strand space is carried out on a particular structure: bundles. A bundle is a causally connected set of nodes.

A bundle must also be causally well-founded: whenever it contains a reception node $-t$ then it also contains a unique transmission node $+t$. On the other hand a transmission node might correspond to many reception nodes or none. The latter possibility corresponds to a kill action by the intruder. Bundles thus take on the structure of acyclic, ordered graphs.

For the strand corresponding to the principal of a given protocol run, we construct all possible bundles containing nodes of the strand. Together, this set of bundles encodes all possible interactions of the environment with that principal in a given run of the protocol.

Reasoning now takes place on this set of bundles. You can think of this as giving the set of all possible worlds consistent with a particular agent's experience of run of the protocol. In particular, notice the highly agent-centric viewpoint: we want to get a handle on what a particular, agent can confidently deduce about relevant but remote events. This is similar in spirit to Bella's notion of 'goal availability' that we will discuss in the next section.

With this framework in place we can go on to prove various security properties of protocols. A number of useful lemmata can also be proved that turn out to have general utility in such proofs. The key to the approach is the fact that bundles form finite, well-founded sets under the causal (partial) ordering and so the standard proof techniques for such structures can be applied. Many of the proofs you will see in the strand spaces literature will look fairly familiar to anyone who has done courses such as set theory and number theory: plenty of induction, plenty of consider-the-smallest-element-of-the-set style reasoning, and so on.

A powerful idea to emerge from this approach is the notion of an authentication test [38]. This is basically a formalization of the basic challenge-response style primitive that is a building block for so many protocols. Thus an agent transmits a uniquely originating term and later receives back another term that is some transformation of the original term. That he gets anything back at all will indicate that he is not entirely alone in the universe, but of course we would like to establish rather more than this. Thus the transformation is usually so designed that it could only be affected by some known entity or maybe set of entities. Typically Anne might transmit a nonce N_a and get back $\{N_a\}_{SK_b}$. Assuming that she can reliably associate PK_b, Bob's public key with Bob, she can verify the returned term. Hence she can, subject to the usual assumptions, conclude that the transformation $N_a \longrightarrow \{N_a\}_{SK_b}$ could only have been done by Bob. Alternatively, she could transmit $\{N_a\}_{PK_b}$ and when she gets N_a back be confident that only Bob could have extracted N_a, again under the usual assumptions that Bob has not compromised his private key and so on. Anne can thus assure herself that Bob is alive and well. More generally, the local knowledge that certain fragments of strand have occurred allows an agent to deduce the occurrence of other, remote fragments of strands.

This kind of reasoning is, of course, quite standard in designing and analyzing security protocols, but the strand-spaces framework allows it to be fully formalized and so put on a firm footing. Another important development in this approach is to address the problem of protocol interactions. It has long been recognized that having a number of different protocols running on a single system can give rise to security problems. In some cases it can give rise to functional problems too of course – so-called feature interactions. The problem is particularly virulent if such protocols share keys. This can give rise to attacks in which Yves uses steps of one protocol as an oracle to provide information or terms that he can use to undermine another protocol. It has been common folklore in the community that if protocols do not share keys then such interactive attacks cannot arise. More precisely if two, different protocols are separately shown to be secure and they do not share any cryptographic material then it should be the case that running them both on a single network does not give rise to any new attacks. Recently, precise statements and proofs have been provided using the strand space framework [30].

A number of protocols have been analyzed using this framework, in some cases revealing new vulnerabilities, in others shedding fresh light on the working of the protocols. The mechanics of the proof tend to be quite intricate and not necessarily easy to follow. On the other hand the approach is very intuitive and does help achieve a deeper understanding of what really makes security protocols tick.

Recently a tool has been developed based of the strand-spaces model called Athena [95]. It is a mix of model-checker and theorem prover. Basing it on the strand-spaces model sidesteps much of the state-space explosion that arises in most model-checking tools due to the interleaving of independent events, though this is is usually handled using partial-order type techniques. The strand-spaces model sidesteps the interleaving problem by not explicitly representing the full traces of the system.

9.9 The inductive approach

In 1996 Paulson [70] introduced the inductive approach with automated support provided by his Isabelle proof assistant. In several respects the underlying, conceptual framework is similar to that of the CSP approach. The key elements are traces: sequences of events that could occur as the protocol agents execute in a hostile environment. Traces are defined inductively from a set of rules that correspond to the possible actions of the agents, including spies. The approach does not involve state enumeration and so the numbers of agents and spies can be regarded as unbounded – and indeed each agent can be allowed to play multiple roles simultaneously.

Security properties such as secrecy and authentication can be stated as predicates over the traces, in a fashion similar to the CSP approach. That a certain property holds of all possible traces for a certain protocol can be proved inductively. This is similar to the rank-function approach, though the mechanics of the proofs are rather different. This does of course mean that as it stands the approach really only works for safety properties, i.e. properties that can be formulated as predicates on traces. However, as we have previously discussed, this works well for most properties of interest, and indeed the CSP approach also concentrates on trace properties.

The approach also allows the incorporation of compromised agents who share their knowledge with the intruder and so-called 'oops' events that model the compromise of a session key.

The original formulation by Paulson did not explicitly model reception events for the legitimate agents as he was initially only interested in reasoning about secrecy, and reception events are not necessary for this purpose as long as the intruder is allowed to monitor all traffic. Omitting them makes the models and reasoning simpler. However, in order to reason about honest agents' knowledge, for example to establish key confirmation properties, it is necessary to model such events. Thus, for example, suppose that you want to be able to establish that after participating in a certain sequence Bob can be confident that Anne knows a session key K and associates it with communication with him. For this you need to be able to model and reason about the reception of corresponding events by Anne. In his recent thesis, Bella [8] extends the original approach explicitly to model reception events to allow such reasoning. He also introduces some further extensions to allow reasoning about time and timestamps, as well as modelling smart cards.

Bella also advances what he calls the principle of 'goal availability'. If a certain security goal is available to an agent this means that the protocol is so designed to ensure that the agent can reach a point at which he has sufficient evidence to infer that the goal has been achieved. In practice, of course, it is typically necessary to rely on some extra assumptions, for example that his peer acts honestly and has not compromised his keys. These are referred to as the minimal-trust assumptions. Clearly it is desirable to so design the protocol to reduce these trust assumptions to the absolute minimum. It is equally clear, however, that in a distributed environment some trust will have to be vested in remote components that are not under your direct control. Indeed, as technology gets ever more sophisticated with mobile code and agents, identifying what exactly is local to any individual and under their control gets steadily more obscure.

Arguably the notion of goal availability has been 'in the air' for some time. You find it implicit in our approach, strand spaces and indeed in the BAN logic. It seems not, however, to have been spelt out explicitly until now.

Spi calculus

The spi-calculus is another fairly new and rather elegant framework for modelling and reasoning about security protocols. It was introduced by Abadi and Gordon in [1]. It is an extension of Milner's π-calculus designed to deal with cryptographic primitives. The π-calculus is a development of Milner's process algebra CCS (Calculus of Communicating Systems). CCS, rather like CSP, deals with fixed topologies of interacting processes. That is to say the processes and network topology are established at the outset and do not change as the interactions unfold. In CSP the topology is established by fixing the alphabets or channels of the various processes. Thus a pair of processes that share an alphabet will have a channel of communication. Conversely, processes with no elements of their alphabets in common will not have any (direct) channels of communication. This is fine for many applications, but increasingly systems allow the establishment of new channels on the fly. The π-calculus allows for such possibilities by allowing channel names to be communicated as well as simple values. Communicating the name of a channel to a process that previously was not aware of this channel allows it to start communicating on that channel. This process is known as scope extrusion.

The behaviour and properties of security protocols can be modelled at a high level of abstraction in the π-calculus. In particular the secrecy of values passed over a channel known only to certain processes can be captured in terms of the π-calculus's scope rules. Furthermore the process of setting up a new channel can be captured by scope extrusion. This can be thought of as a very abstract representation of the process of setting up a new secret channel by establishing cryptographic keys across the channel.

Already we can formalize some security properties. Authentication can be coded in terms of a specification process in which the receiver process 'magically' knows what message to receive from the transmitter process. This is reminiscent of Abrial's high-level 'magical' specifications. We then assert that an implementation that satisfies the authentication property should be equivalent to the 'magical' specification process.

Secrecy is coded in a slightly different way, but again using process equivalence. Here we assert that a protocol maintains secrecy if two instantiations, one with a value M and another with M' transmitted, are indistinguishable to the environment. This is really a form of non-interference: altering the high-level inputs does not result in any observable change at the low-level interface. For both properties, process equivalence is in terms of may-testing.

At this level of abstraction we do not have any representation of the cryptographic primitives that are used to implement the protocols. To be able to reason about the cryptographic primitives Abadi and Gordon extend the syntax and correspondingly the semantics of the π-calculus to express cryptographic terms. They also use new-name creation to model the generation of new nonces and session keys. Now a private channel can be thought of as implemented as a cryptographic channel and channel extrusion as implemented by a suitable key establishment protocol. The notion of equivalence has to be handled rather delicately, just as it must when formalizing secrecy as a non-interference property in the presence of cryptographic channels. This is because strictly speaking there is a causal flow from high to low: different high inputs do lead to different ciphertexts, so the notion of equivalence has to be finessed to avoid processes being distinguished on this basis. The details are rather technical and outside of the scope of this overview. In essence, external tests cannot give different results depending on the value of ciphertexts that they cannot decrypt, and so all encrypted messages are treated as equivalent.

The framework can handle various primitives: symmetric encryption, asymmetric encryption, cryptographic hash functions and signatures.

Currently the approach lacks tool support and the representation of protocols and proofs can be fairly elaborate. One pleasing feature is the way the intruder is modelled simply as an arbitrary environment able to perform any test definable within the language to try to distinguish instantiations of the protocol. This avoids the need to define explicitly the intruder's capabilities and so, arguably, avoids dangers of missing capabilities. On the other hand, limitations on the intruder's capabilities are implicitly coded into the expressiveness of the framework and in particular the richness of the space of tests that can be constructed. It could be argued that for some applications it is better to have an explicit representation of the intruder's capabilities. This allows it to be evaluated more directly and tailored to specific scenarios, for example to situations in which only passive and no active attacks are possible (maybe on certain channels).

9.11 Provable security

Up until now all the frameworks we have discussed have abstracted away from the details of the cryptographic algorithms and primitives.

There are some well-known ways to characterize the security of cryptographic primitives. These involve probability and complexity theory and are quite technical. We will not go into the details here but refer the reader to, for example [9] and [71]. Interestingly they typically boil down to a sort of process equivalence, or at least approximate equivalence. The intruder is thought of as being able to perform an unbounded number of tests, for example by asking for the encryption of some piece of text of his choice. He can do this repeatedly, possibly basing his choice of text on the outcome of previous tests. This is intended to capture what is thought to be the most powerful attack strategies open to the intruder: adaptive chosen-plaintext attacks. Finally he submits two different texts and tries to guess which of the resulting ciphertexts corresponds to which plaintext. If he can do this reliably with significantly better-than-even odds then the system is deemed insecure, otherwise it is deemed secure. Strictly speaking the intruder is deemed to have only 'negligible advantage'. This amounts to placing a tight bound on how much better-than-even odds he can achieve as a function of the amount of work he performs in terms of tests and computation. Again the details are rather technical and outside the scope of this book.

Various attempts have been made to adapt this style of reasoning to cryptographic protocols, as opposed to cryptographic primitives. In essence they boil down to reduction-style arguments: that breaking the protocol would be equivalent to breaking the underlying primitive. Thus, for example, for a Diffie-Hellman style key-establishment protocol one would show that breaking it would imply the ability to solve the Diffie-Hellman problem. The Diffie-Hellman problem is a variant of the discrete log problem: calculating the value of g^{xy} from the knowledge of g^x and g^y. It is currently thought to be intractable, though this has not been proved.

Ideally one would like to combine both styles of analysis: formal and cryptographic. It is clear, however, that a framework that encompassed the aspects of both, says the modelling capability of CSP with the probability and complexity theory of cryptography would almost certainly be intractable. It seems better therefore to be able to relate the results of the two styles of analysis. For examples it would be useful to be able to establish rigorously what is a faithful abstraction of the cryptographic primitives for inclusion in a formal analysis. Alternatively, as suggested by Pfitzmann *et al.* [71], one could try establishing 'cryptographic semantics' to underpin a formal framework.

10 Prospects and wider issues

10.1 Introduction

In this chapter we discuss some of the broader issues, open problems and directions for future research.

10.2 Abstraction of cryptographic primitives

Most of the formal approaches in this area take a very abstract view of the cryptographic primitives. That is to say that they typically treat the cryptographic functions – hashes and so on – as primitives of the data types of messages, for example, and do not concern themselves with any structure they may have or algebraic identities they may satisfy. Of course where the algorithms are known to satisfy certain identities, for example that Vernam encryption is self-inverse, or that RSA is multiplicative, we can incorporate these in our analysis.

By and large cryptographic functions, expecially hash functions and block ciphers, are deliberately constructed to avoid any such simple structure. Structure can so easily be turned to advantage by the cryptanalyst. The most powerful ciphers are those with minimal structure, namely one-time-pads that are pure random.

Thus such assumptions are a reasonable approximation, but clearly only an approximation. In effect we are treating the structure as a free algebra and in particular making implicit assumptions along the lines of:

$$\{M\}_k = \{M'\}_{k'} \ \Rightarrow \ M = M' \text{ and } k = k'$$

In other words: two different plaintexts enciphered with different keys could never give the same ciphertext. This clearly is not true. On the other hand it is a good approximation in a statistical sense: if we were to choose a pair of keys and a pair of plaintexts at random it highly unlikely that the resulting ciphertexts will be equal.

The obvious response is to incorporate the definitions of the cryptographic functions in the models. This is not an attractive course. Firstly, it would vastly complicate the models and certainly in a model-checking context it would render them totally intractable. Second, it would make the analysis highly specific to the particular algorithms under analysis and so it would have to be totally redone if we wanted to substitute alternative algorithms.

A source of difficulty is that our framework, in common with all other practical frameworks for analyzing security protocols, does not deal with probabilities. Furthermore it is very difficult to see how one could introduce probabilities into our framework without rendering it totally intractable.

At the moment the best that our framework and others can do is to incorporate known identities in the models. The problem is knowing that we have identified all the identities, or at least all the relevant identities. Put differently, how do we know that the abstractions of the cryptographic primitives are faithful with regard to the security properties of interest? How do we know that there is not some subtle structure of the cryptographic function that interacts with the protocol in such a way as to give an exploitable vulnerability? Currently there is no good solution to this problem.

10.3   The refinement problem

Another way of thinking of this is as a manifestation of the so-called refinement problem for security. It has long been recognised that secrecy tends not to be preserved by refinement, at least not by refinement in the conventional 'safety' sense.

When we say that design P is a refinement of design Q we are asserting that in some sense P is 'better' than Q and in particular if Q was acceptable as a component of a system then P will be too. The term 'better' here usually means: 'is more predictable'. This is entirely appropriate for safety-style properties where we are concerned with a system not performing certain harmful behaviours, like falling out of the sky. If we know that everything that Q does is acceptable in a certain context then if P is more predictable than Q then it should also be acceptable.

Unfortunately, security is a rather more subtle concept to deal with. To prevent unwanted information flows, predictability is often the last thing that we want. Suppose that Q is high-grade stream cipher. According to the conventional canons of refinement a perfectly acceptable replacement component P would be a device that generates the all-zero stream. This is certainly vastly more predictable than Q and from a functional point of view would be fine: we could still communicate successfully. However, it would clearly blow any security we had right out of the water.

10.4   Combining formal and cryptographic styles of analysis

We have already alluded in Chapter 9 to the desirability of bringing together in some way the formal and cryptanalytic styles of analysis. An alternative approach is to note that there is in fact a convergence of concepts between the two approaches: both are starting to use notions of (testing) equivalence. For example, in the cryptographic camp we see definitions of cryptographic secrecy in terms of tests that an intruder may perform. Informally the intruder is allowed to submit plaintexts of his choice to the crypto system and observe the encrypted outputs. He uses this information to try to make deductions about the key material. His choice of texts to submit can be influenced by previous observations, the so-called adaptive chosen plaintext attack. Eventually the intruder submits a pair of chosen plaintexts to the encryption engine. The corresponding ciphertexts are then returned to him in arbitrary order. If the intruder is unable to guess which is which with significantly better-than-even odds then the encryption is deemed secure. The exact definition of 'significantly better' is couched in terms of complexity theory and need not concern us here.

In the formal approaches, also, people are increasingly thinking of secrecy in terms of various flavours of process equivalence, *see* for example [82]. More precisely the notion of non-interference is used to characterize the absence of information flow. Non-interference in turn is formulated in terms of process equivalence, often in terms of a suitable testing equivalence. This suggests that the notion of testing equivalence might form a possible point of contact between the two styles of analysis.

However, the issue of characterising the secrecy of an encrypted channel in non-interference terms remains problematic. Such channels obviously do not satisfy standard forms of non-interference as the high-level plaintext clearly does influence the ciphertext visible to the low-level user. Furthermore Low can test for equality of ciphertexts even if they are unintelligible to him. The difficulty is that non-interference forbids any causal influence from high to low. It is, however, possible to have causal flows that do not represent any semantic or information flow, as is the case with a secure encrypted channel.

The situation here turns out to be closely related to the idea of data-independence with equality testing that has been developed in the model-checking community, *see* [51]. A process is said to exhibit such data-independence in a given data type if the only operation the process can perform on variables in the data type is equality testing. Thus the absolute values of variables in the data type are irrelevant. This concept has been successfully exploited to reduce the checking of infinite classes of systems and specifications to a finite number of checks with finite models. This is discussed in Section 10.8.

We see though that the concept is actually applicable also to the encryption problem. From Low's point of view a system with a secure encryption over a channel visible to him can be thought of as being having data-independence with equality testing in the data type of that channel. The actual values of the cipher stream are meaningless to him (assuming good, uncompromised cryptography) but he can check for equality of ciphertexts.

Hitherto data-independence (with equality testing) has been given purely syntactic definitions in terms of the particular language in questions. Recent research [52], however, gives a semantic definition of the concept of data-independence with equality testing.

This is cast as a notion form of bisimulation up to isomorphism, or more precisely up to renaming of events of the appropriate type. This would appear to be precisely the form of process equivalence appropriate to encode the notion of an encrypted channel in non-interference terms.

10.5   Dependence on infrastructure assumptions

Great care must be taken in dealing with assumptions incorporated in the models used in any analysis. Ideally we should try to be explicit about any assumptions that the models depend upon. It is essential that engineers thinking of incorporating a particular verified protocol in a real architecture understand these assumptions and are able to check that the architecture does indeed guarantee the assumptions on which the protocol depends.

A good example of the dangers of straying outside the modelling assumptions is where the models assume that there is a suitable infrastructure to ensure that public keys can be reliably associated with principals. Suppose further that we assume that each principal has a unique private/public key pair. If the intruder can tamper with the certification mechanism and fool a principal into associating the wrong public key with another principal then most security properties will be undermined. In particular, if Yves can persuade Bob that his public key is associated with Anne, then he can impersonate Anne to Bob. More subtly, if a user may have several private/public key pairs this may give Yves an extra degree of freedom to launch an attack.

It is not always easy to make all assumptions explicit. Often they are implicit in the structure of the model and may not be obvious. They may also not be easy to express explicitly.

10.6   Conference and group keying

Most of the key establishment protocols in the literature are concerned with setting up secret communication between a pair of users. Some applications, secure group-working for example, require a group (involving more than two participants) to share a common key. Often the schemes are also required to be able to deal efficiently with highly dynamic groups, with agents joining and leaving (or being ejected) frequently, and often also to deal with the merging of groups. A number of protocols to achieve this in a reasonably efficient way have been put forward, for example the papers by Burmester and Desmedt [18, 19] and, more recently in the Cliques project [96]. Most suffer from problems of authentication, performance and scaling.

The techniques and tools for the analysis of such protocols are stretched to deal with the potentially large and undetermined number of agents, as well as the dynamic nature of such schemes. Particularly for the model-checking approaches such as those presented in this book this poses severe challenges. The data-independence techniques described in this chapter may provide a line of attack. Alternatively theorem-proving based approaches, such as the rank-function approach of this book or Paulson's inductive Isabelle-based approach-may be better placed to deal with the open-ended nature of these schemes.

10.7 Quantum cryptography

Besides the revolution in cryptography that has been wrought by public key cryptography we should also mention what could in time become the next major development, arguably even more profound than that of public-key cryptography. Various techniques have been proposed for using quantum mechanical effects in information security. By and large this are still restricted to laboratory experiments, but some are reaching the stage at which real use is in prospect.

Using properties of quantum mechanics, a number of schemes have been proposed to provide confidential communication, either directly by encrypting messages or indirectly by allowing secure key establishment, which can then be used with conventional cryptographic techniques. In some cases, given laws quantum physics like the Heisenberg uncertainty principle, the security provided can be shown to be absolute. The Heisenberg principle asserts, roughly, that any observation of a system necessarily disturbs it. More precisely, the measurement of one system variable will influence the conjugate variable. This can be put to use for security by noting that any attempt to tap a line of communication constitutes an observation and so will inevitably disturb the signals. If the scheme is so arranged as to be able to detect all such disturbances then we can ensure that it is impossible to tap the signals without detection.

This is in contrast to most conventional cryptography where, apart from a couple of exceptions like one-time-pads, security is only ever conditioned.

These techniques exploit the phenomenon of quantum entanglement: correlations between wave functions. One well-known scheme involves Anne generating pairs of photons in such a way as to ensure that their polarizations are correlated. Anne and Bob make measurements of the polarizations according to an ingenious and rather elaborate scheme that ensures that they can detect any interference by Yves or, in the absence of interference, arrive at a shared secret bit stream.

There are however limitations: authenticating quantum key exchange is still problematic. Usually authentication has to take place over a separate, trusted channel. Currently these techniques only work over rather small distances and under favourable conditions. An overview can be found in [73].

The other side of the coin is quantum computation which, if it ever becomes a serious prospect, threatens to undermine much of conventional cryptography. In essence one can perform an arbitrary number of computations in parallel by carefully manipulating super-positions of quantum states. This would blow many of the complexity-theory assumptions underlying both symmetric and asymmetric cryptography out of the water. At the time of writing such techniques still seem to be quite a way off, but seem likely to eventually become feasible for large scale calculations. Currently the record for the factorization of a composite number is 15.

10.8   Data independence

The pragmatics of running model-checkers such as FDR mean, unfortunately, that the sizes of types, such as that of nonces, have to be restricted to far smaller sizes than the types they represent in implementations. Usually they have to be kept down to single figures if the combinatories of how they can create messages of the protocol is not to take other types that have to be considered, such as the overall alphabet size and the set of facts that a potential intruder might learn, beyond the level that can be managed. The models that have been crafted by hand, and which are produced by Casper, therefore allocate a small finite number of these values to each node that has to 'invent' them during a run, so that each time a nonce (say) is required, a node takes one of those remaining from its initial allocation or, if there are none left, simply stops. This use of agents with the capacity for only a finite number of runs means that, while model checkers are rightly regarded as extremely effective tools for finding attacks on protocols, they can only be used to prove that no attack exists on the assumption that each node only engages in a very finite amount of activity. While there are often good intuitive reasons for believing that the limited check would find any attack, these are generally difficult to formalize into a component of a complete proof, and theorem-proving such as the use of rank functions is required to verify the protocol.

This problem has been addressed [77, 78] by the application of *data-independence* techniques [51, 53]. A process P (which makes use of events or messages of type T) is data-independent in the type T if it places no constraints on what T is: the latter can be regarded as a parameter of P. This will be the case if P passes members of the type around, but does not constrain what the type is and may only have its control-flow affected by members of the type in tightly defined ways. The ways in which the CSP models of protocols use types such as keys, nonces and agent identities fall within the scope of this theory.

The techniques are concerned with the mapping of results between processes with different instantiations for T. In particular, they establish conditions on T (generally concerning a lower bound on its size) and on P that allow results concerning $P(T)$ to be deduced for any T' of larger size, even infinite. This means that a relatively small instance of a protocol description, with a particular number of nonces, keys, and users, can be verified on a model-checker, allowing the same results to be concluded for the same model of the protocol instantiated with arbitrarily many nonces, keys, and users.

Furthermore, the CSP models of the protocols themselves can be made more general. Techniques inspired by those used in data independence justify the adaptation of CSP descriptions of protocol models so that agents can perform arbitrarily many protocol runs, one after the other, by cleverly reusing values. The result of these transformations is that values from type T are continually shifted around, and carefully identified with each other, to create room for another value to be created that the program will treat exactly as though it were fresh. For example, once a protocol run has completed, any nonce n used in that run can be 'forgotten' by all of the parties in the network (including the intruder, which has n remapped to a special value *oldnonce*) and can thus be reused as if it is fresh. This is done without curtailing the ability of the intruder to generate attacks (though it may in some circumstances introduce some artificial attacks that are not really possible). Where no attack is found on such a system, it is much easier to argue that the protocol under examination is free from attacks that could be constructed within the model, than it was with the earlier class of limited-run models. However, in practice transforming a CSP model of a protocol in this way by hand is a detailed, time-consuming and error-prone task, and so Casper includes a facility for introducing these transformations automatically [13].

The theory of data independence imposes some conditions on the process P for these results to be applicable. The most important of these is the condition **PosConjEqT** [51], which is a requirement about the results of equality testing. This condition is concerned with the flow of control within the program when a condition is evaluated as part of a conditional statement. It requires that whenever two values are checked for equality, the program should behave as *Stop* if the equality test fails. For example, of the following two processes, P_1 meets this condition, but P_2 does not.

$$P_1 = in?x : T \rightarrow in?y : T \rightarrow if(x = y) \ then \ (a \rightarrow Stop)$$
$$else \ Stop$$

$$P_2 = in?x : T \rightarrow in?y : T \rightarrow if(x = y) \ then \ (a \rightarrow Stop)$$
$$else \ (b \rightarrow Stop)$$

For processes meeting this condition, reducing the size of the type T does not remove any behaviours. This is important for our purposes, since we want to be sure that an analysis of a system with a small instantiation for T will cover all the possibilities present when T is larger. In the case of P_2, which does not meet the condition, when T is of size 1 then b is not possible, but it is possible for larger T. Thus increasing the size of T introduces some new possibilities for P_2.

This kind of condition is normally met by the CSP models of protocol agents with which we are concerned. Agents will often need to check that an incoming value is equal to one they are expecting (such as the response to a nonce challenge). In the presence of this condition we simply model the agent as refusing to participate any further if the incoming value fails the equality check.

In fact a slightly weaker condition is appropriate. The protocol might have to check that some incoming value is not equal to some constant value, such as the agent's own name. Given a set C of such constants involved in inequality checks, the condition **PosConjEqT$'_C$** allows non-*Stop* results for equality tests involving at least one member of C. This will tend to increase the minimum size of an instantiation for T which is sufficient to prove correctness for all larger instantiations T, and hence increase the size of the system that needs to be model-checked.

This condition must also be met by the *Intruder* process. What this means in practice is that there are restrictions on the set of initial knowledge, and on the generates relation $\vdash$:

▪ The initial knowledge set of the intruder can only contain inequality tests (explicit or implicit) of members of our type T with the constants C. For example, if $C = \{Anne, Bob\}$, then allowing all private keys except *Anne*'s and *Bob*'s is allowed, but allowing all except *Anne*'s, *Bob*'s, and *Carol*'s is not.

▪ The deductions that can be made by the intruder must be *positive* – they cannot rely on facts in their antecedent being different. For example, a rule that states

$$m_1 \neq m_2, m_1, m_2, \{m_1\}_k, \{m_2\}_k \vdash k$$

is not positive. On the other hand, the rules we have used in this book are all positive.

Provided these conditions hold, the *Intruder* also meets the **PosConjEqT**$'_C$ condition.

One limitation on the result is that it does not normally allow for Anne or Bob to run more than one session at a time. If it is realistic that they might, then an appropriate number of copies of each should be included in the network. This would in turn increase the number of values required in our types and hence increase the size of the state space to be explored.

In summary, the data-independence techniques give conditions on the CSP protocol descriptions (which will normally be met naturally) that allow results about secrecy and authentication to be established in general by establishing them for a relatively small 'threshold' system. The theory gives limits on how small the system to be checked can be; this will be dependent on the details of the protocol under analysis.

A Background cryptography

In this appendix we provide some further number theoretic and cryptographic background. We omit most of the proofs, since they can be found in any good reference on cryptography or number theory, for example [100].

A number a divides b if there exists a k such that $a.k = b$. In this case we say that a is a *factor* of b.

A prime number is a number greater than 1 divisible only by 1 and itself, for example 3, 5 ,7, etc. It has been known since Euclid that there exists an infinity of primes. Their distribution amongst the integers follows no known pattern, though certain statistical facts are known in the form of the well-known prime number theorem. This states that the number of primes less than or equal to n grows roughly as $n/\ln(n)$.

A number that is not prime is composite and can be written as a unique (up to order) product of prime factors.

The greatest common divisor (gcd) of two numbers m and n is the largest number that is a divisor of both m and n. An efficient algorithm for determining gcds has been known since Euclid, and is named after him.

We also need the idea of modular arithmetic, or arithmetic performed modulo n for a given number n. Here numbers that have the same remainder when divided by n are regarded as equivalent. For any number a and modulus n we define $a \bmod n$ as the unique number r between 0 and $n - 1$ such that a can be written as:

$$a = r + k.n$$

for some k. r is thus the remainder when a is divided by n. For example, suppose that we are working modulo 7, then

$$17(\mathbf{mod}\ 7) = 10(\mathbf{mod}\ 7) = 3$$

Arithmetic operations are reduced modulo n. Thus for example we have:

$$3.5(\mathbf{mod}\ 7) = 15(\mathbf{mod}\ 7) = 1$$

In effect we perform arithmetic on the quotient space of the natural numbers over the appropriate equivalence relation. That such arithmetic is well defined can be shown easily and it obeys analogues of the usual laws of arithmetic: commutativity of addition and multiplication, associativity, distribution laws, and so on. Generalizations of Euclid's algorithm for finding gcds in modular arithmetic are also well known.

The key theorem of modular arithmetic that we need is Fermat's Little Theorem. Fermat's theorem states that for p prime and $a \neq 0 \bmod p$:

$$a^{(p-1)} = 1(\textbf{mod } p)$$

To see this, consider the set

$$\{a.i(\textbf{mod } p) \mid 1 \leqslant i \leqslant (p-1)\}$$

where $a \neq 0(\textbf{mod } p)$. This is simply the same as the set

$$\{i \mid 1 \leqslant i \leqslant (p-1)\}$$

To see this, we note that if $i \neq j(\textbf{mod } p)$ then $a.i \neq a.j(\textbf{mod } p)$ for $a \neq 0(\textbf{mod } p)$. In other words, multiplying a by the numbers $1, \ldots, (p-1)$ modulo p simply permutes the elements. The product of the elements of these sets must therefore be the same:

$$\Pi_{i=1}^{(p-1)}i = \Pi_{i=1}^{(p-1)}a.i = a^{(p-1)}.\Pi_{i=1}^{(p-1)}i(\textbf{mod } p)$$

and so dividing through by $(\Pi_{i=1}^{(p-1)}i)$ yields that $a^{(p-1)} = 1(\textbf{mod } p)$.

If n is the product of two distinct primes p and q, then for any number a and any r we find that

$$a^{(r(p-1)(q-1))+1} = a(\textbf{mod } n) \tag{A.1}$$

To prove this, we first observe for any s that

$$a^s = a(\textbf{mod } p) \wedge a^s = a(\textbf{mod } q) \wedge gcd(p,q) = 1 \Rightarrow a^s = a(\textbf{mod } pq) \tag{A.2}$$

This follows from the fact that p divides $(a^s - a)$ and q divides $(a^s - a)$, and so their product pq must also divide $a^s - a$.

Now by Fermat's Little Theorem we have for $a \neq 0(\textbf{mod } p)$ that

$$a^{p-1} = 1(\textbf{mod } p)$$

and so

$$(a^{(p-1)})^{(r(q-1))} = 1(\textbf{mod } p)$$

Hence multiplying through by a we have for all a (including $a = 0(\textbf{mod } p)$) that

$$a^{(r(p-1)(q-1))+1} = a(\textbf{mod } p)$$

By similar reasoning the same equation holds modulo q, and so by the observation in line A.2 it holds modulo pq, and the result given in line A.1 follows. For example, if $n = 15$, then $(p-1)(q-1) = 8$. We find that $2^9 = 512 = 2$, and $3^9 = 19\,683 = 3$, all modulo 15.

We now have the prerequisites to present the RSA and ElGamal schemes.

A.1 The RSA algorithm

1. Two 'large' primes p and q are chosen and their product $n = pq$ computed.

2. An integer e is chosen that is relatively prime to $(p - 1)(q - 1)$

3. An integer d is found, for example by using the extension to modular arithmetic of Euclid's greatest common divisor algorithm, such that:

$$ed = 1(\textbf{mod } (p - 1)(q - 1)) \qquad \textbf{(A.3)}$$

4. n and e are publicized whilst p, q and d are kept secret.

Encryption of a message $m(\textbf{mod } n)$ can now be performed by anyone knowing the public values n and e by computing:

$$c = m^e(\textbf{mod } n)$$

If the message does not encode to a number less than n then it must be chopped into a suitable number of blocks such that each can be so encoded and each block is enciphered separately.

Decryption is effected by taking the dth power modulo n of the ciphertext (number) which from line A.1 equals the original message:

$$c^d = m^{ed} = m(\textbf{mod } n)$$

To see this, note that from line A.3 above we have:

$$ed = (p - 1)(q - 1) + 1 \qquad \textbf{(A.4)}$$

for some r, but:

$$m^{(p-1)(q-1)} = m(\textbf{mod } n)$$

and so from line A.4:

$$(m^e)^d(\textbf{mod } n) = m(\textbf{mod } n)$$

For example, with $p = 41$ and $q = 17$, we compute $n = 697$ and $(p - 1)(q - 1) = 640$. Choosing $e = 11$, we find $d = 291$ is such that $ed = 3201 = 1(\textbf{mod } 640)$.

The values $n = 697$ and $e = 11$ are published.

To encrypt a message $m = 58$ with e, we compute:

$$m^e(\textbf{mod } n) = 58^{11}(\textbf{mod } 697) = 626$$

Knowledge of d is required to decrypt the message. The calculation is all modulo $n = 697$:

$$626^d = 626^{291} = 58(\textbf{mod } 697)$$

Raising the encrypted message to the power of d regains the original message.

All the operations described above are performed by the legitimate users, and although computationally fairly intensive are quite tractable. Primes can be found reasonably efficiently using various primality-testing algorithms. Besides, these calculations only need to be performed on a once-off basis. Modular exponentiation is quite easy, indeed is reducible to a sequence of multiplications and squarings (with modular reduction at each step). Euclid's algorithm requires very little computation.

On the other hand, finding a suitable d to perform the decryption without knowledge of $(p - 1)(q - 1)$ is thought to be intractable. In turn, finding $(p - 1)(q - 1)$ without knowledge of the factorization of n is also thought intractable. Finally, as long as p and q are suitably chosen, the factorization of n is considered intractable. *See* for example [100].

A.2 The ElGamal public key system

ElGamal's scheme [28] is based on the difficulty of computing discrete logarithms. This is currently considered to be intractable and comparable to the problem of factoring large numbers that underlies RSA. It is quite easy to understand – really no more complicated than RSA and probably about as easy to implement. As far as is currently known (in the open world at any rate) it is cryptographically about as strong as RSA.

A large prime p along with a primitive root a modulo p are made publicly available. A primitive root is one that 'generates' the entire field, so taking successive powers of a modulo p will yield all the integers from 1 to $p - 1$. For a prime p it can be shown that there always exists a primitive root.

A user, Bob say, chooses (or is allocated) a private key $x(b)$ where

$$1 \leqslant x(b) \leqslant p - 1$$

The corresponding public key $y(b)$ is given by:

$$y(b) := a^{x(b)} (\textbf{mod } p)$$

Suppose Anne now wishes to send Bob a message that can be encoded as an integer M in the interval $(1, p - 1)$. To encrypt M 'for Bob's eyes only' she proceeds as follows:

Anne chooses at random an integer k in the interval $(1, p - 1)$ and computes:

$$C_l = a^k \textbf{ mod } p$$
$$K = (y(b))^k \textbf{ mod } p$$
$$C_2 = KM \textbf{ mod } p$$

She transmits the pair C_1, C_2.

In order to decrypt this Bob proceeds as follows:

He calculates K from:

$$K = y(b)^k = a^{x(b)k} = (a^k)^{x(b)} = C_1^{x(b)} \textbf{ mod } p$$

M can now be recovered by solving:

$$C_2 = KM \bmod p$$

In fact K^{-1} can be calculated directly from:

$$K^{-1} = C_l^{(p-1)-x(b)} \bmod p$$

To see this, consider

$$
\begin{aligned}
K.K^{-1} &= C_1^{x(b)}.C_l^{(p-1)-x(b)} \bmod p \\
&= C_1^{p-1} \bmod p \\
&= 1 \bmod p
\end{aligned}
$$

the last equality following from Fermat's Little Theorem.

So M is given directly by:

$$M = C_2.K^{-1} \bmod p$$

As an example, suppose that the prime 71 is chosen for p and the primitive root 7 is chosen for a. Suppose further that Bob chooses for his private key:

$$x(b) = 29$$

Then

$$y(b) = 7^{29} \bmod 71 = 35$$

So we have in summary:

$$p = 71, a = 7, x(b) = 29, y(b) = 35$$

Now suppose that Anne wants to send the message whose numerical representation is $M = 39$ and that the 'random' k that she selects is 21. So:

$$M = 39, k = 21$$

She now computes:

$$
\begin{aligned}
C_l &= 7^{21} \bmod 71 = 46 \\
K &= 35^{21} \bmod 71 = 17 \\
C_2 &= K.M \bmod p = 17.39 \bmod 71 = 24
\end{aligned}
$$

And so she now sends $(46, 24)$.

On receipt Bob first calculates K^{-1} from:

$$K^{-1} = C_1^{(p-1)-x(b)} = 46^{41} \bmod 71 = 46$$

and thence:

$$M = C_2 K^{-1} \bmod p = 24.46 \bmod 71 = 39$$

We see that the legitimate users need do nothing more painful than taking exponents in a finite field for which efficient algorithms exist. Indeed such exponentiation can be reduced to a sequence of squarings and multiplications. For example:

$$7^{21} = (((7^2)^2)^2)^2.(7^2)^2.7$$

Modular reductions can be performed at each step to keep the numbers manageable throughout. The sequence of squarings and multiplications is simply related to the binary representation of the exponent. The reader might like to determine this relationship.

On the other hand it is clear that a malicious agent with a good algorithm for taking discrete logarithms in a finite field would be able to crack the system. No such algorithm is presently known. It has not yet been proven that cracking the ElGamal system is equivalent to taking the discrete logs, but it is thought to be the case.

Note that the cryptogram is twice the length of the plaintext, which could be regarded as a drawback. On the other hand associated with this is a potentially useful probabilistic element in the encryption process, namely that a given plaintext would probably not get enciphered to the same ciphertext twice. The benefit of this is that an eavesdropper with a good guess as to the message cannot verify his guess against the ciphertext without knowing k.

In particular a new k would presumably be chosen for each block where a message needed to be broken up into blocks.

A.3 Complexity theory

We should say a few words about what is meant by a problem being tractable or intractable. The key idea is, for a given algorithm to solve a particular problem, to examine how fast the amount of computation required typically grows with the size of the problem. Take for example Euclid's algorithm for finding the gcd of two numbers, m and n. It can be shown that the number of steps required grows roughly as the log of larger of the two numbers. In fact we can go further and show that the worst case occurs when the input numbers are two successive Fibonacci numbers, in which case the number of steps is the Fibonacci index of the larger number. The Fibonacci numbers grow roughly exponentially with the golden ratio.

Euclid's algorithm is thus regarded as highly efficient – the amount of computation grows roughly as the log on the size of the input. Indeed, any problem for which an algorithm exists for which a polynomial bound can be placed on the rate of growth of the amount of computation as a function of the size of the input is regarded as tractable. Obviously the lower the order of the polynomial the better.

A well-known example of a problem for which even the best algorithms grow exponentially in the size of the input is the travelling salesman problem: given an arbitrary distribution of points on the plane find the shortest Hamiltonian path, that is the shortest path that goes through each point exactly once. The best algorithms do little better than exhaustive search, and the search space grows as the factorial of the number of points. Algorithms that find good approximations more efficiently do exist, but this is not relevant to us.

In fact it is quite common for the search space of a problem to grow exponentially, especially for problems of a combinatorial nature. Usually there is sufficient structure to exploit to give some smarter strategy than exhaustive search. There is, however, a class of problems for which there does not seem to be enough such structure to do significantly better than exhaustive search. The travelling salesman, factorization, and discrete logs all seem to fit in this class.

B The Yahalom protocol in Casper

B.1 The Casper input file

```
#Free variables
a, b : Agent
s : Server
na, nb : Nonce
kab : SessionKey
ServerKey : Agent -> ServerKeys
InverseKeys = (kab, kab), (ServerKey, ServerKey)

#Processes
INITIATOR(a,na) knows ServerKey(a)
RESPONDER(b,s,nb) knows ServerKey(b)
SERVER(s,kab) knows ServerKey

#Protocol description
0.    -> a : b
1.  a -> b : na
2.  b -> s : {a, na, nb}{ServerKey(b)}
3a. s -> a : {b, kab, na, nb}{ServerKey(a)}
3b. s -> b : {a, kab}{ServerKey(b)}
4.  a -> b : {nb}{kab}

#Specification
Secret(a, kab, [b,s])
Secret(b, kab, [a,s])
Agreement(b, a, [na,nb])
-- Agreement(b, a, [kab])
Agreement(a, b, [kab])

#Actual variables
Anne, Bob, Yves : Agent
Jeeves : Server
Kab : SessionKey
Na, Nb : Nonce
InverseKeys = (Kab, Kab)
```

```
#Inline functions
symbolic ServerKey

#System
INITIATOR(Anne, Na)
RESPONDER(Bob, Jeeves, Nb)
SERVER(Jeeves, Kab)

#Intruder Information
Intruder = Yves
IntruderKnowledge = {Anne, Bob, Yves, Jeeves, ServerKey(Yves)}
```

B.2 Casper output

Casper produces the following FDR script from the above description of the protocol
and its requirements.

Data

```
datatype Encryption = Anne | Bob | Yves | Jeeves | Kab | Na | Nb |
   Garbage | ServerKey.Agent | Sq.Seq(Encryption) |
   Encrypt.(ALL_KEYS,Seq(Encryption)) | Hash.(HashFunction,
   Seq(Encryption)) | Xor.(Encryption, Encryption)

ALL_KEYS = Union({SessionKey, ServerKeys})

HashFunction = {}
ATOM = {Anne, Bob, Yves, Jeeves, Kab, Na, Nb, Garbage}

encrypt(m,k) = Encrypt.(k,m)
decrypt(Encrypt.(k1,m),k) = if k == inverse(k1) then m else Garbage
decrypt(_,_) = Garbage
decryptable(Encrypt.(k1,m),k) = k == inverse(k1)
decryptable(_,_) = false
nth(ms,n) = if n == 1 then head(ms) else nth(tail(ms), n - 1)

addGarbage(S) =
   if S=={} then {Garbage}
   else Union({S, {Garbage | Encrypt._ <- S},
               {Garbage | Hash._ <- S},
               {Garbage | Xor._ <- S}})
```

```
-- Types in actual system

Agent = {Anne, Bob, Yves}
Server = {Jeeves}
SessionKey = {Kab}
Nonce = {Na, Nb}
ServerKeys = {ServerKey(arg_1) | arg_1 <- Agent}

inverse(Kab) = Kab
inverse(ServerKey.arg) = ServerKey.arg

ServerKey(arg_1) = ServerKey.(arg_1)
```

Messages

```
datatype Labels =
  Msg1 | Msg2 | Msg3a | Msg3b | Msg4 | Env0

INPUT_INT_MSG4_BODY =
  {(Msg4, Encrypt.(kab, <nb>), <s>) |
     s <- Server, kab <- SessionKey, nb <- Nonce}
INPUT_INT_MSG1_BODY =
  {(Msg1, na,<>) |
     na <- Nonce}
INPUT_INT_MSG2_BODY =
  {(Msg2, Encrypt.(ServerKey(b), <a, na, nb>),<>) |
     a <- Agent, b <- Agent, na <- Nonce, nb <- Nonce}
INPUT_INT_MSG3a_BODY =
  {(Msg3a, Encrypt.(ServerKey(a), <b, kab, na, nb>),<>) |
     a <- Agent, b <- Agent, kab <- SessionKey,
                             na <- Nonce, nb <- Nonce}
INPUT_INT_MSG3b_BODY =
  {(Msg3b, Encrypt.(ServerKey(b), <a, kab>),<>) |
     a <- Agent, b <- Agent, kab <- SessionKey}

INPUT_INT_MSG_BODY =

  Union({
    INPUT_INT_MSG1_BODY,
    INPUT_INT_MSG2_BODY,
    INPUT_INT_MSG3a_BODY,
    INPUT_INT_MSG3b_BODY,
    INPUT_INT_MSG4_BODY
  })
```

```
OUTPUT_INT_MSG4_BODY =
  {(Msg4, Encrypt.(kab, <nb>), <na, s>) |
     na <- Nonce, s <- Server,
                  kab <- SessionKey, nb <- Nonce}

OUTPUT_INT_MSG1_BODY =
  {(Msg1, na,<>) |
     na <- Nonce}
OUTPUT_INT_MSG2_BODY =
  {(Msg2, Encrypt.(ServerKey(b), <a, na, nb>),<>) |
     a <- Agent, b <- Agent, na <- Nonce, nb <- Nonce}
OUTPUT_INT_MSG3a_BODY =
  {(Msg3a, Encrypt.(ServerKey(a), <b, kab, na, nb>),<>) |
     a <- Agent, b <- Agent, kab <- SessionKey,
                            na <- Nonce, nb <- Nonce}
OUTPUT_INT_MSG3b_BODY =
  {(Msg3b, Encrypt.(ServerKey(b), <a, kab>),<>) |
     a <- Agent, b <- Agent, kab <- SessionKey}
OUTPUT_INT_MSG_BODY =
  Union({
    OUTPUT_INT_MSG1_BODY,
    OUTPUT_INT_MSG2_BODY,
    OUTPUT_INT_MSG3a_BODY,
    OUTPUT_INT_MSG3b_BODY,
    OUTPUT_INT_MSG4_BODY
  })

INPUT_MSG1_BODY = {rmb(m) | m <- INPUT_INT_MSG1_BODY}
INPUT_MSG2_BODY = {rmb(m) | m <- INPUT_INT_MSG2_BODY}
INPUT_MSG3a_BODY = {rmb(m) | m <- INPUT_INT_MSG3a_BODY}
INPUT_MSG3b_BODY = {rmb(m) | m <- INPUT_INT_MSG3b_BODY}
INPUT_MSG4_BODY = {rmb(m) | m <- INPUT_INT_MSG4_BODY}
OUTPUT_MSG1_BODY = {rmb(m) | m <- OUTPUT_INT_MSG1_BODY}
OUTPUT_MSG2_BODY = {rmb(m) | m <- OUTPUT_INT_MSG2_BODY}
OUTPUT_MSG3a_BODY = {rmb(m) | m <- OUTPUT_INT_MSG3a_BODY}
OUTPUT_MSG3b_BODY = {rmb(m) | m <- OUTPUT_INT_MSG3b_BODY}
OUTPUT_MSG4_BODY = {rmb(m) | m <- OUTPUT_INT_MSG4_BODY}
INPUT_MSG_BODY =
  Union({
    INPUT_MSG1_BODY,
    INPUT_MSG2_BODY,
    INPUT_MSG3a_BODY,
    INPUT_MSG3b_BODY,
```

```
      INPUT_MSG4_BODY
  })

OUTPUT_MSG_BODY =
  Union({
    OUTPUT_MSG1_BODY,
    OUTPUT_MSG2_BODY,
    OUTPUT_MSG3a_BODY,
    OUTPUT_MSG3b_BODY,
    OUTPUT_MSG4_BODY
  })

MSG_BODY = union(INPUT_MSG_BODY,OUTPUT_MSG_BODY)

ENVMSG0_BODY =
  {(Env0, b, <>) |
     b <- Agent}


ENVMSG_BODY = ENVMSG0_BODY

SenderType ((Msg1,_,_)) = Agent
SenderType ((Msg2,_,_)) = Agent
SenderType ((Msg3a,_,_)) = Server
SenderType ((Msg3b,_,_)) = Server
SenderType ((Msg4,_,_)) = Agent

ReceiverType((Msg1,_,_)) = Agent
ReceiverType((Msg2,_,_)) = Server
ReceiverType((Msg3a,_,_)) = Agent
ReceiverType((Msg3b,_,_)) = Agent
ReceiverType((Msg4,_,_)) = Agent

ALL_PRINCIPALS = Union({Agent, Server})

channel input1:ALL_PRINCIPALS.ALL_PRINCIPALS.INPUT_INT_MSG_BODY
channel output1: ALL_PRINCIPALS.ALL_PRINCIPALS.OUTPUT_INT_MSG_BODY
channel fake: ALL_PRINCIPALS.ALL_PRINCIPALS.INPUT_MSG_BODY
channel intercept: ALL_PRINCIPALS.ALL_PRINCIPALS.OUTPUT_MSG_BODY
channel env : ALL_PRINCIPALS.ENVMSG_BODY

datatype ROLE = INITIATOR_role | RESPONDER_role | SERVER_role

ALL_SECRETS_0 = SessionKey
```

```
ALL_SECRETS = addGarbage(ALL_SECRETS_0)

datatype Signal =
  Claim_Secret.ALL_PRINCIPALS.ALL_SECRETS.Set(ALL_PRINCIPALS) |
  Running1.ROLE.ALL_PRINCIPALS.ALL_PRINCIPALS.Nonce.Nonce |
  Commit1.ROLE.ALL_PRINCIPALS.ALL_PRINCIPALS.Nonce.Nonce |
  Running2.ROLE.ALL_PRINCIPALS.ALL_PRINCIPALS.SessionKey |
  Commit2.ROLE.ALL_PRINCIPALS.ALL_PRINCIPALS.SessionKey

channel signal : Signal
```

Definitions of agents

```
INITIATOR_0(a, na) =
  [] b : Agent @ env.a.(Env0, b,<>) ->
  output1.a.b.(Msg1, na,<>) ->
  [] kab : SessionKey @ [] nb : Nonce @ [] s : Server @
    input1.s.a.(Msg3a, Encrypt.(ServerKey(a), <b, kab, na, nb>),<>) ->
  output1.a.b.(Msg4, Encrypt.(kab, <nb>),<na, s>) ->
  SKIP

INITIATOR(a, na) =
  INITIATOR_0(a, na)
    [[input1.s.a.m <-fake.s.a.rmb(m) |
        s <- Server, m <- INPUT_INT_MSG3a_BODY]]
    [[output1.a.b.m <- intercept.a.b.rmb(m) |
        b <- Agent, m <- OUTPUT_INT_MSG1_BODY]]
    [[output1.a.b.m <- intercept.a.b.rmb(m) |
        b <- Agent, m <- OUTPUT_INT_MSG4_BODY]]

RESPONDER_0(b, s, nb) =
  [] a : Agent @ [] na : Nonce @ input1.a.b.(Msg1, na,<>) ->
  output1.b.s.(Msg2, Encrypt.(ServerKey(b), <a, na, nb>),<>) ->
  [] kab : SessionKey @
    input1.s.b.(Msg3b, Encrypt.(ServerKey(b), <a, kab>),<>) ->
  input1.a.b.(Msg4, Encrypt.(inverse(kab), <nb>),<s>) ->
  SKIP

RESPONDER(b, s, nb) =
  RESPONDER_0(b, s, nb)
    [[input1.a.b.m <-fake.a.b.rmb(m) |
        a <- Agent, m <- INPUT_INT_MSG1_BODY]]
    [[input1.s.b.m <-fake.s.b.rmb(m) |
        s <- Server, m <- INPUT_INT_MSG3b_BODY]]
```

```
      [[input1.a.b.m <-fake.a.b.rmb(m) |
          a <- Agent, m <- INPUT_INT_MSG4_BODY]]
      [[output1.b.s.m <- intercept.b.s.rmb(m) |
          s <- Server, m <- OUTPUT_INT_MSG2_BODY]]

SERVER_0(s, kab) =
  [] a : Agent @ [] b : Agent @ [] na : Nonce @ [] nb : Nonce @
    input1.b.s.(Msg2, Encrypt.(ServerKey(b), <a, na, nb>),<>) ->
  output1.s.a.(Msg3a, Encrypt.(ServerKey(a), <b, kab, na, nb>),<>) ->
  output1.s.b.(Msg3b, Encrypt.(ServerKey(b), <a, kab>),<>) ->
  SKIP

SERVER(s, kab) =
  SERVER_0(s, kab)
    [[input1.b.s.m <-fake.b.s.rmb(m) |
        b <- Agent, m <- INPUT_INT_MSG2_BODY]]
    [[output1.s.a.m <- intercept.s.a.rmb(m) |
        a <- Agent, m <- OUTPUT_INT_MSG3a_BODY]]
    [[output1.s.b.m <- intercept.s.b.rmb(m) |
        b <- Agent, m <- OUTPUT_INT_MSG3b_BODY]]
```

Facts and deductions

```
Fact_1 =
  Union({
    {Garbage},
    Nonce,
    Agent,
    SessionKey,
    ServerKeys,
    {Encrypt.(ServerKey(b), <a, na, nb>) |
        a <- Agent, b <- Agent, na <- Nonce, nb <- Nonce},
    {Encrypt.(ServerKey(a), <b, kab, na, nb>) |
        a <- Agent, b <- Agent, kab <- SessionKey,
                                na <- Nonce, nb <- Nonce},
    {Encrypt.(ServerKey(b), <a, kab>) |
        a <- Agent, b <- Agent, kab <- SessionKey},
    {Encrypt.(kab, <nb>) |
        kab <- SessionKey, nb <- Nonce}
  })


laws = {(Garbage, Garbage)}

external mtransclose
```

```
renaming = mtransclose(laws, Fact_1)

external relational_inverse_image
external relational_image
ren = relational_inverse_image(renaming)

-- renaming for facts
applyRenaming0(a) =
  let S = ren(a)
  within if card(S)==0 then a else elsing(S)

elsing({x}) = x

-- renaming for events
applyRenaming(Sq.ms) =
  if member(Sq.ms, Fact_1) then applyRenaming0(Sq.ms)
  else Sq.<applyRenaming0(m) | m <- ms>
applyRenaming(a) = applyRenaming0(a)

rmb((l,m,extras)) =
(l, applyRenaming(m), <applyRenaming(e) | e <- extras>)

domain = {a | (_,a) <- renaming}

applyRenamingToSet(X) =
  union({elsing(ren(a)) | a <- inter(X,domain)},  diff(X, domain))

applyRenamingToDeductions(S) =
  {(applyRenaming0(f), applyRenamingToSet(X)) | (f,X) <- S}
```

intruder's knowledge and deductions

```
unSq (Sq.ms) = set(ms)
unSq (m) = {m}

IK0 = {Anne, Bob, Yves, Jeeves, ServerKey(Yves), Garbage}

unknown(S) = diff(S,IK0)

Deductions_0 =
  Union({SqDeductions, UnSqDeductions,
         EncryptionDeductions, DecryptionDeductions,
         VernEncDeductions, VernDecDeductions,
```

```
                 UserDeductions, FnAppDeductions, HashDeductions})

SqDeductions =
  {(Sq.fs, unknown(set(fs))) | Sq.fs <- Fact_1}

UnSqDeductions =
  {(f, unknown({Sq.fs})) | Sq.fs <- Fact_1, f <- unknown(set(fs))}

EncryptionDeductions =
  {(Encrypt.(k,fs), unknown(union({k}, set(fs)))) |
      Encrypt.(k,fs) <- Fact_1}

DecryptionDeductions =
  {(f, unknown({Encrypt.(k,fs), inverse(k)})) |
      Encrypt.(k,fs) <- Fact_1, f <- unknown(set(fs))}

VernEncDeductions =
  {(Xor.(m1,m2), unknown(union(unSq(m1), unSq(m2)))) |
      Xor.(m1,m2) <- Fact_1}

VernDecDeductions =
    {(m11, union(unknown(unSq(m2)), {Xor.(m1,m2)})) |
        Xor.(m1,m2) <- Fact_1, m11 <- unSq(m1)}
UserDeductions = {}


FnAppDeductions = {}

HashDeductions = {(Hash.(f, ms), set(ms)) | Hash.(f, ms) <- Fact_1}

components((_, Sq.ms, _)) =
  if member(Sq.ms, Fact_1) then {Sq.ms} else set(ms)
components((_, m,_)) = {m}
```

Close-up knowledge and deductions

```
subset(A,B) = inter(A,B) == A

Seeable = Union({unknown(components(m)) | m <- MSG_BODY})

Close(IK, ded, fact) =
  let IK1 =
        union(IK, {f | (f,fs) <- ded, subset(fs,IK)})
      ded1 =
```

```
            {(f,fs) | (f,fs) <- ded, not (member(f,IK)),
                        subset(fs,fact)}
        fact1 = Union({IK, {f | (f,fs) <- ded}, Seeable})
    within
    if card(IK)==card(IK1) and card(ded)==card(ded1)
       and card(fact)==card(fact1)
    then (IK, {(f,diff(fs,IK)) | (f,fs) <- ded}, fact)
    else Close(IK1, ded1, fact1)

Deductions_1 = {(f,fs) | (f,fs) <- Deductions_0,
                            not (member(f,fs))}


(IK1, Deductions, KnowableFact) =
  Close(applyRenamingToSet(IK0),
        applyRenamingToDeductions(Deductions_1),
        applyRenamingToSet(Fact_1))

print IK1
print KnowableFact
print Deductions
```

The intruder

```
second((_,m,_)) = m
INTRUDER_MSG_BODY = {second(m) | m <- MSG_BODY}
dummyDeds = {(Garbage,{Garbage})}
Deductions' = if Deductions=={} then dummyDeds else Deductions
-- Don't you hate hacks like this?
channel leak : addGarbage(ALL_SECRETS)
channel hear, say : INTRUDER_MSG_BODY
channel infer : Deductions'

IGNORANT(f,ms,fss,ds) =
   hear?m:ms -> KNOWS(f,ms,ds)
   []
   ([] fs : fss @ infer.(f,fs) -> KNOWS(f,ms,ds))

KNOWS(f,ms,ds) =
  hear?m:ms -> KNOWS(f,ms,ds)
  []
  say?m:ms -> KNOWS(f,ms,ds)
  []
  infer?(f1,fs) : ds -> KNOWS(f,ms,ds)
```

```
  []
  member(f,ALL_SECRETS) & leak.f -> KNOWS(f,ms,ds)

f_ms_fss_ds_s =
  let rid = relational_image(Deductions)
  within {(f,
           {m | m <- INTRUDER_MSG_BODY, member(f,unSq(m))},
           rid(f),
           {x | x_@@(_,fs) <- Deductions, member(f, fs)}) |
              f <- diff(KnowableFact,IK1)}

AlphaL(f,ms,fss,ds) =
  Union({(if member(f,ALL_SECRETS) then {leak.f} else {}),
         {hear.m, say.m | m <- ms},
         {infer.(f,fs) | fs <- fss},
         {infer.(f1,fs) | (f1,fs) <- ds}})

transparent chase

INTRUDER_0 =
  (|| (f,ms,fss,ds) : f_ms_fss_ds_s @
         [AlphaL(f,ms,fss,ds)] IGNORANT(f,ms,fss,ds))
  \ {|infer|}

INTRUDER_1 =
  chase(INTRUDER_0)
    [[hear.(second(m)) <- intercept.A.B.m |
        m <- OUTPUT_MSG_BODY, A <- SenderType(m), B <- ReceiverType(m)]]
    [[say.(second(m)) <- fake.A.B.m |
        m <- INPUT_MSG_BODY, A <- SenderType(m), B <- ReceiverType(m)]]

SAY_KNOWN =
  ([] f : inter(IK1, ALL_SECRETS) @ leak.f -> SAY_KNOWN)
  []
  ([] m : {m | m <- OUTPUT_MSG_BODY, subset(components(m),IK1)} @
     let ST = SenderType(m)
         RT = ReceiverType(m)
     within
      (intercept?A:diff(ST,{Yves})?B:RT!m -> SAY_KNOWN))
  []
  ([] m : {m | m <- INPUT_MSG_BODY, subset(components(m),IK1)} @
     let ST = SenderType(m)
         RT = ReceiverType(m)
     within
```

```
                    (fake?A:ST?B:RT!m -> SAY_KNOWN))

        INTRUDER =
          (INTRUDER_1 [|{|intercept.Yves|}|] STOP) ||| SAY_KNOWN
```

Process representing Anne

```
Alpha_INITIATOR_Anne =
  Union({
    {|intercept.Anne.A.m | A <- ALL_PRINCIPALS, m <- MSG1_BODY|},
    {|intercept.Anne.A.m | A <- ALL_PRINCIPALS, m <- MSG4_BODY|},
    {|fake.A.Anne.m | A <- ALL_PRINCIPALS, m <- MSG3a_BODY|}
  })

INITIATOR_Anne = INITIATOR(Anne, Na)

Alpha_Anne = {|intercept.Anne.A, fake.A.Anne | A <- ALL_PRINCIPALS|}

AGENT_Anne =
  INITIATOR_Anne
```

Process representing Bob

```
Alpha_RESPONDER_Bob =
  Union({
    {|intercept.Bob.A.m | A <- ALL_PRINCIPALS, m <- MSG2_BODY|},
    {|fake.A.Bob.m | A <- ALL_PRINCIPALS, m <- MSG1_BODY|},
    {|fake.A.Bob.m | A <- ALL_PRINCIPALS, m <- MSG3b_BODY|},
    {|fake.A.Bob.m | A <- ALL_PRINCIPALS, m <- MSG4_BODY|}
  })

RESPONDER_Bob = RESPONDER(Bob, Jeeves, Nb)

Alpha_Bob = {|intercept.Bob.A, fake.A.Bob | A <- ALL_PRINCIPALS|}

AGENT_Bob =
  RESPONDER_Bob
```

Process representing Jeeves

```
Alpha_SERVER_Jeeves =
  Union({
```

```
        {|intercept.Jeeves.A.m | A <- ALL_PRINCIPALS, m <- MSG3a_BODY|},
        {|intercept.Jeeves.A.m | A <- ALL_PRINCIPALS, m <- MSG3b_BODY|},
        {|fake.A.Jeeves.m | A <- ALL_PRINCIPALS, m <- MSG2_BODY|}
    })

SERVER_Jeeves = SERVER(Jeeves, Kab)

Alpha_Jeeves = {|intercept.Jeeves.A, fake.A.Jeeves |
                                    A <- ALL_PRINCIPALS|}

AGENT_Jeeves =
  SERVER_Jeeves
```

Complete system

```
SYSTEM_0 =
  (AGENT_Anne
    |||
  (AGENT_Bob
    |||
  AGENT_Jeeves))

SYSTEM = SYSTEM_0 [| {|intercept, fake|} |] INTRUDER
```

Systems specifications

```
Sigma = {|fake, intercept, env, leak|}

-- Secret specifications

SECRET_SPEC_0(s) =
  signal.Claim_Secret?A!s?Bs ->
    (if member(Yves, Bs) then SECRET_SPEC_0(s) else SECRET_SPEC_1(s))
    []
  leak.s -> SECRET_SPEC_0(s)

SECRET_SPEC_1(s) = signal.Claim_Secret?A!s?Bs -> SECRET_SPEC_1(s)

AlphaS(s) =
  union({|signal.Claim_Secret.A.s | A <- ALL_PRINCIPALS|}, {leak.s})

Alpha_SECRETS = {|leak, signal.Claim_Secret|}

SECRET_SPEC = (|| s : ALL_SECRETS @ [AlphaS(s)] SECRET_SPEC_0(s))
```

```
assert SECRET_SPEC [T= SYSTEM_S\ diff(Events,Alpha_SECRETS)
c
-- Authentication specifications

AuthenticateRESPONDERToINITIATORAgreement_na_nb(b) =
  signal.Running1.RESPONDER_role.b?a?na?nb ->
  signal.Commit1.INITIATOR_role.a.b.na.nb -> STOP

AlphaAuthenticateRESPONDERToINITIATORAgreement_na_nb(b) =
  {|signal.Running1.RESPONDER_role.b.a,
    signal.Commit1.INITIATOR_role.a.b |
      a <- Agent|}

AuthenticateINITIATORToRESPONDERAgreement_kab(a) =
  signal.Running2.INITIATOR_role.a?b?kab ->
  signal.Commit2.RESPONDER_role.b.a.kab -> STOP

AlphaAuthenticateINITIATORToRESPONDERAgreement_kab(a) =
  {|signal.Running2.INITIATOR_role.a.b,
    signal.Commit2.RESPONDER_role.b.a |
      b <- Agent|}

AuthenticateRESPONDERAnneToINITIATORAgreement_na_nb =
  STOP

assert AuthenticateRESPONDERAnneToINITIATORAgreement_na_nb [T=
  SYSTEM_1 \
   diff(Events,
        AlphaAuthenticateRESPONDERToINITIATORAgreement_na_nb(Anne))

AuthenticateRESPONDERBobToINITIATORAgreement_na_nb =
  AuthenticateRESPONDERToINITIATORAgreement_na_nb(Bob)

assert AuthenticateRESPONDERBobToINITIATORAgreement_na_nb [T=
  SYSTEM_1 \
   diff(Events,
        AlphaAuthenticateRESPONDERToINITIATORAgreement_na_nb(Bob))

AuthenticateINITIATORAnneToRESPONDERAgreement_kab =
  AuthenticateINITIATORToRESPONDERAgreement_kab(Anne)

assert AuthenticateINITIATORAnneToRESPONDERAgreement_kab [T=
  SYSTEM_2 \
   diff(Events,
```

```
            AlphaAuthenticateINITIATORToRESPONDERAgreement_kab(Anne))

AuthenticateINITIATORBobToRESPONDERAgreement_kab =
  STOP

assert AuthenticateINITIATORBobToRESPONDERAgreement_kab [T=
  SYSTEM_2 \
   diff(Events,
        AlphaAuthenticateINITIATORToRESPONDERAgreement_kab(Bob))




SYSTEM_1 = SYSTEM
[[intercept.b.s.rmb((Msg2, Encrypt.(ServerKey(b), <a, na, nb>), <>))
    <- signal.Running1.RESPONDER_role.b.a.
            applyRenaming(na).applyRenaming(nb),
  intercept.a.b.rmb((Msg4, Encrypt.(kab, <nb>), <na, s>))
    <- signal.Commit1.INITIATOR_role.a.b.
            applyRenaming(na).applyRenaming(nb) |
      b <- Agent, s <- Server, a <- Agent, na <- Nonce, nb <- Nonce,
    kab <- SessionKey]]

SYSTEM_2 = SYSTEM
[[intercept.a.b.rmb((Msg4, Encrypt.(kab, <nb>), <na, s>))
    <- signal.Running2.INITIATOR_role.a.b.applyRenaming(kab),
  fake.a.b.rmb((Msg4, Encrypt.(kab, <nb>), <s>))
    <- signal.Commit2.RESPONDER_role.b.a.applyRenaming(kab) |
      a <- Agent, b <- Agent, na <- Nonce,
      s <- Server, kab <- SessionKey, nb <- Nonce]]

SYSTEM_S = SYSTEM
[[intercept.a.b.rmb((Msg4, Encrypt.(kab, <nb>), <na, s>))
    <- signal.Claim_Secret.a.kab.{b, s},
fake.a.b.rmb((Msg4, Encrypt.(kab, <nb>), <s>))
    <- signal.Claim_Secret.b.kab.{a, s}
  | a <- Agent, b <- Agent, na <- Nonce,
    s <- Server, kab <- SessionKey, nb <- Nonce]]
```

C CyberCash rank function analysis

In Chapter 8, a number of simplifications were applied to the CyberCash main sequence protocol. The overall effect of these simplifications is to reduce the protocol to versions that can be easily understood with respect to the properties under consideration. The main aspects of the protocol have in each case been retained to ensure that the protocol still meets its original requirement, yet it is simple enough to apply standard analysis techniques. In this appendix we use the rank-function technique to verify the protocol.

C.1 Secrecy

We first consider the secrecy property required of this protocol. Some details of the transaction (such as its value) are available to eavesdroppers in the original protocol, and hence are not required to be kept secret. However, some care is taken to keep the card number secret, and we will take this as the secrecy property that is required for the protocol: that if the customer interacts with an honest merchant then the intruder cannot learn *cardNumber*. (Clearly if the customer interacts with a dishonest merchant or the intruder posing as a merchant then no guarantees can be expected concerning secrecy of the card number.)

We will provide a rank function that demonstrates that the protocol indeed satisfies this property. To do this, we must consider the CSP descriptions of the protocol agents. These descriptions use variables to hold the values expected in the protocol. A list of these variables and the values they expect to hold is given in Figure C.1.

The CSP description of a single customer run of the simplified protocol, with merchant mr, session key kcs, amount am and card number cn is as follows:

$$Cust_{cu}(mr, kcs, am, cn) =$$
$$receive.mr.cu?(mci.ma) \rightarrow$$
$$if\ merchant(mci) = mr$$
$$then\ send.cu!mr!\ (id.ma.mci.tr.\{kcs\}_{pkCyberKey}.\{am.cn.mci.cu.ma.tr\}_{kcs})$$
$$\rightarrow receive.mr.cu.(mci.ma.tr.cu.\{cn.am\}_{kcs}) \rightarrow Stop$$
$$else\ Stop$$

The function $merchant(mci)$ yields the merchant that the Cyberbank associates with mci. We assume that the customer has some way of checking that mci corresponds to the merchant mr.

A customer has a single card number for all the different runs. A general description of a customer cu (who interacts only with honest merchants) is therefore

269

am	*Amount*
cn	*CardNumber*
mci	*MerchantCcId*
ma	*MerchantAmount*
tr	*Transaction*
mt	*MerchantTransaction*
cu	*Id* (= customer's name)
mr	*MerchantId* (= merchant's name)
cb	*Cyberbank*
kcs	a customer's session key
kms	a merchant's session key
pkCyberKey(cu)	an assymetric key known only to customer *cu*, whose inverse is known to Cyberbank
pkCyberKey(mr)	an assymetric key known only to merchant *mr*, whose inverse is known to Cyberbank

Figure C.1 Variables in the CSP description of CyberCash

as follows:

$$Customer_{cu}(cardNumber) = \left|\left|\right|_{mr \in HM, kcs \in KEYS_{cu}, am} Cust_{cu}(mr, kcs, am, cn)\right.$$

HM is the set of honest merchants, and $KEYS_{cu}$ is the set of session keys cu has available for use in this protocol with the Cyberbank. There is one potential run for each of these session keys.

The behaviour of a single run of an honest merchant mr with session key kms is described as follows:

$$Merchantrun_{mr}(kms) =$$
$$\square_{cu,ma} send.mr!cu!(mci.ma)$$
$$\rightarrow receive.cu.mr?(cu.ma.mci.tr.x.y)$$
$$\rightarrow send.mr!cb! \ (mci.mt.x.y.\{kms\}_{pkCyberKey(mr)}.cu.ma.mci.mt.tr$$
$$\rightarrow receive.cb.mr? \ (mci.mt.\{cn.ma.cu.mr.tr\}_{kms}.z$$
$$\rightarrow send.mr!cu!(mci.ma.tr.cu.z) \rightarrow Stop$$

Then a merchant's behaviour is simply an interleaving of arbitrarily many runs:

$$Merchant_{mr} = \left|\left|\right|_{kms \in KEYS_{mr}} Merchantrun_{mr}(kms)\right.$$

$KEYS_{mr}$ is the set of session keys that merchant mr has available to use with Cyberbank. There is one potential run for each of these.

Finally, the Cyberbank's role in the protocol is described as follows:

$Cyber =$

$\left|\left|\right|\right|_{n\in\mathbb{N}} \square_{mr}$ $receive.mr.cb?(\ mci.mt.\{kcs\}_{pkCyberKey}.\{am.cn.mci.cu.ma.tr\}_{kcs}.$
$\{kms\}_{pkCyberKey(mr)}.cu.ma.mci.mt.tr)$

$\rightarrow$ *if* $mr = merchant(mci)$

then $send.cb.m!(\ mci.mt.\{cn.ma.cu.mr.tr\}_{kms}.$
$\{cn.am\}_{kcs})$
$\rightarrow Stop$

else Stop

As noted above, the function $merchant(mci)$ yields the merchant associated with mci. The bank must check that this corresponds to the signature on the incoming message, since this provides the guarantee that the key kms was generated by that merchant.

We aim to prove that if $CardNumber_0$ is customer cu_0's card number, then this can never be obtained by the intruder. The secrecy property we will prove is

$$Secrecy(tr) = \neg(leak.CardNumber_0 \text{ in } tr)$$

To establish this, it is sufficient to exhibit a rank function that

- gives $CardNumber_0$ a rank of 0;
- gives all the intruder's initial knowledge a rank of 1;
- ensures that the set of positive-ranked messages is closed under the $\vdash$ relation;
- is such that the processes $Customer_{cu}$ for any cu, $Merchant_{mr}$ for any mr, and $Cyber$ all maintain positive rank.

We will also need to use the fact that no two customers have the same card number; so no other customer will be able to divulge $CardNumber_0$.

Constructing the rank function

We now construct the rank function. In fact, every message need only have rank 0 or 1. We begin by examining the messages that are transmitted in the protocol. We firstly observe that the plaintext $CardNumber_0$ must have rank 0. However, it can legitimately appear in runs of the protocol encrypted under session keys kms and kcs, so such encrypted appearances must have rank 1 (or greater). To prevent the intruder from decrypting these messages, we must ensure that all such kms and kcs sessions keys are not available to the intruder: they must have rank 0. This must be true for any session key of the customer cu_0, and also for any session key of any honest merchant. These keys are sent, encrypted under $pkCyberKey$ and $pkCyberKey(mr)$, to the Cyberbank, so it is essential that the intruder cannot decrypt these messages: the inverse keys $skCyberKey$ and $skCyberKey(mr)$ must have rank 0. (If any of them have rank 1 then we have e.g. that $skCyberkey(mr)$ has rank 1. Since $\{kms\}_{pkCyberKey(mr)}$ also has rank 1 as a legitimate message in the protocol, and since $\{skCyberKey(mr), \{kms\}_{pkCyberKey(mr)}\} \vdash kms$, closure of positive rank under $\vdash$ requires that kms has rank 1, which we do not want.)

All other plaintext messages – all other information except keys – can have rank 1. Most plaintext can be transmitted unencrypted in the simplified protocol.

We now consider the protocol participants. The customer creates two encrypted messages, which are both sent out as part of the second message of the protocol. They must be given rank 1 to ensure that all customers preserve positive message rank:

▩ $\{kcs\}_{pkCyberKey}$. We can ensure that this has positive rank by stipulating that all messages encrypted with $pkCyberKey$ have positive rank, whatever the rank of kcs.

▩ $\{am.cn.mci.cu.ma.tr\}_{kcs}$. There are two possibilities: if kcs is one of cu_0's session keys, then the message was generated by $Cust_{cu_0}$ and so it contains $CardNumber_0$ – both key and content have rank 0. The alternative is that neither kcs nor the content of the message have rank 0. Hence we can give this message a rank of 1 if either contents and key both have rank 0, or if they both have rank 1. It will have rank 0 otherwise. Observe that if kcs is one of cu_0's session keys then mci must correspond to an honest merchant, since we assume that cu_0 only communicates with honest merchants. In considering the Cyberbank below we will need to use the fact that a dishonest mci cannot appear in such a message encrypted with kcs, and so such messages will also have to be given rank 0.

The merchant only creates one encrypted message: $\{kms\}_{pkCyberKey(mr)}$. We must ensure that this message always has rank 1. If the merchant is honest, then kms has rank 0 and so does $pkCyberKey(mr)$. If the merchant is not honest, then both keys have rank 1. Thus if both keys have the same rank then their combination here can be given rank 1. Other combinations are not possible, and so can be given rank 0.

Finally, we consider the Cyberbank. This receives a number of encrypted message components, and then transmits transformed versions of them.

If the messages it receives have rank 1, then the components it transmits must have rank 1. They are:

▩ $\{cn.am\}_{kcs}$. Here we require that if $cn = CardNumber_0$ then kcs has rank 0, since otherwise the intruder could extract $CardNumber_0$. Thus we again give this message a rank of 1 if the ranks of its contents and encryption key are the same. We can prove that the Cyberbank maintains positive-message rank by establishing that $CardNumber_0$ can indeed only be sent out encrypted under a key with rank 0. To see this, observe that one of the (positive-rank) messages received is $\{am.CardNumber_0.mci.cu.ma.tr\}_{kcs}$. Since the content of this message has rank 0 (since it contains $CardNumber_0$), the key kcs must also have rank 0.

▩ $\{cn.ma.cu.mr.tr\}_{kms}$. If kms has rank 0 then we can give the encrypted message rank 1 whatever the rank of the contents, since the contents can never be extracted. If kms has rank 1 then we can expect that the contents of the message can be extracted by the intruder. We would expect that only contents with positive rank should be encrypted by such keys. Hence we give this message positive rank if either *kms* has rank 0, or if the message has positive rank. To establish that *Cyber* maintains positive message rank, we consider a run in which this message is transmitted.

If *kms* has rank 0, then the transmitted encrypted message has positive rank.

If *kms* has rank 1 then since $\{kms\}_{pkCyberKey(mr)}$ has positive rank, it follows that $pkCyberKey(mr)$ has positive rank and hence that $mr \notin HM$. Also, the boolean guard means that $mr = merchant(mcl)$ where is the value of another field in the received message. However, one of the (positive-rank) message components received by *Cyber* is $\{am.cn.mci.cu.ma.tr\}_{kcs}$. If $cn = CardNumber_0$ then this message must have rank 0, since $merchant(mci) \notin HM$. (This is where we use the fact pointed out earlier that the customer is assumed to interact only with honest merchants.) Hence *cn* cannot be $CardNumber_0$. So the text inside the transmitted message has rank 1; and thus so does the entire transmitted message.

The rank function resulting from these considerations is given in Figure C.2. It meets all of the required conditions, and hence establishes that the simplified protocol ensures the secrecy property. This means that the full CyberCash Main Sequence protocol ensures secrecy of the card number.

C.2 Authentication

There are a number of different authentication requirements we might be interested in, at least one for each of the participants in the protocol.

We will focus on the following three:

- The merchant is authenticated to the customer. This gives the customer an assurance that the merchant he considers to be the other party in the protocol is indeed the other party.

- The merchant authenticates the Cyberbank. This gives the merchant an assurance that the transaction has passed through the Cyberbank and hence that the transaction amount will be transferred.

- The Cyberbank authenticates the customer. This gives the Cyberbank an assurance that the transaction really does involve the customer mentioned in the protocol, and hence that a transfer of funds from that customer is appropriate.

In each case, we insert additional *Running* and *Commit* specification signals into the protocol, in order to capture the requirement that *Running* signal must precede the corresponding *Commit* signals. These are illustrated in Figures C.3, C.5 and C.7. The properties we will establish are:

$$\rho_0(u) = 1$$

$$\rho_0(t) = \begin{cases} 0 & \text{if } t = CardNumber_0 \\ 1 & \text{otherwise} \end{cases}$$

$$\rho_0(pk) = \begin{cases} 0 & \text{if } pk = pkCyberKey(mr) \text{ for } mr \in HM \\ 1 & \text{otherwise} \end{cases}$$

$$\rho_0(sk) = \begin{cases} 0 & \text{if } sk = skCyberKey(mr) \text{ for } mr \in HM \text{ or } sk = skCyberKey \\ 1 & \text{otherwise} \end{cases}$$

$$\rho_0(shk) = \begin{cases} 0 & \text{if } shk \in KEYS_{cu_0} \text{ or } shk \in KEYS_{mr} \text{ for } mr \in HM \\ 1 & \text{otherwise} \end{cases}$$

$$\rho(\{m\}_k) = \begin{cases} 1 & \text{if } k = pkCyberKey \\ & \text{or } k = KEYS_{mr} \text{ for some } mr \in HM \\ & \text{or } \rho(m) = \rho(k) \wedge (\rho(k) = 0 \wedge m = am.cn.mci.cu.ma.tr \\ & \qquad\qquad\qquad \Rightarrow merchant(mci) \in HM) \\ 0 & \text{otherwise} \end{cases}$$

$$\rho(m_1.m_2) = \min\{\rho(m_1), \rho(m_2)\}$$

Figure C.2 Rank function for verification of Simplified CyberCash Protocol Secrecy property

■ *Running_Cust.cu_0.mr_0.am_0.ma_0.cn_0* precedes *Commit_Cyber.cu_0.mr_0.am_0.ma_0.cn_0*

■ *Running_Cyber.cu_0.mr_0.ma_0.cn_0* precedes *Commit_Merch.cu_0.mr_0.ma_0.cn_0*

■ *Running_Merch.cu_0.mr_0.ma_0* precedes *Commit_Cust.cu_0.mr_0.ma_0*

The choices of the parameters on which agreement is required will be discussed as the properties are established in detail.

Authenticating the customer to the bank

We first consider the authentication of an arbitrary customer cu_0 to the Cyberbank: the Cyberbank obtains a guarantee that the customer mentioned in the transaction really is involved. More precisely, it establishes that if it is required to process a transaction signed by cu_0, then cu_0 really did request that transaction.

We insert the signal *Running_Cust.cu.mr.am.ma.cn* before customer *cu*'s first transmitted message. To authenticate this message is to authenticate that *cu* is running the protocol apparently with *mr*, in order to make a payment of *am* on card *cn*.

For the Cyberbank to establish authentication, it will have to commit to the transaction at some stage. In fact it can be at any point after receipt of message

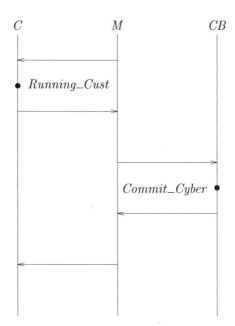

Figure C.3 Inserting messages to authenticate *C* to *CB*

3 of the protocol. We place the signal *Commit_Cyber.cu.mr.ma.am.cn* before the response message (though it could equally well go after). The introduction of these two specification signals is illustrated in Figure C.3.

Then the authentication property we aim to establish is that the system guarantees the following property for arbitrary cu_0, mr_0, am_0, ma_0, and cn_0:

$$Running\_Cust.cu_0.mr_0.am_0.ma_0.cn_0$$
$$\textsf{precedes}\quad Commit\_Cyber.cu_0.mr_0.am_0.ma_0.cn_0$$

The introduction of the appropriate signal is introduced into the description of an individual customer run as follows:

$Cust_{cu}(mr, kcs, am, cn) =$
$\quad receive.mr.cu?\{mci\}_{SK(mr)}.ma$
$\quad \to signal!Running\_Cust.cu.mr.am.ma.cn$
$\quad \to send.cu!mr!\ cu.ma.mci.tr.\{kcs\}_{pkCyberKey}.\{\{am.cn.mci.cu.ma.tr\}_{kcs}\}_{SK(cu)}$
$\quad \to receive.mr.cu.(mci.ma.tr.cu.\{cn.am\}_{kcs})$
$\quad \to Stop$

The description of *Cyber* is also augmented with a signal, as follows:

$Cyber =$
$\square_{mr}$ *receive.mr.cb? mci.mt.* $\{kcs\}_{pkCyberKey}$.*am.cn.*
$\qquad \{\{am.cn.mci.cu.ma.tr\}_{kcs}\}_{SK(cu)}$.
$\qquad \{kms\}_{pkCyberKey(mr)}$.*cu.ma.mci.tr.*
$\qquad \{cu.ma.mci.mt.tr\}_{SK(mr)}$
$\rightarrow$ *if mr = merchant(mci)*
$\qquad$ *then signal!Commit_Cyber.cu.mr.am.ma.cn*
$\qquad\qquad \rightarrow send.cb.mr! mci.mt.*
$\qquad\qquad\qquad \{cn.ma.cu.mr.tr\}_{kms}.\{cn.am\}_{kcs} \rightarrow Stop$
$\qquad$ *else Stop*

This version of the protocol is correct provided the merchant variable *mr* ranges over honest names again (in other words, that the merchants *Cyber* deals with are honest). If not, a dishonest merchant can fool the customer into paying someone else (i.e. cu_0 thinks he is paying mr_0, but mr_0 has signed mci_1, which belongs to mr_1, and so the payment gets switched so that mr_1 gets paid instead of mr_0).

To establish that the required authentication property holds in this case, it is sufficient to find a valid rank function on the system in which a particular $Running\_Cust.cu_0.mr_0.am_0.ma_0.cn_0$ is blocked and cannot occur. We require that $Commit\_Cyber.cu_0.mr_0.am_0.ma_0.cn_0$ must have rank 0: that it cannot occur if the signal it is authenticating does not occur.

Constructing the rank function

We must find a rank function that meets the following conditions:

- gives $Commit\_Cyber.cu_0.mr_0.am_0.ma_0.cn_0$ a rank of 0;
- gives all the intruder's initial knowledge a rank of 1;
- ensures that the set of positive-ranked messages is closed under the $\vdash$ relation;
- is such that the processes $Customer_{cu_0}$ maintains positive message rank when blocked on performing $Running\_Cust.cu_0.mr_0.am_0.ma_0.cn_0$;
- is such that $Customer_{cu}$ for any $cu \neq cu_0$, $Merchant_{mr}$ for any mr, and $Cyber$ all maintain positive rank.

The rank function in this situation is quite straightforward to construct. Authentication relies on the signature of the customer cu_0 on the appropriate message. Hence we firstly give the signature key $SK(cu_0)$ a rank of 0 to reflect the fact that this key is not available to the intruder. Since $Customer_{cu_0}$ is blocked on $Running\_Cust.cu_0.mr_0.am_0.ma_0.cn_0$ we can give a rank of 0 to any messages signed by cu_0 that have thus become blocked. These will be messages of the form $\{\{am_0.cn_0.mci.cu_0.ma.tr\}_{kcs}\}_{SK(cu_0)}$ for which $merchant(mci) = mr_0$ (since the customer is assumed to be able to check that mci and mr match). Such messages will be given a rank of 0. All other encryptions simply retain the rank of their contents. No other encryptions are relevant to this authentication property.

$$\rho_0(u) = 1$$
$$\rho_0(t) = 1$$
$$\rho_0(k) = \begin{cases} 0 & \text{if } k = SK(cu_0) \\ 1 & \text{otherwise} \end{cases}$$

$$\rho(\{m\}_k) = \begin{cases} 0 & \text{if } k = SK(cu_0) \text{ and } m = am_0.cn_0.mci.cu_0.ma_0.tr \\ & \text{for some } tr, merchant(mci) = mr_0 \\ \rho(m) & \text{otherwise} \end{cases}$$
$$\rho(m_1.m_2) = \min\{\rho(m_1), \rho(m_2)\}$$
$$\rho(signal) = \begin{cases} 0 & \text{if } signal = Commit\_Cyber.cu_0.mr_0.am_0.ma_0.cn_0 \\ 1 & \text{otherwise} \end{cases} \}$$

Figure C.4 Rank function for verification of Simplified CyberCash Protocol Authentication property of Customer to Cyberbank

The rank function of Figure C.4 is suitable to establish this property.

It is clear that the *Customer* processes preserve message rank: the only messages of rank 0 that could have been generated are now blocked.

It is equally clear that the *Merchant* processes preserve message rank – they do not introduce any messages of rank 0.

Finally, if *Cyber* produces a signal *Commit_Cyber.cu.mr.am.ma.cn* then this must follow receipt of a message $\{\{am.cn.mci.cu.ma.tr\}_{kcs}\}_{SK(cu)}$ in which we have $merchant(mci) = mr$. The only way the Cyberbank can produce a signal of rank 0 is to have previously received a corresponding message that has rank 0. Hence it maintains positive-message rank.

Authenticating Cyberbank to the merchant

Any particular merchant mr_0 requires a guarantee by the end of the protocol that the transfer of funds from cu_0 to mr_0 has been registered by the Cyberbank. Hence the merchant wishes the signal $Commit\_Merch.cu_0.mr_0.ma_0.cn_0$ to authenticate the signal $Running\_Cyber.cu_0.mr_0.ma_0, cn_0$ provided by *Cyber* after the third message of the protocol, as illustrated in Figure C.5.

The *Commit_Merch* signal is inserted into the CSP description of *Merchant* as follows:

$$Merchant_{mr}(cu, ma) =$$
$$send.mr!cu!mci.ma$$
$$\rightarrow receive.cu.mr?(cu.ma.mci.tr.x.am.cn.y)$$
$$\rightarrow send.mr!cb! mci.mt.x.am.cn.y.$$
$$\{kms\}_{pkCyberKey(mr)}.cu.ma.mci.mt.$$
$$\{cu.ma.mci.mt.tr\}_{SK(mr)}$$
$$\rightarrow receive.cb.mr?(mci.mt.\{cn.ma.cu.mr.tr\}_{kms}.z)$$
$$\rightarrow send.mr!cu!(mci.ma.tr.cu.z)$$
$$\rightarrow signal.Commit\_Merch.cu.mr.ma.cn \rightarrow Stop$$

Figure C.5 Inserting messages to authenticate *CB* to *M*

and the *Running_Cyber* signal that it authenticates is inserted into the description of *Cyber* as follows:

$Cyber =$
$\quad \square_{mr} \ receive.mr.cb? \ (mci.mt.\{kcs\}_{pkCyberKey}.am.cn.$
$\qquad\qquad \{\{am.cn.mci.cu.ma.tr\}_{kcs}\}_{SK(cu)}.$
$\qquad\qquad \{kms\}_{pkCyberKey(mr)}.cu.ma.mci.tr.$
$\qquad\qquad \{cu.ma.mci.mt.tr\}_{SK(mr)})$
$\quad \rightarrow signal!Running\_Cyber.cu.mr.ma.cn$
$\quad \rightarrow if \ merchant(mci) = mr$
$\qquad then \ send.cb.mr!(mci.mt.\{cn.ma.cu.mr.tr\}_{kms}.\{cn.am\}_{kcs}) \rightarrow Stop$
$\qquad else \ Stop$

Then we wish to show that

$Running\_Cyber.cu_0.mr_0.ma_0.cn_0$ **precedes** $Commit\_Merch.cu_0.mr_0.ma_0.cn_0$

Constructing the rank function

We must find a rank function that meets the following conditions:

- gives $Commit\_Merch.cu_0.mr_0.ma_0.cn_0$ a rank of 0;

- gives all the intruder's initial knowledge a rank of 1;

$$\rho_0(u) = 1$$
$$\rho_0(t) = 1$$
$$\rho_0(pk) = \begin{cases} 0 \text{ if } pk = pkCyberKey(mr_0) \\ 1 \text{ otherwise} \end{cases}$$

$$\rho_0(sk) = \begin{cases} 0 \text{ if } sk = skCyberKey(mr_0) \\ 1 \text{ otherwise} \end{cases}$$

$$\rho_0(shk) = \begin{cases} 0 \text{ if } shk \in KEYS_{mr_0} \\ 1 \text{ otherwise} \end{cases}$$

$$\rho(\{m\}_k) = \begin{cases} 1 \text{ if } m \in KEYS_{mr_0} \text{ and } k = pkCyberkey(mr_0) \\ 0 \text{ if } k \in KEYS_{mr_0} \text{ and } m = cn_0.ma_0.cu_0.mr_0.tr \text{ for some } tr \\ \rho(m) \quad \text{otherwise} \end{cases}$$
$$\rho(m_1.m_2) = \min\{\rho(m_1), \rho(m_2)\}$$
$$\rho(signal) = \begin{cases} 0 \text{ if } signal = Commit\_Merch.cu_0.mr_0.ma_0.cn_0 \\ 1 \text{ otherwise} \end{cases}$$

Figure C.6 Rank function for verification of Simplified CyberCash Protocol Authentication property of Cyberbank to merchant

■ ensures that the set of positive-ranked messages is closed under the ⊢ relation;

■ is such that the process *Cyber* maintains positive-message rank when blocked on performing $Running\_Cyber.cu_0.mr_0.ma_0$;

■ is such that the processes $Customer_{cu}$ for any $cu \neq cu_0$, and $Merchant_{mr}$ for any mr.

Authentication here relies on the fact that the session keys $shk \in KEYS_{mr_0}$ are not available to the intruder, and that the intruder cannot obtain them from the messages that pass. These keys will therefore have rank 0. A message encrypted under such a key must therefore have come from the Cyberbank, the only party other than the merchant who is given the key.

If the *Running_Cyber* signal is blocked, then messages that are of the form $\{cn_0.ma_0.cu_0.mr_0.tr\}_{kms}$ will not be produced by *Cyber*. Since these messages are used by *Merchant* to authenticate the transaction, they should be given rank 0.

The rank function of Figure C.6 is then suitable to establish this authentication property.

The *Customer* process clearly maintains positive-message rank, since it only ever sends out messages of rank 1.

To show that the *Cyber* process blocked on *Running_Cyber*.$cu_0.mr_0.ma_0.cn_0$ maintains positive message rank, we need only to show that it cannot transmit any messages of the form $\{cn_0.ma_0.cu_0.mr_0.tr\}_{kms}$. And this follows immediately from the blocking of the *Running_Cyber* signal.

The protocol messages transmitted by *Merchant* all have positive rank. To transmit the signal *Commit_Merch*.$cu_0.mr_0.ma_0.cn_0$ the merchant must previously have received $\{cn_0.ma_0.cu_0.mr_0.tr\}_{kms}$ with $kms \in KEYS_{mr_0}$ (since the key must be the one sent out). But this message received message has rank 0. Hence if *Merchant* only receives messages of rank 1 then it will only transmit messages of rank 1, and so it maintains positive-message rank.

Authenticating the merchant to the customer

Finally, we wish the protocol to enable an arbitrary cu_0 to authenticate mr_0: that cu_0 can be confident at the end of a protocol run that mr_0 has been involved in a run with cu_0, and that they agree on the amount. The CSP description of the *Cust* process will therefore insert a *Commit_Cust.cu.mr.ma* signal at the end of the protocol run, and the *Merchant* process will insert *Running_Merch.cu.mr.ma* after the second message. As observed above, receipt of the fifth message by the customer provides no guarantees that the merchant has received or sent the fourth message. Hence the best we can expect is for the customer's completion of the run to authenticate that the merchant was involved in the run at an earlier stage. These signals are inserted into the protocol as illustrated in Figure C.7.

The CSP descriptions are amended as follows:

$$Merchant_{mr}(cu, ma) =$$
$$send.mr!cu!mci.ma$$
$$\rightarrow receive.cu.mr?(cu.ma.mci.tr.x.am.cn.y)$$
$$\rightarrow signal.Running\_Merch.cu.mr.ma$$
$$\rightarrow send.m!cb! \, (mci.mt.x.am.cn.y.$$
$$\{kms\}_{pkCyberKey(mr)}.cu.ma.mci.mt.$$
$$\{cu.ma.mci.mt.tr\}_{SK(mr)})$$
$$\rightarrow receive.cb.mr?(mci.mt.\{cn.ma.cu.mr.tr\}_{kms}.z)$$
$$\rightarrow send.mr!cu!mci.ma.tr.cu.z \rightarrow Stop$$

In the description of $Merchant_{mr}$, we assume that the *mci* generated by the merchant is a valid *MerchantCcId* for that merchant. In other words, $merchant(mci) = mr$.

$$Cust_{cu}(mr, kcs, am, cn) =$$
$$receive.mr.cu?\{mci\}_{SK(mr)}.ma$$
$$\rightarrow send.cu!mr! \, cu.ma.mci.tr.\{kcs\}_{pkCyberKey}.$$
$$\{\{am.cn.mci.cu.ma.tr\}_{kcs}\}_{SK(cu)}$$
$$\rightarrow receive.mr.cu.(mci.ma.tr.cu.\{cn.am\}_{kcs})$$
$$\rightarrow signal!Commit\_Cust.cu.mr.ma$$
$$\rightarrow Stop$$

Figure C.7 Inserting messages to authenticate M to C

Then we are concerned with the property

$$Running\_Merch.cu_0.mr_0.ma_0 \textbf{ precedes } Commit\_Cust.cu_0.mr_0.ma_0$$

for arbitrary customer cu_0, merchant mr_0, and merchant amount ma_0.

Constructing the rank function

In this case it is best to split consideration of $Customer_{cu_0}$ and consider the different possibilities for $Cust_{cu_0}(mr, kcs, am, cn)$ independently, as discussed in Chapter 7. Those cases in which $mr \neq mr_0$ or $ma \neq ma_0$ can never result in the signal $Commit\_Cust.cu_0.mr_0.ma_0$, and so they do not need to be further considered: the protocol running with these cases trivially meets the authentication property.

We thus focus on the case in which $ma = ma_0$ and $mr = mr_0$. We must find a rank function that meets the following conditions:

- gives $Commit\_Cust.cu_0.mr_0.am_0$ a rank of 0;
- gives all the intruder's initial knowledge a rank of 1;
- ensures that the set of positive ranked messages is closed under the $\vdash$ relation;
- is such that the process $Merchant_{mr_0}$ maintains positive-message rank when blocked on performing $Running\_Merch.cu_0.mr_0.ma_0$;

$$\rho_0(u) = 1$$
$$\rho_0(t) = 1$$
$$\rho_0(pk) = \begin{cases} 0 & \text{if } pk = PKCyberKey(cu_0) \\ 1 & \text{otherwise} \end{cases}$$

$$\rho_0(sk) = \begin{cases} 0 & \text{if } sk = SK(cu_0) \text{ or } sk = SK(mr_0) \text{ or } sk = SKCyberkey(cu_0) \\ 1 & \text{otherwise} \end{cases}$$

$$\rho_0(shk) = \begin{cases} 0 & \text{if } shk \in KEYS_{cu_0} \\ 1 & \text{otherwise} \end{cases}$$

$$\rho(\{m\}_k) = \begin{cases} 1 & \text{if } k = SK(mr_0) \text{ and } m = mci \\ & \text{for some } mci \text{ with } merchant(mci) = mr_0 \\ 1 & \text{if } k = SK(cu_0) \text{ and } m = am.cn.mci.cu_0.ma_0.tr \\ & \text{for some } am, cn, \text{ and } mci \text{ and } merchant(mci) = mr_0 \\ 1 & \text{if } k = pkCyberkey(cu_0) \text{ and } m \in KEYS_{cu_0} \\ 0 & \text{if } k = SK(mr_0) \text{ and } m = cu_0.ma_0.mci.mt.tr \\ & \text{for some } mci, mt, tr \\ 0 & \text{if } m = cn_0.am_0, \text{ and } k \in KEYS_{cu_0} \\ \min\{\rho(m), \rho(k)\} & \text{otherwise} \end{cases}$$

$$\rho(m_1.m_2) = \min\{\rho(m_1), \rho(m_2)\}$$

$$\rho(signal) = \begin{cases} 0 & \text{if } signal = Commit\_Cust.cu_0.mr_0.ma_0 \\ 1 & \text{otherwise} \end{cases}$$

Figure C.8 Rank function for verification of Simplified CyberCash Protocol Authentication property of merchant to customer

■ is such that the process $Cust_{cu}(mr_0, kcs, am_0, cn)$, $Customer_{cu}$ for $cu \neq cu_0$, $Merchant_{mr}$ for any $mr \neq mr_0$, and *Cyber* all maintain positive message rank.

A suitable rank function is given in Figure C.8.

$Merchant_{mr_0}$ blocked on $Running\_Merch.cu_0.mr_0.ma_0$ maintains positive-message rank since it does not transmit anything of rank 0. Similarly, the other *Merchant* processes do not generate anything of rank 0 to transmit.

$Customer_{cu}$ processes for which $cu \neq cu_0$ only generate messages of positive rank.

$Cust_{cu_0}(mr_0, kcs, am_0, cn_0)$ maintains positive rank, since the first messages it transmits have positive rank, and the signal can only occur after receipt of a message of rank 0.

Cyber preserves positive-message rank if we can show that it can only transmit the rank 0 message $\{cn_0.am_0\}_{kcs}$ (with $kcs \in KEYS_{cu_0}$) if it has received at least one message of rank 0. In order to transmit this message it must have received messages of the form:

- $\{kcs\}_{pkCyberKey(cu)}$ (where $kcs \in KEYS_{cu_0}$)
- $\{am_0.cn_0.mci.cu.ma.tr\}\}_{SK(cu)}$
- $\{cu.ma.mci.mt.tr\}_{SK(mr)}$

with $merchant(mci) = mr$. For the first of these messages to have rank 1, we must have $cu = cu_0$. Then for the second to have rank 0, we must have $ma = ma_0$ and $merchant(mci) = mr_0$. But this gives the last message a rank of 0 since then $mr = mr_0$ (since $merchant(mci) = mr$), $cu = cu_0$, and $ma = ma_0$. Hence *Cyber* cannot transmit that message without first receiving some message of rank 0. Thus *Cyber* maintains positive message rank.

Bibliography

[1] M. Abadi and A. D. Gordon. A calculus for cryptographic protocols: the spi calculus. *Information and Computation*, 148, 1999.

[2] M. Abadi and R. Needham. Prudent engineering practice for cryptographic protocols. *IEEE Transactions on Software Engineering*, 22(1), 1996.

[3] M. Abadi and M. Tuttle. A semantics for a logic of authentication. *Proceedings of the 10th Annual ACM Symposium on Principles of Distributed Computing*, 1991.

[4] R. Anderson, B. Crispo, J. H. Lee, C. Manifavas, V. Matyas Jr., and F. A. P. Petitcolas. *The Global Internet Trust Register*. MIT Press, 1999.

[5] R. Anderson and R. Needham. Programming Satan's computer. In J. van Leeuwen (ed.) *Computer Science Today*, volume 1000 of *LNCS*. Springer, 1995.

[6] N. Asokan, V. Shoup, and M. Waidner. Asynchronous protocols for optimistic fair exchange. *IEEE Symposium on Research in Security and Privacy*, 1998.

[7] R. Bayer and E. McCreight. Organisation and maintenance of large ordered indexes. *Acta Informatica*, 1, 1972.

[8] G. Bella. *Inductive Verification of Cryptographic Protocols*. PhD thesis, Cambridge University, 2000.

[9] M. Bellare and P. Rogaway. Entity authentication and key distribution. *CRYPTO '93*, number 773 in *LNCS*. Springer, 1994.

[10] P. Bieber and N. Boulahia-Cuppens. Formal development of authentication protocols. *BCS-FACS Sixth Refinement Workshop*, 1994.

[11] S. Brackin. A HOL extension of GNY for automatically analyzing cryptographic protocols. *9th IEEE Computer Security Foundations Workshop*, 1996.

[12] S. Brackin. Automatic formal analysis of two large commercial protocols. *DIMACS Workshop on Design and Formal Verification of Security Protocols*, 1997.

[13] P. Broadfoot, G. Lowe, and A. W. Roscoe. Automating data independence. *European Symposium on Research in Computer Security*, number 1895 in *LNCS*. Springer, 2000.

[14] S. D. Brookes, A. W. Roscoe, and D. J. Walker. *An operational semantics for CSP*. Technical report, Oxford University, 1988.

[15] J. W. Bryans and S. A. Schneider. CSP, PVS, and a recursive authentication protocol. *DIMACS Workshop on Design and Formal Verification of Security Protocols*, 1997.

[16] J. A. Bull and D. J. Otway. *The authentication protocol.* Technical Report DRA/CIS3/PROJ/CORBA/SC/1/CSM/436-04/03, Defence Research Agency, 1997.

[17] J. R. Burch, E. M. Clarke, K. L. McMillan, D. L. Dill, and L. J. Hwang. Symbolic model checking: 10^{20} states and beyond. *Information and Computation*, 98(2), 1992.

[18] M. Burmester and Y. Desmedt. A secure and efficient conference key distribution system. *EUROCRYPT*, 1994.

[19] M. Burmester and Y. Desmedt. Efficient and secure conference key distribution. *Security Protocols Workshop*, 1996.

[20] M. Burrows, M. Abadi, and R. Needham. A logic of authentication. *Proceedings of the Royal Society of London*, 426, 1989. A preliminary version appeared as Digital Equipment Corporation Systems Research Center report No. 39, 1989.

[21] D. Chaum. The dining cryptographers problem: unconditional sender and recipient untraceability. *Journal of Cryptology*, 1, 1988.

[22] D. E. Denning and G. M. Sacco. Timestamps in key distribution protocols. *Communications of the ACM*, 24(8), 1981.

[23] W. Diffie and M. E. Hellman. New directions in cryptography. *IEEE Transactions on Information Theory*, 22, 1976.

[24] W. Diffie, P. C. van Oorschot, and M. J. Wiener. Authentication and authenticated key exchanges. *Designs, Codes and Cryptography*, 2, 1992.

[25] D. Dolev and A. C. Yao. On the security of public key protocols. *IEEE Transactions on Information Theory*, 29(2), 1983.

[26] B. Donovan, P. Norris, and G. Lowe. Analyzing a library of security protocols using Casper and FDR. *Workshop on Formal Methods and Security Protocols*, Trento, Italy, 1999.

[27] B. Dutertre and S. A. Schneider. Embedding CSP in PVS. An application to authentication protocols. *Theorem proving in Higher Order Logics*, number 1275 in *LNCS*. Springer, 1997.

[28] T. ElGamal. A public-key cryptosystem and a signature scheme based on discrete logarithms. *IEEE Transactions on Information Theory*, 31, 1985.

[29] N. Evans and S. A. Schneider. Analysing time-dependent security properties in CSP using PVS. *European Symposium on Research in Computer Security*, number 1895 in *LNCS*. Springer, 2000.

[30] F. J. Thayer Fábrega, J. C. Herzog, and J. D. Guttman. Strand spaces: why is a security protocol correct? *IEEE Computer Society Symposium on Security and Privacy*, 1998.

[31] R. Focardi, A. Ghelli and R. Gorrieri. Using non-interference for the analysis of security protocols. In *DIMACS Workshop on Design and Formal Verification of Security Protocols*, 1997.

[32] R. Focardi and R. Gorrieri. A classification of security properties for process algebras. *Journal of Computer Security*, 3(1), 1995.

[33] R. Focardi and R. Gorrieri. The compositional security checker: a tool for the verification of information flow properties. *IEEE Transactions on Software Engineering*, 23(9), 1997.

[34] M. Franklin and M. Reiter. A linear protocol failure for RSA with exponent three. *CRYPTO '95 Rump Session*, 1995.

[35] D. Gollmann. What do we mean by entity authentication? *IEEE Computer Society Symposium on Research in Security and Privacy*, 1996.

[36] D. Gollmann. On the verification of cryptographic protocols – a tale of two committees. *DERA/RHUL Workshop on Secure Architectures and Information Flow*, volume 32 of *ENTCS*, 1999.

[37] L. Gong, R. Needham, and R. Yahalom. Reasoning about belief in cryptographic protocols. *IEEE Computer Society Symposium on Research in Security and Privacy*, 1990.

[38] J. D. Guttman and F. J. Thayer Fábrega. Authentication tests and the normal, efficient penetrator. *IEEE Computer Society Symposium on Research in Security and Privacy*, 2000.

[39] J. A. Heather and S. A. Schneider. Towards automatic verification of security protocols on an unbounded network. *13th IEEE Computer Security Foundations Workshop*, 2000.

[40] M. Hennessy. *Algebraic Theory of Processes*. MIT Press, 1988.

[41] C. A. R. Hoare. *Communicating Sequential Processes*. Prentice-Hall, 1985.

[42] G. Holzmann. *Design and Validation of Computer Protocols*. Prentice-Hall, 1991.

[43] Tzonelih Hwang, Narn-Yih Lee, Chuan-Ming Li, Ming-Yung Ko, and Yung-Hsiang Chen. Two attacks on Neuman-Stubblebine authentication protocols. *Information Processing Letters*, 53, 1995.

[44] ISO/IEC JTC1. Information technology – open systems interconnection – security frameworks in open system, part 4: Non-repudiation, 1995. ISO/IEC DIS 10181-4, 1995.

[45] D. Kahn. *The Code-Breakers*. Simon & Schuster, 1997.

[46] A. Kehne, J. Schönwälder, and H. Landendörfer. A nonce-based protocol for multiple authentications. *Operating Systems Review*, 26(4), 1992.

[47] R. Kemmerer. Using formal verification techniques to analyze encryption protocols. *IEEE Computer Society Symposium on Security and Privacy*, 1987.

[48] R. Kemmerer and Z. Dang. Using the ASTRAL model checker for cryptographic protocol analysis. *DIMACS Workshop on Design and Formal Verification of Security Protocols*, 1997.

[49] R. Kemmerer, C. Meadows, and J. Millen. Three systems for cryptographic protocol analysis. *Journal of Cryptology*, 7(2), 1994.

[50] X. Lai. On the design and security of block ciphers. In J. L. Massey (ed.) *EHT Series in Information Technology*, volume 1. Technische Hochschulke (Zurich), 1992.

[51] R. Lazić. *A Semantic Study of Data Independence with Applications to the Mechanical Verification of Concurrent Systems*. D.Phil, Oxford University, 1998.

[52] R. Lazić and D. Novak. A unifying approach to data-independence. *11th International Conference on Concurrency Theory*, number 1877 in *LNCS*. Springer, 2000.

[53] R. S. Lazić and A. W. Roscoe. A semantic study of data independence with applications to model-checking. Submitted for publication, 1998.

[54] G. Lowe. Breaking and fixing the Needham-Schroeder public-key protocol using FDR. *Proceedings of TACAS*, number 1055 in *LNCS*. Springer, 1996. Also in *Software – Concepts and Tools*, 17:93–102, 1996.

[55] G. Lowe. Some new attacks upon security protocols. 9th *IEEE Computer Security Foundations Workshop*, 1996.

[56] G. Lowe. Casper: A compiler for the analysis of security protocols. *10th IEEE Computer Security Foundations Workshop*, 1997.

[57] G. Lowe. A hierarchy of authentication specifications. *10th IEEE Computer Security Foundations Workshop*, 1997.

[58] G. Lowe. Casper: A compiler for the analysis of security protocols. *Journal of Computer Security*, 6, 1998.

[59] G. Lowe. *Defining information flow*. Technical Report 1999/3, Department of Mathematics and Computer Science, University of Leicester, 1999.

[60] G. Lowe and M. L. Hui. Safe simplifying transformations for security protocols. *12th IEEE Computer Security Foundations Workshop*, 1999.

[61] G. Lowe and A. W. Roscoe. Using CSP to detect errors in the TMN protocol. *IEEE Transactions in Software Engineering*, 23(10), 1997.

[62] K. McMillan. *Symbolic model checking*. Kluwer Academic Publishers, 1993.

[63] A. J. Menezes, P. C. Van Oorschot, and S. A. Vanstone. *Handbook of Applied Cryptography*. CRC Press, 1996.

[64] J. Millen. Common authentication protocol specification language, CAPSL. `www.csl.sri.com/ millen/capsl/abstract.html`, 1998.

[65] S. P. Miller, C. Neumann, J. I. Schiller, and J. H. Saltzer. Kerberos authentication and authorization system. Project Athena Technical Plan Section E.2.1, MIT, 1987.

[66] R. Milner. *Communication and Concurrency*. Prentice-Hall, 1989.

[67] National Institute for Standards and Technology. Advanced encryption standard. `http://csrc.nist.gov/encryption/aes/`.

[68] R. Needham and M. Schroeder. Using encryption for authentication in large networks of computers. *Communications of the ACM*, 21(12), 1978.

[69] L. Paulson. Mechanised proofs for a recursive authentication protocol. *10th IEEE Computer Security Foundations Workshop*, 1997.

[70] L. Paulson. The inductive approach to verifying cryptographic protocols. *Journal of Computer Security*, 6, 1998.

[71] B. Pfitzmann, M. Schunter, and M. Waidner. Cryptographic security of reactive systems. *DERA/RHUL Workshop on Secure Architectures and Information Flow*, volume 32 of *ENTCS*, 1999.

[72] B. Pfitzmann and M. Waidner. A general framework for formal notions of 'secure' system. *Hildesheimer Informatik-Berichte* 11/94, Institut für Informatik, Universität Hildesheim, 1994.

[73] S. J. D. Phoenix and P. D. Townsend. Quantum cryptography and secure optical communication. *BT Technical Journal*, 11(2), 1993.

[74] R. Rivest, A. Shamir and L. Adleman. A method for obtaining digital signatures and public-key cryptosystems. *Communications of the ACM*, 21(2), 1978.

[75] A. W. Roscoe. *A mathematical theory of communicating processes*. D.Phil, Oxford University, 1982.

[76] A. W. Roscoe. *The Theory and Practice of Concurrency*. Prentice-Hall, 1997.

[77] A. W. Roscoe. Proving security protocols with model checkers by data independence techniques. *11th Computer Security Foundations Workshop*, 1998.

[78] A. W. Roscoe and P. J. Broadfoot. Proving security protocols with model checkers by data independence techniques. *Journal of Computer Security*, 1999.

[79] A. W. Roscoe, P. H. B. Gardiner, M. H. Goldsmith, J. R. Hulance, D. M. Jackson, and J. B. Scattergood. Hierarchical compression for model-checking CSP *or* how to check 10^{20} dining philosophers for deadlock. *First TACAS*, number 1019 in *LNCS*. Springer, 1995.

[80] A. W. Roscoe, J. C. P. Woodcock, and L. Wulf. Non-interference through determinism. *Journal of Computer Security*, 4(1), 1996.

[81] P. Y. A. Ryan and S. A. Schneider. An attack on a recursive authentication protocol: A cautionary tale. *Information Processing Letters*, 1998.

[82] P. Y. A. Ryan and S. A. Schneider. Process algebra and non-interference. *Journal of Computer Security*, 2000. Also in *12th IEEE Computer Security Foundations Workshop*, 1999.

[83] J. B. Scattergood. *Tools for CSP and Timed CSP*. D.Phil, Oxford University, 1997.

[84] S. A. Schneider. Security properties and CSP. *IEEE Computer Society Symposium on Security and Privacy*, 1996.

[85] S. A. Schneider. Formal analysis of a non-repudiation protocol. *11th IEEE Computer Security Foundations Workshop*, 1998.

[86] S. A. Schneider. Verifying authentication protocols in CSP. *IEEE Transactions on Software Engineering*, 1998.

[87] S. A. Schneider. *Concurrent and Real-time Systems: the CSP Approach*. Addison-Wesley, 1999.

[88] S. A. Schneider and A. Sidiropoulos. CSP and anonymity. *European Symposium on Research in Computer Security*, 1996.

[89] B. Schneier. *Applied Cryptography*. John Wiley, 1995.

[90] G. Seroussi, N. P. Smart, and I. F. Blake. *Elliptic Curves in Cryptography*. Number 265 in *London Mathematical Society Lecture Note Series*. Cambridge University Press, 1999.

[91] N. Shankar, S. Owre, and J. M. Rushby. *The PVS proof checker: A reference manual*. Technical report, Computer Science Laboratory, SRI International, 1993.

[92] C. Shannon. Communication theory of secrecy systems. *Bell Systems Technical Journal*, 28(4), 1949.

[93] G. J. Simmons. Cryptanalysis and protocol failures. *Communications of the ACM*, 37(11), 1994.

[94] S. Singh. *The Code Book*. Fourth Estate, 1999.

[95] D. Song, S. Berezin, and A. Perrig. Athena, a novel approach to efficient automatic security protocol analysis. *Journal of Computer Security*, 2000.

[96] M. Steiner, G. Tsudik, and M. Waidner. CLIQUES: A new approach to group key agreement. *18th IEEE International Conference on Distributed Computing Systems*, 1998.

[97] D. R. Stinson. *Cryptography: Theory and Practice*. CRC Press, 1995.

[98] P. Syverson and P. Van Oorschot. On unifying some cryptographic protocol logics. *IEEE Computer Society Symposium on Research in Security and Privacy*, 1994.

[99] M. Tatebayashi, N. Matsuzaki, and D. B. Newman, Jr. Key distribution protocol for digital mobile communication systems. *Advances in Cryptology: Proceedings of Crypto '89*, volume 435 of *LNCS*. Springer, 1990.

[100] D. Welsh. *Codes and Cryptography*. Oxford University Press, 1988.

[101] J. T. Yantchev. ARC – a tool for efficient refinement and equivalence checking for CSP. *IEEE Second International Conference on Algorithms and Architectures for Parallel Processing*, 1996.

[102] Jianying Zhou and D. Gollmann. A fair non-repudiation protocol. *IEEE Computer Society Symposium on Security and Privacy*, 1996.

[103] P. R. Zimmermann. *The Official PGP User's Guide*. MIT Press, 1995.

Notation in protocol descriptions

Lower case is used for variables: message components and keys that are generated in a particular run (e.g. nonces, session keys). Lower case is also used for agent names in the general description of the run. e.g. k_{ab} for a session key generated in that run.

Upper case is used for constants: items that are fixed for all runs (e.g. long-term session keys, the name of the server, public and secret agent keys). So PK_a for a's public key, SK_a for a's secret key, PK_J for Jeeves' public key (since the functions PK and SK from agents' names to keys are constant). If K is upper case then the key is fixed prior to communication, e.g. K_{AB}. If it is lower case, e.g. k_{ab} then it is a key being set up by the protocol under consideration and is not known to the agents in advance.

a, b	agent variables
A, B	particular given agent names
k	key variable
pk	public key variable
sk	secret key variable
shk	shared key variable
k_{ab}	a shared session key
n	nonce variable
n_a	a nonce supposedly generated by agent a
t	text variable
$Agent$	the set of agent names
$Honest$	the set of names of honest agents
Key	the set of keys
$Nonce$	the set of nonces
$Nonce\_I_a$	a's set of nonces for use in initiator runs
$Nonce\_R_a$	a's set of nonces for use in responder runs
$\{m\}_k$ or $encrypt(k, m)$	message m encrypted under key k
$g(\!|m|\!)$	message m hashed under hash function g
$m_1.m_2$	the concatenation of m_1 and m_2
$X \vdash f$	f can be constructed from the facts in X

$I(A)$	the intruder masquerading as agent A. In $I(A) \rightarrow B : M$, I initiates messge M making it appear to come from A. In $B \rightarrow I(A) : M$, I intercepts a message M intended for A.
$ServerKey(a)$	a's long-term key shared with the trusted server
PK_a	agent a's public key
SK_a	agent a's secret key
IK	the intruder's initial knowledge
$Init$	CSP description of a protocol initiator role single run
$Initiator(a, n_a)$	initiator role with agent a and nonce n_a
$Resp$	CSP description of a protocol responder role single run
$Responder(b, n_b)$	responder role with agent b and nonce n_b
$User$	CSP description of all a user's possible protocol runs together
$Serv$	CSP description of a single server protocol run
$Server$	CSP description of the complete server behaviour in a protocol
$Intruder$	CSP description of the hostile environment
$System$	CSP description of the protocol in the hostile environment
$send.i.j.m$	CSP event: agent i transmitting message m for delivery to agent j
$receive.i.j.m$	CSP event: agent j taking delivery of message m apparently from agent i
$signal.claim.a.b.f$	a specification event in a protocol description marking a significant stage of the protocol execution a is running apparently with b
$signal.Claim\_Secret.a.b.f$	a specification event marking the point at which the agent a executing the protocol apparently with b is claimed to have established secrecy of fact f
$signal.Running\_role.a.b.f$	a specification event marking the point at which the agent a in the particular role executing the protocol apparently with b is deemed to be running the protocol with parameters f
$signal.Commit\_role.a.b.f$	a specification event inserted into a protocol description to mark the point at which the agent a in the particular role executing the protocol apparently with b is deemed to have successfully completed the protocol with parameters f
$role$	roles used in this book are $Initiator$, $Responder$, $Server$, $Customer$, $Merchant$, $CyberBank$ and abbreviations of these

Index

Numbers in brackets indicate relevant figures contained within the page range; 'n' refers to a note on the page shown.